ENGAGING
THE
PSALMS

1   2   3   4   5   6   7   8   9   10   30   29   28   27   26   25   24   23   22   21

ENGAGING THE PSALMS

A GUIDE FOR REFLECTION AND PRAYER

CONCORDIA PUBLISHING HOUSE · SAINT LOUIS

CONTENTS

INTRODUCTION

The Psalms are (mostly) short and quickly read. Throughout these 150 songs, the reader experiences the full range of the human experience. Through them, we understand what being God's child is like in all the stages and times of life. As such, the small section of Scripture that makes up the Psalms forms a wonderful introduction to more in-depth Bible reading. At the same time, their richness appeals to Christians of all ages and all levels of maturity.

Martin Luther identified the Psalms as a summary of the Bible. He was not alone. Throughout the history of God's people, the Psalms have served as a foundational core of personal and corporate meditation as well as reflection on God's life-giving Word.

Why use the Book of Psalms, and why should you start now? It is critical that you begin by understanding that the Psalms (or sacred songs) are God's Word, and God's Word gives life. In discovering and rediscovering the richness of the Book of Psalms, God will enrich your daily discipleship. The depths of God's Word are unending; as you hear, read, and consider the Psalms, the Holy Spirit will continually form your faith and transform how you understand the Christian life. There has never been a better time to take a break from the routines of life, open the pages of this book, and spend some time meditating on God's Word.

The Psalter constituted the first hymnal, as it were, for God's people. Recognizing this fact, a generous selection of psalms is located first in *Lutheran Service Book*. All the hymns written later and included further on in the hymnal take their place in the tradition begun by the Lord Himself when by inspiration He gave the Psalms.

The Psalms remain contemporary. They are also *your* songs—not merely the sentiments of ancient people. These songs speak compellingly, even frighteningly, of sin and the consequences of living in a sinful world. They also soothe your troubled heart with the grace and forgiveness of God and His promised Messiah—Jesus, our Lord.

Rev. Dr. Pete Jurchen,
Editor

PREFACE TO THE
ENGLISH STANDARD VERSION

The Bible

"This Book [is] the most valuable thing that this world affords. Here is Wisdom; this is the royal Law; these are the lively Oracles of God." With these words the Moderator of the Church of Scotland hands a Bible to the new monarch in Britain's coronation service. These words echo the King James Bible translators, who wrote in 1611, "God's sacred Word . . . is that inestimable treasure that excelleth all the riches of the earth." This assessment of the Bible is the motivating force behind the publication of the English Standard Version.

Translation Legacy

The English Standard Version (ESV) stands in the classic mainstream of English Bible translations over the past half-millennium. The fountainhead of that stream was William Tyndale's New Testament of 1526; marking its course were the King James Version of 1611 (KJV), the English Revised Version of 1885 (RV), the American Standard Version of 1901 (ASV), and the Revised Standard Version of 1952 and 1971 (RSV). In that stream, faithfulness to the text and vigorous pursuit of precision were combined with simplicity, beauty, and dignity of expression. Our goal has been to carry forward this legacy for this generation and generations to come.

To this end each word and phrase in the ESV has been carefully weighed against the original Hebrew, Aramaic, and Greek, to ensure the fullest accuracy and clarity and to avoid under-translating or overlooking any nuance of the original text. The words and phrases themselves grow out of the Tyndale–King James legacy, and most recently out of the RSV, with the 1971 RSV text providing the starting point for our work. Archaic language has been brought into line with current usage and significant corrections have been made in the translation of key texts. But throughout, our goal has been to retain the depth of meaning and enduring quality of language that have made their indelible mark on the English-speaking world and have defined the life and doctrine of its church over the last five centuries.

Translation Philosophy

The ESV is an "essentially literal" translation that seeks as far as possible to reproduce the precise wording of the original text and the personal style of each Bible writer. As such, its emphasis is on "word-for-word" correspondence, at the same time taking full account of differences in grammar, syntax, and idiom between current literary English and the original languages. Thus it seeks to be transparent to the original text, letting the reader see as directly as possible the structure and exact force of the original.

In contrast to the ESV, some Bible versions have followed a "thought-for-thought" rather than "word-for-word" translation philosophy, emphasizing "dynamic equivalence" rather than the "essentially literal" meaning of the original. A "thought-for-thought" translation is of necessity more inclined to reflect the interpretive views of the translator and the influences of contemporary culture.

Every translation is at many points a trade-off between literal precision and readability, between "formal equivalence" in expression and "functional equivalence" in communication, and the ESV is no exception. Within this framework we have sought to be "as literal as possible" while maintaining clarity of expression and literary excellence. Therefore, to the extent that plain English permits and the meaning in each case allows, we have sought to use the same English word for important recurring words in the original; and, as far as grammar and syntax allow, we have rendered Old Testament passages cited in the New in ways that show their correspondence. Thus in each of these areas, as well as throughout the Bible as a whole, we have sought to capture all the echoes and overtones of meaning that are so abundantly present in the original texts.

As an essentially literal translation, taking into account grammar and syntax, the ESV thus seeks to carry over every possible nuance of meaning in the original words of Scripture into our own language. As such, the ESV is ideally suited for in-depth study of the Bible. Indeed, with its commitment to literary excellence, the ESV is equally well suited for public reading and preaching, for private reading and reflection, for both academic and devotional study, and for Scripture memorization.

Translation Principles and Style

The ESV also carries forward classic translation principles in its literary style. Accordingly it retains theological terminology—words such as grace, faith, justification, sanctification, redemption, regeneration, reconciliation, propitiation—because of their central importance for Christian doctrine and also because the underlying Greek words were already becoming key words and technical terms among Christians in New Testament times.

The ESV lets the stylistic variety of the biblical writers fully express itself—from the exalted prose that opens Genesis, to the flowing narratives of the historical books, to the rich metaphors and dramatic imagery of the poetic books, to the ringing rhetoric in the prophetic books, to the smooth elegance of Luke, to the profound simplicities of John, and the closely reasoned logic of Paul.

In punctuating, paragraphing, dividing long sentences, and rendering connectives, the ESV follows the path that seems to make the ongoing flow of thought clearest in English. The biblical languages regularly connect sentences by frequent repetition of words such as "and," "but," and "for," in a way that goes beyond the conventions of current literary English. Effective translation, however, requires that these links in the original be reproduced so that the flow of the argument will be transparent to the reader. We have therefore normally translated these connectives, though occasionally we have varied the rendering by using alternatives (such as "also," "however," "now," "so," "then," or "thus") when they better express the linkage in specific instances.

In the area of gender language, the goal of the ESV is to render literally what is in the original. For example, "anyone" replaces "any man" where there is no word corresponding to "man" in the original languages, and "people" rather than "men" is regularly used where the original languages refer to both men and women. But the words "man" and "men" are retained where a male meaning component is part of the original Greek or Hebrew. Likewise, the word "man" has been retained where the original text intends to convey a clear contrast between "God" on the one hand and "man" on the other hand, with "man" being used in the collective sense of the whole human race (see Luke 2:52). Similarly, the English word "brothers" (translating the Greek word αδελπηοι) is retained as an important familial form of address between fellow-Jews and fellow-Christians in the first century. A recurring note is included to indicate that the term "brothers" (αδελπηοι) was often used in Greek to refer to both men and women, and to indicate the specific instances in the text where this is the case. In addition, the English word "sons" (translating the Greek word ηυιοι) is retained in specific instances because the underlying Greek term usually includes a male meaning component and it was used as a legal term in the adoption and inheritance laws of first-century Rome. As used by the apostle Paul, this term refers to the status of all Christians, both men and women, who, having been adopted into God's family, now enjoy all the privileges, obligations, and inheritance rights of God's children.

The inclusive use of the generic "he" has also regularly been retained, because this is consistent with similar usage in the original languages and because an essentially literal translation would be impossible without it.

In each case the objective has been transparency to the original text, allowing the reader to understand the original on its own terms rather than in the terms of our present-day Western culture.

The Translation of Specialized Terms

The Greek word Χηριστοσ has been translated consistently as "Christ." Although the term originally meant simply "anointed," among Jews in New Testament times it had specifically come to designate the Messiah, the great Savior that God had promised to raise up. In other New Testament contexts, however, especially among Gentiles, Χηριστοσ ("Christ") was on its way to becoming a proper name. It is important, therefore, to keep the context in mind in understanding the various ways that Χηριστοσ ("Christ") is used in the New Testament. At the same time, in accord with its "essentially literal" translation philosophy, the ESV has retained consistency and concordance in the translation of Χηριστοσ ("Christ") throughout the New Testament.

Second, a particular difficulty is presented when words in biblical Greek refer to ancient practices and institutions that do not correspond directly to those in the modern world. Such is the case in the translation of δουλοσ, a term which is often rendered "slave." This term, however, actually covers a range of relationships that requires a range of renderings—"slave," "bondservant," or "servant"—depending on the context. Further, the word "slave" currently carries associations with the often brutal and dehumanizing institution of slavery particularly in nineteenth-century America. For this reason, the ESV translation of the word δουλοσ has been undertaken with particular attention to its meaning in each specific context. In New Testament times, a δουλοσ is often best described as a "bondservant"—that is, someone in the Roman Empire officially bound under contract to serve his master for seven years (except for those in Caesar's household in Rome who were contracted for fourteen years). When the contract expired, the person was freed, given his wage that had been saved by the master, and officially declared a freedman. The ESV usage thus seeks to express the most fitting nuance of meaning in each context. Where absolute ownership by a master is envisaged (as in Romans 6), "slave" is used; where a more limited form of servitude is in view, "bondservant" is used (as in 1 Corinthians 7:21–24); where the context indicates a wide range of freedom (as in John 4:51), "servant" is preferred. Footnotes are generally provided to identify the Greek and the range of meaning that this term may carry in each case. The issues involved in translating the Greek word δουλοσ apply also to the Greek word συνδουλοσ, translated in the text as "fellow servant."

Third, it is sometimes suggested that Bible translations should capitalize pronouns referring to deity. It has seemed best not to capitalize deity pronouns in the ESV, however, for the following reasons: first, there is nothing in the original Greek manuscripts that corresponds to such capitalization; second, the practice of capitalizing deity pronouns in English Bible translations is a recent innovation, which began only in the mid-twentieth century; and, third, such capitalization is absent from the KJV Bible and the whole stream of Bible translations that the ESV carries forward.

A fourth specialized term, the word "behold," usually has been retained as the most common translation for the Greek word ιδου, which means something like "Pay careful attention to what follows! This is important!" Other than the word "behold," there is no single word in English that fits well in most contexts. Although "Look!" and "See!" and "Listen!" would be workable in some contexts, in many others these words lack sufficient weight and dignity. Given the principles of "essentially literal" translation, it is important not to leave ιδου completely untranslated and so to lose the intended emphasis in the original language. The older and more formal word "behold" has usually been retained, therefore, as the best available option for conveying the original weight of meaning.

Textual Basis and Resources

The ESV New Testament is based on the Greek text in the 2014 editions of the *Greek New Testament* (5th corrected ed.), published by the United Bible Societies (UBS), and *Novum Testamentum Graece* (28th ed., 2012), edited by Nestle and Aland. In a few difficult cases in the New Testament, the ESV has followed a Greek text different from the text given preference in the UBS/Nestle-Aland 28th edition. Throughout, the translation team has benefited greatly from the massive textual resources that have become readily available recently, from new insights into biblical laws and culture, and from current advances in Greek lexicography and grammatical understanding.

Textual Footnotes

The footnotes that are included in most editions of the ESV are therefore an integral part of the ESV translation, informing the reader of textual variations and difficulties and showing how these have been resolved by the ESV translation team. In addition to this, the footnotes indicate significant alternative readings and occasionally provide an explanation for technical terms or for a difficult reading in the text.

Publishing Team

The ESV publishing team has included more than a hundred people. The fourteen-member Translation Oversight Committee benefited from the work of more than fifty biblical experts serving as Translation Review Scholars and from the comments of the more than fifty members of the Advisory Council, all of which was carried out under the auspices of the Crossway Board of Directors. This hundred-plus-member team shares a common commitment to the truth of God's Word and to historic Christian orthodoxy and is international in scope, including leaders in many denominations.

To God's Honor and Praise

We know that no Bible translation is perfect; but we also know that God uses imperfect and inadequate things to his honor and praise. So to our triune God and to his people we offer what we have done, with our prayers that it may prove useful, with gratitude for much help given, and with ongoing wonder that our God should ever have entrusted to us so momentous a task.

Soli Deo Gloria!—To God alone be the glory!
The Translation Oversight Committee

FEATURES OF THE FOOTNOTES

TEXTUAL FOOTNOTES

Several kinds of footnotes related to the ESV text are provided throughout the ESV Bible to assist the reader. These footnotes appear at the bottom of the page and are indicated in the ESV text by a superscript *number* that *follows* the word or phrase to which the footnote applies (e.g., "Isaac[2]"). Superscript *letters* that *precede* a word indicate cross-references (see explanation on the following page).

The footnotes included in the ESV Bible are an integral part of the text and provide important information concerning the understanding and translation of the text. The footnotes fall mainly into four categories, as illustrated in the examples below.

Types of Textual Footnotes

(1) *Alternative Translations.* Footnotes of this kind provide alternative translations for specific words or phrases when there is a strong possibility that such words or phrases could be translated in another way, such as: "Or *keep awake*" (see Matt. 26:38); and "Or *down payment*" (see Eph. 1:14). In such cases, the translation deemed to have the stronger support is in the text while other possible renderings are given in the note.

(2) *Explanation of Greek and Hebrew Terms.* Notes of this kind relate primarily to the meaning of specific Greek or Hebrew terms, as illustrated by the following examples:

(a) Notes about the meaning of names in the original languages, such as: "*Isaac* means *he laughs*" (see Gen. 17:19); and "*Simeon* sounds like the Hebrew for *heard*" (see Gen. 29:33).

(b) Notes that give the literal translation of a Greek or Hebrew word or phrase deemed too awkward to be used in the English text, such as: "Greek *girding up the loins of your mind*" (see 1 Pet. 1:13).

(c) Notes indicating that absolute certainty of the meaning of a word or phrase is not possible given our best understanding of the original language (e.g., Hebrew words occurring so infrequently in the Old Testament that their meaning cannot be determined with certainty). Such words are identified with a note stating that "The meaning of the Hebrew is uncertain" (see, e.g., Josh. 17:11).

(d) Notes that indicate the specialized use of a Greek word, such as: "brothers," translating the Greek word *adelphoi* (see, e.g., the extended note on Rom. 1:13, corresponding to the first occurrence of *adelphoi* in any New Testament book, and the abbreviated note, e.g., on Rom. 7:1, corresponding to subsequent occurrences of *adelphoi* in any New Testament book); and "sons," translating the Greek word *huioi* (see, e.g., Rom. 8:14). See also the discussion of *adelphoi* and *huioi* in the Preface.

(3) *Other Explanatory Notes.* Footnotes of this kind provide clarifying information as illustrated by the following examples:

(a) Notes clarifying additional meanings that may not otherwise be apparent in the text, such as: "*Leprosy* was a term for several skin diseases; see Leviticus 13."

(b) Notes clarifying important grammatical points that would not otherwise be apparent in English, such as: "In Hebrew *you* is plural in verses 1–5" (see Gen. 3:1).

(c) Notes clarifying when the referent for a pronoun has been supplied in the English text, such as: "Greek *he*" (see, e.g., Mark 1:43).

(d) Notes giving English equivalents for weights, measures, and monetary values.

(4) *Technical Translation Notes.* Footnotes of this kind indicate how decisions have been made in the translation of difficult Hebrew and Greek passages. Such notes occasionally include technical terms. For an explanation of these terms the reader is referred to standard Bible study reference works. See further the section in the Preface on "Textual Basis and Resources" for an explanation of the original-language texts used in the translation of the ESV Bible and how the translation of difficult passages has been resolved.

HOW TO USE THIS BOOK

You may notice that this book is arranged a bit differently than other books that encourage personal and group Bible study. First, the bulk of this book is the text of the 150 ancient Psalms. You may also notice, however, that immediately following the text of each psalm, this book incorporates personal reflection spaces on the Word as well as applications through prayer into daily life. Each one-page reflection gives a basic introduction to the psalm and a structured way to pray, meditate on, and apply the psalm to daily life. The specific form of the reflection pages is based on two methods of meditating on Scripture and prayer that come from the Lutheran tradition.

The first of these methods is based on the key Lutheran understanding of the study of God's Word: *oratio, meditatio, tentatio.* These three Latin words can be roughly translated as *prayer, meditation,* and *struggle.* Luther advocated for this method from reading the Psalms themselves (specifically Psalm 119). To study in this way, said Luther, was to participate in the way that God makes theologians. Therefore, this book naturally uses this three-fold approach as a model for helping you reflect on God's Word. For the sake of simplifying and making the process easier to remember, in this book, we refer to these steps as three *R*s: Request the Spirit's Help in Prayer, Read and Repeat the Word, and Return to the Lord in Prayer.

Request the Spirit's Help in Prayer
It is important to prepare yourself before digging into the Holy Scriptures. We trust that the Holy Spirit works through God's Word. In following David's example from the Psalms, we learn to humble ourselves before God before meditating on His Word. If possible, find a quiet space and time where you can prepare yourself to receive the gifts of God's Word. Pray that God would help you to view Scripture as not simply another piece of information, but rather the Means of Grace by which He creates and sustains faith for life. Pray that God's Word would form and transform your mind so that by receiving it you may better understand who He is, who you are, and what He has done for you. A list of prayers for you to use, if you desire, can be found on pages 450–53 in this book.

Read and Repeat God's Word
The second step in the process is spending time reading and repeating the words of the psalm. For the Christian, meditation on God's Word is not glancing over the text once and then coming to your own conclusions. Instead, meditating on God's Word, following David's example from the Psalms, includes going over the text again and again. Read it once to yourself, then

consider reading it out loud. Look over the words for details, especially what the author is saying and the impact that the words of the text have on you.

Consider underlining or highlighting sentences as you go or circling important words in the text itself. As you do, consider also reflecting in writing to the given prompts on the page. What words or phrases stick out to you? How do those words or phrases reveal the poet's purpose for the psalm? What effect does this psalm have on you as you meditate on it? Many Christians throughout history have found great benefit to jotting down their reflections in writing, and by so doing, you can better organize your thoughts.

Space is provided in this book for you to do just that. In addition, by taking some time to reflect and meditate on the words of the psalm through writing, you will also record your meditation for later. As you return to the book and the psalm in the future, you will be able to continue to build your understanding of the depths of the text.

Timothy Saleska, in his Concordia Commentary *Psalms 1–50*, offers excellent advice for how to read the Psalms and enjoy the experience. He suggests:

1. When you read a psalm, remember to continually stop and ask yourself, *"What is the poet doing?"* What is the force of his language? Is he confessing or praising or condemning or predicting or commanding or encouraging or something else? Why is he repeating himself? Why does he keep rewording? Why this metaphor or figure of speech? What does he intend for me to understand?

2. *What am I doing* as I read his psalm? Ask yourself questions like these: What connections am I making on the basis of my own experiences and understanding? What conclusions am I drawing? What judgments am I making? What questions do I have? What do I not understand? Can I identify with the circumstances of the voice in the psalm, or does his experience sound foreign to me? All of this involves reading yourself even as you are reading the text.

3. I have tried to show that interpretation of a psalm takes place on both a cognitive as well as an affective level. Sometimes subtle. Sometimes bold. The poet expresses his emotions and feelings, his desires and needs through his language. He shows you the inner landscape of his heart, and this is part of the meaning of the psalm. . . . A psalm gives us not just propositional truth but also affective and relational truth.

4. We read the Psalms with an expectation that the language of these poems is complex, and we find that meaning can take multiple directions. This is different than the way a judge, for example, is taught to read legal texts such as the Constitution, statutes, legal precedents, and so on. The goal of members of the legal community is to *resolve* interpretive disputes. In their interpretations, they seek to derive single lines of meaning from their particular texts. That is, to put it more bluntly, the aim of judges (and communities like scientists) is to constrict meaning.

We read poetry with the expectation that meaning will take many directions. We expect that the Psalms will offer us any number of interpretive possibilities. So we are on the lookout for (and are satisfied to find) ambiguities, ironies, paradoxes. From one end of a psalm to the other, there are all kinds of things to see and think about. This is not a problem (instead, it's a pleasure) if we remember that one vital purpose of the Psalms is to enable us to reflect deeply on the complex and many-sided nature of truth, to contemplate life's paradoxes, and to give voice to our—often conflicting—emotions and experiences. These texts can open up conversations around the important theological and anthropological questions they raise. (Saleska, *Psalms 1–50*, Concordia Commentary [St. Louis: Concordia Publishing House, 2020], 27–28)

Return to the Lord in Prayer
The third step in the process is, translated roughly from German, to struggle with the text. The devil, the world, and the sinful flesh will never cease working to tempt God's people away from the faith. In addition, once God's people receive God's Word, Satan's attacks will surely intensify. However, you do not need to fear; this wrestling against the lies and temptations of these ancient enemies is another way that God forms our faith and life. What the devil tries to do often backfires, as the faith that God has planted in our hearts through His Word grows and flourishes as we continually meditate on it. This struggle also continually draws us back time and again to God's Word, which once again forms our faith and life.

In this book, each section titled "Return to the Lord in Prayer" has three parts that will equip you and help you focus your attention toward God. This section is meant to help you prepare to go back to your daily walk of faith. First, for each psalm, there is a devotional meditation paragraph. This text will help you dig into the deeper meaning of the psalm. It will also highlight the Law, which shows us our sin and the wrath of God, and the Gospel, which shows us our Savior, Jesus Christ, and brings God's grace and favor. This meditation is not meant to be a substitute for your own meditation on

God's Word; instead, it is an extra aid to help you get the most out of your meditation as you look to Christ in the Psalms.

The second part of this section is a space for prayers and notes. Here you are encouraged to look at the psalm upon which you have just meditated and the content of God's Word that you have received as the fuel for your prayers. Though there are different prayer prompts written with particular psalms in mind, many of them follow a three-step pattern for prayer. These three steps are as follows: (1) giving thanks to God, (2) confessing sins, and then (3) bringing your requests to God. This pattern of praying is based on suggestions from Luther himself on how to pray. This prayer pattern makes up the second method of meditation from the Lutheran tradition that is incorporated in this book. Often, the prompts for the prayers of request are divided into four categories based on the major vocations, or callings, through which God uses His people to love and serve their neighbor: the household, work or livelihood, the congregation, and society. Other times, the prayer section is left more open-ended, but you can use any pattern you so choose for prayer. This section also has space to write down words or phrases specific to your prayers, and you are encouraged to do some writing to help organize your thoughts and prayers.

The last part of the "Return to the Lord in Prayer" section is a final prayer at the bottom of the page, which you can use as a way to close out your period of meditating on the psalm.

The three Rs—Request, Read and Repeat, and Return—should help you better understand the rhythms of receiving the gifts of God's Word for life. These are included to help you get the most out of reading the Psalms, but feel free to use them or not, as you decide. The real purpose of this book is to help you develop the attitudes, skills, understandings, and habits of meditating on God's Word. As you grow as a lifelong learner of God's Word, meditating on and storing up the Scriptures in your heart, the Holy Spirit will strengthen and aid you as you walk daily in the Christian faith and life.

You will also notice that throughout the book are a variety of articles and other resources that are meant to help you better understand the Psalms. These are interspersed at strategic locations throughout the book, and hopefully, they will be helpful for you as you dig in and seek to understand the nuances of this incredible treasure.

Finally, the concluding pages of this volume include a section with five different Bible studies that can be used in large and small groups. These Bible studies are designed to be simple and easy to use, with suggested reading plans for each of the Bible studies. Consider using these as a springboard to help get your learners more deeply engaged in the lifelong process of meditating on the Psalms.

INTRODUCING THE BOOK OF PSALMS

No other book of the Bible is quite like the book we know as the Psalms. The Book of Psalms is not one continuous writing, broken into chapters. It consists of independent units. Rather than a single author, it has multiple authors. Although some of them are identified, a third of the Psalms say nothing regarding authorship. This article will help you get to know the lay of the land in this unique book.

Organization

The book's name comes from the Greek *psalmos*, which generally means a song sung with a stringed instrument. An alternate name, *psalterion*, came into English as "psalter," which is used as another name for the entire collection. The 150 psalms are divided into five books, containing from seventeen to forty-four psalms each. The psalms comprising each book come from a variety of sources. At the conclusion of the last psalm in each of the first four books, there is some form of blessing of God, followed by an "amen" (Psalm 41:13; 72:18–19; 89:52; 106:48).

The circumstances surrounding the compilation of the five books of the Psalter are not clear. Chronology was not the organizing principle. The oldest entry, Psalm 90, composed by Moses, appears in the same book (Book Four) as several of David's psalms. It could be that each book existed on its own at one time. For instance, Psalm 14 (Book One) appears in essentially the same form in Psalm 53 (Book Two). Other examples of such borrowing of materials between books of the Psalter can be found in Psalm 40 and 70, and 57/60 and 108. It remains a mystery precisely when all five books were eventually brought together. This compilation had to have taken place by the third century BC since the translation of the Hebrew Psalter into Greek includes all of the psalms in the order we know—although several psalms are combined into one and several other psalms are divided into two.

Outline

BOOK	PRINCIPAL AUTHORS	POSSIBLE HISTORICAL CONTEXT
I. Psalms 1–41	Intensely personal psalms of David	Life of David; 11th century BC; time of the tabernacle
II. Psalms 42–72	Psalms of David and the kingdom; nationalistic	Reigns of David and Solomon; 11th and 10th centuries BC; time of the first temple
III. Psalms 73–89	Psalms of Asaph and the Sons of Korah; nationalistic	Reign of Solomon; 10th century BC; some difficult to date
IV. Psalms 90–106	Anonymous psalms and laments	Historical context less clear; some of the psalms refer to earlier writers such as Moses (Psalm 90) and David (for example, Psalm 122), but others refer to the time of exile in Babylon (Psalm 137), 6th century BC
V. Psalms 107–50	Songs of ascents and praise; psalms of David	

Headings

Many of the psalms have headings identifying authorship or circumstances of composition. Nearly half of the psalms are identified as having been written by David. The account of 1 Chronicles 16 suggests that he also wrote Psalm 96 and portions of Psalm 105.

Others wrote psalms as well. One psalm is attributed to Moses (90) and two to Solomon (72; 127). Asaph, a cymbal player in 1 Chronicles 15:19, composed a dozen psalms (50; 73–83). The Sons of Korah, who were descendants of Korah the Levite and in charge of the threshold of the tent of meeting (1 Chronicles 9:19), are responsible for eleven psalms (42; 44–49; 84–85; 87–88).

Names in the Psalms

NAME	PSALM ASSOCIATION	CONTRIBUTION
Moses: died around 1406 BC. Prophet who led Israel out of Egypt and received God's Law.	Psalm 90	Moses led or provided for leadership in worship at the beginning of Israel's independence (Exodus 15).
David: 1040–970 BC. Second king of Israel; warrior, prophet, and poet.	Psalms 3–9; 10?; 11–32; 34–41; 51–65; 68–70; 86; 101; 103; 108–10; 122; 124; 131; 133; 138–45	David appointed 4,000 singers and musicians for the tabernacle. About half of all the psalms are attributed to David.
Jeduthun (Ethan): Time of David; family of Merari?	Psalm 39	Levites/prophets appointed by David for praise at the tabernacle (1 Chronicles 25:1–3, 6). They used harps, lyres, and cymbals as accompaniment. Different family groups cast lots to determine when they would serve.
Heman: Time of David; family of Kohath.	Psalm 88	
Asaph: Time of David and Solomon; family of Gershon.	Psalms 50; 73–83	
Sons of Korah: Time of David and Solomon.	Psalms 42; 44–49; 84–85; 87–88	Doorkeepers and musicians of the tabernacle and temple.
Solomon: died 931 BC. Israel's third king; wrote Proverbs, Song of Solomon, and Ecclesiastes.	Psalms 72; 127	Builder of the first temple; 3,000 proverbs and 1,005 songs, but very few psalms, are attributed to Solomon.
Ethan: Time of Solomon.	Psalm 89	An Ezrahite, renowned for wisdom (1 Kings 4:31).
Anonymous: Some of these psalms connect with the psalm that precedes them. Most anonymous psalms are in Book Five of the Psalter.	Psalms 1–2; 10?; 33; 43; 66–67; 71; 91–100; 102; 104–7; 111–21; 123; 125–26; 128–30; 132; 134–37; 146–50	Psalms 113–18 form the "Egyptian Hallel" of later Jewish liturgy, used at festivals. Psalms 120–36 form the "Great Hallel."

Occasionally, psalm headings refer to specific historical occasions. The heading for Psalm 51 indicates that it was written when David was called to repentance for his sins of adultery and murder. Knowing the situation contributes to understanding the psalm. More than a dozen other psalms of David provide similar kinds of references (for example, Psalms 52 and 57).

Many psalm headings include instructions with meanings that are not always clear. Six psalms, for example, include the description *miktam*, which may refer to a song inscribed on a tablet or to a poem of memorable thoughts. Thirteen psalms have the heading *maskil*, which may have meant a psalm intended for teaching or meditation. Musical terms include *Gittith*, *Sheminith*, and *Shiggaion*. Nothing definite can be said about these. The same holds true for other designations, such as *According to Lilies* (Psalm 45) or *According to The Dove on Far-off Terebinths* (Psalm 56). In any case, these headings remind us that the psalms were intended to be sung, not just spoken.

Another term that appears in numerous places within the psalm texts themselves is *Selah*. Various meanings have been suggested for this word. It appears to be some sort of musical or liturgical direction, perhaps calling on the singers to pause in order to ponder the text.

Hebrew Names for Psalms

HEBREW NAME	POSSIBLE ENGLISH TRANSLATION	EXAMPLES FROM PSALMS
Mizmor	"Psalm"; refers to sound made by strings of a harp	Psalm 3; 4; etc.
Shir	Song	Psalm 18
Shir yedidoth	Song of love	Psalm 45
Shir hammaloth	Song of ascents	Psalms 120–34
Shir tehillah	Song of praise	Psalm 145
Tepillah	Prayer	Psalms 17; 86
Miktam	(meaning unknown)	Psalms 16; 56–60
Maskil	Skilled or artistic piece?	Psalms 32; 42; 45; 52–55; 74; 78; 88–89; 142
Shiggaion	(meaning unknown)	Psalm 7

Musical Instruments

References to musical instruments are made throughout the Book of Psalms and elsewhere in the Old Testament. The importance of making music is evident: "David and all Israel were celebrating before God with all their might, with song and lyres and harps and tambourines and cymbals and trumpets" (1 Chronicles 13:8). At times, the psalm prescripts give titles of tunes. Examples include "The Death of the Son" (9); "The Doe of the Morning" (22); "Lilies" (45; 69); "The Dove on Far-off Terebinths" (56), "Do Not Destroy" (57–59; 75), "Lily of the Covenant" (60; 80), and "Suffering of Affliction" (88). Such titles inspire the imagination, pointing to the range of sorrow, beauty, and joy expressed in ancient Israelite music.

Our knowledge of ancient instruments is limited, but some generalizations can be made. Of primary importance were stringed instruments with various numbers of strings. A ten-stringed lyre or harp is mentioned in Psalm 144:9. When David served in Saul's court, he played the lyre to soothe the king's troubled soul (1 Samuel 16:23). Hebrew has a variety of words for stringed instruments, but harps seem to be the basic instruments of worship. Large orchestras were formed for special services (see 2 Chronicles 5:12–13).

Another category was wind instruments. Chief among them was the *shofar*, the ram's horn, often translated as "trumpet." The priests blew this horn as Israel marched around Jericho (Joshua 6). Only two or three notes could be sounded by such instruments. Other blown instruments included pipes, similar to flutes, and reed-type instruments.

Finally, there were percussive instruments, including tambourines and cymbals (Psalm 150:4–5). The three most famous Levitical musicians, Asaph, Heman, and Ethan, were cymbal players (1 Chronicles 15:19). Another instrument was the castanets (2 Samuel 6:5). The Jewish Talmud records that the Levites usually played cymbals for beating time, nine soprano harps for melody, and two bass harps (see 1 Chronicles 25:1, 6).

Below is a list of different instruments or musical terms described in either the psalms themselves or in the superscript (or headings) of different psalms. Consider using this list as a reference as you engage in meditation on the different psalms.

bell   Small bronze bells were sewn to the hem of the high priest's garment so that they sounded as he walked (see Exodus 28:33–35).

castanets   Small shells or pieces of wood or ivory fastened to thumb and finger and then clicked together (see 2 Samuel 6:5).

choir   The chief "instrument" for praising God is the human voice, which can make music in combination with God's own Word (see Nehemiah 12:40 for more). See *voice*.

choirmaster   Probably a liturgical notation, indicating either that the director of music should collect the psalm for Israel's worship services or that the leader of the Levitical choir should speak this psalm (for more, see 1 Chronicles 23:5, 30; 25; Nehemiah 11:17).

clapping   Even hands can keep rhythm in praise to God (see Psalm 47:1).

cymbals   Copper or bronze percussion instruments (1 Chronicles 15:19). The Hebrew term describes "ringing" or "resounding" (see Psalm 150:5).

dance   Hebrew words for *dance* mean to skip, hop, leap, and whirl. Dances could be performed in a circle. Women are described dancing together (for example, in Exodus 15:20). David danced in priestly garb when the ark was brought to Jerusalem (2 Samuel 6:14–16). This is the only specific reference to male dancing.

flute In Hebrew *chalil*; from a term meaning "to pierce" or "to bore." A double-piped flute with holes bored in it for creating different musical notes (see 1 Samuel 10:5–6). Numerous clay figurines have been discovered depicting the playing of this instrument.

harp In Hebrew *nebel*. The name refers to the instrument's shape, like that of a bottle or jar. It was a large instrument with ten or twelve strings of varying length, which were plucked (see Psalm 33:2).

lute In Hebrew *kinor*. Smaller than the harp, with five or so strings, which were plucked or strummed with a plectrum.

lyre See *lute*.

pipes See *flute*.

Selah This Hebrew word is untranslatable. It is used mainly in the first two books of Psalms, and probably refers to the accompaniment of the harps during the psalm.

strings See *harp*.

tambourine The Hebrew term includes hand drums. These were usually played by women (Exodus 15:20), as shown by numerous clay figurines of women playing such instruments

trumpet In Hebrew *shofar*, or "ram's horn." The most frequently mentioned instrument in the Bible, it had both religious and military uses. Priests sounded the trumpet to call people to worship (Psalms 81:3–4; 98:6). Its loud blast was used as a signal rather than as music (see 2 Samuel 6:15). Trumpets were not played with other instruments.

trumpet(s) In Hebrew *chatsotserah*, or "bugle." This instrument, made of silver or bronze, was long and straight and had limited musical range. Like the *shofar*, this instrument had sacred and military functions. It marked the progress of the offerings (Numbers 10:1–10; Psalm 98:6). Trumpets were not played with other instruments.

voice Most common and best instrument of music, because it can convey God's Word (see 2 Chronicles 29:27–28; Psalm 47:6). See *choir.*

Some Protestant churches do not use musical instruments to accompany their singing and even forbid their use in worship. They argue that the New Testament does not teach the use of musical instruments for worship. The Psalms clearly record how important instrumental music was for worshipers who gathered at the temple (for example, Psalm 47; 150). Likewise, the Book of Revelation notes the use of musical instruments in heaven! (Note the mention of harps in Revelation 5:8; 15:2; and trumpets in Revelation 8:2, 6, 13.)

Categories of the Psalms
Some psalms are marked in their headings, or superscripts, into a thematic category of psalms. The best example of this is the Psalms of Ascents, Psalms 120–134. Other psalms have been categorized over the years into different themes; some psalms fall into two or more categories. A selection of these different psalms and how they are categorized can be found below.

1. Wisdom psalms: 1; 19:8–15; 34; 37; 49; 73; 78; 111; 112; 119; 127; 128; 133; 139

2. Messianic/royal psalms: 2; 20; 21; 45; 72; 89; 101; 110; 132; 144; and enthronement psalms: 47; 93; 96–99

3. Individual laments: 3–7; 10–14; 16; 17; 22; 25–28; 31; 35; 36; 38–43; 51–59; 61–64; 69; 71; 73; 86; 88; 102; 109; 130

4. Community laments: 44; 60; 74; 77; 79; 80; 83; 85; 89; 90; 94; 123; 126; 129; 137

5. Imprecatory psalms: 35; 69; 79; 109

6. Individual psalms of praise: 9; 18; 30–32; 40; 66; 92; 116; 138

7. Psalms of trust: 23; 27; 62; 63; 71; and 131

8. Community psalms of praise: 106; 124; 129

ENGAGING THE PSALMS: A GUIDE FOR REFLECTION AND PRAYER

9. Hymns/psalms of descriptive praise: 8; 19; 29; 33; 57; 65; 66; 89; 100; 103; 104; 111; 113; 117; 134–36; 139; 145–50

10. Psalms of creation: 8; 19; 104; 39

11. Psalms of Zion: 46; 48; 76; 84; and 87

12. Liturgical psalms: 24; 66; 107; 118; 121; 122. Psalms 120–34 are Songs of Ascents to the temple for the Feast of Weeks. The Hallel psalms (113–18) were sung at the Passover meal and at other major festivals.

Parallelism

Psalms are written in a specific style of poetry. Unlike English poetry, which is distinguished by meter and rhyme, Hebrew poetry has no rhyme scheme. Any sense of meter is better described as balance between two parallel parts of connected thoughts.

There are three main types of Hebrew parallelism:

1. *Synonymous parallelism* repeats the thought in the first line by using synonymous language in the second, often intensifying the emotion.
    > The heavens declare the glory of God,
    >> and the sky above proclaims His handiwork.
    > (Psalm 19:1)

2. *Antithetic parallelism* contrasts two opposite ideas. It is found in both Psalms and Proverbs.
    > In the *morning* it *flourishes* and is *renewed*;
    >> in the *evening* it *fades* and *withers*.
    > (Psalm 90:6, emphasis added)

3. In *synthetic parallelism*, the second statement adds to what is presented in the first. Not quite parallel in meaning, the succeeding lines carry the thought a little further.
    > Blessed is the man
    >> who *walks* not in the counsel of the wicked,
    >> nor *stands* in the way of sinners,
    >> nor *sits* in the seat of scoffers.
    > (Psalm 1:1, emphasis added)

Take some time to get to know these three different kinds of parallelism. As you meditate on the Psalms, it will be helpful to reflect. What kind of parallel is the author using, and what might that tell you about the meaning of the psalm?

PSALMS

PSALM 1

1   Blessed is the man[a]
    who walks not in the counsel of the wicked,
  nor stands in the way of sinners,
    nor sits in the seat of scoffers;
2   but his delight is in the law[b] of the LORD,
    and on his law he meditates day and night.

3   He is like a tree
    planted by streams of water
  that yields its fruit in its season,
    and its leaf does not wither.
  In all that he does, he prospers.
4   The wicked are not so,
    but are like chaff that the wind drives away.

5   Therefore the wicked will not stand in the judgment,
    nor sinners in the congregation of the righteous;
6   for the LORD knows the way of the righteous,
    but the way of the wicked will perish.

---

a   Psalm 1:1 The singular Hebrew word for *man (ish)* is used here to portray a representative example of a godly person; see Preface
b   Psalm 1:2 Or *instruction*

The author and date of Psalm 1 are unknown. Based on the psalm's high regard for God's Word, the author may have been a scholar of the Law.

⊛ REQUEST THE SPIRIT'S HELP IN PRAYER

⊛ READ AND REPEAT THE WORD

What words or phrases stick out to you? How do those words or phrases reveal the poet's purpose for the psalm? What effect does this psalm have on you as you meditate on it?

⊛ RETURN TO THE LORD IN PRAYER

Psalm 1 shows us the destiny of both the righteous and the wicked. The wicked, all sinners, will receive judgment. Yet God has provided a different way. He sets us on the way of righteousness through His Word. The Means of Grace forever remind us that through the death and resurrection of Jesus Christ, our destination is certain. We will stand holy before God in the final judgment as the congregation of the righteous.

LORD GOD, I THANK YOU:

MERCIFUL GOD, I CONFESS TO YOU:

PRAYERS OF REQUEST
For members of my household to delight in the Lord, I pray:

For faithfulness in my everyday work, I pray:

For my congregation, I pray:

For my neighbor in the world, I pray:

NOTES:

O Lord, bless our meditation on the accomplished fact of our salvation through Christ Jesus. Amen.

PSALM 2

1　Why do the nations rage[a]
　　　and the peoples plot in vain?
2　The kings of the earth set themselves,
　　　and the rulers take counsel together,
　　　against the LORD and against his Anointed, saying,
3　"Let us burst their bonds apart
　　　and cast away their cords from us."

4　He who sits in the heavens laughs;
　　　the Lord holds them in derision.
5　Then he will speak to them in his wrath,
　　　and terrify them in his fury, saying,
6　"As for me, I have set my King
　　　on Zion, my holy hill."

7　I will tell of the decree:
　　　The LORD said to me, "You are my Son;
　　　　today I have begotten you.
8　Ask of me, and I will make the nations your heritage,
　　　and the ends of the earth your possession.
9　You shall break[b] them with a rod of iron
　　　and dash them in pieces like a potter's vessel."

10　Now therefore, O kings, be wise;
　　　be warned, O rulers of the earth.
11　Serve the LORD with fear,
　　　and rejoice with trembling.
12　Kiss the Son,
　　　lest he be angry, and you perish in the way,
　　　for his wrath is quickly kindled.
　　　Blessed are all who take refuge in him.

a　Psalm 2:1 Or *nations noisily assemble*
b　Psalm 2:9 Revocalization yields (compare Septuagint) *You shall rule*

Psalm 2 is ascribed to David in Acts 4:25, perhaps because the whole Psalter is associated with him. The context of the psalm may be David's coronation or the coronation of one of Jerusalem's other kings. The beginning verses may hint at some of King David's later wars, perhaps from 2 Samuel 8; 10.

◉ REQUEST THE SPIRIT'S HELP IN PRAYER

◉ READ AND REPEAT THE WORD

What words or phrases stick out to you? How do those words or phrases reveal the poet's purpose for the psalm? What effect does this psalm have on you as you meditate on it?

◉ RETURN TO THE LORD IN PRAYER

Those who plot against God's elect and anointed ones incite God's wrath. The Lord, not human beings, anointed Israel's king and elected this nation for His plan of salvation. Ultimately, the Messiah—which means "Anointed One"—was born from the nation of Israel. God preserved Israel so that through one of David's descendants, Mary, the Savior of humankind was born (for more, see Genesis 3:15). Those "who take refuge in Him" (v. 12), trusting in Him through faith for their salvation, are truly blessed.

PRAYERS:

Lord Jesus, despite our miserable and constant rebellion, You rescue us from sin. Lead us to embrace Your gracious rule with joyful hearts. Amen.

PSALM 3

1   O LORD, how many are my foes!
      Many are rising against me;
2   many are saying of my soul,
      "There is no salvation for him in God."   *Selah* [a]

3   But you, O LORD, are a shield about me,
      my glory, and the lifter of my head.
4   I cried aloud to the LORD,
      and he answered me from his holy hill.   *Selah*

5   I lay down and slept;
      I woke again, for the LORD sustained me.
6   I will not be afraid of many thousands of people
      who have set themselves against me all around.

7   Arise, O LORD!
      Save me, O my God!
  For you strike all my enemies on the cheek;
      you break the teeth of the wicked.

8   Salvation belongs to the LORD;
      your blessing be on your people!   *Selah*

---

a   Psalm 3:2 The meaning of the Hebrew word *Selah*, used frequently in the Psalms, is uncertain. It may be a musical or liturgical direction

This psalm of David describes Absalom's attempt to undermine his father's rule (2 Samuel 15–17). Thus, it was written toward the end of David's reign.

⚜ REQUEST THE SPIRIT'S HELP IN PRAYER

⚜ READ AND REPEAT THE WORD

What words or phrases stick out to you? How do those words or phrases reveal the poet's purpose for the psalm? What effect does this psalm have on you as you meditate on it?

⚜ RETURN TO THE LORD IN PRAYER

This psalm recounts a dark period in David's life. His enemies, including his own son, have overwhelmed and opposed him. Despite his foes' claim that David's sins preclude him from salvation, David remains confident that God will protect and deliver him. Despite our miserable condition and certain end, God shields us from our foes, lifts us, and directs our eyes to His great mercy, displayed in the cross of Christ. He assures us that salvation belongs to Him and is given to those who trust in Him.

LORD GOD, I THANK YOU:

MERCIFUL GOD, I CONFESS TO YOU:

PRAYERS OF REQUEST
For those in my household and in my family both near and far, I pray:

That I may remain focused and faithful in my everyday work, I pray:

For the sick and hurting in my congregation, I pray:

For my neighbor and those who suffer in society, I pray:

NOTES:

"You, O LORD, are a shield about me, my glory, and the lifter of my head. . . . Arise, O LORD! Save me, O my God!" (Psalm 3:3, 7). Amen.

PSALM 4

To the choirmaster: with stringed instruments. A Psalm of David.

1   Answer me when I call, O God of my righteousness!
     You have given me relief when I was in distress.
     Be gracious to me and hear my prayer!

2   O men,[a] how long shall my honor be turned into shame?
     How long will you love vain words and seek after lies? *Selah*
3   But know that the LORD has set apart the godly for himself;
     the LORD hears when I call to him.

4   Be angry,[b] and do not sin;
     ponder in your own hearts on your beds,
     and be silent.   *Selah*
5   Offer right sacrifices,
     and put your trust in the LORD.

6   There are many who say, "Who will show us some good?
     Lift up the light of your face upon us, O LORD!"
7   You have put more joy in my heart
     than they have when their grain and wine abound.

8   In peace I will both lie down and sleep;
     for you alone, O LORD, make me dwell in safety.

---

a   Psalm 4:2 Or *O men of rank*
b   Psalm 4:4 Or *Be agitated*

Psalm 4 was for the director of Israel's worship services, or perhaps it was to be spoken or sung by the director of a liturgical choir.

⊚ REQUEST THE SPIRIT'S HELP IN PRAYER

⊚ READ AND REPEAT THE WORD

What words or phrases stick out to you? How do those words or phrases reveal the poet's purpose for the psalm? What effect does this psalm have on you as you meditate on it?

....

....

....

....

....

....

....

⊚ RETURN TO THE LORD IN PRAYER

David complains that his enemies are speaking ill of him as king in an attempt to shame him. He reminds them that God sets apart the godly from those who behave in such a manner. How often do we find ourselves speaking ill of people in positions of authority, of colleagues, and of peers? God's Word condemns unjust complaints. Through David, God encourages us to turn from our sinful ways and "trust in the LORD" (Psalm 4:5). Such trust brings peace of mind and eternal peace.

LORD GOD, YOU HAVE CREATED ME, REDEEMED ME BY THE BLOOD OF CHRIST, AND GIVEN ME FAITH AND NEW LIFE THROUGH THE POWER OF THE HOLY SPIRIT. I BRING MY PRAYERS BEFORE YOU, ESPECIALLY PRAYERS FOR TRUST IN YOU AND YOUR WORD AND FOR PEACE. I ESPECIALLY PRAY:

....

....

....

....

....

....

"You alone, O LORD, make me dwell in safety" (Psalm 4:8).
Teach me to judge rightly and dwell in peace. Amen.

To the choirmaster: for the flutes. A Psalm of David.

1   Give ear to my words, O Lord;
        consider my groaning.
2   Give attention to the sound of my cry,
        my King and my God,
        for to you do I pray.
3   O Lord, in the morning you hear my voice;
        in the morning I prepare a sacrifice for you[a] and watch.

4   For you are not a God who delights in wickedness;
        evil may not dwell with you.
5   The boastful shall not stand before your eyes;
        you hate all evildoers.
6   You destroy those who speak lies;
        the Lord abhors the bloodthirsty and deceitful man.

7   But I, through the abundance of your steadfast love,
        will enter your house.
    I will bow down toward your holy temple
        in the fear of you.
8   Lead me, O Lord, in your righteousness
        because of my enemies;
        make your way straight before me.

9   For there is no truth in their mouth;
        their inmost self is destruction;
    their throat is an open grave;
        they flatter with their tongue.
10 Make them bear their guilt, O God;
        let them fall by their own counsels;
    because of the abundance of their transgressions cast them out,
        for they have rebelled against you.

11 But let all who take refuge in you rejoice;
        let them ever sing for joy,
    and spread your protection over them,
        that those who love your name may exult in you.
12 For you bless the righteous, O Lord;
        you cover him with favor as with a shield.

a   Psalm 5:3 Or *I direct my prayer to you*

This psalm of David, written for the choirmaster, was written to include flutes. These were likely double-piped instruments with holes bored into them to create different notes.

◉ REQUEST THE SPIRIT'S HELP IN PRAYER

◉ READ AND REPEAT THE WORD

What words or phrases stick out to you? How do those words or phrases reveal the poet's purpose for the psalm? What effect does this psalm have on you as you meditate on it?

....

....

....

....

....

....

....

....

....

◉ RETURN TO THE LORD IN PRAYER

Boasting and deceit inevitably lead to destruction. David's petition reveals that God leads us out of such sins and covers us with His favor. God declares us righteous and covers us with His favor through faith in Christ's atoning sacrifice for all of our sins.

LORD GOD, I THANK YOU:

....

....

MERCIFUL GOD, I CONFESS TO YOU:

....

....

GOD OUR REFUGE, I ALSO PRAY TODAY:

....

....

Lord Jesus Christ, You are the light of the world; You alone are the way to eternal life. Restrain the corrupters of Your Word and all the enemies of Your truth. Preserve the truth of Your Gospel in these latter days, through faithful teachers who will lead us in the way everlasting. Grant us to serve You in steadfast faith and in good conscience. Amen.

Psalm 5 is a psalm of prayer against the false teachers and the rebellious spirits. It harshly condemns both their glistening teaching and their works, by which—under the name of God—they do great harm to the pure Word of God and the true worship of God. The psalm prays for the righteous, that is, for the pure Word of God and the pure worship of God. In the last verse it promises that such a prayer will be heard and the rebellious spirits will be condemned.

This psalm belongs to the Second and Third Commandments, in which we are commanded to keep both God's name and God's Word holy. It belongs to the First and Second Petitions of the Lord's Prayer, in which we pray that God's name, honor, and kingdom will be advanced. (Martin Luther)

HOW LONG, O LORD, HOW LONG?

Often, things are not as they seem. Seeds planted in the ground appear to be dead, but the experienced farmer or gardener knows that beneath the surface a miracle is taking place. The seed is preparing to sprout and begin its growth. Things are not as they seem.

So it is in the Christian life. While one might logically expect life to be good for God's children, this is not always the case. Often, it seems to be quite the opposite, as though God has abandoned His followers and hidden Himself from them. That is the sense one gets when reading the psalms of lament, especially those of David.

David's Lament

Considering David's struggles, it's not surprising to hear him wrestle with God. For example, in Psalm 6, David voices his confidence in God's deliverance. Yet he also expresses the agony of waiting for God to act: "My soul also is greatly troubled. But You, O LORD—how long?" (v. 3). David continues, "I am weary with my moaning; every night I flood my bed with tears; I drench my couch with my weeping. My eye wastes away because of grief; it grows weak because of all my foes" (vv. 6–7). David's confidence, however, remains solely in the Lord, even in the face of seeming abandonment: "The LORD has heard my plea; the LORD accepts my prayer" (v. 9).

Asaph's Lament

Of the various types of psalms, psalms of lament, including Psalm 6, are by far the most numerous. They are not limited to David's psalms. Psalm 77, written by Asaph, provides an excellent example of how God's faithful people struggle during times of doubt. "Will the Lord spurn forever, and never again be favorable? Has His steadfast love forever ceased? Are His promises at an end for all time? Has God forgotten to be gracious? Has He in anger shut up His compassion?" (vv. 7–9).

To the one who is undergoing trial and hardship, the answer to such questions might seem a disheartening yes. But believers cling in faith to a deeper, more profound truth—namely, that God will not abandon His faithful. In that light, the psalmist confesses, "Then I said, 'I will appeal to this, to the years of the right hand of the Most High.' I will remember the deeds of the LORD; yes, I will remember Your wonders of old. I will ponder all Your work, and meditate on Your mighty deeds" (vv. 10–12).

Even when all evidence points to the contrary, the psalmist—and the Christian—appeals to God's saving deeds, confident that He will carry us through even the worst trials.

How Long?

One of the phrases frequently used in the psalms of lament is "How long?" We see it in Psalm 6. Consider other examples:

> How long, O LORD? Will You forget me forever? How long will You hide Your face from me? How long must I take counsel in my soul and have sorrow in my heart all the day? How long shall my enemy be exalted over me? (Psalm 13:1–2)

> How long, O Lord, will You look on? Rescue me from their destruction, my precious life from the lions! (Psalm 35:17)

> How long, O God, is the foe to scoff? (Psalm 74:10)

In each case, the heartfelt plea to God is followed by a confident confession of faith:

> But I have trusted in Your steadfast love; my heart shall rejoice in Your salvation. I will sing to the LORD, because He has dealt bountifully with me. (Psalm 13:5–6)

> I will thank You in the great congregation; in the mighty throng I will praise You. (Psalm 35:18)

> Yet God my King is from of old, working salvation in the midst of the earth. (Psalm 74:12)

Psalm 22

Perhaps the most famous of the psalms of lament is Psalm 22. Better known as a messianic psalm, it expresses feelings of anguish and abandonment that sometimes accompany us in times of severe trial: "My God, my God, why have You forsaken me? Why are You so far from saving me, from the words of my groaning? O my God, I cry by day, but You do not answer, and by night, but I find no rest" (vv. 1–2).

Have you ever felt this way? Of course, no one can know the utter abandonment that our Lord underwent as He bore the sin of the world on the cross. Even in our own moments of agony, though, we can confess, "Yet You are holy, enthroned on the praises of Israel. In You our fathers trusted; they trusted, and You delivered them. To You they cried and were rescued; in You they trusted and were not put to shame" (vv. 3–5).

Like Jesus, whose confidence was completely in His Father, you can confidently trust that God will deliver you from your tribulations.

Theology of the Cross

Early in the Reformation, Martin Luther had to wrestle with suffering. In a collection of theses on grace and good works that Luther prepared for a disputation at Heidelberg, he wrote, "He deserves to be called a theologian, however, who comprehends the visible and manifest things of God seen through suffering and the cross" (AE 31:40). In the explanation of the following thesis, Luther wrote, "This is clear: He who does not know Christ does not know God hidden in suffering. . . . God can be found only in suffering and the cross, as has already been said" (AE 31:53).

The more Luther studied Scripture, including the Psalms, the more he came to realize that God's true heart of mercy is found not in the grand and obvious works of His creation but rather in the sufferings of Christ, who bore the world's sin. Those who think that evidence of God's approval is found in one's success, Luther says, are not theologians of the cross; they are theologians of glory. Luther could find great comfort in promises such as this passage from Hebrews 4:15–16:

> We do not have a high priest who is unable to sympathize with our weaknesses, but one who in every respect has been tempted as we are, yet without sin. Let us then with confidence draw near to the throne of grace, that we may receive mercy and find grace to help in time of need.

As you study and meditate upon the Psalms, always keep your eyes fixed on Jesus. Like the psalmist, you, too, will experience hardships and trials in life. Difficult things will happen to you: things that you have brought upon yourself through your sins, evils that others do to you, and events in nature or different sicknesses or diseases that seem to happen for no reason at all. Though Christians ultimately know that God is in control of all things, this often is little comfort when God does not tell us why, and it is not a good habit to speculate and try to come up with reasons for God when He gives none. Instead, we can call evil what it is, and instead fix our eyes and minds on what we do know: that Christ suffered and died for you to give you the gifts of forgiveness, life, and salvation. Fix your eyes on Him in your laments, trials, and suffering, remembering that He understands your pain and struggle more than you know. Pray to Him in all things. Look forward to the day when Jesus will return to destroy the power of sin, death, and the devil once and for all. He will restore a new creation, free from all suffering and death, for His people.

PSALM 6

To the choirmaster: with stringed instruments; according to The
Sheminith.[a] A Psalm of David.

1 O LORD, rebuke me not in your anger,
   nor discipline me in your wrath.
2 Be gracious to me, O LORD, for I am languishing;
   heal me, O LORD, for my bones are troubled.
3 My soul also is greatly troubled.
   But you, O LORD—how long?

4 Turn, O LORD, deliver my life;
   save me for the sake of your steadfast love.
5 For in death there is no remembrance of you;
   in Sheol who will give you praise?

6 I am weary with my moaning;
   every night I flood my bed with tears;
   I drench my couch with my weeping.
7 My eye wastes away because of grief;
   it grows weak because of all my foes.

8 Depart from me, all you workers of evil,
   for the LORD has heard the sound of my weeping.
9 The LORD has heard my plea;
   the LORD accepts my prayer.
10 All my enemies shall be ashamed and greatly troubled;
   they shall turn back and be put to shame in a moment.

a   Psalm 6:1 Probably a musical or liturgical term

Psalm 6 is one of seven penitential psalms, or psalms of confession and repentance. The other psalms of this type are Psalms 32; 38; 51; 102; 130; and 143. The exact context of this prayer for deliverance is uncertain.

❀ REQUEST THE SPIRIT'S HELP IN PRAYER

❀ READ AND REPEAT THE WORD

What words or phrases stick out to you? How do those words or phrases reveal the poet's purpose for the psalm? What effect does this psalm have on you as you meditate on it?

❀ RETURN TO THE LORD IN PRAYER

David pleads with the Lord for deliverance from anxiety, physical discomfort, and sickness caused by a growing awareness of his sinful condition. Luther referred to such mental torment as *Anfechtung*, a German term for the state of despair and doubt we human beings experience when coming to terms with the consequences of our failure to meet the demands of God's Law. Scripture clearly reveals that the result of sin is death, as beautifully described in Romans 6:23, but how seriously do we take this threat? Consider this: nearly two thousand years ago, our sinful condition was so desperate that God sent His own Son to pay the price. God be praised! Through faith in Christ's redemption, our sins have been forgiven.

MERCIFUL GOD, I AM UNWORTHY OF FORGIVENESS, LIFE, AND SALVATION, YET IN CHRIST, YOU HAVE FORGIVEN ME MY SINS. TRUSTING THAT YOU DESIRE TO HEAR MY PRAYER, I CONFESS TO YOU THAT I HAVE SINNED:

*Lord, hear my plea and accept my prayer through
the merits of Jesus, who prays for me. Amen.*

PSALM 7

A Shiggaion[a] of David, which he sang to the LORD concerning the words of Cush, a Benjaminite.

1 O LORD my God, in you do I take refuge;
  save me from all my pursuers and deliver me,
2 lest like a lion they tear my soul apart,
  rending it in pieces, with none to deliver.

3 O LORD my God, if I have done this,
  if there is wrong in my hands,
4 if I have repaid my friend[b] with evil
  or plundered my enemy without cause,
5 let the enemy pursue my soul and overtake it,
  and let him trample my life to the ground
  and lay my glory in the dust. *Selah*

6 Arise, O LORD, in your anger;
  lift yourself up against the fury of my enemies;
  awake for me; you have appointed a judgment.
7 Let the assembly of the peoples be gathered about you;
  over it return on high.

8 The LORD judges the peoples;
  judge me, O LORD, according to my righteousness
  and according to the integrity that is in me.
9 Oh, let the evil of the wicked come to an end,
  and may you establish the righteous—
  you who test the minds and hearts,[c]
  O righteous God!
10 My shield is with God,
  who saves the upright in heart.
11 God is a righteous judge,
  and a God who feels indignation every day.

a Psalm 7:1 Probably a musical or liturgical term
b Psalm 7:4 Hebrew *the one at peace with me*
c Psalm 7:9 Hebrew *the hearts and kidneys*

12 If a man^d does not repent, God^e will whet his sword;
    he has bent and readied his bow;
13 he has prepared for him his deadly weapons,
    making his arrows fiery shafts.
14 Behold, the wicked man conceives evil
    and is pregnant with mischief
    and gives birth to lies.
15 He makes a pit, digging it out,
    and falls into the hole that he has made.
16 His mischief returns upon his own head,
    and on his own skull his violence descends.

17 I will give to the LORD the thanks due to his righteousness,
    and I will sing praise to the name of the LORD, the Most High.

d Psalm 7:12 Hebrew *he*
e Psalm 7:12 Hebrew *he*

The title of Psalm 7 includes the word *Shiggaion,* a rare Hebrew word, which is possibly a liturgical term or usage. Some scholars argue that it borrows from an ancient Assyrian (or Akkadian) word that means "to complain" or "to lament." The other name in the title is Cush, a Benjaminite. Since Cush was from the tribe of Benjamin, he was almost certainly an ally of David's enemy Saul, and his words prompted David to write this psalm.

⊛ REQUEST THE SPIRIT'S HELP IN PRAYER

⊛ READ AND REPEAT THE WORD

What words or phrases stick out to you? How do those words or phrases reveal the poet's purpose for the psalm? What effect does this psalm have on you as you meditate on it?

⊛ RETURN TO THE LORD IN PRAYER

David, confident of his righteousness, petitions the Lord to judge him and his enemies justly. He repeatedly asserts that the righteousness of God's justice must destroy unrepentant sinners, and he compares God's wrath to that of a soldier preparing to meet his foe. What a startling image for those who refuse to repent of their sins! Yet the Lord also offers salvation through Christ Jesus, for which God's people rejoice.

PRAYERS:

*O God, readily forgive and turn away Your righteous
indignation from me. Put a new song on my lips: "Praise to
the name of the LORD, the Most High" (Psalm 7:17). Amen.*

Psalm 7 is also a psalm of prayer. It laments over slanderers who accuse the saints and their teachings as being riotous, opposed to the authorities, and disturbing the peace. In this way Shimei the Benjaminite (2 Samuel 16:5–14) slandered the pious David as if David had stolen King Saul's kingdom. In the same way, Christ was also accused before Pilate, and even now slanderers defame the Gospel. David fights against this affliction with prayer and cries to God of his innocence. By David's own example, he shows us that such a prayer was granted, so that we might have comfort. The psalm also threatens the slanderers and oppressors and holds before them the example of those who perish before they accomplished the evil they intended. It belongs, like the preceding psalm, in the Second Commandment and the First Petition. (Martin Luther)

PSALM 8

To the choirmaster: according to The Gittith.[a] A Psalm of David.

1   O LORD, our Lord,
     how majestic is your name in all the earth!
    You have set your glory above the heavens.
2   Out of the mouth of babies and infants,
    you have established strength because of your foes,
     to still the enemy and the avenger.

3   When I look at your heavens, the work of your fingers,
     the moon and the stars, which you have set in place,
4   what is man that you are mindful of him,
     and the son of man that you care for him?

5   Yet you have made him a little lower than the
  heavenly beings[b]
    and crowned him with glory and honor.
6   You have given him dominion over the works of your hands;
    you have put all things under his feet,
7   all sheep and oxen,
    and also the beasts of the field,
8   the birds of the heavens, and the fish of the sea,
    whatever passes along the paths of the seas.

9   O LORD, our Lord,
    how majestic is your name in all the earth!

a   Psalm 8:1 Probably a musical or liturgical term
b   Psalm 8:5 Or *than God*; Septuagint *than the angels*

22

The meaning of the word *Gittith* in the title is unclear. Perhaps it points to a kind of musical instrument or particular melody. References to the moon and stars in this psalm make it especially appropriate for evening worship.

◉ REQUEST THE SPIRIT'S HELP IN PRAYER

◉ READ AND REPEAT THE WORD

What words or phrases stick out to you? How do those words or phrases reveal the poet's purpose for the psalm? What effect does this psalm have on you as you meditate on it?

◉ RETURN TO THE LORD IN PRAYER

Of this psalm, Luther wrote:

> David concludes this psalm just the way he began it. He thanks the Lord, our Ruler, for His great and inestimable blessing, for establishing such a kingdom and calling and gathering His church, which gloriously praises His name throughout the world and thanks Him in heaven. Let us follow the example of this singer of praises as he prophesies to us. The Lord is our Ruler, too, and His kingdom is established and founded from the mouths of babes and sucklings. We entered it by Baptism, and we are called to it daily through Word and Gospel. With David we also hope to come to where we shall see the heavens, the work of His fingers, the moon and the stars which He will prepare. He won the kingdom with great trouble and anguish. Now He is crowned with honor and adornment and has everything under His feet. For this we give God our praise and thanks, but especially for the fact that He has brought us to a light and knowledge that does not spring up out of human reason but out of Christ. He is our Sun, who died for us and was raised from the dead, lives and reigns, so that through Him we might be saved. To this end may God help us all. Amen. Glory to God alone. (AE 12:135–36)

LORD GOD, TODAY I BRING BEFORE YOU MY PRAYERS:

PSALM 9

[a]To the choirmaster: according to Muth-labben.[b] A Psalm of David.

1   I will give thanks to the LORD with my whole heart;
      I will recount all of your wonderful deeds.
2   I will be glad and exult in you;
      I will sing praise to your name, O Most High.

3   When my enemies turn back,
      they stumble and perish before[c] your presence.
4   For you have maintained my just cause;
      you have sat on the throne, giving righteous judgment.

5   You have rebuked the nations; you have made the
    wicked perish;
      you have blotted out their name forever and ever.
6   The enemy came to an end in everlasting ruins;
      their cities you rooted out;
      the very memory of them has perished.

7   But the LORD sits enthroned forever;
      he has established his throne for justice,
8   and he judges the world with righteousness;
      he judges the peoples with uprightness.

9   The LORD is a stronghold for the oppressed,
      a stronghold in times of trouble.
10 And those who know your name put their trust in you,
      for you, O LORD, have not forsaken those who seek you.

11 Sing praises to the LORD, who sits enthroned in Zion!
      Tell among the peoples his deeds!
12 For he who avenges blood is mindful of them;
      he does not forget the cry of the afflicted.

---

a   Psalm 9:1 Psalms 9 and 10 together follow an acrostic pattern, each stanza beginning with the successive letters
    of the Hebrew alphabet. In the Septuagint they form one psalm
b   Psalm 9:1 Probably a musical or liturgical term
c   Psalm 9:3 Or *because of*

13 Be gracious to me, O Lord!
> See my affliction from those who hate me,
> O you who lift me up from the gates of death,
14 that I may recount all your praises,
> that in the gates of the daughter of Zion
> I may rejoice in your salvation.

15 The nations have sunk in the pit that they made;
> in the net that they hid, their own foot has been caught.
16 The Lord has made himself known; he has executed judgment;
> the wicked are snared in the work of their own hands.
> *Higgaion.*[d] *Selah*

17 The wicked shall return to Sheol,
> all the nations that forget God.

18 For the needy shall not always be forgotten,
> and the hope of the poor shall not perish forever.

19 Arise, O Lord! Let not man prevail;
> let the nations be judged before you!
20 Put them in fear, O Lord!
> Let the nations know that they are but men!　*Selah*

---

d　Psalm 9:16 Probably a musical or liturgical term

Psalms 9 and 10 are understood by many scholars to comprise one psalm. Some commentators suggest that the psalm was composed later in David's lifetime, after the ark of the covenant was brought to and permanently kept in Jerusalem, as referenced in verse 11. *Muth-labben* is likely a musical notation.

⊛ REQUEST THE SPIRIT'S HELP IN PRAYER

⊛ READ AND REPEAT THE WORD

What words or phrases stick out to you? How do those words or phrases reveal the poet's purpose for the psalm? What effect does this psalm have on you as you meditate on it?

⊛ RETURN TO THE LORD IN PRAYER

"The wicked are snared in the work of their own hands" (v. 16), David observes in this psalm. How timeless is this truth! How often do we dig ourselves deeper into sin just to cover up a previous sin? Ultimately, our sin carries the most frightening of consequences: death and damnation. However, as David reminds us, if we acknowledge our sin and God's wonderful deeds on our behalf, especially through Christ, we can be confident of His mercy toward us. We, too, can "be glad and exult" (v. 2) in His name.

LORD GOD, I THANK YOU:

MERCIFUL GOD, I CONFESS TO YOU:

PRAYERS OF REQUEST
For members of my household to delight in the Lord, I pray:

For faithfulness in my everyday work, I pray:

For my congregation, I pray:

For my neighbor in the world, I pray:

Dear Lord Jesus, through praise and thanksgiving, we continually recount Your wonderful deeds. Amen.

Psalm 9 is also a prophecy of the people of Christ, the Holy Christian Church. They suffer, following the example of Christ, and their blood is continually being shed. However, the psalm gives this prophecy thankfully and comfortingly, so that it might well be called a psalm of thanks and comfort. The Christians (and especially the holy martyrs) here thank God and are comforted by the fact that God never leaves them. No, the more they are persecuted, the more He multiplies them, as some of the persecutors convert and become Christians and the others perish. This psalm belongs in the First Commandment and in the Second Petition. (Martin Luther)

PSALM 10

1 Why, O LORD, do you stand far away?
  Why do you hide yourself in times of trouble?

2 In arrogance the wicked hotly pursue the poor;
  let them be caught in the schemes that they have devised.
3 For the wicked boasts of the desires of his soul,
  and the one greedy for gain curses[a] and renounces
  the LORD.
4 In the pride of his face[b] the wicked does not seek him;[c]
  all his thoughts are, "There is no God."
5 His ways prosper at all times;
  your judgments are on high, out of his sight;
  as for all his foes, he puffs at them.
6 He says in his heart, "I shall not be moved;
  throughout all generations I shall not meet adversity."
7 His mouth is filled with cursing and deceit and oppression;
  under his tongue are mischief and iniquity.
8 He sits in ambush in the villages;
  in hiding places he murders the innocent.
  His eyes stealthily watch for the helpless;
9   he lurks in ambush like a lion in his thicket;
  he lurks that he may seize the poor;
    he seizes the poor when he draws him into his net.
10 The helpless are crushed, sink down,
  and fall by his might.
11 He says in his heart, "God has forgotten,
  he has hidden his face, he will never see it."

12 Arise, O LORD; O God, lift up your hand;
  forget not the afflicted.
13 Why does the wicked renounce God
  and say in his heart, "You will not call to account"?
14 But you do see, for you note mischief and vexation,
  that you may take it into your hands;
  to you the helpless commits himself;
  you have been the helper of the fatherless.
15 Break the arm of the wicked and evildoer;
  call his wickedness to account till you find none.

---

a   Psalm 10:3 Or *and he blesses the one greedy for gain*
b   Psalm 10:4 Or *of his anger*
c   Psalm 10:4 Or *the wicked says, "He will not call to account"*

16 The Lord is king forever and ever;
    the nations perish from his land.
17 O Lord, you hear the desire of the afflicted;
    you will strengthen their heart; you will incline your ear
18 to do justice to the fatherless and the oppressed,
    so that man who is of the earth may strike terror no more.

For more on this psalm, read the introduction to Psalm 9, its counterpart.

⊛ REQUEST THE SPIRIT'S HELP IN PRAYER

⊛ READ AND REPEAT THE WORD

What words or phrases stick out to you? How do those words or phrases reveal the poet's purpose for the psalm? What effect does this psalm have on you as you meditate on it?

⊛ RETURN TO THE LORD IN PRAYER

The psalmist confidently prays that God will root out those who are wicked and take advantage of the weak and poor throughout Israel. He asks God to dispense justice, so that these wicked men "may strike terror no more" (v. 18). Such behavior, David reminds us, will be called into account. There is hope, however, whether we have taken advantage of the weak or have been the victim of oppression. The Lord has compassion on those oppressed by sin.

PRAYERS:

In mercy, Lord, bring "justice to the fatherless and the oppressed" (Psalm 10:18). Eradicate terror and injustice from the earth. Forgive us, and come quickly to establish Your kingdom. Amen.

PSALM 11

To the choirmaster. Of David.

1   In the LORD I take refuge;
    how can you say to my soul,
      "Flee like a bird to your mountain,
2   for behold, the wicked bend the bow;
      they have fitted their arrow to the string
      to shoot in the dark at the upright in heart;
3   if the foundations are destroyed,
      what can the righteous do?"[a]

4   The LORD is in his holy temple;
      the LORD's throne is in heaven;
      his eyes see, his eyelids test the children of man.
5   The LORD tests the righteous,
      but his soul hates the wicked and the one who loves
      violence.
6   Let him rain coals on the wicked;
      fire and sulfur and a scorching wind shall be the portion
      of their cup.
7   For the LORD is righteous;
    he loves righteous deeds;
      the upright shall behold his face.

---

a   Psalm 11:3 Or *for the foundations will be destroyed; what has the righteous done?*

Psalm 11 was written during a time in which the danger posed by David's enemies was so great that even the king's counselors encouraged him to retreat into hiding, likely during the events of 2 Samuel 15–17.

◉ REQUEST THE SPIRIT'S HELP IN PRAYER

◉ READ AND REPEAT THE WORD

What words or phrases stick out to you? How do those words or phrases reveal the poet's purpose for the psalm? What effect does this psalm have on you as you meditate on it?

◉ RETURN TO THE LORD IN PRAYER

In this psalm, David confesses his confidence in the Lord's unmovable favor. The Lord, David writes, "tests the righteous" (v. 5). Our faith is often tested and often found wanting. God's faithfulness and mercy toward us, however, never weaken or fail. Despite our lack of faith and even our wicked deeds, He extends His grace as a refuge from our sinful nature and the sinful works of others. He does so audibly and visibly through Word and Sacrament, as a testament of His great and unending love for us.

LORD GOD, I THANK YOU:

MERCIFUL GOD, I CONFESS TO YOU:

PRAYERS OF REQUEST
For members of my household to delight in the Lord, I pray:

For faithfulness in my everyday work, I pray:

For my congregation, I pray:

For my neighbor in the world, I pray:

In You, O Lord, we take refuge. Though we are found wanting for righteousness, save us by the righteousness of Christ. Amen.

PSALM 12

To the choirmaster: according to The Sheminith.[a] A Psalm of David.

1   Save, O LORD, for the godly one is gone;
      for the faithful have vanished from among the children
      of man.
2   Everyone utters lies to his neighbor;
      with flattering lips and a double heart they speak.

3   May the LORD cut off all flattering lips,
      the tongue that makes great boasts,
4   those who say, "With our tongue we will prevail,
      our lips are with us; who is master over us?"

5   "Because the poor are plundered, because the needy groan,
      I will now arise," says the LORD;
      "I will place him in the safety for which he longs."
6   The words of the LORD are pure words,
      like silver refined in a furnace on the ground,
      purified seven times.

7   You, O LORD, will keep them;
      you will guard us[b] from this generation forever.
8   On every side the wicked prowl,
      as vileness is exalted among the children of man.

---

a   Psalm 12:1 Probably a musical or liturgical term
b   Psalm 12:7 Or *guard him*

The word *Sheminith* in the title literally means "the eighth." Though likely about a musical note, the meaning of the word is uncertain. As a youth, David was repeatedly mistreated by King Saul, as found in 1 Samuel 18:6–11. Later, King David was the target of further intrigues, including the famous one involving his son Absalom (2 Samuel 15–18). This psalm recalls those and other similar experiences.

❀ REQUEST THE SPIRIT'S HELP IN PRAYER

❀ READ AND REPEAT THE WORD

What words or phrases stick out to you? How do those words or phrases reveal the poet's purpose for the psalm? What effect does this psalm have on you as you meditate on it?

❀ RETURN TO THE LORD IN PRAYER

In this psalm, we hear David cry for help in the face of treachery and deceit. Unchecked wickedness sometimes leads us to doubt that God is watching out for us. Such despair is a great evil and can ruin our souls. However, it can also help us to appreciate our complete dependence on God and His unfailing promises to save and defend us, which are ultimately fulfilled for us in Christ.

LORD GOD, I THANK YOU:

MERCIFUL GOD, I CONFESS TO YOU:

PRAYERS OF REQUEST
For members of my household to delight in the Lord, I pray:

For faithfulness in my everyday work, I pray:

For my congregation, I pray:

For my neighbor in the world, I pray:

*Lord, use the surrounding evil and the threats they pose
to drive us once again to a lively hope in our promised
salvation; through Christ Jesus, our Lord. Amen.*

PSALM 13

To the choirmaster. A Psalm of David.

1 How long, O LORD? Will you forget me forever?
     How long will you hide your face from me?
2 How long must I take counsel in my soul
     and have sorrow in my heart all the day?
   How long shall my enemy be exalted over me?

3 Consider and answer me, O LORD my God;
     light up my eyes, lest I sleep the sleep of death,
4 lest my enemy say, "I have prevailed over him,"
     lest my foes rejoice because I am shaken.

5 But I have trusted in your steadfast love;
     my heart shall rejoice in your salvation.
6 I will sing to the LORD,
     because he has dealt bountifully with me.

Psalm 13 is best understood as having been written while David was being pursued by King Saul. On numerous occasions during Saul's pursuit, David was nearly killed.

⊛ REQUEST THE SPIRIT'S HELP IN PRAYER

⊛ READ AND REPEAT THE WORD

What words or phrases stick out to you? How do those words or phrases reveal the poet's purpose for the psalm? What effect does this psalm have on you as you meditate on it?

....

....

....

....

⊛ RETURN TO THE LORD IN PRAYER

In moments of fear and frustration, our prayers can easily slip into blaming God for our problems. Asking "How long, O LORD?" (v. 1) is understandable. Casting blame on the Lord and reproving His failure to act according to our wishes and timetables, however, comes close to blasphemy. When our prayers question God and His ways, we do well to remember that Jesus not only commanded us to pray but also graciously promised to hear our prayers and intercede for us before the Father. No matter how weak our prayers or deep our frustration, Jesus' grace makes up for their shortcomings.

LORD GOD, I THANK YOU:
....

MERCIFUL GOD, I CONFESS TO YOU:
....

PRAYERS OF REQUEST
For members of my household to delight in the Lord, I pray:
....

For faithfulness in my everyday work, I pray:
....

For my congregation, I pray:
....

For my neighbor in the world, I pray:
....

*Lord Jesus, You conquered death and the grave; You can
handle anything, including our impatient or even disrespectful
prayers. Teach us to know that You are greater than all things,
so that we may pray confidently, "Your will be done." Amen.*

PSALM 14

To the choirmaster. Of David.

1   The fool says in his heart, "There is no God."
        They are corrupt, they do abominable deeds;
        there is none who does good.

2   The Lord looks down from heaven on the children of man,
        to see if there are any who understand,[a]
        who seek after God.

3   They have all turned aside; together they have
    become corrupt;
        there is none who does good,
        not even one.

4   Have they no knowledge, all the evildoers
        who eat up my people as they eat bread
        and do not call upon the Lord?

5   There they are in great terror,
        for God is with the generation of the righteous.
6   You would shame the plans of the poor,
        but[b] the Lord is his refuge.

7   Oh, that salvation for Israel would come out of Zion!
        When the Lord restores the fortunes of his people,
        let Jacob rejoice, let Israel be glad.

a   Psalm 14:2 Or *that act wisely*
b   Psalm 14:6 Or *for*

Psalm 14 provides repeated and strong warnings against unbelief. It gives a vivid picture of what the righteous, God's chosen people, ought always to avoid.

⊛ REQUEST THE SPIRIT'S HELP IN PRAYER

⊛ READ AND REPEAT THE WORD

What words or phrases stick out to you? How do those words or phrases reveal the poet's purpose for the psalm? What effect does this psalm have on you as you meditate on it?

⊛ RETURN TO THE LORD IN PRAYER

Atheism and spirituality without religion are increasingly accepted beliefs—indeed, they are even fashionable in modern societies. However, they are destructive and lead finally to moral abandon and eternal death. Because this psalm clarifies the depth of human sinfulness, it also illumines the greatness in Jesus' redemption. He atoned for all the sins of all people and graciously calls all, even the most sinful, to forgiveness and eternal life.

LORD GOD, I THANK YOU:

MERCIFUL GOD, I CONFESS TO YOU:

PRAYERS OF REQUEST
For members of my household to delight in the Lord, I pray:

For faithfulness in my everyday work, I pray:

For my congregation, I pray:

For my neighbor in the world, I pray:

NOTES:

*Lord Jesus, when we despair because of the world's
increasing hostility or indifference to You, help us also
to see the greatness of Your love and grace. Amen.*

PSALM 15

A Psalm of David.

1   O LORD, who shall sojourn in your tent?
       Who shall dwell on your holy hill?

2   He who walks blamelessly and does what is right
       and speaks truth in his heart;
3   who does not slander with his tongue
       and does no evil to his neighbor,
       nor takes up a reproach against his friend;
4   in whose eyes a vile person is despised,
       but who honors those who fear the LORD;
       who swears to his own hurt and does not change;
5   who does not put out his money at interest
       and does not take a bribe against the innocent.
       He who does these things shall never be moved.

Many scholars think that Psalm 15 was a temple entry prayer that reminded the Israelites of their need for holiness in God's presence. Lutheran theologian Martin Chemnitz wrote about this psalm, "He is not describing the cause of our justification or the means of apprehending righteousness, nor the form wherein our righteousness actually consists, but He is describing it by its fruits and who they are who have attained true righteousness and dwell in the church of God" (*LTh* 2:641).

❧ REQUEST THE SPIRIT'S HELP IN PRAYER

❧ READ AND REPEAT THE WORD

What words or phrases stick out to you? How do those words or phrases reveal the poet's purpose for the psalm? What effect does this psalm have on you as you meditate on it?

....

....

....

....

....

....

❧ RETURN TO THE LORD IN PRAYER

Sincerity and the righteous treatment of others, as taught in the Ten Commandments, are emphasized as the foundation to genuine worship. At times, sad to say, we come to worship God in an unworthy manner. For example, we may remain unreconciled with others or persist in behaviors we know to be wrong. As God's true temple and the Mercy Seat where full forgiveness is freely given, our Lord Jesus Christ still calls us to Himself. Through His grace, we are made right with God and counted worthy to stand before the Father's throne.

PRAYERS: ....

....

....

....

....

....

Almighty God, grant that all our worship and life may be acceptable in Your sight; through Jesus Christ, our Lord. Amen.

PSALM 16

A Miktam[a] of David.

1   Preserve me, O God, for in you I take refuge.
2   I say to the LORD, "You are my Lord;
     I have no good apart from you."

3   As for the saints in the land, they are the excellent ones,
     in whom is all my delight.[b]

4   The sorrows of those who run after[c] another god
    shall multiply;
     their drink offerings of blood I will not pour out
     or take their names on my lips.

5   The LORD is my chosen portion and my cup;
     you hold my lot.
6   The lines have fallen for me in pleasant places;
     indeed, I have a beautiful inheritance.

7   I bless the LORD who gives me counsel;
     in the night also my heart instructs me.[d]
8   I have set the LORD always before me;
     because he is at my right hand, I shall not be shaken.

9   Therefore my heart is glad, and my whole being[e] rejoices;
     my flesh also dwells secure.
10   For you will not abandon my soul to Sheol,
     or let your holy one see corruption.[f]

11   You make known to me the path of life;
     in your presence there is fullness of joy;
     at your right hand are pleasures forevermore.

a   Psalm 16:1 Probably a musical or liturgical term
b   Psalm 16:3 Or *To the saints in the land, the excellent in whom is all my delight, I say:*
c   Psalm 16:4 Or *who acquire*
d   Psalm 16:7 Hebrew my *kidneys instruct me*
e   Psalm 16:9 Hebrew *my glory*
f   Psalm 16:10 Or *see the pit*

The meaning of the term *Miktam* in the title is unknown. Of this psalm, Luther wrote that it was "a prophecy of the suffering and resurrection of Christ, as the apostles themselves powerfully indicate (Acts 2:25 and 13:35)" (*RPL*, p. 42).

⊛ REQUEST THE SPIRIT'S HELP IN PRAYER

⊛ READ AND REPEAT THE WORD

What words or phrases stick out to you? How do those words or phrases reveal the poet's purpose for the psalm? What effect does this psalm have on you as you meditate on it?

⊛ RETURN TO THE LORD IN PRAYER

Psalm 16 praises the Lord for numerous earthly blessings but moves toward a climactic expression of hope for life in God's presence beyond the grave. Far too often, our prayers are simply laundry lists of earthly desires. This psalm reminds us of our greater need to thank and praise God and make spiritual blessings a priority. Those who have the Lord have the source of all good things, even everlasting life. We who are in Christ have been set at God's right hand, where we can never be removed.

LORD GOD, FOR MY EARTHLY BLESSINGS, I THANK YOU:

MERCIFUL GOD, FOR YOUR FAITHFULNESS TO ME, ESPECIALLY IN JESUS CHRIST, I PRAISE YOU:

THAT I MAY ALWAYS THANK YOU FOR THE GIFT OF SALVATION IN JESUS CHRIST, I PRAY:

Lord, keep us in Your presence throughout our earthly pilgrimage so that we may come to the fullness of Your joy in heaven and the new creation; through Jesus Christ, our resurrected Lord. Amen.

Psalm 17

A Prayer of David.

1 Hear a just cause, O Lord; attend to my cry!
   Give ear to my prayer from lips free of deceit!
2 From your presence let my vindication come!
   Let your eyes behold the right!

3 You have tried my heart, you have visited me by night,
   you have tested me, and you will find nothing;
   I have purposed that my mouth will not transgress.
4 With regard to the works of man, by the word of your lips
   I have avoided the ways of the violent.
5 My steps have held fast to your paths;
   my feet have not slipped.

6 I call upon you, for you will answer me, O God;
   incline your ear to me; hear my words.
7 Wondrously show[a] your steadfast love,
   O Savior of those who seek refuge
   from their adversaries at your right hand.

8 Keep me as the apple of your eye;
   hide me in the shadow of your wings,
9 from the wicked who do me violence,
   my deadly enemies who surround me.

10 They close their hearts to pity;
   with their mouths they speak arrogantly.
11 They have now surrounded our steps;
   they set their eyes to cast us to the ground.
12 He is like a lion eager to tear,
   as a young lion lurking in ambush.

13 Arise, O Lord! Confront him, subdue him!
   Deliver my soul from the wicked by your sword,
14 from men by your hand, O Lord,
   from men of the world whose portion is in this life.[b]
   You fill their womb with treasure;[c]
   they are satisfied with children,
   and they leave their abundance to their infants.

15 As for me, I shall behold your face in righteousness;
   when I awake, I shall be satisfied with your likeness.

---

a Psalm 17:7 Or *Distinguish me by*
b Psalm 17:14 Or *from men whose portion in life is of the world*
c Psalm 17:14 Or *As for your treasured ones, you fill their womb*

Psalm 17 is possibly another of David's cries for deliverance during the time King Saul was trying to kill him, as recorded throughout 1 Samuel.

⊛ REQUEST THE SPIRIT'S HELP IN PRAYER

⊛ READ AND REPEAT THE WORD

What words or phrases stick out to you? How do those words or phrases reveal the poet's purpose for the psalm? What effect does this psalm have on you as you meditate on it?

⊛ RETURN TO THE LORD IN PRAYER

In this psalm, David begs for protection from a bloodthirsty enemy. A tragic consequence of the world's fall into sin is that we often suffer through no particular fault of our own. The Book of Job presents the classic case of one who suffers innocently. Though we don't always know the particulars about why some people suffer and others don't, we know that God cares about our suffering and has chosen to do something about it. God is able to turn injustice into good, which is best illustrated by Jesus' innocent death on the cross. That horrible miscarriage of justice at the cross worked life and salvation for all people.

LORD GOD, I THANK YOU:

MERCIFUL GOD, I CONFESS TO YOU:

PRAYERS OF REQUEST
For members of my household to delight in the Lord, I pray:

For faithfulness in my everyday work, I pray:

For my congregation, I pray:

For my neighbor in the world, I pray:

Lord, keep our eyes fixed on Jesus, the author and perfecter of our faith. He saved us by enduring great injustice and now sits at Your right hand. Amen.

PSALM 18

To the choirmaster. A Psalm of David, the servant of the Lord, who
addressed the words of this song to the Lord on the day when
the Lord delivered him from the hand of all his enemies, and
from the hand of Saul. He said:

1 I love you, O Lord, my strength.
2 The Lord is my rock and my fortress and my deliverer,
 my God, my rock, in whom I take refuge,
 my shield, and the horn of my salvation, my stronghold.
3 I call upon the Lord, who is worthy to be praised,
 and I am saved from my enemies.

4 The cords of death encompassed me;
 the torrents of destruction assailed me;[a]
5 the cords of Sheol entangled me;
 the snares of death confronted me.

6 In my distress I called upon the Lord;
 to my God I cried for help.
 From his temple he heard my voice,
 and my cry to him reached his ears.

7 Then the earth reeled and rocked;
 the foundations also of the mountains trembled
 and quaked, because he was angry.
8 Smoke went up from his nostrils,[b]
 and devouring fire from his mouth;
 glowing coals flamed forth from him.
9 He bowed the heavens and came down;
 thick darkness was under his feet.
10 He rode on a cherub and flew;
 he came swiftly on the wings of the wind.
11 He made darkness his covering, his canopy around him,
 thick clouds dark with water.
12 Out of the brightness before him
 hailstones and coals of fire broke through his clouds.

13 The Lord also thundered in the heavens,
 and the Most High uttered his voice,
 hailstones and coals of fire.
14 And he sent out his arrows and scattered them;
 he flashed forth lightnings and routed them.

---

a Psalm 18:4 Or *terrified me*
b Psalm 18:8 Or *in his wrath*

15 Then the channels of the sea were seen,
    and the foundations of the world were laid bare
at your rebuke, O LORD,
    at the blast of the breath of your nostrils.

16 He sent from on high, he took me;
    he drew me out of many waters.
17 He rescued me from my strong enemy
    and from those who hated me,
    for they were too mighty for me.
18 They confronted me in the day of my calamity,
    but the LORD was my support.
19 He brought me out into a broad place;
    he rescued me, because he delighted in me.

20 The LORD dealt with me according to my righteousness;
    according to the cleanness of my hands he rewarded me.
21 For I have kept the ways of the LORD,
    and have not wickedly departed from my God.
22 For all his rules^c were before me,
    and his statutes I did not put away from me.
23 I was blameless before him,
    and I kept myself from my guilt.
24 So the LORD has rewarded me according to my righteousness,
    according to the cleanness of my hands in his sight.

25 With the merciful you show yourself merciful;
    with the blameless man you show yourself blameless;
26 with the purified you show yourself pure;
    and with the crooked you make yourself seem tortuous.
27 For you save a humble people,
    but the haughty eyes you bring down.
28 For it is you who light my lamp;
    the LORD my God lightens my darkness.
29 For by you I can run against a troop,
    and by my God I can leap over a wall.
30 This God—his way is perfect;^d
    the word of the LORD proves true;
    he is a shield for all those who take refuge in him.

31 For who is God, but the LORD?
    And who is a rock, except our God?—
32 the God who equipped me with strength
    and made my way blameless.
33 He made my feet like the feet of a deer
    and set me secure on the heights.

c   Psalm 18:22 Or *just decrees*
d   Psalm 18:30 Or *blameless*

34 He trains my hands for war,
    so that my arms can bend a bow of bronze.
35 You have given me the shield of your salvation,
    and your right hand supported me,
    and your gentleness made me great.
36 You gave a wide place for my steps under me,
    and my feet did not slip.
37 I pursued my enemies and overtook them,
    and did not turn back till they were consumed.
38 I thrust them through, so that they were not able to rise;
    they fell under my feet.
39 For you equipped me with strength for the battle;
    you made those who rise against me sink under me.
40 You made my enemies turn their backs to me,[e]
    and those who hated me I destroyed.
41 They cried for help, but there was none to save;
    they cried to the LORD, but he did not answer them.
42 I beat them fine as dust before the wind;
    I cast them out like the mire of the streets.

43 You delivered me from strife with the people;
    you made me the head of the nations;
    people whom I had not known served me.
44 As soon as they heard of me they obeyed me;
    foreigners came cringing to me.
45 Foreigners lost heart
    and came trembling out of their fortresses.

46 The LORD lives, and blessed be my rock,
    and exalted be the God of my salvation—
47 the God who gave me vengeance
    and subdued peoples under me,
48 who rescued me from my enemies;
    yes, you exalted me above those who rose against me;
    you delivered me from the man of violence.

49 For this I will praise you, O LORD, among the nations,
    and sing to your name.
50 Great salvation he brings to his king,
    and shows steadfast love to his anointed,
    to David and his offspring forever.

e   Psalm 18:40 Or *You gave me my enemies' necks*

Psalm 18 is a royal thanksgiving hymn, with the twin themes of gratitude and praise permeating the text. Along with a variant form of Psalm 18, the description in the title also appears in 2 Samuel 22:1, which provides the historical setting for the psalm.

⚙ REQUEST THE SPIRIT'S HELP IN PRAYER

⚙ READ AND REPEAT THE WORD

What words or phrases stick out to you? How do those words or phrases reveal the poet's purpose for the psalm? What effect does this psalm have on you as you meditate on it?

⚙ RETURN TO THE LORD IN PRAYER

David exults, "The LORD . . . is worthy to be praised" (v. 3). This truth makes our failures to render Him thanks and praise a grievous affront. In this psalm, David recounts a time when the very cords of death were dragging him down into the abyss. The deliverance God provided him reminds us of our own victory over the grave, achieved for us by the risen Lord Jesus.

LORD GOD, I THANK YOU:

MERCIFUL GOD, I CONFESS TO YOU:

PRAYERS OF REQUEST
For members of my household to delight in the Lord, I pray:

For faithfulness in my everyday work, I pray:

For my congregation, I pray:

For my neighbor in the world, I pray:

*Grant me Your grace, Lord Jesus, that I may fervently
sing the praises of what You have done and so
make Your name known to all people. Amen.*

PSALM 19

To the choirmaster. A Psalm of David.

1   The heavens declare the glory of God,
      and the sky above[a] proclaims his handiwork.
2   Day to day pours out speech,
      and night to night reveals knowledge.
3   There is no speech, nor are there words,
      whose voice is not heard.
4   Their voice[b] goes out through all the earth,
      and their words to the end of the world.
   In them he has set a tent for the sun,
5   which comes out like a bridegroom leaving his chamber,
      and, like a strong man, runs its course with joy.
6   Its rising is from the end of the heavens,
      and its circuit to the end of them,
      and there is nothing hidden from its heat.

7   The law of the LORD is perfect,[c]
      reviving the soul;
   the testimony of the LORD is sure,
      making wise the simple;
8   the precepts of the LORD are right,
      rejoicing the heart;
   the commandment of the LORD is pure,
      enlightening the eyes;
9   the fear of the LORD is clean,
      enduring forever;
   the rules[d] of the LORD are true,
      and righteous altogether.
10 More to be desired are they than gold,
      even much fine gold;
   sweeter also than honey
      and drippings of the honeycomb.
11 Moreover, by them is your servant warned;
      in keeping them there is great reward.

12 Who can discern his errors?
      Declare me innocent from hidden faults.
13 Keep back your servant also from presumptuous sins;
      let them not have dominion over me!

a   Psalm 19:1 Hebrew *the expanse*; compare Genesis 1:6–8
b   Psalm 19:4 Or *Their measuring line*
c   Psalm 19:7 Or *blameless*
d   Psalm 19:9 Or *just decrees*

> Then I shall be blameless,
>   and innocent of great transgression.
>
> 14 Let the words of my mouth and the meditation of my heart
>   be acceptable in your sight,
>   O LORD, my rock and my redeemer.

Luther describes Psalm 19 as "a prophecy. It speaks of how the Gospel would spread to the entire world, as far as the heavens extend. Day and night it would be spread, not only in Hebrew but in all languages" (*RPL*, p. 51).

❀ REQUEST THE SPIRIT'S HELP IN PRAYER

❀ READ AND REPEAT THE WORD

What words or phrases stick out to you? How do those words or phrases reveal the poet's purpose for the psalm? What effect does this psalm have on you as you meditate on it?

....

....

....

....

❀ RETURN TO THE LORD IN PRAYER

The heavens continually declare God's praise, and the forces of nature daily show forth His glory as they faithfully carry out the duties He has assigned them. Sadly, we so often fail in the fulfillment of our divinely appointed tasks. The heavens are marvelous, and nature's testimony to the greatness of the Creator is eloquent, but God's forgiveness and grace as revealed in His Word are even more glorious.

LORD GOD, I THANK YOU:

....

....

MERCIFUL GOD, I CONFESS TO YOU:

....

....

RIGHTEOUS GOD, TODAY I ALSO PRAY:

....

....

> *"Let the words of my mouth and the meditation of my heart*
>   *be acceptable in Your sight, O LORD, my rock and my*
>   *redeemer" (Psalm 19:14); through Christ Jesus. Amen.*

PSALM 20

To the choirmaster. A Psalm of David.

1   May the LORD answer you in the day of trouble!
      May the name of the God of Jacob protect you!
2   May he send you help from the sanctuary
      and give you support from Zion!
3   May he remember all your offerings
      and regard with favor your burnt sacrifices!   *Selah*

4   May he grant you your heart's desire
      and fulfill all your plans!
5   May we shout for joy over your salvation,
      and in the name of our God set up our banners!
    May the LORD fulfill all your petitions!

6   Now I know that the LORD saves his anointed;
      he will answer him from his holy heaven
      with the saving might of his right hand.
7   Some trust in chariots and some in horses,
      but we trust in the name of the LORD our God.
8   They collapse and fall,
      but we rise and stand upright.

9   O LORD, save the king!
      May he answer us when we call.

Psalm 20 is possibly an antiphonal prayer: that is, a prayer where two groups of people take turns going back and forth praying the lines. This psalm may have been offered before King David led his troops into battle. It was likely used in times of peace as well, just as the British regularly sing "God Save the Queen."

⊛ REQUEST THE SPIRIT'S HELP IN PRAYER

⊛ READ AND REPEAT THE WORD

What words or phrases stick out to you? How do those words or phrases reveal the poet's purpose for the psalm? What effect does this psalm have on you as you meditate on it?

⊛ RETURN TO THE LORD IN PRAYER

In the psalm, we hear the people's desire for God's blessing on their king as he prepares to lead them into battle. In modern, developed countries, we are easily tempted to place our confidence in certain leaders and technological wonders rather than in God. Doing so, however, is little more than old-fashioned idolatry. When we humbly pray for the authorities God has placed over us, He unfailingly answers and acts on our behalf in accord with His good and gracious will.

LORD GOD, I THANK YOU:

MERCIFUL GOD, I CONFESS TO YOU:

PRAYERS OF REQUEST
For members of my household to delight in the Lord, I pray:

For faithfulness in my everyday work, I pray:

For my congregation, I pray:

For my neighbor in the world, I pray:

Guide and direct our rulers, O King of kings and Lord of lords, so that they ever acknowledge You rather than trust in their earthly might. Lead us in the way of righteousness and peace. Amen.

PSALM 21

To the choirmaster. A Psalm of David.

1 O LORD, in your strength the king rejoices,
     and in your salvation how greatly he exults!
2 You have given him his heart's desire
     and have not withheld the request of his lips.   *Selah*
3 For you meet him with rich blessings;
     you set a crown of fine gold upon his head.
4 He asked life of you; you gave it to him,
     length of days forever and ever.
5 His glory is great through your salvation;
     splendor and majesty you bestow on him.
6 For you make him most blessed forever;[a]
     you make him glad with the joy of your presence.
7 For the king trusts in the LORD,
     and through the steadfast love of the Most High
     he shall not be moved.

8 Your hand will find out all your enemies;
     your right hand will find out those who hate you.
9 You will make them as a blazing oven
     when you appear.
   The LORD will swallow them up in his wrath,
     and fire will consume them.
10 You will destroy their descendants from the earth,
     and their offspring from among the children of man.
11 Though they plan evil against you,
     though they devise mischief, they will not succeed.
12 For you will put them to flight;
     you will aim at their faces with your bows

13 Be exalted, O LORD, in your strength!
     We will sing and praise your power.

---

a Psalm 21:6 Or *make him a source of blessing forever*

Luther wrote, "The 21st psalm is a prophecy of the kingdom of Christ, the kingdom that is and remains eternally and spiritually before God" (*RPL*, p. 54).

❋ REQUEST THE SPIRIT'S HELP IN PRAYER

❋ READ AND REPEAT THE WORD

What words or phrases stick out to you? How do those words or phrases reveal the poet's purpose for the psalm? What effect does this psalm have on you as you meditate on it?

❋ RETURN TO THE LORD IN PRAYER

Psalm 21 not only offers thanks to God for Israel's king (vv. 1–7) but also encourages the king with promises of the Lord's blessing (vv. 8–12). Part of our Christian responsibility, as this psalm and the apostle Paul remind us (Romans 13:1–7), is to offer thanksgiving and petitions on behalf of our ruling authorities. Failing to do so is an act of ingratitude. The Scriptures testify that God establishes and uses the various governments of the world not only to serve His people's earthly needs but also to further the spread of the Gospel.

LORD GOD, FOR MY EARTHLY BLESSINGS, I THANK YOU:

MERCIFUL GOD, I CONFESS TO YOU:

PRAYERS OF REQUEST
For my neighbor in the world, especially for those in authority over me in society, I pray:

"God bless our native land; Firm may she ever stand Through storm and night. . . . Thou who art ever nigh, Guarding with watchful eye, To Thee aloud we cry: God save the state!" Amen. (LSB 965:1–2)

Psalm 22

To the choirmaster: according to The Doe of the Dawn.
A Psalm of David.

1 My God, my God, why have you forsaken me?
  Why are you so far from saving me, from the words of
  my groaning?
2 O my God, I cry by day, but you do not answer,
  and by night, but I find no rest.

3 Yet you are holy,
  enthroned on the praises[a] of Israel.
4 In you our fathers trusted;
  they trusted, and you delivered them.
5 To you they cried and were rescued;
  in you they trusted and were not put to shame.

6 But I am a worm and not a man,
  scorned by mankind and despised by the people.
7 All who see me mock me;
  they make mouths at me; they wag their heads;
8 "He trusts in the LORD; let him deliver him;
  let him rescue him, for he delights in him!"

9 Yet you are he who took me from the womb;
  you made me trust you at my mother's breasts.
10 On you was I cast from my birth,
  and from my mother's womb you have been my God.
11 Be not far from me,
  for trouble is near,
  and there is none to help.

12 Many bulls encompass me;
  strong bulls of Bashan surround me;
13 they open wide their mouths at me,
  like a ravening and roaring lion.

14 I am poured out like water,
  and all my bones are out of joint;
  my heart is like wax;
  it is melted within my breast;

---

a Psalm 22:3 Or *dwelling in the praises*

15 my strength is dried up like a potsherd,
        and my tongue sticks to my jaws;
        you lay me in the dust of death.

16 For dogs encompass me;
        a company of evildoers encircles me;
        they have pierced my hands and feet[b]—
17 I can count all my bones—
        they stare and gloat over me;
18 they divide my garments among them,
        and for my clothing they cast lots.

19 But you, O LORD, do not be far off!
        O you my help, come quickly to my aid!
20 Deliver my soul from the sword,
        my precious life from the power of the dog!
21 Save me from the mouth of the lion!
    You have rescued[c] me from the horns of the wild oxen!

22 I will tell of your name to my brothers;
        in the midst of the congregation I will praise you:
23 You who fear the LORD, praise him!
        All you offspring of Jacob, glorify him,
        and stand in awe of him, all you offspring of Israel!
24 For he has not despised or abhorred
        the affliction of the afflicted,
    and he has not hidden his face from him,
        but has heard, when he cried to him.

25 From you comes my praise in the great congregation;
        my vows I will perform before those who fear him.
26 The afflicted[d] shall eat and be satisfied;
        those who seek him shall praise the LORD!
        May your hearts live forever!

27 All the ends of the earth shall remember
        and turn to the LORD,
    and all the families of the nations
        shall worship before you.
28 For kingship belongs to the LORD,
        and he rules over the nations.

---

b   Psalm 22:16 Some Hebrew manuscripts, Septuagint, Vulgate, Syriac; most Hebrew manuscripts *like a lion* [they are at] *my hands and feet*
c   Psalm 22:21 Hebrew *answered*
d   Psalm 22:26 Or *The meek*

29 All the prosperous of the earth eat and worship;
     before him shall bow all who go down to the dust,
     even the one who could not keep himself alive.
30 Posterity shall serve him;
     it shall be told of the Lord to the coming generation;
31 they shall come and proclaim his righteousness to a people
   yet unborn,
     that he has done it.

The reference to the "The Doe of the Dawn" before the psalm possibly indicates the name of the tune that accompanied this text. According to the Early Church Father Justin Martyr, "The whole Psalm refers . . . to Christ" (*ANF* 1:248).

⊛ REQUEST THE SPIRIT'S HELP IN PRAYER

⊛ READ AND REPEAT THE WORD

What words or phrases stick out to you? How do those words or phrases reveal the poet's purpose for the psalm? What effect does this psalm have on you as you meditate on it?

⊛ RETURN TO THE LORD IN PRAYER

Facing great opposition, the psalmist initially feels that God has forsaken him and is ignoring his prayers. After remembering God's faithfulness and deliverance, he believes that God will deliver him, and he commits himself to telling that message to others. We, too, may feel alone and forsaken by God. Truly, we deserve to be forsaken by Him because of our sinfulness. But as this psalm foretells, God Himself came to be our Redeemer. While many human beings have shared this feeling of being forsaken by God, this psalm finds its greatest fulfillment in Jesus Christ, who spoke it from the cross (Matthew 27:46). Christ truly was forsaken by His Father and died alone so that we could be reconciled to our God. We are never alone because our crucified, resurrected Savior is with us.

LORD GOD, FOR SENDING YOUR SON, JESUS, TO DIE FOR ME AND REDEEM ME FROM DEATH, I THANK YOU. TRUSTING IN YOUR ETERNAL MERCY AND FAITHFULNESS, I BRING MY PRAYERS TO YOU:

Loving Savior, Your death and resurrection have made us Your people. Lead us to proclaim Your constant care. Amen.

The 22nd psalm is a prophecy of the suffering and resurrection of Christ and a prophecy of the Gospel, which the entire world shall hear and receive. Beyond all other texts, it clearly shows Christ's torment on the cross, that He was pierced hand and foot and His limbs stretched out so that His bones could have been counted. Nowhere in the other prophets can one find so clear a description. It is indeed one of the chief psalms. It belongs in the First Commandment, for it promises a new worship of God. It is in the First and Second Petitions. (Martin Luther)

SHEEP AND SHEPHERDS

Unquestionably, of the 150 psalms, Psalm 23 is the most familiar. It has been used on countless occasions, especially at funerals. It is still on the lips of many, in the version they learned from the King James Bible. Even those who are only Christian in name may know a line or two.

But how well do we really know this psalm? For further insight, it is worthwhile to dig into the subject of sheep and shepherds in the Bible.

Old Testament Sheep and Shepherds

Psalm 23 is just one place to find sheep and shepherds. The Pentateuch (the first five books of the Bible) contains numerous references to sheep. Beginning with Abraham, various covenants between individuals were sealed with the exchange of sheep or other animals (Genesis 21:27). Sheep were often listed among one's possessions (Genesis 12:16; Job 1:3). Of course, sheep were used for sacrifice (Exodus 12:5; Leviticus 1:10). When the temple was dedicated, Solomon sacrificed 120,000 sheep in addition to thousands of other animals (1 Kings 8:63)!

As for the appearances of shepherds in the Old Testament, we are taken right to the beginning, where Abel, the son of Adam and Eve, is described as "a keeper of sheep" (Genesis 4:2). Jacob's sons, the brothers of Joseph, were also shepherds (Genesis 47:3). Best known of all the shepherds, of course, is David, son of Jesse (1 Samuel 16:11).

Elsewhere, the words *sheep* and *shepherds* are used figuratively. When God spoke to Moses about his eventual death, Moses said, "Let the LORD, the God of the spirits of all flesh, appoint a man over the congregation, . . . who shall lead them out and bring them in, that the congregation of the LORD may not be as sheep that have no shepherd" (Numbers 27:16–17). By way of contrast, in the days of wicked King Ahab, the people were described "as sheep that have no shepherd" (1 Kings 22:17; 2 Chronicles 18:16). The parallel with the crowds following Jesus is impossible to miss: "When [Jesus] saw the crowds, He had compassion for them, because they were harassed and helpless, like sheep without a shepherd" (Matthew 9:36; see also Mark 6:34).

Time and again, the image of shepherd and sheep is used to describe the relationship of a leader to the people. David the shepherd was to be shepherd of God's people (2 Samuel 5:2; 1 Chronicles 11:2). The prophets, too, were to be shepherds for God's people. In Jeremiah and Ezekiel, much attention is given to this relationship. God condemned the prophets who were misleading the people: "'Woe to the shepherds who destroy and scatter the sheep of My pasture!' declares the LORD" (Jeremiah 23:1). God would not tolerate false shepherds. In the midst of the many condemnations, however, Jeremiah also delivers God's promises: "I will give you shepherds after My own heart, who will feed you with knowledge and understanding" (Jeremiah 3:15); "I will set shepherds over them who will care for them, and they shall fear no more" (Jeremiah 23:4). Ezekiel also delivered a sharp denunciation of the false shepherds, concluding with this word of promise: "As a shepherd seeks out his flock when he is among his sheep that have been scattered, so will I seek out My sheep, and I will rescue them from all places where they have been scattered" (Ezekiel 34:12).

New Testament Sheep and Shepherds

Christ took up the sheep/shepherd relationship in two primary passages. The first is the parable of the lost sheep (Matthew 18:12–14; Luke 15:4–7). Here, our Lord's emphasis is on the responsibility of the shepherd who, through some negligence of his own, has lost one of his flock. The shepherd turns it around, as it were, and risks all to return the sheep to the fold. He invites his neighbors to rejoice with him, showing the sheep's value in his eyes.

The second place where sheep and shepherd stand front and center in the New Testament is in John 10. Jesus calls Himself the Good Shepherd, making it plain that He is the Lord and Shepherd in Psalm 23. The relationship of sheep to shepherd is key, with the sheep following the familiar voice of the one who protects and cares for them. As in the parable of the lost sheep, the shepherd puts his very life on the line. He lays it down for the sheep (John 10:11). Mission comes into focus as Jesus speaks of other sheep who are not of the fold, sheep He must also bring in (John 10:16).

We could examine many other biblical passages. Some utter strong words of condemnation, while others present Gospel comfort. For God's children, there can be no greater comfort than knowing that the Lord is their reliable and true Shepherd. In Revelation, this image is set in heaven itself, where the Lamb of God who takes away the world's sin is also our Shepherd! "The Lamb in the midst of the throne will be their shepherd, and He will guide them to springs of living water, and God will wipe away every tear from their eyes" (Revelation 7:17). It would be hard to doubt that this was how David understood heaven when he wrote, "Surely goodness and mercy shall follow me all the days of my life, and I shall dwell in the house of the LORD forever" (Psalm 23:6).

Some Final Food for Thought about Shepherds in the Bible

New Testament scholar Kenneth Bailey spent four decades living and teaching in the Middle East. In *Finding the Lost: Cultural Keys to Luke 15* (CPH, 1992), Bailey provides insights into the relationship of sheep and shepherds that bear on the interpretation of Psalm 23 and related texts.

One of his more interesting points concerns Jesus' phrase about the shepherd laying the lost sheep on his shoulders to carry it home (Luke 15:5). When a sheep gets lost, Bailey explains, it becomes terrified. It sits down in the closest sheltered place, shaking and bleating. After it is found, it remains so nervous that it cannot stand, not even with the shepherd. The shepherd must carry the sheep on his back—up to seventy pounds of animal! In a real sense, the shepherd risks his own neck to save the sheep.

In the early centuries of Christianity, while crucifixion was still being practiced, crosses were considered too horrifying for symbolic use in worship. Often, the alternate symbol was a shepherd carrying a large sheep. Of special interest are several sculptures from this period in which the sheep is as large as or even larger than the shepherd. The sculptors knew that such proportions were inaccurate. The distortion was intentional. Just as the cross eventually became the symbol of Christ's sacrifice, so this symbol of the shepherd carrying the large sheep reminded early Christians of the great price paid for their redemption.

PSALM 23

A Psalm of David.

1   The Lord is my shepherd; I shall not want.
2   He makes me lie down in green pastures.
He leads me beside still waters.[a]
3   He restores my soul.
He leads me in paths of righteousness[b]
     for his name's sake.

4   Even though I walk through the valley of the shadow
of death,[c]
     I will fear no evil,
for you are with me;
     your rod and your staff,
     they comfort me.

5   You prepare a table before me
     in the presence of my enemies;
you anoint my head with oil;
     my cup overflows.
6   Surely[d] goodness and mercy[e] shall follow me
     all the days of my life,
and I shall dwell[f] in the house of the Lord
     forever.[g]

---

a   Psalm 23:2 Hebrew *beside waters of rest*
b   Psalm 23:3 Or *in right paths*
c   Psalm 23:4 Or *the valley of deep darkness*
d   Psalm 23:6 Or *Only*
e   Psalm 23:6 Or *steadfast love*
f   Psalm 23:6 Or *shall return to dwell*
g   Psalm 23:6 Hebrew *for length of days*

Of this iconic and well-loved psalm, Luther wrote that it was "a psalm of thanks in which a Christian heart praises and thanks God for teaching him and keeping him on the right way, comforting and protecting him in every danger through His Holy Word" (*RPL*, p. 59).

⊛ REQUEST THE SPIRIT'S HELP IN PRAYER

⊛ READ AND REPEAT THE WORD

What words or phrases stick out to you? How do those words or phrases reveal the poet's purpose for the psalm? What effect does this psalm have on you as you meditate on it?

....

....

....

....

....

⊛ RETURN TO THE LORD IN PRAYER

In faith, David declares that since Yahweh is his shepherd, he "shall not want" (Psalm 23:1). Our Good Shepherd lovingly provides everything that we need in this life, but we often fail to recognize that these gifts come from Him. Instead, we focus on things that we want but do not need. How wonderful that our Shepherd does not withhold His blessings from us! He cares for these needs and more: He gives us His own Son!

GOOD SHEPHERD, I THANK YOU:...

GOOD SHEPHERD, I CONFESS TO YOU:...

....

PRAYERS OF REQUEST
For members of my household to delight in the Lord, I pray:...........................

For faithfulness in my everyday work, I pray:...

For my congregation, I pray:..

For my neighbor in the world, I pray:...

....

Good Shepherd, open our eyes to see Your blessings. Open our ears to hear Your voice. Open our hearts that we may love You. Amen.

PSALM 24

A Psalm of David.

1   The earth is the LORD's and the fullness thereof,[a]
     the world and those who dwell therein,
2   for he has founded it upon the seas
     and established it upon the rivers.

3   Who shall ascend the hill of the LORD?
     And who shall stand in his holy place?
4   He who has clean hands and a pure heart,
     who does not lift up his soul to what is false
     and does not swear deceitfully.
5   He will receive blessing from the LORD
     and righteousness from the God of his salvation.
6   Such is the generation of those who seek him,
     who seek the face of the God of Jacob.[b]   *Selah*

7   Lift up your heads, O gates!
     And be lifted up, O ancient doors,
     that the King of glory may come in.
8   Who is this King of glory?
     The LORD, strong and mighty,
     the LORD, mighty in battle!
9   Lift up your heads, O gates!
     And lift them up, O ancient doors,
     that the King of glory may come in.
10 Who is this King of glory?
     The LORD of hosts,
     he is the King of glory!   *Selah*

---

a   Psalm 24:1 Or *and all that fills it*
b   Psalm 24:6 Septuagint, Syriac, and two Hebrew manuscripts; Masoretic Text *who seek your face, Jacob*

Psalm 24, which may have been written for the return of the ark of the covenant to the tabernacle (2 Samuel 6:12–15), calls God's people to worship, noting His creation and glory.

⊛ REQUEST THE SPIRIT'S HELP IN PRAYER

⊛ READ AND REPEAT THE WORD

What words or phrases stick out to you? How do those words or phrases reveal the poet's purpose for the psalm? What effect does this psalm have on you as you meditate on it?

⊛ RETURN TO THE LORD IN PRAYER

Those who worship the Lord need "clean hands and a pure heart" (v. 4). Sinful human beings are neither prepared nor worthy to be in God's presence or worship Him. Yet God forgives us, covers us with Christ's righteousness, and enables us to worship Him. This is why worship begins with Confession and Absolution. By God's grace, we worship with clean hands and a pure heart.

LORD GOD, I THANK YOU:

MERCIFUL GOD, I CONFESS TO YOU:

PRAYERS OF REQUEST
For members of my household to delight in the Lord, I pray:

For faithfulness in my everyday work, I pray:

For my congregation, I pray:

For my neighbor in the world, I pray:

Merciful Lord, I confess all my sins to You, trusting in Your promises. Forgive me, for Jesus' sake. Amen.

PSALM 25

^aOf David.

1   To you, O LORD, I lift up my soul.
2   O my God, in you I trust;
     let me not be put to shame;
     let not my enemies exult over me.
3   Indeed, none who wait for you shall be put to shame;
     they shall be ashamed who are wantonly treacherous.

4   Make me to know your ways, O LORD;
     teach me your paths.
5   Lead me in your truth and teach me,
     for you are the God of my salvation;
     for you I wait all the day long.

6   Remember your mercy, O LORD, and your steadfast love,
     for they have been from of old.
7   Remember not the sins of my youth or my transgressions;
     according to your steadfast love remember me,
     for the sake of your goodness, O LORD!

8   Good and upright is the LORD;
     therefore he instructs sinners in the way.
9   He leads the humble in what is right,
     and teaches the humble his way.
10 All the paths of the LORD are steadfast love and faithfulness,
     for those who keep his covenant and his testimonies.

11 For your name's sake, O LORD,
     pardon my guilt, for it is great.
12 Who is the man who fears the LORD?
     Him will he instruct in the way that he should choose.
13 His soul shall abide in well-being,
     and his offspring shall inherit the land.
14 The friendship^b of the LORD is for those who fear him,
     and he makes known to them his covenant.
15 My eyes are ever toward the LORD,
     for he will pluck my feet out of the net.

---

a   Psalm 25:1 This psalm is an acrostic poem, each verse beginning with the successive letters of the Hebrew alphabet
b   Psalm 25:14 Or *The secret counsel*

16 Turn to me and be gracious to me,
       for I am lonely and afflicted.
17 The troubles of my heart are enlarged;
       bring me out of my distresses.
18 Consider my affliction and my trouble,
       and forgive all my sins.

19 Consider how many are my foes,
       and with what violent hatred they hate me.
20 Oh, guard my soul, and deliver me!
       Let me not be put to shame, for I take refuge in you.
21 May integrity and uprightness preserve me,
       for I wait for you.

22 Redeem Israel, O God,
       out of all his troubles.

Psalm 25, another of David, is written as an acrostic. In this particular style, the first letter of the first line begins with the first letter of the Hebrew alphabet, and each subsequent statement in the psalm is followed by the next letter of the Hebrew alphabet, and so on until the end.

- ● REQUEST THE SPIRIT'S HELP IN PRAYER

- ● READ AND REPEAT THE WORD

What words or phrases stick out to you? How do those words or phrases reveal the poet's purpose for the psalm? What effect does this psalm have on you as you meditate on it?

....

....

....

....

....

....

....

- ● RETURN TO THE LORD IN PRAYER

In this psalm, David prays, "For You I wait all the day long" (v. 5). God promises to answer our prayers, but we may be impatient or tempted to question His answers. Even when our faithfulness fails, God is faithful. He hears our prayers and truly acts for our good. In faith, we patiently wait for Him.

PRAYERS: ....

....

....

....

....

....

....

....

NOTES: ....

....

....

....

Almighty God, give us trust and patience to wait for You and faith to believe Your promises. In Jesus' name, I pray. Amen.

The 25th psalm is a psalm of prayer in which the righteous pray that God will make them godly, forgive their sins, guard them from sin and shame, and finally deliver them from all enemies and all evil. Along with this the psalm mocks the false, self-centered spirits and teachers. It belongs to the Second Commandment and the Second Petition. (Martin Luther)

PSALM 26

Of David.

1   Vindicate me, O LORD,
      for I have walked in my integrity,
      and I have trusted in the LORD without wavering.
2   Prove me, O LORD, and try me;
      test my heart and my mind.[a]
3   For your steadfast love is before my eyes,
      and I walk in your faithfulness.

4   I do not sit with men of falsehood,
      nor do I consort with hypocrites.
5   I hate the assembly of evildoers,
      and I will not sit with the wicked.

6   I wash my hands in innocence
      and go around your altar, O LORD,
7   proclaiming thanksgiving aloud,
      and telling all your wondrous deeds.

8   O LORD, I love the habitation of your house
      and the place where your glory dwells.
9   Do not sweep my soul away with sinners,
      nor my life with bloodthirsty men,
10   in whose hands are evil devices,
      and whose right hands are full of bribes.

11   But as for me, I shall walk in my integrity;
      redeem me, and be gracious to me.
12   My foot stands on level ground;
      in the great assembly I will bless the LORD.

---

a   Psalm 26:2 Hebrew *test my kidneys and my heart*

The words and emotions of Psalm 26 evoke the plea of a man who has been falsely accused of wrongdoing. This psalm may have been sung by worshipers as they entered the temple gates as a way to prepare for worship.

⚜ REQUEST THE SPIRIT'S HELP IN PRAYER

⚜ READ AND REPEAT THE WORD

What words or phrases stick out to you? How do those words or phrases reveal the poet's purpose for the psalm? What effect does this psalm have on you as you meditate on it?

⚜ RETURN TO THE LORD IN PRAYER

In faith, David worships, proclaiming God's wondrous deeds. He loves worship and being in God's presence (v. 8). In worship, we sometimes focus on ourselves instead of God. God calls us to repentance so that He may bless us and forgive us. Strengthened in faith, we respond by telling others of the great things He has done.

LORD GOD, I THANK YOU:

MERCIFUL GOD, I CONFESS TO YOU:

PRAYERS OF REQUEST
For members of my household to delight in the Lord, I pray:

For faithfulness in my everyday work, I pray:

For my congregation, I pray:

For my neighbor in the world, I pray:

Blessed Trinity, forgive us and empower us to worship You in faith and joy. Amen.

PSALM 27

Of David.

1   The LORD is my light and my salvation;
     whom shall I fear?
  The LORD is the stronghold[a] of my life;
     of whom shall I be afraid?

2   When evildoers assail me
     to eat up my flesh,
  my adversaries and foes,
     it is they who stumble and fall.

3   Though an army encamp against me,
     my heart shall not fear;
  though war arise against me,
     yet[b] I will be confident.

4   One thing have I asked of the LORD,
     that will I seek after:
  that I may dwell in the house of the LORD
     all the days of my life,
  to gaze upon the beauty of the LORD
     and to inquire[c] in his temple.

5   For he will hide me in his shelter
     in the day of trouble;
  he will conceal me under the cover of his tent;
     he will lift me high upon a rock.

6   And now my head shall be lifted up
     above my enemies all around me,
  and I will offer in his tent
     sacrifices with shouts of joy;
  I will sing and make melody to the LORD.

a   Psalm 27:1 Or *refuge*
b   Psalm 27:3 Or *in this*
c   Psalm 27:4 Or *meditate*

7 Hear, O LORD, when I cry aloud;
    be gracious to me and answer me!
8 You have said, "Seek^{d} my face."
    My heart says to you,
      "Your face, LORD, do I seek."^{e}
9 Hide not your face from me.
    Turn not your servant away in anger,
      O you who have been my help.
    Cast me not off; forsake me not,
      O God of my salvation!
10 For my father and my mother have forsaken me,
    but the LORD will take me in.

11 Teach me your way, O LORD,
    and lead me on a level path
    because of my enemies.
12 Give me not up to the will of my adversaries;
    for false witnesses have risen against me,
    and they breathe out violence.

13 I believe that I shall look^{f} upon the goodness of the LORD
    in the land of the living!
14 Wait for the LORD;
    be strong, and let your heart take courage;
    wait for the LORD!

---

d   Psalm 27:8 The command (*seek*) is addressed to more than one person
e   Psalm 27:8 The meaning of the Hebrew verse is uncertain
f   Psalm 27:13 Other Hebrew manuscripts *Oh! Had I not believed that I would look*

When reading through Psalm 27, note the change of mood. The first six verses express David's confidence in God, but the rest are a prayer for God's help, forgiveness, and guidance. This structure may indicate that this psalm was used as part of the liturgy of worship in the tabernacle. If so, a sacrifice and prayer may have been offered after verse 6, the turning point in the psalm.

◉ REQUEST THE SPIRIT'S HELP IN PRAYER

◉ READ AND REPEAT THE WORD

What words or phrases stick out to you? How do those words or phrases reveal the poet's purpose for the psalm? What effect does this psalm have on you as you meditate on it?

....

....

....

....

◉ RETURN TO THE LORD IN PRAYER

David recognizes that when the Lord is on his side, he has nothing to fear. Human beings are prone to fearful responses. We worry about problems in this life, acting as if we face them alone. Yet God is our light and our salvation. Since He has redeemed us, we have nothing to fear. "If God is for us, who can be against us?" (Romans 8:31).

LORD GOD, I THANK YOU FOR YOUR FAITHFULNESS TO ME AT ALL TIMES:

....

....

....

MERCIFUL GOD, I CONFESS TO YOU THAT I AM OFTEN FEARFUL OF THIS LIFE, AND I FAIL TO TRUST IN YOU. TODAY I LAY MY FEARS AND ANXIETIES AT YOUR FEET:

....

....

....

*O Christ, my light and my salvation, comfort
me and strengthen my faith. Amen.*

The 27th psalm is a psalm of thanks. However, it also prays much and gives us comfort against the false teachers who give a false witness, blaspheming without any hesitation. For only entirely foolhardy saints would give a witness, bold and impudent, before God—from whom they have no command! Yet we see it daily: the more foolish and unlearned the people are, the more bold and audacious they are to preach and to teach the whole world. No one knows anything; they alone know all. They prepare themselves to make war and revolt against the true saints and God-fearers. This psalm belongs in the Second and First Commandments and in the First and Second Petitions. (Martin Luther)

PSALM 28

Of David.

1 To you, O Lord, I call;
   my rock, be not deaf to me,
 lest, if you be silent to me,
   I become like those who go down to the pit.
2 Hear the voice of my pleas for mercy,
   when I cry to you for help,
 when I lift up my hands
   toward your most holy sanctuary.[a]

3 Do not drag me off with the wicked,
   with the workers of evil,
 who speak peace with their neighbors
   while evil is in their hearts.
4 Give to them according to their work
   and according to the evil of their deeds;
 give to them according to the work of their hands;
   render them their due reward.
5 Because they do not regard the works of the Lord
   or the work of his hands,
 he will tear them down and build them up no more.

6 Blessed be the Lord!
   For he has heard the voice of my pleas for mercy.
7 The Lord is my strength and my shield;
   in him my heart trusts, and I am helped;
 my heart exults,
   and with my song I give thanks to him.

8 The Lord is the strength of his people;[b]
   he is the saving refuge of his anointed.
9 Oh, save your people and bless your heritage!
   Be their shepherd and carry them forever.

---

a Psalm 28:2 Hebrew *your innermost sanctuary*
b Psalm 28:8 Some Hebrew manuscripts, Septuagint, Syriac; most Hebrew manuscripts *is their strength*

Psalm 28 is a prayer for help, followed by words of praise in anticipation of God's answer. It may come from the time when Absalom, David's son, rebelled against David (2 Samuel 15–18). David is troubled by his enemies' duplicity and lack of faith, fearing for his life (Psalm 28:1). These words also apply to other trying times. Faced with affliction, we rely on God's help and anticipate His blessing.

⚜ REQUEST THE SPIRIT'S HELP IN PRAYER

⚜ READ AND REPEAT THE WORD

What words or phrases stick out to you? How do those words or phrases reveal the poet's purpose for the psalm? What effect does this psalm have on you as you meditate on it?

⚜ RETURN TO THE LORD IN PRAYER

Facing personal crisis, David realizes he is unable to protect and save himself. He needs God to be his strength and shield. As sinners, we cannot save ourselves. We recognize our helplessness and need for God's grace. Our Savior comes, giving us His strength and protecting us from our enemies by paying the penalty for our sins.

LORD GOD, I THANK YOU:

MERCIFUL GOD, I CONFESS TO YOU:

PRAYERS OF REQUEST
For members of my household to delight in the Lord, I pray:

For faithfulness in my everyday work, I pray:

For my congregation, I pray:

For my neighbor in the world, I pray:

Lord Jesus, my strength and my shield, I trust in You.
Be my shepherd and carry me forever. Amen.

PSALM 29

A Psalm of David.

1   Ascribe to the Lord, O heavenly beings,[a]
        ascribe to the Lord glory and strength.
2   Ascribe to the Lord the glory due his name;
        worship the Lord in the splendor of holiness.[b]

3   The voice of the Lord is over the waters;
        the God of glory thunders,
        the Lord, over many waters.
4   The voice of the Lord is powerful;
        the voice of the Lord is full of majesty.

5   The voice of the Lord breaks the cedars;
        the Lord breaks the cedars of Lebanon.
6   He makes Lebanon to skip like a calf,
        and Sirion like a young wild ox.

7   The voice of the Lord flashes forth flames of fire.
8   The voice of the Lord shakes the wilderness;
        the Lord shakes the wilderness of Kadesh.

9   The voice of the Lord makes the deer give birth[c]
        and strips the forests bare,
        and in his temple all cry, "Glory!"

10 The Lord sits enthroned over the flood;
        the Lord sits enthroned as king forever.
11 May the Lord give strength to his people!
        May the Lord bless[d] his people with peace!

a   Psalm 29:1 Hebrew *sons of God,* or *sons of might*
b   Psalm 29:2 Or *in holy attire*
c   Psalm 29:9 Revocalization yields *makes the oaks to shake*
d   Psalm 29:11 Or *The Lord will give . . . The Lord will bless*

Luther interpreted this psalm of David as "a prophecy of the Gospel, that it shall resound with power throughout the world. . . . He established the flood, Baptism, in which the old Adam is drowned and the new man arises" (*RPL*, p. 70).

❋ REQUEST THE SPIRIT'S HELP IN PRAYER

❋ READ AND REPEAT THE WORD

What words or phrases stick out to you? How do those words or phrases reveal the poet's purpose for the psalm? What effect does this psalm have on you as you meditate on it?

....

....

....

....

❋ RETURN TO THE LORD IN PRAYER

God's power can be terrifying. The sound of His voice brings forth creation, shakes the mountains and trees, and unleashes the great flood that destroyed the earth. We sinners might be destroyed by the power of His holy, powerful voice. Yet "the Word became flesh and dwelt among us" (John 1:14). God came to us in Jesus to speak His love and grace. In Baptism, flood and voice combine to cleanse us; indeed, this psalm was traditionally used at Baptisms. Hearing His gracious voice, we join heaven and earth in praise.

LORD GOD, I THANK YOU FOR THE GIFT OF BAPTISM, IN WHICH YOU CALLED ME TO BE YOUR OWN. I CONFESS TO YOU THAT I HAVE NOT FAITH-FULLY LIVED IN THAT BAPTISMAL IDENTITY. TODAY I CONFESS TO YOU:

....

PRAYERS OF REQUEST
Living in my baptismal grace, today I pray for my household:
....

That I may faithfully fulfill my vocations at work, I pray:
....

For my congregation, those baptized who gather around the Means of Grace, I pray:
....

That I may lovingly and faithfully engage my neighbor, I pray:
....

O Word of God, You became flesh to be our Savior.
Let us hear Your powerful voice. Amen.

PSALM 30

A Psalm of David. A song at the dedication of the temple.

1   I will extol you, O LORD, for you have drawn me up
     and have not let my foes rejoice over me.
2   O LORD my God, I cried to you for help,
     and you have healed me.
3   O LORD, you have brought up my soul from Sheol;
     you restored me to life from among those who go down to
     the pit.[a]

4   Sing praises to the LORD, O you his saints,
     and give thanks to his holy name.[b]
5   For his anger is but for a moment,
     and his favor is for a lifetime.[c]
   Weeping may tarry for the night,
     but joy comes with the morning.

6   As for me, I said in my prosperity,
     "I shall never be moved."
7   By your favor, O LORD,
     you made my mountain stand strong;
   you hid your face;
     I was dismayed.

8   To you, O LORD, I cry,
     and to the Lord I plead for mercy:
9   "What profit is there in my death,[d]
     if I go down to the pit?[e]
   Will the dust praise you?
     Will it tell of your faithfulness?
10 Hear, O LORD, and be merciful to me!
     O LORD, be my helper!"

11 You have turned for me my mourning into dancing;
     you have loosed my sackcloth
     and clothed me with gladness,
12 that my glory may sing your praise and not be silent.
     O LORD my God, I will give thanks to you forever!

a   Psalm 30:3 Or *to life, that I should not go down to the pit*
b   Psalm 30:4 Hebrew *to the memorial of his holiness* (see Exodus 3:15)
c   Psalm 30:5 Or *and in his favor is life*
d   Psalm 30:9 Hebrew *in my blood*
e   Psalm 30:9 Or *to corruption*

As recorded in 2 Samuel 24 and 1 Chronicles 21, David, near the end of his reign as king, took a census of all men capable of fighting, indicating a reliance on human power over God's strength. As a consequence for this rebellion, a plague came on Israel, and seventy thousand men died. In repentance, David bought land, built an altar, and offered a sacrifice to the Lord. This psalm was likely written to dedicate this land, the place where God's temple would later be built. This is also the site where, traditionally, God commanded Abraham to sacrifice Isaac some thousand years before David, and where God provided a ram in place of Isaac. All these details contribute to the historic and symbolic importance of the site, where God time and again shows mercy to His people, pointing His people to the coming Messiah.

◉ REQUEST THE SPIRIT'S HELP IN PRAYER

◉ READ AND REPEAT THE WORD

What words or phrases stick out to you? How do those words or phrases reveal the poet's purpose for the psalm? What effect does this psalm have on you as you meditate on it?

◉ RETURN TO THE LORD IN PRAYER

David summarizes his feelings and God's response in verse 5. Sorrowful times in life are sometimes caused by things outside of our control and sometimes by our own sins. Trusting in God's deliverance, David knows that the sorrow he feels will be replaced with joy as God comforts him. We, too, are confident in God's promise to comfort us and dry our tears (Revelation 7:17).

PRAYERS:

O God, comfort me with Your presence and fill me with joy. Amen.

PSALM 31

To the choirmaster. A Psalm of David.

1   In you, O Lord, do I take refuge;
     let me never be put to shame;
     in your righteousness deliver me!
2   Incline your ear to me;
     rescue me speedily!
  Be a rock of refuge for me,
     a strong fortress to save me!

3   For you are my rock and my fortress;
     and for your name's sake you lead me and guide me;
4   you take me out of the net they have hidden for me,
     for you are my refuge.
5   Into your hand I commit my spirit;
     you have redeemed me, O Lord, faithful God.

6   I hate[a] those who pay regard to worthless idols,
     but I trust in the Lord.
7   I will rejoice and be glad in your steadfast love,
     because you have seen my affliction;
     you have known the distress of my soul,
8   and you have not delivered me into the hand of the enemy;
     you have set my feet in a broad place.

9   Be gracious to me, O Lord, for I am in distress;
     my eye is wasted from grief;
     my soul and my body also.
10 For my life is spent with sorrow,
     and my years with sighing;
  my strength fails because of my iniquity,
     and my bones waste away.

11 Because of all my adversaries I have become a reproach,
     especially to my neighbors,
  and an object of dread to my acquaintances;
     those who see me in the street flee from me.
12 I have been forgotten like one who is dead;
     I have become like a broken vessel.

---

a   Psalm 31:6 Masoretic Text; one Hebrew manuscript, Septuagint, Syriac, Jerome *You hate*

13 For I hear the whispering of many—
    terror on every side!—
  as they scheme together against me,
    as they plot to take my life.

14 But I trust in you, O Lord;
    I say, "You are my God."
15 My times are in your hand;
    rescue me from the hand of my enemies and from my
    persecutors!
16 Make your face shine on your servant;
    save me in your steadfast love!
17 O Lord, let me not be put to shame,
    for I call upon you;
  let the wicked be put to shame;
    let them go silently to Sheol.
18 Let the lying lips be mute,
    which speak insolently against the righteous
    in pride and contempt.

19 Oh, how abundant is your goodness,
    which you have stored up for those who fear you
  and worked for those who take refuge in you,
    in the sight of the children of mankind!
20 In the cover of your presence you hide them
    from the plots of men;
  you store them in your shelter
    from the strife of tongues.

21 Blessed be the Lord,
    for he has wondrously shown his steadfast love to me
    when I was in a besieged city.
22 I had said in my alarm,[b]
    "I am cut off from your sight."
  But you heard the voice of my pleas for mercy
    when I cried to you for help.

23 Love the Lord, all you his saints!
    The Lord preserves the faithful
    but abundantly repays the one who acts in pride.
24 Be strong, and let your heart take courage,
    all you who wait for the Lord!

b Psalm 31:22 Or *in my haste*

Though uncertain, due to the context of the psalm, Psalm 31 was perhaps written when Saul's forces were pursuing David (for example, 1 Samuel 23).

❀ REQUEST THE SPIRIT'S HELP IN PRAYER

❀ READ AND REPEAT THE WORD

What words or phrases stick out to you? How do those words or phrases reveal the poet's purpose for the psalm? What effect does this psalm have on you as you meditate on it?

❀ RETURN TO THE LORD IN PRAYER

David says that he hates those who trust in worthless idols; he trusts in the Lord (v. 6). Too often, we devote our lives to worthless things and despise the things of God. Yet even as God delivered David from his sin and enemies, so He delivers us as well. Christ paid for our idolatry and indifference. His Spirit gives us the gift of faith so that we trust in the only true God. Now we join David in rejoicing in God's great salvation.

LORD GOD, I THANK YOU FOR YOUR FAITHFULNESS TO ME IN ALL TIMES, EVEN WHEN I WORSHIP FALSE IDOLS. I CONFESS TO YOU THAT I HAVE OFTEN MADE IDOLS OF YOUR CREATION, WHICH DRAWS MY HEART AND ATTENTION AWAY FROM YOU. I ESPECIALLY CONFESS THESE SINS:

TRUSTING IN YOUR MERCY AND IN YOUR FORGIVENESS, I ALSO PRAY:

O triune God, strengthen my faith so that I may ever worship You alone. Amen.

The 31st psalm is a universal psalm of thanks, a psalm of prayer, and a psalm of comfort, all at the same time. It is spoken in the person of Christ and of His saints, who, on account of the Word of God, are plagued their entire lives—inwardly with fears and troubles; outwardly with persecutions, slander, and contempt. Yet they are comforted and delivered by God out of all of them. This psalm belongs in the Second and Third Commandments and in the First and Second Petitions. (Martin Luther)

PSALM 32

A Maskil[a] of David.

1 Blessed is the one whose transgression is forgiven,
  whose sin is covered.
2 Blessed is the man against whom the LORD counts no iniquity,
  and in whose spirit there is no deceit.

3 For when I kept silent, my bones wasted away
  through my groaning all day long.
4 For day and night your hand was heavy upon me;
  my strength was dried up[b] as by the heat of summer. *Selah*

5 I acknowledged my sin to you,
  and I did not cover my iniquity;
  I said, "I will confess my transgressions to the LORD,"
  and you forgave the iniquity of my sin. *Selah*

6 Therefore let everyone who is godly
  offer prayer to you at a time when you may be found;
  surely in the rush of great waters,
  they shall not reach him.
7 You are a hiding place for me;
  you preserve me from trouble;
  you surround me with shouts of deliverance. *Selah*

8 I will instruct you and teach you in the way you should go;
  I will counsel you with my eye upon you.
9 Be not like a horse or a mule, without understanding,
  which must be curbed with bit and bridle,
  or it will not stay near you.

10 Many are the sorrows of the wicked,
  but steadfast love surrounds the one who trusts in the LORD.
11 Be glad in the LORD, and rejoice, O righteous,
  and shout for joy, all you upright in heart!

a Psalm 32:1 Probably a musical or liturgical term
b Psalm 32:4 Hebrew *my vitality was changed*

Psalm 32 is a penitential psalm of Confession and Absolution, and it is often grouped with other penitential psalms (6; 38; 51; 102; 130; 143). Luther saw these psalms as instructive in the sense of wisdom and understanding within a spiritual and holy context over against a worldly context.

⦿ REQUEST THE SPIRIT'S HELP IN PRAYER

⦿ READ AND REPEAT THE WORD

What words or phrases stick out to you? How do those words or phrases reveal the poet's purpose for the psalm? What effect does this psalm have on you as you meditate on it?

....
....
....
....
....
....
....

⦿ RETURN TO THE LORD IN PRAYER

Of this psalm, Luther wrote, "The beginning of this psalm teaches two things: first, that all are in sins [no one is righteous] and no one is blessed; second, that no one is capable of meriting the forgiveness of sin, but it is the Lord alone who forgives freely by not imputing [guilt]" (AE 10:147). This psalm also shows the physical, mental, and spiritual implications of being silent in sin. God calls us to confess our sins quickly with contrite hearts in order to receive Absolution. Only He can relieve the troubled heart. "If we confess our sins, He is faithful and just to forgive us our sins and to cleanse us from all unrighteousness" (1 John 1:9).

LORD GOD, TO YOU I CONFESS MY SINS, SPECIFICALLY THE FOLLOWING:

....
....
....
....
....
....

Lord Jesus Christ, grant me the honesty to examine my life
according to Your Ten Commandments. Show me my sin,
that I may know and feel it in my heart and disdain it. Most
of all, grant forgiveness by Your gracious hand. Amen.

PSALM 33

1 Shout for joy in the LORD, O you righteous!
   Praise befits the upright.
2 Give thanks to the LORD with the lyre;
   make melody to him with the harp of ten strings!
3 Sing to him a new song;
   play skillfully on the strings, with loud shouts.

4 For the word of the LORD is upright,
   and all his work is done in faithfulness.
5 He loves righteousness and justice;
   the earth is full of the steadfast love of the LORD.

6 By the word of the LORD the heavens were made,
   and by the breath of his mouth all their host.
7 He gathers the waters of the sea as a heap;
   he puts the deeps in storehouses.

8 Let all the earth fear the LORD;
   let all the inhabitants of the world stand in awe of him!
9 For he spoke, and it came to be;
   he commanded, and it stood firm.

10 The LORD brings the counsel of the nations to nothing;
    he frustrates the plans of the peoples.
11 The counsel of the LORD stands forever,
    the plans of his heart to all generations.
12 Blessed is the nation whose God is the LORD,
    the people whom he has chosen as his heritage!

13 The LORD looks down from heaven;
    he sees all the children of man;
14 from where he sits enthroned he looks out
    on all the inhabitants of the earth,
15 he who fashions the hearts of them all
    and observes all their deeds.
16 The king is not saved by his great army;
    a warrior is not delivered by his great strength.
17 The war horse is a false hope for salvation,
    and by its great might it cannot rescue.

18 Behold, the eye of the LORD is on those who fear him,
    on those who hope in his steadfast love,
19 that he may deliver their soul from death
    and keep them alive in famine.

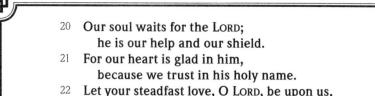

20 Our soul waits for the Lord;
   he is our help and our shield.
21 For our heart is glad in him,
   because we trust in his holy name.
22 Let your steadfast love, O Lord, be upon us,
   even as we hope in you.

The reference to Psalm 33 as "a new song" in verse 3 suggests a national deliverance, such as Judah experienced in the time of Jehoshaphat (2 Chronicles 20) or Hezekiah (2 Kings 19). As such, this psalm is a great song of praise toward God, most likely accompanied by the voices of the Levitical choir, mentioned in 1 Chronicles 16:7–36; 25:1.

⊛ REQUEST THE SPIRIT'S HELP IN PRAYER

⊛ READ AND REPEAT THE WORD

What words or phrases stick out to you? How do those words or phrases reveal the poet's purpose for the psalm? What effect does this psalm have on you as you meditate on it?

⊛ RETURN TO THE LORD IN PRAYER

God's people are always to put their trust in Him alone and not in arms, generals, national defenses, and so on. Through His Word and Spirit, almighty God grants us faith in Christ and His steadfast love. Thus, He gives us hope in our hearts and minds and certainty of His salvation in His Son, Jesus Christ. All praise, laud, and worship belong to our God, the Father, Son, and Holy Spirit.

PRAYERS:

O Lord Jesus Christ, through Your precious blood You redeemed me, a lost and condemned creature, and You called me to be Your very own. Renew my heart in righteousness and holiness so that I may praise and adore You. Amen.

The 33rd psalm is a psalm of thanks to God in general for His blessings, for helping His faithful people in all kinds of distress, and for not letting them perish. He is able to help because He made all things and still creates all things with a word, so that nothing is impossible with Him. God is also so good and true that He will help and willingly helps, as He has promised in the First Commandment: "I will be your God," that is, I will be your comfort, help, salvation, life, and all good things, and I will stand against anything that would do you harm. That's what it means to "be God."

But the psalmist particularly thanks and praises the mighty blessing of God, that He guides the whole world, even the hearts, thoughts, intentions, anger, and fury of the kings and princes, not as they will, but as He wills. And He finally frustrates all their intentions, so that they accomplish nothing as they really want. What they intend to do against the righteous He immediately turns aside and overthrows. This is the particular joy and comfort of His saints against the arrogant and overweening insolence, the thrashing and threats of the raging nobles and the ruthless tyrants, who suppose that they can with threats devour all the saints of God and hurl God Himself down from heaven. But before they have half begun, they lie in the dust. Consider the people of Sodom against Lot, Sennacherib the King, and our tyrants today—how totally countless intentions have been dashed up till now. (Martin Luther)

ACROSTIC PSALMS

An alphabetic acrostic is a literary technique in which a writer organizes a section so that the first letter of each line uses the letters of the Hebrew alphabet in order. This device is used in various places in the Old Testament, especially the psalms.

First, observe the Hebrew alphabet, which is written from right to left:

א ב ג ד ה

Now, consider the first six verses of Psalm 34, read right to left:

אֲבָרֲכָה אֶת־יְהוָה בְּכָל־עֵת תָּמִיד תְּהִלָּתוֹ בְּפִי׃
בַּיהוָה תִּתְהַלֵּל נַפְשִׁי יִשְׁמְעוּ עֲנָוִים וְיִשְׂמָחוּ׃
גַּדְּלוּ לַיהוָה אִתִּי וּנְרוֹמְמָה שְׁמוֹ יַחְדָּו׃
דָּרַשְׁתִּי אֶת־יְהוָה וְעָנָנִי וּמִכָּל־מְגוּרוֹתַי הִצִּילָנִי׃
הִבִּיטוּ אֵלָיו וְנָהָרוּ וּפְנֵיהֶם אַל־יֶחְפָּרוּ׃

Each line, a verse of Psalm 34, begins with a successive letter of the Hebrew alphabet. Other acrostic psalms include Psalms 9–10; 25; 37; 111; 112; and 145.

The most thorough example is found in Psalm 119. Divided into twenty-two sections according to the twenty-two letters of the Hebrew alphabet, each section contains eight verses. Every verse in a section begins with the same Hebrew letter.

Why did authors write in this way? The alphabetical scheme may have provided a helpful device for teaching or memorizing. Such a scheme may also have made these sections easier to pass on orally. It took skill to write an acrostic psalm. Holy Scripture, while always more than mere literature, is certainly never less.

PSALM 34

[a]Of David, when he changed his behavior before Abimelech, so that he drove him out, and he went away.

1   I will bless the LORD at all times;
       his praise shall continually be in my mouth.
2   My soul makes its boast in the LORD;
       let the humble hear and be glad.
3   Oh, magnify the LORD with me,
       and let us exalt his name together!

4   I sought the LORD, and he answered me
       and delivered me from all my fears.
5   Those who look to him are radiant,
       and their faces shall never be ashamed.
6   This poor man cried, and the LORD heard him
       and saved him out of all his troubles.
7   The angel of the LORD encamps
       around those who fear him, and delivers them.

8   Oh, taste and see that the LORD is good!
       Blessed is the man who takes refuge in him!
9   Oh, fear the LORD, you his saints,
       for those who fear him have no lack!
10 The young lions suffer want and hunger;
       but those who seek the LORD lack no good thing.

11 Come, O children, listen to me;
       I will teach you the fear of the LORD.
12 What man is there who desires life
       and loves many days, that he may see good?
13 Keep your tongue from evil
       and your lips from speaking deceit.
14 Turn away from evil and do good;
       seek peace and pursue it.

15 The eyes of the LORD are toward the righteous
       and his ears toward their cry.
16 The face of the LORD is against those who do evil,
       to cut off the memory of them from the earth.
17 When the righteous cry for help, the LORD hears

a   Psalm 34:1 This psalm is an acrostic poem, each verse beginning with the successive letters of the Hebrew alphabet

and delivers them out of all their troubles.
18 The LORD is near to the brokenhearted
and saves the crushed in spirit.

19 Many are the afflictions of the righteous,
but the LORD delivers him out of them all.
20 He keeps all his bones;
not one of them is broken.
21 Affliction will slay the wicked,
and those who hate the righteous will be condemned.
22 The LORD redeems the life of his servants;
none of those who take refuge in him will be condemned.

The reference in the superscript where David changed his behavior can be found in Scripture in 1 Samuel 21:10–15.

⊛ REQUEST THE SPIRIT'S HELP IN PRAYER

⊛ READ AND REPEAT THE WORD

What words or phrases stick out to you? How do those words or phrases reveal the poet's purpose for the psalm? What effect does this psalm have on you as you meditate on it?

⊛ RETURN TO THE LORD IN PRAYER

The Lord turns His countenance of favor toward His children, saves them, and blesses them. The Lord turns His countenance away from the wicked and condemns them to eternal death, though His will is to save all people by grace through faith in Christ.

PRAYERS:

Dear heavenly Father, blessed are those who hear Your Word and fear You, for they seek Your grace and righteousness. Move us to praise and worship You with joyful hearts because of Your Word, Jesus, so that we might inherit life everlasting. Amen.

The 34th psalm is a psalm of thanks, much like the preceding psalm. It offers us the history of David as an example for all the righteous so we might learn from him that God never despises the cries of His saints. Moreover, it teaches us to fear God and no one else; further, to be on our guard against false teachers, against curses, grumblings, and slander. We should have patience, bless enemies rather than curse them, wish them all good, do good to them rather than evil, and so (as much as in us lies) to live at peace with all people, whether they are evil or godly. For it is certain (the psalmist says) that the righteous will suffer many things. It cannot be otherwise. If you will be righteous, you must take up your cross and suffer. This is how it must be.

On the other hand, it is certain that the Lord will truly help us out of all these afflictions, that none of the least of your bones will be taken away or missing. Yes, even the hairs of the head are numbered. Although the bones of the saints in their martyrdom were often broken, some of them burnt to ashes, and many more decaying in their graces, they will yet return and not remain eternally broken or be called broken. Rather, for a time they will be broken, but afterward they will all again be more whole and healthy than they formerly were.

This is the first psalm that speaks about angels, that they attend to the righteous and wait on us. They are not simply with us or around us. The angels are like an army—armed soldiers encamped around us, pitching their tents, keeping watch, and fighting for us against the devil and all his minions. This is a great and excellent comfort for all who believe, as the prophet Elisha, following this verse, made clear with his clear and correct example (2 Kings 6:17). But this verse is taken from Genesis 32:1–2, where the angels encounter the patriarch Jacob, because of which he called that city "army" or "camp." For they were his troops and camped around him as a protection, as the psalm here states. (Martin Luther)

THOSE "POLITICALLY INCORRECT" PSALMS

We live in an age where political correctness rules the day. What may have started as a way to minimize giving offense is now viewed by many as the chief criterion by which speech is to be judged, even at the price of the truth. All speech is affected by this maxim. The Church does not stand immune from the pressures imposed by political correctness. Pressures from gender issues in particular impact speech about God Himself. They also cause significant problems in handling subjects such as marriage.

In an age that wants to minimize offense of any kind, what is the Church supposed to do with the category of psalms known as the imprecatory psalms? What answer would we have if someone accused us of promoting the murder of babies, quoting from one of the psalms:

> O daughter of Babylon, doomed to be destroyed,
>   blessed shall he be who repays you
>   with what you have done to us!
> Blessed shall he be who takes your little ones
>   and dashes them against the rock! (Psalm 137:8–9)

Definitions

A basic definition of *imprecation*, from which we get the title of "imprecatory" psalms, is "an act of calling down a curse on one's enemies or praying for the defeat of that enemy." There are six psalms that are generally recognized as thoroughgoing imprecatory psalms (35; 58; 69; 83; 109; 137; all but Psalms 83 and 137 are by David). The enemies described in these psalms vary, but generally, they fall into three categories.

First, there are psalms that speak against the nations that had treated Israel harshly. These were the nations that had as their goal the destruction of Israel:

> For behold, Your enemies make an uproar;
>   those who hate You have raised their heads.
> They lay crafty plans against Your people;
>   they consult together against Your treasured ones.
> They say, "Come, let us wipe them out as a nation;
>   let the name of Israel be remembered no more!"
>   (Psalm 83:2–4)

Given that God had promised to send the Messiah through the nation of Israel, the destruction of Israel would not do. Since these enemies were often too numerous and too powerful for the Israelites to defeat, the psalmist singles them out and calls on the Lord to defeat them.

Second, the psalmist might focus on being betrayed by a friend. Psalms 35 and 109 by David are good examples of this type of imprecatory psalm: "In return for my love they accuse me, but I give myself to prayer. So they reward me evil for good, and hatred for my love" (Psalm 109:4–5). In these psalms, the reader senses that an injustice needs to be righted. The imprecations can get quite personal, including calls for creditors to seize the possessions of individuals, for posterity to be cut off, and even for children to become fatherless (Psalm 109:6–15).

The third type of imprecatory psalm is directed against those who abuse a godly trust. Nothing can be more detrimental to society than a ruler or judge who abuses his authority for personal gain. Thus, David writes, "Do you indeed decree what is right, you gods [or "you mighty lords"]? Do you judge the children of man uprightly? No, in your hearts you devise wrongs; your hands deal out violence on earth" (Psalm 58:1–2). In calling on God for vengeance, the psalmist seeks justice from the true Judge of Israel.

Other Imprecations in the Bible

Imprecations in the Bible are not limited to the Psalter. Centuries after David, the prophet Jeremiah was continually hounded by false prophets who sought to discredit him. On several occasions, he spoke curses against them (Jeremiah 15:15; 17:18; 20:12). The most forceful imprecation is found in Jeremiah 18:21–23, in which he used language reminiscent of the imprecatory psalms.

Perhaps more surprising are several such statements in the New Testament. In his Letter to the Galatians, the apostle Paul bemoans how his readers have been swayed from the truth by false teachers. In no uncertain terms, he writes, "I wish those who unsettle you would emasculate themselves!" (Galatians 5:12). Similarly, at the beginning of this same epistle, he writes, "If anyone is preaching to you a gospel contrary to the one you received, let him be accursed" (Galatians 1:9). In every case, these curses, just like those mentioned in the Psalms, call upon God to intervene, lest the truth be turned to falsehood.

Imprecatory Psalms and the Christian

Many readers feel uncomfortable with the bluntness of the imprecatory psalms. They have suggested that these psalms have no place in the life of the Christian. God is, after all, a God of love. This truth is the constant witness of the New Testament. Since that is so, we must ask how prayers that call for such violence can be reconciled with our Lord's command to love one another (John 15:12; Romans 12:10).

A careful examination of these psalms reveals that the curses, while directed at specific persons or nations, are directed at evil that is directly opposed to God. The nations that sought Israel's destruction, for example, are directly at odds with God's plan of salvation. Their evil must be thwarted, so the psalmist makes the case to God that He must act. If the evil nation will repent, then so will God—in the sense that He will withhold His wrath. Such was the example of the Ninevites, who heeded Jonah's call to repentance (Jonah 3).

The turning of the enemy's heart is always the preferred goal. Even in a psalm as caustic as Psalm 83, the psalmist says:

> Fill their faces with shame,
>   that they may seek Your name, O LORD.
> Let them be put to shame and dismayed forever;
>   let them perish in disgrace,
> that they may know that You alone,
>   whose name is the LORD,
>   are the Most High over all the earth. (Psalm 83:16–18)

Where hearts are turned toward God, Christians will rejoice, even as the angels in heaven do whenever a sinner repents (Luke 15:10). Still, where evil continues to hold sway, Christians can continue to pray that God will thwart evil and cause justice to be done.

Praying the Imprecatory Psalms

Christians should understand that the violent outbursts in these psalms are not prescriptions for the behavior of God's people but illustrations of emotions that God's people will indeed experience. Christians today who lose loved ones to war or to violent criminals will have these same feelings of anger and revenge. Praying the imprecatory psalms can help God's people express their anguish before God rather than act out their feelings in an unjust way. Imprecatory psalms prayed alongside psalms of repentance and hope can guide troubled hearts through the feelings they cannot escape.

God called Israel to be a blessing to all nations (Genesis 12:3). He has likewise called us to bear witness to His grace. Along with this high calling, our knowledge of God's approaching judgment on the wicked and our painful experiences in life drives us to anticipate the day of wrath, which will end injustices. For these reasons, the imprecatory psalms still have an important role to play in the prayers of God's people. Go ahead and pray the imprecatory psalms, knowing and confessing that you are a sinner in need of God's mercy and grace as much as anyone else in this world. Pray these psalms in faith in the crucified and risen Christ too, knowing and believing that in Him all your enemies have been conquered.

PSALM 35

Of David.

1   Contend, O LORD, with those who contend with me;
      fight against those who fight against me!
2   Take hold of shield and buckler
      and rise for my help!
3   Draw the spear and javelin[a]
      against my pursuers!
  Say to my soul,
      "I am your salvation!"

4   Let them be put to shame and dishonor
      who seek after my life!
  Let them be turned back and disappointed
      who devise evil against me!
5   Let them be like chaff before the wind,
      with the angel of the LORD driving them away!
6   Let their way be dark and slippery,
      with the angel of the LORD pursuing them!

7   For without cause they hid their net for me;
      without cause they dug a pit for my life.[b]
8   Let destruction come upon him when he does not know it!
  And let the net that he hid ensnare him;
      let him fall into it—to his destruction!

9   Then my soul will rejoice in the LORD,
      exulting in his salvation.
10   All my bones shall say,
      "O LORD, who is like you,
  delivering the poor
      from him who is too strong for him,
      the poor and needy from him who robs him?"

11   Malicious[c] witnesses rise up;
      they ask me of things that I do not know.
12   They repay me evil for good;
      my soul is bereft.[d]

a   Psalm 35:3 Or *and close the way*
b   Psalm 35:7 The word *pit* is transposed from the preceding line; Hebrew *For without cause they hid the pit of their net for me; without cause they dug my life*
c   Psalm 35:11 Or *Violent*
d   Psalm 35:12 Hebrew *it is bereavement to my soul*

13 But I, when they were sick—
 I wore sackcloth;
 I afflicted myself with fasting;
I prayed with head bowed^e on my chest.
14 I went about as though I grieved for my friend or my
  brother;
as one who laments his mother,
 I bowed down in mourning.

15 But at my stumbling they rejoiced and gathered;
 they gathered together against me;
wretches whom I did not know
 tore at me without ceasing;
16 like profane mockers at a feast,^f
 they gnash at me with their teeth.

17 How long, O Lord, will you look on?
 Rescue me from their destruction,
 my precious life from the lions!
18 I will thank you in the great congregation;
 in the mighty throng I will praise you.

19 Let not those rejoice over me
 who are wrongfully my foes,
and let not those wink the eye
 who hate me without cause.
20 For they do not speak peace,
 but against those who are quiet in the land
 they devise words of deceit.
21 They open wide their mouths against me;
 they say, "Aha, Aha!
 Our eyes have seen it!"

22 You have seen, O Lord; be not silent!
 O Lord, be not far from me!
23 Awake and rouse yourself for my vindication,
 for my cause, my God and my Lord!
24 Vindicate me, O Lord, my God,
 according to your righteousness,
 and let them not rejoice over me!
25 Let them not say in their hearts,
 "Aha, our heart's desire!"
Let them not say, "We have swallowed him up."

e Psalm 35:13 Or *my prayer shall turn back*
f Psalm 35:16 The meaning of the Hebrew phrase is uncertain

26 Let them be put to shame and disappointed altogether
   who rejoice at my calamity!
   Let them be clothed with shame and dishonor
   who magnify themselves against me!

27 Let those who delight in my righteousness
   shout for joy and be glad
   and say evermore,
   "Great is the LORD,
   who delights in the welfare of his servant!"
28 Then my tongue shall tell of your righteousness
   and of your praise all the day long.

Psalm 35 is most likely set during Saul's time (see 1 Samuel 20; 23–26). It appears that men close to David had developed a destructive disdain for him, and someone sought David's life and slandered him. In 1 Samuel 24:12, 15, David appeals to God as the righteous judge, and this psalm may have been written around that time.

◉ REQUEST THE SPIRIT'S HELP IN PRAYER

◉ READ AND REPEAT THE WORD

What words or phrases stick out to you? How do those words or phrases reveal the poet's purpose for the psalm? What effect does this psalm have on you as you meditate on it?

◉ RETURN TO THE LORD IN PRAYER

David appeals to God Almighty as divine warrior and righteous judge. He prays that God will come to his defense and rescue him from those who were once close friends but who now accuse, slander, and condemn him with malice. The Lord forbids that we accuse an innocent person (Eighth Commandment), which would cause him or her to be wrongly punished in body, property, or reputation (see Proverbs 22:1). He bids us to err on the side of the Gospel in the case of our neighbor, unless guilt is clear (see Matthew 18:15–18). As we endeavor to treat our neighbors fairly and with mercy, our merciful Lord justifies us according to His righteousness.

PRAYERS:

O Lord Jesus Christ, Son of God, Savior of the world, move us, we pray, to shun lies and to speak well of our neighbor. Build a strong bulwark around our name, reputation, and integrity so that we might be protected from malicious gossip and deceitful tongues; through Jesus Christ, our Lord. Amen.

PSALM 36

To the choirmaster. Of David, the servant of the LORD.

1   Transgression speaks to the wicked
    deep in his heart;[a]
there is no fear of God
    before his eyes.
2   For he flatters himself in his own eyes
    that his iniquity cannot be found out and hated.
3   The words of his mouth are trouble and deceit;
    he has ceased to act wisely and do good.
4   He plots trouble while on his bed;
    he sets himself in a way that is not good;
    he does not reject evil.

5   Your steadfast love, O LORD, extends to the heavens,
    your faithfulness to the clouds.
6   Your righteousness is like the mountains of God;
    your judgments are like the great deep;
    man and beast you save, O LORD.

7   How precious is your steadfast love, O God!
    The children of mankind take refuge in the shadow
    of your wings.
8   They feast on the abundance of your house,
    and you give them drink from the river of your delights.
9   For with you is the fountain of life;
    in your light do we see light.

10 Oh, continue your steadfast love to those who know you,
    and your righteousness to the upright of heart!
11 Let not the foot of arrogance come upon me,
    nor the hand of the wicked drive me away.
12 There the evildoers lie fallen;
    they are thrust down, unable to rise.

a   Psalm 36:1 Some Hebrew manuscripts, Syriac, Jerome (compare Septuagint); most Hebrew manuscripts *in my heart*

Though the superscriptions on the psalms, "to the choirmaster" and "of David," are common in the psalms, Psalm 36 adds the superscript, "the servant of the LORD." This helps to emphasize how David served in an official capacity as a leader and instructor of the people.

⊛ REQUEST THE SPIRIT'S HELP IN PRAYER

⊛ READ AND REPEAT THE WORD

What words or phrases stick out to you? How do those words or phrases reveal the poet's purpose for the psalm? What effect does this psalm have on you as you meditate on it?

....

....

....

....

....

....

....

⊛ RETURN TO THE LORD IN PRAYER

In this psalm, we see a contrast between the wicked and the children of God. On one hand, someone who is wicked does not fear God, does not acknowledge his sin, and sets his heart on evil ways. The children of God, however, are those who are saved by God, who take refuge in Him, and drink from the fountain of life that He alone gives. Jesus, the fulfillment of God's epic plan of salvation, is the true water of life, and He has given His life for us, making us God's children. As His children, we are then to trust in God's steadfast love, avoiding any temptations to wickedness or arrogance that tempt us to abandon our faith.

LORD GOD, THAT YOU WOULD SHELTER ME IN THE STEADFASTNESS OF YOUR LOVE AND KEEP ME FROM TEMPTATIONS TO WICKEDNESS, I PRAY:

....

....

....

....

O heavenly Father, we rely on Your grace and protection in the midst of sin and the wicked works of those who test our faith. Your Word is truth. Do not allow courage to build in the hearts of Your enemies, who despise Your Word and Your Son. Do not let them proudly boast, "Where is your God?" Answer, we pray, those who oppress Your Holy Word. Amen.

PSALM 37

[a]Of David.

1   Fret not yourself because of evildoers;
      be not envious of wrongdoers!
2   For they will soon fade like the grass
      and wither like the green herb.

3   Trust in the LORD, and do good;
      dwell in the land and befriend faithfulness.[b]
4   Delight yourself in the LORD,
      and he will give you the desires of your heart.

5   Commit your way to the LORD;
      trust in him, and he will act.
6   He will bring forth your righteousness as the light,
      and your justice as the noonday.

7   Be still before the LORD and wait patiently for him;
      fret not yourself over the one who prospers in his way,
      over the man who carries out evil devices!

8   Refrain from anger, and forsake wrath!
      Fret not yourself; it tends only to evil.
9   For the evildoers shall be cut off,
      but those who wait for the LORD shall inherit the land.

10 In just a little while, the wicked will be no more;
      though you look carefully at his place, he will not be there.
11 But the meek shall inherit the land
      and delight themselves in abundant peace.

12 The wicked plots against the righteous
      and gnashes his teeth at him,
13 but the Lord laughs at the wicked,
      for he sees that his day is coming.

---

a   Psalm 37:1 This psalm is an acrostic poem, each stanza beginning with the successive letters of the Hebrew alphabet
b   Psalm 37:3 Or *and feed on faithfulness*, or *and find safe pasture*

14 The wicked draw the sword and bend their bows
   to bring down the poor and needy,
   to slay those whose way is upright;
15 their sword shall enter their own heart,
   and their bows shall be broken.

16 Better is the little that the righteous has
   than the abundance of many wicked.
17 For the arms of the wicked shall be broken,
   but the Lord upholds the righteous.

18 The Lord knows the days of the blameless,
   and their heritage will remain forever;
19 they are not put to shame in evil times;
   in the days of famine they have abundance.

20 But the wicked will perish;
   the enemies of the Lord are like the glory of the pastures;
   they vanish—like smoke they vanish away.

21 The wicked borrows but does not pay back,
   but the righteous is generous and gives;
22 for those blessed by the Lord[c] shall inherit the land,
   but those cursed by him shall be cut off.

23 The steps of a man are established by the Lord,
   when he delights in his way;
24 though he fall, he shall not be cast headlong,
   for the Lord upholds his hand.

25 I have been young, and now am old,
   yet I have not seen the righteous forsaken
   or his children begging for bread.
26 He is ever lending generously,
   and his children become a blessing.

27 Turn away from evil and do good;
   so shall you dwell forever.
28 For the Lord loves justice;
   he will not forsake his saints.
   They are preserved forever,
   but the children of the wicked shall be cut off.
29 The righteous shall inherit the land
   and dwell upon it forever.

c   Psalm 37:22 Hebrew *by him*

30 The mouth of the righteous utters wisdom,
    and his tongue speaks justice.
31 The law of his God is in his heart;
    his steps do not slip.

32 The wicked watches for the righteous
    and seeks to put him to death.
33 The LORD will not abandon him to his power
    or let him be condemned when he is brought to trial.

34 Wait for the LORD and keep his way,
    and he will exalt you to inherit the land;
    you will look on when the wicked are cut off.

35 I have seen a wicked, ruthless man,
    spreading himself like a green laurel tree.[d]
36 But he passed away,[e] and behold, he was no more;
    though I sought him, he could not be found.

37 Mark the blameless and behold the upright,
    for there is a future for the man of peace.
38 But transgressors shall be altogether destroyed;
    the future of the wicked shall be cut off.

39 The salvation of the righteous is from the LORD;
    he is their stronghold in the time of trouble.
40 The LORD helps them and delivers them;
    he delivers them from the wicked and saves them,
    because they take refuge in him.

d   Psalm 37:35 The identity of this tree is uncertain
e   Psalm 37:36 Or *But one passed by*

Psalm 37 is an acrostic poem, with approximately two verses for each letter of the alphabet. It provides teaching and comfort in a similar way to the Book of Proverbs. It reconciles the tension between the prosperity of the wicked and the slander of the righteous, as we read in Psalm 36. The psalm focuses on how leaders should trust in the Lord above all things.

◉ REQUEST THE SPIRIT'S HELP IN PRAYER

◉ READ AND REPEAT THE WORD

What words or phrases stick out to you? How do those words or phrases reveal the poet's purpose for the psalm? What effect does this psalm have on you as you meditate on it?

....

....

....

....

◉ RETURN TO THE LORD IN PRAYER

This psalm stresses two things: the righteous are blessed by God in due season, and divine punishment will overtake the wicked. Our Lord does not abandon us, His children, to the schemes of the wicked, but on the Last Day, He will fulfill our salvation and eternally deliver us from our enemies of sin, death, and the devil.

LORD GOD, I THANK YOU: ....

MERCIFUL GOD, I CONFESS TO YOU: ....

....

PRAYERS OF REQUEST
For wisdom to trust You in my household, I pray: ....

For my work and livelihood, I pray: ....

For my congregation, I pray: ....

For wisdom in loving my neighbor in the world, I pray: ....

....

Heavenly Father, You have begun Your good work in us. Continue, we pray, to fill us with the wisdom and knowledge of Your life-giving Word. Grant that our cross and sufferings may direct our hearts and minds to You, O Christ, our sure and blessed hope. Amen.

PSALM 38

A Psalm of David, for the memorial offering.

1 O LORD, rebuke me not in your anger,
      nor discipline me in your wrath!
2 For your arrows have sunk into me,
      and your hand has come down on me.

3 There is no soundness in my flesh
      because of your indignation;
   there is no health in my bones
      because of my sin.
4 For my iniquities have gone over my head;
      like a heavy burden, they are too heavy for me.

5 My wounds stink and fester
      because of my foolishness,
6 I am utterly bowed down and prostrate;
      all the day I go about mourning.
7 For my sides are filled with burning,
      and there is no soundness in my flesh.
8 I am feeble and crushed;
      I groan because of the tumult of my heart.

9 O Lord, all my longing is before you;
      my sighing is not hidden from you.
10 My heart throbs; my strength fails me,
      and the light of my eyes—it also has gone from me.
11 My friends and companions stand aloof from my plague,
      and my nearest kin stand far off.

12 Those who seek my life lay their snares;
      those who seek my hurt speak of ruin
      and meditate treachery all day long.

13 But I am like a deaf man; I do not hear,
      like a mute man who does not open his mouth.
14 I have become like a man who does not hear,
      and in whose mouth are no rebukes.

15 But for you, O Lord, do I wait;
    it is you, O Lord my God, who will answer.
16 For I said, "Only let them not rejoice over me,
    who boast against me when my foot slips!"

17 For I am ready to fall,
    and my pain is ever before me.
18 I confess my iniquity;
    I am sorry for my sin.
19 But my foes are vigorous, they are mighty,
    and many are those who hate me wrongfully.
20 Those who render me evil for good
    accuse me because I follow after good.

21 Do not forsake me, O Lord!
    O my God, be not far from me!
22 Make haste to help me,
    O Lord, my salvation!

Psalm 38, another acrostic, is one of the seven penitential psalms, or psalms of repentance. Jewish tradition has the second half of the psalm as a liturgical prayer that accompanied the memorial offering (see Leviticus 24:7; Psalm 70:1). In this psalm, David knows he has sinned and attributes his suffering to God's wrath.

⊕ REQUEST THE SPIRIT'S HELP IN PRAYER

⊕ READ AND REPEAT THE WORD

What words or phrases stick out to you? How do those words or phrases reveal the poet's purpose for the psalm? What effect does this psalm have on you as you meditate on it?

⊕ RETURN TO THE LORD IN PRAYER

The Lord chastises His children in order to turn them from temptation and sin and to keep them safe and faithful to Him. Sin that is not confessed becomes a burden on our bodies and souls and causes great despair. The Law accuses us and shows us our sin (see Romans 3:20; 7:7). Here we see that God's divine will is ultimately for our good as believers. "O Lord, my salvation!" (Psalm 38:22) is the beautiful confession that through the healing balm of the Lord's mercy, there is deliverance and absolution.

MERCIFUL GOD, I HAVE SINNED AND DONE WHAT IS EVIL IN YOUR SIGHT. TODAY I CONFESS TO YOU THAT I HAVE SINNED:

O Lord God Almighty, we are in Your hands. You pronounce us sinners, and we accept the truth of Your Word. May we be quick to confess our sin. Thank You for leading us to this confession through Your Law and promises. Keep us alive, O blessed and faithful Redeemer, for in You alone do we trust. Amen.

The 38th psalm is a psalm of prayer in which the psalmist laments over his sins, on account of which his conscience despairs and is greatly afflicted and can see nothing but God's arrows, that is, God's anger, threats, death, and hell. These sorrows consume marrow and bone, strength and fluids. They disfigure the appearance and the complexion and alter one's total understanding and demeanor. To truly feel one's sins and despair over a guilty conscience is the torture above all torture. Moreover, outward persecutors add to this "comfort," pursuing the righteous in their conscience and boasting that God is with them and against the righteous. And because God here holds back His comfort, this terror in the heart follows, that God is angry with them on account of their sins. (Martin Luther)

PSALM 39

To the choirmaster: to Jeduthun. A Psalm of David.

1 I said, "I will guard my ways,
    that I may not sin with my tongue;
I will guard my mouth with a muzzle,
    so long as the wicked are in my presence."
2 I was mute and silent;
    I held my peace to no avail,
and my distress grew worse.
3   My heart became hot within me.
As I mused, the fire burned;
    then I spoke with my tongue:

4 "O Lord, make me know my end
    and what is the measure of my days;
    let me know how fleeting I am!
5 Behold, you have made my days a few handbreadths,
    and my lifetime is as nothing before you.
Surely all mankind stands as a mere breath!   *Selah*
6   Surely a man goes about as a shadow!
Surely for nothing[a] they are in turmoil;
    man heaps up wealth and does not know who will gather!

7 "And now, O Lord, for what do I wait?
    My hope is in you.
8 Deliver me from all my transgressions.
    Do not make me the scorn of the fool!
9 I am mute; I do not open my mouth,
    for it is you who have done it.
10 Remove your stroke from me;
    I am spent by the hostility of your hand.
11 When you discipline a man
    with rebukes for sin,
you consume like a moth what is dear to him;
    surely all mankind is a mere breath!   *Selah*

12 "Hear my prayer, O Lord,
    and give ear to my cry;
    hold not your peace at my tears!
For I am a sojourner with you,
    a guest, like all my fathers.
13 Look away from me, that I may smile again,
    before I depart and am no more!"

a   Psalm 39:6 Hebrew *Surely as a breath*

Whereas Psalm 38 spoke of silence before the enemy, Psalm 39 speaks of silence before God. Both are prayers in times of illness; both acknowledge sin and express deep trust in God. The superscript mentions Jeduthun, who was one of David's three musicians (as seen in 1 Chronicles 6:44; 15:16–17; 16:41–42; 25:1, 6; 2 Chronicles 5:12; 35:15) Why this psalm was put into Jeduthun's (Ethan's) hands is unclear, as is David's specific life situation when writing it.

⊕ REQUEST THE SPIRIT'S HELP IN PRAYER

⊕ READ AND REPEAT THE WORD

What words or phrases stick out to you? How do those words or phrases reveal the poet's purpose for the psalm? What effect does this psalm have on you as you meditate on it?

....

....

....

....

⊕ RETURN TO THE LORD IN PRAYER

Veiled in uncertainty is a flickering faith that puts its hope in God and in His strength. God promises to rescue all who call on His name. In the midst of this life of vapors, phantoms, and threats, we often push God away. Despite this, He hears and answers our prayers. We are His children through His Word and Holy Baptism, and He is our safe harbor and anchor of salvation and protection.

LORD GOD, I THANK YOU:

....

....

MERCIFUL GOD, I CONFESS TO YOU:

....

....

FAITHFUL GOD, I ALSO PRAY TO YOU TODAY:

....

....

> *Heavenly Father, what would we be if You forsook*
> *us—if You withdrew Your Word and Your hand?*
> *Enlighten us with Your Word. Let us walk in the light*
> *of Your blessed Son, our Lord Jesus Christ. Amen.*

PSALM 40

To the choirmaster. A Psalm of David.

1 I waited patiently for the LORD;
  he inclined to me and heard my cry.
2 He drew me up from the pit of destruction,
  out of the miry bog,
 and set my feet upon a rock,
  making my steps secure.
3 He put a new song in my mouth,
  a song of praise to our God.
 Many will see and fear,
  and put their trust in the LORD.

4 Blessed is the man who makes
  the LORD his trust,
 who does not turn to the proud,
  to those who go astray after a lie!
5 You have multiplied, O LORD my God,
  your wondrous deeds and your thoughts toward us;
  none can compare with you!
 I will proclaim and tell of them,
  yet they are more than can be told.

6 In sacrifice and offering you have not delighted,
  but you have given me an open ear.[a]
 Burnt offering and sin offering
  you have not required.
7 Then I said, "Behold, I have come;
  in the scroll of the book it is written of me:
8 I delight to do your will, O my God;
  your law is within my heart."

9 I have told the glad news of deliverance[b]
  in the great congregation;
 behold, I have not restrained my lips,
  as you know, O LORD.
10 I have not hidden your deliverance within my heart;
  I have spoken of your faithfulness and your salvation;
 I have not concealed your steadfast love and your faithfulness
  from the great congregation.

a Psalm 40:6 Hebrew *ears you have dug for me*
b Psalm 40:9 Hebrew *righteousness*; also verse 10

11 As for you, O LORD, you will not restrain
        your mercy from me;
    your steadfast love and your faithfulness will
        ever preserve me!
12 For evils have encompassed me
        beyond number;
    my iniquities have overtaken me,
        and I cannot see;
    they are more than the hairs of my head;
        my heart fails me.

13 Be pleased, O LORD, to deliver me!
        O LORD, make haste to help me!
14 Let those be put to shame and disappointed altogether
        who seek to snatch away my life;
    let those be turned back and brought to dishonor
        who delight in my hurt!
15 Let those be appalled because of their shame
        who say to me, "Aha, Aha!"

16 But may all who seek you
        rejoice and be glad in you;
    may those who love your salvation
        say continually, "Great is the LORD!"
17 As for me, I am poor and needy,
        but the Lord takes thought for me.
    You are my help and my deliverer;
        do not delay, O my God!

Psalm 40 appears to be from an earlier time in David's life when he was an outlaw fleeing from Saul, who sought to kill David time and again.

⊛ REQUEST THE SPIRIT'S HELP IN PRAYER

⊛ READ AND REPEAT THE WORD

What words or phrases stick out to you? How do those words or phrases reveal the poet's purpose for the psalm? What effect does this psalm have on you as you meditate on it?

⊛ RETURN TO THE LORD IN PRAYER

One who has fallen away from God now cries out for His fatherly kindness and mercy. As saint and sinner, we are unable to keep God's Law perfectly, though He requires that we do so. By the power of His Word and Spirit and by faith, He instills in us a new desire. Our Lord Christ kept the Law perfectly and died on our behalf so that we might live with Him in His kingdom.

LORD GOD, I THANK YOU:

MERCIFUL GOD, I CONFESS TO YOU:

PRAYERS OF REQUEST
For members of my household to delight in the Lord, I pray:

For faithfulness in my everyday work, I pray.

For my congregation, I pray:

For my neighbor in the world, I pray:

O my Lord, help me, that by Your grace I might learn Your Commandments more completely each day. Preserve me, I earnestly pray, that by Your Holy Spirit I will never become ungrateful and seek after the world's vanity or other gods, but cling truly and solely to You, dear God and Father. Amen.

The 40th psalm is a beautiful psalm of prayer in which Christ Himself laments His sufferings and calls for rescue from death. It clearly prophesies that He alone does God's will and fulfills the Law, and that this is written about Him in the book of Moses. Christ dissolves and abolishes the old Law of sacrifices and its holiness by which God's will was not fulfilled. God alone does everything for us; nothing is done by our work or sacrifices. He therefore promises and establishes the New Testament in which the justification of the believers will be preached in the great congregation, that is, in the entire world, and not the justification by sacrifices or our works. For works and sacrifices make only arrogant and false saints whose hope is not in God or in His grace, but in their lies and false holiness. (Martin Luther)

PSALM 41

To the choirmaster. A Psalm of David.

1 Blessed is the one who considers the poor![a]
    In the day of trouble the LORD delivers him;
2 the LORD protects him and keeps him alive;
    he is called blessed in the land;
    you do not give him up to the will of his enemies.
3 The LORD sustains him on his sickbed;
    in his illness you restore him to full health.[b]

4 As for me, I said, "O LORD, be gracious to me;
    heal me,[c] for I have sinned against you!"
5 My enemies say of me in malice,
    "When will he die, and his name perish?"
6 And when one comes to see me, he utters empty words,
    while his heart gathers iniquity;
    when he goes out, he tells it abroad.
7 All who hate me whisper together about me;
    they imagine the worst for me.[d]

8 They say, "A deadly thing is poured out[e] on him;
    he will not rise again from where he lies."
9 Even my close friend in whom I trusted,
    who ate my bread, has lifted his heel against me.
10 But you, O LORD, be gracious to me,
    and raise me up, that I may repay them!

11 By this I know that you delight in me:
    my enemy will not shout in triumph over me.
12 But you have upheld me because of my integrity,
    and set me in your presence forever.

13 Blessed be the LORD, the God of Israel,
    from everlasting to everlasting!
    Amen and Amen.

a   Psalm 41:1 Or *weak*
b   Psalm 41:3 Hebrew *you turn all his bed*
c   Psalm 41:4 Hebrew *my soul*
d   Psalm 41:7 Or *they devise evil against me*
e   Psalm 41:8 Or *has fastened*

In this psalm, David is sick, and his enemies are vengeful. Because of this, Psalm 41 can likely be placed within the time of the rebellion of David's son Absalom. For more, read 2 Samuel 14–15.

⊛ REQUEST THE SPIRIT'S HELP IN PRAYER

⊛ READ AND REPEAT THE WORD

What words or phrases stick out to you? How do those words or phrases reveal the poet's purpose for the psalm? What effect does this psalm have on you as you meditate on it?

⊛ RETURN TO THE LORD IN PRAYER

Two experiences afflict David: he is sick, and he suffers at the hands of enemies (traitors) who want his throne and his life. The Lord allows suffering in our lives so that our sins might be punished in the temporal sense, though we often cannot tell why we are suffering. Whatever the case, repent of your sins and pray for the Lord's mercy and guidance according to His Word. The Lord is gracious and merciful toward His precious children. Though His discipline may never seem to end, we know His love and mercy still abound for us.

LORD GOD, I THANK YOU:

MERCIFUL GOD, I CONFESS TO YOU:

PRAYERS OF REQUEST
For members of my household to delight in the Lord, I pray:

For faithfulness in my everyday work, I pray:

For my congregation, I pray:

For my neighbor in the world, I pray:

> *Dear Father, thank You for Your infinite love and goodness toward us, Your dear children. Even when we are disciplined, we know You love us. Keep us in Your Word, in faith and in prayer. Amen.*

PSALM 42

To the choirmaster. A Maskil[a] of the Sons of Korah.

1 As a deer pants for flowing streams,
    so pants my soul for you, O God.
2 My soul thirsts for God,
    for the living God.
When shall I come and appear before God?[b]
3 My tears have been my food
    day and night,
while they say to me all the day long,
    "Where is your God?"
4 These things I remember,
    as I pour out my soul:
how I would go with the throng
    and lead them in procession to the house of God
with glad shouts and songs of praise,
    a multitude keeping festival.

5 Why are you cast down, O my soul,
    and why are you in turmoil within me?
Hope in God; for I shall again praise him,
    my salvation[c] 6 and my God.

My soul is cast down within me;
    therefore I remember you
from the land of Jordan and of Hermon,
    from Mount Mizar.
7 Deep calls to deep
    at the roar of your waterfalls;
all your breakers and your waves
    have gone over me.
8 By day the LORD commands his steadfast love,
    and at night his song is with me,
    a prayer to the God of my life.
9 I say to God, my rock:
    "Why have you forgotten me?
Why do I go mourning
    because of the oppression of the enemy?"

---

a   Psalm 42:1 Probably a musical or liturgical term
b   Psalm 42:2 Revocalization yields *and see the face of God*
c   Psalm 42:5 Hebrew *the salvation of my face*; also verse 11 and 43:5

10 As with a deadly wound in my bones,
    my adversaries taunt me,
    while they say to me all the day long,
    "Where is your God?"

11 Why are you cast down, O my soul,
    and why are you in turmoil within me?
    Hope in God; for I shall again praise him,
    my salvation and my God.

Psalms 42 and 43 appear separately, but they are connected by a common refrain and lament. Psalm 43 has no superscription, indicating that the two psalms are meant to be understood together. The two psalms form three cycles focused on intense yearning for God and communion with Him at the temple. In distress, the psalmist wishes only for the temple in Jerusalem, the Lord's earthly location. Of the psalm, Luther wrote, "[The psalmist] desires to come to God's house and be comforted by the face of God. . . . For God's house is that place where God's Word is, and God's face is His presence through which He makes Himself known and, by means of His Word, reveals His grace" (*RPL*, pp. 105–6). The term *Maskil* in the superscript may indicate a skilled or artistic piece. The phrase "Sons of Korah" indicates descendants of Levi who served as temple musicians (1 Chronicles 6:1, 22, 31).

⊛ REQUEST THE SPIRIT'S HELP IN PRAYER

⊛ READ AND REPEAT THE WORD

What words or phrases stick out to you? How do those words or phrases reveal the poet's purpose for the psalm? What effect does this psalm have on you as you meditate on it?

⊛ RETURN TO THE LORD IN PRAYER

The psalmist despairs at the seeming victory of the godless as well as his separation from God's merciful presence at the temple. We, too, should desire God's presence, hear His Word in public worship, and receive the salvation that He gives in the Word. In the midst of our suffering and troubles, and against all appearances to the contrary, our Lord Jesus is our Savior. He dwells among us in preaching and in Communion to save us.

PRAYERS:

*O living God, I thirst for Your mercy. Answer my
prayer, for You are my salvation. Amen.*

PSALM 43

1   Vindicate me, O God, and defend my cause
      against an ungodly people,
  from the deceitful and unjust man
      deliver me!
2   For you are the God in whom I take refuge;
      why have you rejected me?
  Why do I go about mourning
      because of the oppression of the enemy?

3   Send out your light and your truth;
      let them lead me;
  let them bring me to your holy hill
      and to your dwelling!
4   Then I will go to the altar of God,
      to God my exceeding joy,
  and I will praise you with the lyre,
      O God, my God.

5   Why are you cast down, O my soul,
      and why are you in turmoil within me?
  Hope in God; for I shall again praise him,
      my salvation and my God.

For more on Psalm 43, read the introduction to Psalm 42.

⊛ REQUEST THE SPIRIT'S HELP IN PRAYER

⊛ READ AND REPEAT THE WORD

What words or phrases stick out to you? How do those words or phrases reveal the poet's purpose for the psalm? What effect does this psalm have on you as you meditate on it?

⊛ RETURN TO THE LORD IN PRAYER

The psalmist desires vindication for the cause of his sufferings. He asks God for the light and truth that come from His dwelling so that he might return to His sanctuary in joyful worship. In an ungodly world, you, too, are assailed by sin, death, and the devil. Yet God will comfort you by His life-sustaining Word.

LORD GOD, I THANK YOU:

MERCIFUL GOD, I CONFESS TO YOU:

PRAYERS OF REQUEST
For members of my household to delight in the Lord, I pray:

For faithfulness in my everyday work, I pray:

For my congregation, I pray:

For my neighbor in the world, I pray:

*Lead me to Your dwelling, O God, my God, and open
my mouth with Your praise and song. Amen.*

PSALM 44

To the choirmaster. A Maskil[a] of the Sons of Korah.

1 O God, we have heard with our ears,
   our fathers have told us,
 what deeds you performed in their days,
   in the days of old:
2 you with your own hand drove out the nations,
   but them you planted;
 you afflicted the peoples,
   but them you set free;
3 for not by their own sword did they win the land,
   nor did their own arm save them,
 but your right hand and your arm,
   and the light of your face,
   for you delighted in them.

4 You are my King, O God;
   ordain salvation for Jacob!
5 Through you we push down our foes;
   through your name we tread down those who
   rise up against us.
6 For not in my bow do I trust,
   nor can my sword save me.
7 But you have saved us from our foes
   and have put to shame those who hate us.
8 In God we have boasted continually,
   and we will give thanks to your name forever.   *Selah*

9 But you have rejected us and disgraced us
   and have not gone out with our armies.
10 You have made us turn back from the foe,
   and those who hate us have gotten spoil.
11 You have made us like sheep for slaughter
   and have scattered us among the nations.
12 You have sold your people for a trifle,
   demanding no high price for them.
13 You have made us the taunt of our neighbors,
   the derision and scorn of those around us.
14 You have made us a byword among the nations,
   a laughingstock[b] among the peoples.

---

a   Psalm 44:1 Probably a musical or liturgical term
b   Psalm 44:14 Hebrew *a shaking of the head*

15 All day long my disgrace is before me,
   and shame has covered my face
16 at the sound of the taunter and reviler,
   at the sight of the enemy and the avenger.

17 All this has come upon us,
   though we have not forgotten you,
   and we have not been false to your covenant.
18 Our heart has not turned back,
   nor have our steps departed from your way;
19 yet you have broken us in the place of jackals
   and covered us with the shadow of death.
20 If we had forgotten the name of our God
   or spread out our hands to a foreign god,
21 would not God discover this?
   For he knows the secrets of the heart.
22 Yet for your sake we are killed all the day long;
   we are regarded as sheep to be slaughtered.

23 Awake! Why are you sleeping, O Lord?
   Rouse yourself! Do not reject us forever!
24 Why do you hide your face?
   Why do you forget our affliction and oppression?
25 For our soul is bowed down to the dust;
   our belly clings to the ground.
26 Rise up; come to our help!
   Redeem us for the sake of your steadfast love!

Psalm 44 is a lament in which Israel complains to God after suffering some national calamity or military defeat. They are chastened and confused that God has permitted this disaster to befall them.

⊕ REQUEST THE SPIRIT'S HELP IN PRAYER

⊕ READ AND REPEAT THE WORD

What words or phrases stick out to you? How do those words or phrases reveal the poet's purpose for the psalm? What effect does this psalm have on you as you meditate on it?

....

....

....

....

....

....

⊕ RETURN TO THE LORD IN PRAYER

The psalmist recounts God's past faithfulness but complains that God is now against His people, letting them suffer defeat despite their faithfulness to Him. They petition Him to help them once more. As we undergo affliction, we are tempted to believe that God has deserted us or is unfairly punishing us. God is always for you despite everything you see, feel, or think to the contrary. God is not sleeping; rather, He always helps, redeems, and loves. Indeed, "He . . . did not spare His own Son but gave Him up for us all" (Romans 8:32).

MERCIFUL GOD, HEAVENLY FATHER, YOUR WAYS ARE NOT OUR WAYS, AND THERE IS SO MUCH THAT WE DO NOT UNDERSTAND. TRUSTING IN YOUR ULTIMATE MERCY AND GRACE TO US IN JESUS CHRIST, I BRING MY PRAYERS TO YOU THIS DAY:

....

....

....

....

....

....

....

Awake, O Lord, and come to our side. Amen.

The 44th psalm is a general psalm of prayer in which all the saints, especially the New Testament saints, lament that they are persecuted by the heathen and tyrants and would be slaughtered. They cry out that God has given them over to this, as if He had abandoned them. Formerly He had helped them with great wonders, and no harm came to them from persecutions. But they are now even persecuted on their own account, that is, for God's sake, as if they had done all kinds evil. In summary, this psalm is the sighing of the spirit. It rebukes the flesh, which murmurs against God that it is judged unrighteous and is so poorly governed (according to reason) that the godly, who ought to be helped, are allowed to suffer, and the evil, who ought to be punished, are elevated.
(Martin Luther)

PSALM 45

To the choirmaster: according to Lilies. A Maskil[a] of the
Sons of Korah; a love song.

1   My heart overflows with a pleasing theme;
      I address my verses to the king;
      my tongue is like the pen of a ready scribe.

2   You are the most handsome of the sons of men;
      grace is poured upon your lips;
      therefore God has blessed you forever.
3   Gird your sword on your thigh, O mighty one,
      in your splendor and majesty!

4   In your majesty ride out victoriously
      for the cause of truth and meekness and righteousness;
      let your right hand teach you awesome deeds!
5   Your arrows are sharp
      in the heart of the king's enemies;
      the peoples fall under you.

6   Your throne, O God, is forever and ever.
      The scepter of your kingdom is a scepter of uprightness;
7   you have loved righteousness and hated wickedness.
  Therefore God, your God, has anointed you
      with the oil of gladness beyond your companions;
8   your robes are all fragrant with myrrh and aloes and cassia.
  From ivory palaces stringed instruments make you glad;
9   daughters of kings are among your ladies of honor;
      at your right hand stands the queen in gold of Ophir.

10   Hear, O daughter, and consider, and incline your ear:
      forget your people and your father's house,
11   and the king will desire your beauty.
  Since he is your lord, bow to him.
12   The people[b] of Tyre will seek your favor with gifts,
      the richest of the people.[c]

a   Psalm 45:1 Probably a musical or liturgical term
b   Psalm 45:12 Hebrew *daughter*
c   Psalm 45:12 Or *The daughter of Tyre is here with gifts, the richest of people seek your favor*

13 All glorious is the princess in her chamber, with robes inter-
woven with gold.

14   In many-colored robes she is led to the king,
with her virgin companions following behind her.

15 With joy and gladness they are led along
as they enter the palace of the king.

16 In place of your fathers shall be your sons;
you will make them princes in all the earth.

17 I will cause your name to be remembered in all generations;
therefore nations will praise you forever and ever.

Psalm 45 is a royal psalm celebrating the marriage of the ideal king to his bride. It also shows the close connection between the song of the temple, where God dwelled, and the royal court, where His king sat enthroned. It enlarges the scope of the messianic prophecy recorded in Psalm 2 (see Psalm 2:1–11; 2 Samuel 7 for further reading). The prayer addressed to God (vv. 3, 6), as well as to this king (vv. 1, 7), depicts the anointed one in a way that would have exceeded any Davidic king. Whoever the king of the original setting is, he foreshadows that future One who is "greater than Solomon" (Matthew 12:42). Our Lord Jesus Christ gave Himself up for and is intimately united with His Bride, the Church (Ephesians 5:25–27).

The superscript, "according to Lilies," is likely a name for a specific melody, and the reference to a love song likely indicates, as Luther wrote, a "wedding lyric" (AE 12:200). The title is actually plural, meaning "a song of loves," referring to bridal virgins or maidens, including the bride herself. Alternatively, it is possibly a reference to accompaniment for the female vocal (or soprano) range. The psalm likely contains features of the wedding ceremony.

⊛ Request the Spirit's Help in Prayer

⊛ Read and Repeat the Word

What words or phrases stick out to you? How do those words or phrases reveal the poet's purpose for the psalm? What effect does this psalm have on you as you meditate on it?

....

....

....

....

⊛ Return to the Lord in Prayer

The psalmist uses a royal wedding to portray God our King and the fulfillment of His kingdom in His Son. The grand picture of this King and this marriage—illustrating Christ and His Bride, the Church—stands in contrast to the hard realities of suffering and death that we continue to see in the Church and endure in life. Behind the weak appearances of our life in the Church, Jesus Christ forgives, cleanses, and nourishes us by the baptismal washing and holy food that He gives for His Bride (Ephesians 5:26, 29).

Prayers:

....

....

....

Though our lives are yet hidden with Christ in God, Your throne and reign, O God, are forever and ever. Amen.

The 45th psalm is a prophecy of the Gospel and the kingdom of Christ, adorned with magnificent, splendid, and powerful words. For it portrays Christ as a king—with all kingly splendor, very handsome, well-spoken, well-adorned, well-armored, successful in war, righteous, gentle, gracious, having likewise a fine castle, a grand host of ladies-in-waiting, a beautiful queen, and children forever. This all is nothing else than a spiritual picture of the Gospel of Christ, His Spirit, grace, Church, and eternal life, of war against sin, death, Law, devil, flesh, world, and all evil.

The psalm also clearly proclaims that the Old Testament shall come to an end. For it calls on the daughters to forget their father's house and people and call on this king as the one God, of which there is no other God. It gives Him also the honor of the First Commandment, namely prayer, and it names Him clearly as the true God, acknowledging Him to be the eternal king who rules in righteousness and takes sins away. An eternal king can only be God Himself.
(Martin Luther)

PSALM 46

To the choirmaster. Of the Sons of Korah. According to Alamoth.[a]
A Song.

1   God is our refuge and strength,
     a very present[b] help in trouble.
2   Therefore we will not fear though the earth gives way,
     though the mountains be moved into the heart of the sea,
3   though its waters roar and foam,
     though the mountains tremble at its swelling.   *Selah*

4   There is a river whose streams make glad the city of God,
     the holy habitation of the Most High.
5   God is in the midst of her; she shall not be moved;
     God will help her when morning dawns.
6   The nations rage, the kingdoms totter;
     he utters his voice, the earth melts.
7   The LORD of hosts is with us;
     the God of Jacob is our fortress.   *Selah*

8   Come, behold the works of the LORD,
     how he has brought desolations on the earth.
9   He makes wars cease to the end of the earth;
     he breaks the bow and shatters the spear;
     he burns the chariots with fire.
10 "Be still, and know that I am God.
     I will be exalted among the nations,
     I will be exalted in the earth!"
11 The LORD of hosts is with us;
     the God of Jacob is our fortress.   *Selah*

---

a   Psalm 46:1 Probably a musical or liturgical term
b   Psalm 46:1 Or *well proved*

Psalm 46 is a song of complete trust in God as a strong refuge, particularly in the face of crisis. It is also the basis of Luther's best-known hymn. The "Most High" (v. 4), the "LORD of hosts . . . [and] the God of Jacob" (v. 7) has chosen to dwell in an earthly location. By God's grace, "the city of God" (v. 4) was among His people Israel (vv. 5, 7) in Jerusalem on Mount Zion. Luther paraphrased this psalm in the hymn "A Mighty Fortress Is Our God," asking the question, "Ask ye, Who is this?" and answering boldly, "Jesus Christ it is, Of Sabaoth Lord, And there's none other God" (*LSB* 656:2). The title in the superscript, "A Song," suggests perhaps it was meant for a vocal arrangement, without instrumental accompaniment.

◈ REQUEST THE SPIRIT'S HELP IN PRAYER

◈ READ AND REPEAT THE WORD

What words or phrases stick out to you? How do those words or phrases reveal the poet's purpose for the psalm? What effect does this psalm have on you as you meditate on it?

◈ RETURN TO THE LORD IN PRAYER

The almighty and Most High God controls nature, safeguards His chosen city against attacking foes, and stands over all nations at war. He is our sure fortress. In mercy, He makes Himself accessible and is, therefore, "God with us." As individuals and as the Church, we experience many troubles in this life on account of the devil, the world, and our own sinful nature. Yet amid every crisis of body or soul, God is with us in His Son so that we may face every upheaval.

LORD GOD, OUR MIGHTY FORTRESS, TODAY I THANK YOU:

MERCIFUL GOD, OUR REFUGE AND STRENGTH, I CONFESS TO YOU:

LORD OF HOSTS, OUR PRESENT HELP IN TROUBLE, TODAY I ALSO PRAY:

O Lord, make us know You as our refuge and strength,
our very present help in every trouble. Amen.

PSALM 47

To the choirmaster. A Psalm of the Sons of Korah.

1   Clap your hands, all peoples!
      Shout to God with loud songs of joy!
2   For the LORD, the Most High, is to be feared,
      a great king over all the earth.
3   He subdued peoples under us,
      and nations under our feet.
4   He chose our heritage for us,
      the pride of Jacob whom he loves.   *Selah*

5   God has gone up with a shout,
      the LORD with the sound of a trumpet.
6   Sing praises to God, sing praises!
      Sing praises to our King, sing praises!
7   For God is the King of all the earth;
      sing praises with a psalm![a]

8   God reigns over the nations;
      God sits on his holy throne.
9   The princes of the peoples gather
      as the people of the God of Abraham.
    For the shields of the earth belong to God;
      he is highly exalted!

a   Psalm 47:7 Hebrew *maskil*

Psalm 47 is a psalm in praise of both the kingship of the Lord and the universal reign of "the God of Abraham" (v. 9). The psalmist addresses no less than "all peoples" (v. 1), insisting that all should praise the Lord for what He has done in Israel. Of this, Luther wrote, "The 47th psalm is a prophecy of Christ, that He shall rise up and become king over all the world without a battle, simply through shouts, songs, and trumpet calls, that is, through the joyful preaching of the Gospel, just as the walls of Jericho fell by trumpet blasts and shouts, without any weapons at all" (*RPL*, p. 116). The psalm indicates a liturgical procession ("gone up" to the temple mount, in v. 5) and was possibly used in the temple worship during a chief festival, such as the Feast of Tabernacles, Weeks, or Booths, which included "the sound of a trumpet" (v. 5; see also Leviticus 23:34).

⊛ REQUEST THE SPIRIT'S HELP IN PRAYER

⊛ READ AND REPEAT THE WORD

What words or phrases stick out to you? How do those words or phrases reveal the poet's purpose for the psalm? What effect does this psalm have on you as you meditate on it?

⊛ RETURN TO THE LORD IN PRAYER

All nations are called to praise God for what He has done for Israel. Israel is called to praise Him as their great King, demonstrating His universal rule and salvation. God's promised salvation is for all nations and has been carried out in time and history by His Son, who became man precisely to be "lifted up" on the cross and so "draw all people" to Himself (John 12:32).

PRAYERS AND NOTES:

Sing praises to our God, for He is the King of all the earth, which He has saved through His Son. Amen.

PSALM 48

A Song. A Psalm of the Sons of Korah.

1   Great is the LORD and greatly to be praised
      in the city of our God!
   His holy mountain, 2 beautiful in elevation,
      is the joy of all the earth,
   Mount Zion, in the far north,
      the city of the great King.
3   Within her citadels God
      has made himself known as a fortress.

4   For behold, the kings assembled;
      they came on together.
5   As soon as they saw it, they were astounded;
      they were in panic; they took to flight.
6   Trembling took hold of them there,
      anguish as of a woman in labor.
7   By the east wind you shattered
      the ships of Tarshish.
8   As we have heard, so have we seen
      in the city of the LORD of hosts,
   in the city of our God,
      which God will establish forever.   *Selah*

9   We have thought on your steadfast love, O God,
      in the midst of your temple.
10   As your name, O God,
      so your praise reaches to the ends of the earth.
   Your right hand is filled with righteousness.
11   Let Mount Zion be glad!
   Let the daughters of Judah rejoice
      because of your judgments!

12   Walk about Zion, go around her,
      number her towers,
13   consider well her ramparts,
      go through her citadels,
   that you may tell the next generation
14   that this is God,
   our God forever and ever.
      He will guide us forever.[a]

---

a   Psalm 48:14 Septuagint; another reading is (compare Jerome, Syriac) *He will guide us beyond death*

Psalm 48 is a Song of Zion that, like previous psalms (46–47), takes up the theme that the Lord Most High, the "great king over all the earth" (Psalm 47:2) dwells in Jerusalem, "the city of our God" (Psalm 48:1, 8). No specific event or attack is named; the psalm breathes a setting greater than just a local conflict. Accordingly, this place is the "joy of all the earth" (v. 2), a "fortress" against every enemy (v. 3), and the place of His "steadfast love" (v. 9) for His congregation. Jewish writings collected in the Mishnah indicate that the Levitical choir sang Psalm 48 (Psalm 47 in the Septuagint) as the assigned psalm for the second day of the week for the morning and evening sacrifices (see 2 Chronicles 2:4) before the temple was destroyed in AD 70 (Tamid 7:4).

◉ Request the Spirit's Help in Prayer

◉ Read and Repeat the Word

What words or phrases stick out to you? How do those words or phrases reveal the poet's purpose for the psalm? What effect does this psalm have on you as you meditate on it?

◉ Return to the Lord in Prayer

The Lord of heaven and earth makes His abode with humankind, where He is a strong fortress that shatters every enemy. He is, therefore, worthy of all praise, and we rightly "tell the next generation" (v. 13) what He has done. What Mount Zion and temple worship were for ancient Israel, Christ's Church at worship is for us—the place where God mercifully dwells to save by His Word.

Prayers of Request
For members of my household, that we may praise You, I pray:

For steadfastness in my everyday work, I pray:

For my congregation, that we may faithfully praise You, I pray:

For my neighbor in the world, that all may follow Your ways, I pray:

May we consider well Your steadfast love,
O God, in the midst of Your temple. Amen.

PSALM 49

To the choirmaster. A Psalm of the Sons of Korah.

1 Hear this, all peoples!
    Give ear, all inhabitants of the world,
2 both low and high,
    rich and poor together!
3 My mouth shall speak wisdom;
    the meditation of my heart shall be understanding.
4 I will incline my ear to a proverb;
    I will solve my riddle to the music of the lyre.

5 Why should I fear in times of trouble,
    when the iniquity of those who cheat me surrounds me,
6 those who trust in their wealth
    and boast of the abundance of their riches?
7 Truly no man can ransom another,
    or give to God the price of his life,
8 for the ransom of their life is costly
    and can never suffice,
9 that he should live on forever
    and never see the pit.

10 For he sees that even the wise die;
    the fool and the stupid alike must perish
    and leave their wealth to others.
11 Their graves are their homes forever,[a]
    their dwelling places to all generations,
    though they called lands by their own names.
12 Man in his pomp will not remain;
    he is like the beasts that perish.

13 This is the path of those who have foolish confidence;
    yet after them people approve of their boasts.[b]   *Selah*
14 Like sheep they are appointed for Sheol;
    death shall be their shepherd,
    and the upright shall rule over them in the morning.
        Their form shall be consumed in Sheol, with no place
        to dwell.
15 But God will ransom my soul from the power of Sheol,
    for he will receive me.   *Selah*

---

a   Psalm 49:11 Septuagint, Syriac, Targum; Hebrew *Their inward thought was that their homes were forever*
b   Psalm 49:13 Or *and of those after them who approve of their boasts*

16 Be not afraid when a man becomes rich,
   when the glory of his house increases.
17 For when he dies he will carry nothing away;
   his glory will not go down after him.
18 For though, while he lives, he counts himself blessed
   —and though you get praise when you do well for
   yourself—
19 his soul will go to the generation of his fathers,
   who will never again see light.
20 Man in his pomp yet without understanding is like the
   beasts that perish.

Psalm 49 is a wisdom psalm that instructs on the futility of wealth and worldliness, which stand in contrast to God's power to redeem from death. The refrain "Man in his pomp . . . is like the beasts that perish" (vv. 12, 20) points to the certainty of death (for example, "the pit," v. 9; "Sheol," v. 15). The psalm teaches God's power to ransom the soul out of death. Wisdom (see Proverbs 8:22–31) is ultimately fulfilled in and personified by Jesus Christ (for more, read Matthew 11:19; Luke 11:49; 1 Corinthians 1:24, 30).

❁ REQUEST THE SPIRIT'S HELP IN PRAYER

❁ READ AND REPEAT THE WORD

What words or phrases stick out to you? How do those words or phrases reveal the poet's purpose for the psalm? What effect does this psalm have on you as you meditate on it?

....

....

....

❁ RETURN TO THE LORD IN PRAYER

Wealth and earthly goods cannot buy off death. Those who foolishly rely on them find a very different end than those whose fortune and trust is in the Lord. In a culture saturated with great personal and national prosperity, our own relative wealth and advantage easily become false gods to which we look for all good things. Neither the god of money nor any person can pay the ransom price for sin or overcome death. Christ alone has done this for us by His death and resurrection.

Thanks be to God, who has ransomed my soul from the power of the grave and made me rich in blessings. Amen.

PSALM 50

A Psalm of Asaph.

1 The Mighty One, God the LORD,
  speaks and summons the earth
  from the rising of the sun to its setting.
2 Out of Zion, the perfection of beauty,
  God shines forth.

3 Our God comes; he does not keep silence;[a]
  before him is a devouring fire,
  around him a mighty tempest.
4 He calls to the heavens above
  and to the earth, that he may judge his people:
5 "Gather to me my faithful ones,
  who made a covenant with me by sacrifice!"
6 The heavens declare his righteousness,
  for God himself is judge!   Selah

7 "Hear, O my people, and I will speak;
  O Israel, I will testify against you.
  I am God, your God.
8 Not for your sacrifices do I rebuke you;
  your burnt offerings are continually before me.
9 I will not accept a bull from your house
  or goats from your folds.
10 For every beast of the forest is mine,
  the cattle on a thousand hills.
11 I know all the birds of the hills,
  and all that moves in the field is mine.

12 "If I were hungry, I would not tell you,
  for the world and its fullness are mine.
13 Do I eat the flesh of bulls
  or drink the blood of goats?
14 Offer to God a sacrifice of thanksgiving,[b]
  and perform your vows to the Most High,
15 and call upon me in the day of trouble;
  I will deliver you, and you shall glorify me."

---

a Psalm 50:3 Or *May our God come, and not keep silence*
b Psalm 50:14 Or *Make thanksgiving your sacrifice to God*

16 But to the wicked God says:
    "What right have you to recite my statutes
    or take my covenant on your lips?
17 For you hate discipline,
    and you cast my words behind you.
18 If you see a thief, you are pleased with him,
    and you keep company with adulterers.

19 "You give your mouth free rein for evil,
    and your tongue frames deceit.
20 You sit and speak against your brother;
    you slander your own mother's son.
21 These things you have done, and I have been silent;
    you thought that I[c] was one like yourself.
    But now I rebuke you and lay the charge before you.

22 "Mark this, then, you who forget God,
    lest I tear you apart, and there be none to deliver!
23 The one who offers thanksgiving as his sacrifice glorifies me;
    to one who orders his way rightly
    I will show the salvation of God!"

c   Psalm 50:21 Or *that the I* AM

This psalm is of Asaph, one of the Levites appointed by David to provide music for the temple services (see 1 Chronicles 15:16–24; 25:1; 2 Chronicles 29:30). It is separated from the rest of the Asaph psalms (73–83) that begin Book Three of the Book of Psalms. God speaks in the first person (vv. 5, 7–15, 16–23). Our eyes should be drawn to the piling up of divine names from the beginning: verse 1, "The Mighty One" (*'El*); "God" (*'Elohim*); "the LORD" (*Yahweh*)—a combination found elsewhere only in Joshua 22:22; "judge" (v. 6); "Most High" (v. 14); "I AM" (v. 21 footnote); and "God" (the rare Hebrew word *'eloah*, v. 22). The divine judge is calling His people to account! The psalm gives an almost visionary scene that depicts a past, present, and future revelation of God.

❀ REQUEST THE SPIRIT'S HELP IN PRAYER

❀ READ AND REPEAT THE WORD

What words or phrases stick out to you? How do those words or phrases reveal the poet's purpose for the psalm? What effect does this psalm have on you as you meditate on it?

❀ RETURN TO THE LORD IN PRAYER

God comes as a judge to reprimand His people for the unbelief that hides behind careless ritualism and hypocritical religiosity. We mask our sin by hiding behind false piety or merely going through the motions of Christian worship (confessing, hearing, communing), ignoring the deadly seriousness of sin. Sin is not magically waved away; true repentance turns away from sin as the horror and poison that it is, and clings to the perfect, once-for-all sacrifice of God's Son dying on the cross.

GOD OF ALL CREATION, TURN THE HEARTS OF YOUR PEOPLE FROM SIN TO TRUE REPENTANCE AND JOY IN OUR SALVATION. TODAY I ESPECIALLY PRAY:

O Lord, we receive Jesus and all the benefits of His sacrifice in Word and Sacrament. We praise and glorify You for this great salvation! Amen.

Psalm 50 is a psalm of instruction that tells us of the true worship of God and true sacrifice in contrast to the false saints. They value their own sacrifices and worship highly, as if God must surely be thankful and indebted to them. God, however, reverses this. He intends for His goodness and help to be so highly esteemed that we will be thankful and indebted to Him.

Likewise, when the psalm commands that vows be fulfilled, this does not mean absurd self-chosen vows, but those that are commanded in the Ten Commandments, especially in the First and Second—that we praise God, that we trust in Him, call on Him, praise and thank Him as our only God, and the like. Of this, the raving saints and the hypocrites know nothing.

Mark well the clear words with which the psalm closes. The last verse teaches us that to call upon God in distress and thank Him is the true worship, the most pleasing offering, and the right way to salvation. (Martin Luther)

LAW AND GOSPEL IN THE PSALMS

Have you ever noticed how God sometimes seems to be talking out of both sides of His mouth? At one place in Scripture, He speaks a condemning word. A bit further on comes a message of comfort and grace. What does this mean?

God is, in a sense, speaking two opposing messages to us: His Law and His Gospel. In the Law, God reveals His will for us, while in the Gospel, He reveals what He has done to fulfill the Law for us. To speak of "Law and Gospel" is not simply to equate the Old Testament with the Law and the New Testament with the Gospel. Throughout Scripture, including in the Psalms, God speaks to us both His word of judgment and His word of promise.

Law and Gospel in the Psalms

Compare the Ten Commandments and the Apostles' Creed. The Ten Commandments teach us what we should do. The Creed summarizes God's acts and gifts for us: the Father gave His Son to redeem us, and the Holy Spirit calls us to faith in Christ and bestows Christ's righteousness on us.

It is amazing how frequently Law and Gospel are found in the Psalter, especially in psalms where sin is confessed and God's forgiveness is spoken, such as in the penitential psalms. Perhaps one of the most succinct examples, a familiar one from the Divine Service, is in Psalm 32:5: "I acknowledged my sin to You, and I did not cover my iniquity; I said, 'I will confess my transgressions to the LORD,' and You forgave the iniquity of my sin."

The Law of God, with its demands to be holy as the Lord is holy, leaves us with one of two possibilities: we can either reject the Law's demands and live in a state of unbelief, or we can acknowledge the truthfulness of God's guilty verdict on us. That is what confession of sin is all about, admitting that God's Law speaks the truth about me: I am a sinner.

When that word of judgment from God puts me to death, then I am ready to hear His other word, the word of forgiveness: the Gospel.

How Many Ways to Say "Good News"?

Particularly striking in the Psalter are the many ways in which the Gospel is portrayed. Staying with Psalm 32, verses 1–2 offer three distinct images for our salvation.

1. Our sin is described as being forgiven—much as a debt is forgiven so that the debtor is free from all obligations.

2. Our sin is described as being covered. Although the Law condemns us and strips us bare of any defenses, our sins

are covered by the blood of Christ. When the Father looks at us, He sees His beloved Son who has borne not only our sin but also the sin of the whole world.

3. The language of justification is used: "Blessed is the man against whom the LORD counts no iniquity" (Psalm 32:2). Our sins are not counted against us but against Christ, for "the LORD has laid on Him the iniquity of us all" (Isaiah 53:6). What is counted (or imputed) to our account is Christ's innocence and righteousness. "For our sake He made Him to be sin who knew no sin, so that in Him we might become the righteousness of God" (2 Corinthians 5:21). Note that the apostle Paul quoted Psalm 32:1–2 in Romans 4:7–8.

Dramatic Distinction

The Psalms are filled with examples of the distinction between the Law and the Gospel. What is more, the distinction is often portrayed in colorful and dramatic ways. Consider Psalm 51, another of the penitential psalms. The heading to this psalm indicates that it originated from David's encounter with the prophet Nathan when David's sins of adultery and murder were exposed. The prophet showed no mercy as he nailed David with the particulars of his transgressions: "You are the man!" (2 Samuel 12:7; see vv. 7–12). David had no place to hide but was beaten down until he uttered the simplest of confessions: "I have sinned against the LORD" (v. 13). In reply, Nathan ceased his application of God's Law and offered the comfort of the Gospel instead: "The LORD also has put away your sin; you shall not die" (2 Samuel 12:13).

In this setting, consider the opening verses of Psalm 51. What is the source of David's hope? Nothing other than God's steadfast love and abundant mercy. He has nowhere else to turn. With confidence in that mercy, David can ask for cleansing, which is yet another image of God's merciful dealing with us. Later in the psalm, David asks God: "Create in me a clean heart, O God" (v. 10), well-known words from the Offertory in the Divine Service.

So God does speak out of both sides of His mouth, with words that condemn and forgive. He speaks them to you also through the Psalms. The good news is that His forgiving word most clearly reveals His fatherly heart of love in Christ Jesus.

PSALM 51

To the choirmaster. A Psalm of David, when Nathan the prophet
went to him, after he had gone in to Bathsheba.

1   Have mercy on me,[a] O God,
    according to your steadfast love;
  according to your abundant mercy
    blot out my transgressions.
2   Wash me thoroughly from my iniquity,
    and cleanse me from my sin!

3   For I know my transgressions,
    and my sin is ever before me.
4   Against you, you only, have I sinned
    and done what is evil in your sight,
  so that you may be justified in your words
    and blameless in your judgment.
5   Behold, I was brought forth in iniquity,
    and in sin did my mother conceive me.
6   Behold, you delight in truth in the inward being,
    and you teach me wisdom in the secret heart.

7   Purge me with hyssop, and I shall be clean;
    wash me, and I shall be whiter than snow.
8   Let me hear joy and gladness;
    let the bones that you have broken rejoice.
9   Hide your face from my sins,
    and blot out all my iniquities.
10   Create in me a clean heart, O God,
    and renew a right[b] spirit within me.
11   Cast me not away from your presence,
    and take not your Holy Spirit from me.
12   Restore to me the joy of your salvation,
    and uphold me with a willing spirit.

13   Then I will teach transgressors your ways,
    and sinners will return to you.
14   Deliver me from bloodguiltiness, O God,
    O God of my salvation,
  and my tongue will sing aloud of your righteousness.
15   O Lord, open my lips,
    and my mouth will declare your praise.

---

a   Psalm 51:1 Or *Be gracious to me*
b   Psalm 51:10 Or *steadfast*

16 For you will not delight in sacrifice, or I would give it;
        you will not be pleased with a burnt offering.
17 The sacrifices of God are a broken spirit;
        a broken and contrite heart, O God, you will not despise.

18 Do good to Zion in your good pleasure;
        build up the walls of Jerusalem;
19 then will you delight in right sacrifices,
        in burnt offerings and whole burnt offerings;
        then bulls will be offered on your altar.

Psalm 51 is the fourth of seven penitential psalms, or psalms of repentance (6; 32; 38; 51; 102; 130; 143). David confesses his sin with Bathsheba in this intensely personal lament that has become significant for the Church's liturgy (vv. 10–12 are used in the Offertory; v. 15 is used in the opening sentences of Matins and Vespers and as the Introit for Ash Wednesday). David not only explains sin and its deadly consequences as powerfully present in all people, but he also unfolds God's re-creative mercy as He works repentance and forgiveness. David's confession (read 2 Samuel 11:1–12:25) is intended for public worship, for the whole nation to pray.

✸ REQUEST THE SPIRIT'S HELP IN PRAYER

✸ READ AND REPEAT THE WORD

What words or phrases stick out to you? How do those words or phrases reveal the poet's purpose for the psalm? What effect does this psalm have on you as you meditate on it?

✸ RETURN TO THE LORD IN PRAYER

This anguished cry of confession from the depths of guilt finds God's absolution and renewal on the certain footing of grace alone (*sola gratia*). Sin is an inheritance, born in us, ever damaging us. None of our works can ever set us free from terror, despair, or death. However, God has blotted out even the worst of our sins—adultery and murder—by Jesus' sacrifice. **Prayers of thanksgiving, confession, and request:**

Holy Spirit, create me new again, giving joy for sadness. Have mercy on me, O God, and cleanse me from my sin. Amen.

PSALM 52

To the choirmaster. A Maskil[a] of David, when Doeg, the
Edomite, came and told Saul, "David has come to the house of
Ahimelech."

1 Why do you boast of evil, O mighty man?
    The steadfast love of God endures all the day.
2 Your tongue plots destruction,
    like a sharp razor, you worker of deceit.
3 You love evil more than good,
    and lying more than speaking what is right.   *Selah*
4 You love all words that devour,
    O deceitful tongue.

5 But God will break you down forever;
    he will snatch and tear you from your tent;
    he will uproot you from the land of the living.   *Selah*
6 The righteous shall see and fear,
    and shall laugh at him, saying,
7 "See the man who would not make
    God his refuge,
  but trusted in the abundance of his riches
    and sought refuge in his own destruction!"[b]

8 But I am like a green olive tree
    in the house of God.
  I trust in the steadfast love of God
    forever and ever.
9 I will thank you forever,
    because you have done it.
  I will wait for your name, for it is good,
    in the presence of the godly.

---

a Psalm 52:1 Probably a musical or liturgical term
b Psalm 52:7 Or *in his work of destruction*

The title of Psalm 52 recounts a very specific event in David's life. Chief of Saul's herdsmen, Doeg denounced Ahimelech the priest to Saul after he saw the fugitive David receive aid from him (from 1 Samuel 21:1–9). In response, bloodthirsty Saul declared Ahimelech guilty by association with David and ordered Doeg to slaughter Ahimelech, his family, eighty-five priests, and the whole city of Nob (1 Samuel 22:6–23). This psalm, then, is a deeply personal lament of David as he speaks directly to a vicious enemy. He fearlessly faces this evil one, who has a twisted sense of morality. David announces God's judgment and comforts himself in God's "steadfast love" (Psalm 52:1). The tone is similar to that of Isaiah 22:15–19.

❀ REQUEST THE SPIRIT'S HELP IN PRAYER

❀ READ AND REPEAT THE WORD

What words or phrases stick out to you? How do those words or phrases reveal the poet's purpose for the psalm? What effect does this psalm have on you as you meditate on it?

....

....

....

....

❀ RETURN TO THE LORD IN PRAYER

Confident prayer remembers God's promises, and it trusts and waits on God's justice and love. In an unbelieving world, the wicked attack what is good, boast, and even thrive in their evil. Does God care? Yes! God has overruled the way of the wicked by sending His own Son to suffer and even die at the hand of evil people so that, by His death and resurrection, He might comfort us by His enduring love.

STEADFAST GOD, TODAY I THANK YOU: ....

....

LORD GOD, I CONFESS TO YOU: ....

....

LORD OF HOSTS, WHO HAS CONQUERED THE POWER OF THE ANCIENT ENE-MIES OF SIN, DEATH, AND SATAN FOR ME THROUGH CHRIST, TODAY I ALSO PRAY: ....

....

....

"I will thank You forever, because You have done it. I will wait for Your name, for it is good" (Psalm 52:9). Amen.

PSALM 53

To the choirmaster: according to Mahalath. A Maskil[a] of David.

1 The fool says in his heart, "There is no God."
   They are corrupt, doing abominable iniquity;
   there is none who does good.

2 God looks down from heaven
   on the children of man
 to see if there are any who understand,[b]
   who seek after God.

3 They have all fallen away;
   together they have become corrupt;
 there is none who does good,
   not even one.

4 Have those who work evil no knowledge,
   who eat up my people as they eat bread,
   and do not call upon God?

5 There they are, in great terror,
   where there is no terror!
 For God scatters the bones of him who encamps against you;
   you put them to shame, for God has rejected them.

6 Oh, that salvation for Israel would come out of Zion!
   When God restores the fortunes of his people,
   let Jacob rejoice, let Israel be glad.

a   Psalm 53:1 Probably musical or liturgical terms
b   Psalm 53:2 Or *who act wisely*

Psalm 53 is remarkably similar to Psalm 14, with the notable change that in verses 2, 4, 5, and 6, the divine name LORD (*Yahweh*) is replaced, as one would expect in Book Two of the Psalter, by the term *God* (*Elohim*). The superscription of Psalm 53 is more elaborate than that of Psalm 14. The order of the stories about men in 1 Samuel (ch. 22 for Doeg; ch. 25 for Nabal; ch. 26 for the Ziphites) is duplicated in three psalms: Psalm 52 for Doeg; Psalm 53 for the "fool" (the Hebrew word *nabal*); Psalm 54 for the Ziphites. The other title in the superscript, *Mahalath* (which also appears in Psalm 88), may mean a musical setting or a melody about sorrow.

⚜ REQUEST THE SPIRIT'S HELP IN PRAYER

⚜ READ AND REPEAT THE WORD

What words or phrases stick out to you? How do those words or phrases reveal the poet's purpose for the psalm? What effect does this psalm have on you as you meditate on it?

⚜ RETURN TO THE LORD IN PRAYER

When evil fools encamp against God's people, He saves and restores them. We are all foolishly corrupt, doing iniquity and not good. We do not understand or seek after God in the ways He gives Himself. We all fall away from Him. The salvation that comes for us out of Zion is Jesus, who took our foolishness—our iniquity and corruption, our sin and death—and saved us by the seeming foolishness of His cross (1 Corinthians 1:18–25).

PRAYERS:

Though we have all alike become corrupt, O God, send Your salvation and restore our fortunes in Christ. Amen.

PSALM 54

To the choirmaster: with stringed instruments. A Maskil[a] of
David, when the Ziphites went and told Saul, "Is not David
hiding among us?"

1 O God, save me by your name,
   and vindicate me by your might.
2 O God, hear my prayer;
   give ear to the words of my mouth.

3 For strangers[b] have risen against me;
   ruthless men seek my life;
   they do not set God before themselves.   *Selah*

4 Behold, God is my helper;
   the Lord is the upholder of my life.
5 He will return the evil to my enemies;
   in your faithfulness put an end to them.

6 With a freewill offering I will sacrifice to you;
   I will give thanks to your name, O LORD, for it is good.
7 For he has delivered me from every trouble,
   and my eye has looked in triumph on my enemies.

---

a   Psalm 54:1 Probably a musical or liturgical term
b   Psalm 54:3 Some Hebrew manuscripts and Targum *insolent men* (compare Psalm 86:14)

Psalm 54 is another brief lament of David during yet another experience of betrayal (such as in Psalm 52) that nonetheless ends with thanksgiving and confidence in God's sure deliverance. Luther commented that this was "a psalm of prayer against the persecutors who seek the life of the godly on account of the Word of God. Thus Saul and those in Ziph had attempted to kill David on account of the Word of God, through which he had been called and consecrated to be king. The psalmist prays for deliverance from his enemies and for vengeance upon them" (*RPL*, p. 129). As David fled from Saul's murderous intent, he hid in the wilderness of Ziph in the southern part of Judah. In order to gain favor from Saul, the Ziphites betrayed David's whereabouts (1 Samuel 23:15–24; 26:1), which prompted David to write the psalm.

❀ REQUEST THE SPIRIT'S HELP IN PRAYER

❀ READ AND REPEAT THE WORD

What words or phrases stick out to you? How do those words or phrases reveal the poet's purpose for the psalm? What effect does this psalm have on you as you meditate on it?

❀ RETURN TO THE LORD IN PRAYER

The psalmist prays for deliverance amid persecution from family and even strangers! He is confident that God will help, as He always has. In times of sudden testing and unexpected trouble, we easily become disillusioned and wonder if God has abandoned us. However, in every trouble, God is our sure helper. The deliverance He provides in Christ, who Himself knew persecution and death, makes us triumphant despite every appearance to the contrary.

TRIUMPHANT GOD, TODAY I THANK YOU:

LORD GOD, OUR DELIVERER, TODAY I CONFESS TO YOU:

MERCIFUL GOD, OUR HELPER, TODAY I ALSO PRAY:

> *God, thank You for being my helper and
> the upholder of my life. Amen.*

PSALM 55

To the choirmaster: with stringed instruments. A Maskil[a] of David.

1   Give ear to my prayer, O God,
        and hide not yourself from my plea for mercy!
2   Attend to me, and answer me;
        I am restless in my complaint and I moan,
3   because of the noise of the enemy,
        because of the oppression of the wicked.
    For they drop trouble upon me,
        and in anger they bear a grudge against me.

4   My heart is in anguish within me;
        the terrors of death have fallen upon me.
5   Fear and trembling come upon me,
        and horror overwhelms me.
6   And I say, "Oh, that I had wings like a dove!
        I would fly away and be at rest;
7   yes, I would wander far away;
        I would lodge in the wilderness;   *Selah*
8   I would hurry to find a shelter
        from the raging wind and tempest."

9   Destroy, O Lord, divide their tongues;
        for I see violence and strife in the city.
10 Day and night they go around it
        on its walls,
    and iniquity and trouble are within it;
11   ruin is in its midst;
    oppression and fraud
        do not depart from its marketplace.

12 For it is not an enemy who taunts me—
        then I could bear it;
    it is not an adversary who deals insolently with me—
        then I could hide from him.
13 But it is you, a man, my equal,
        my companion, my familiar friend.
14 We used to take sweet counsel together;
        within God's house we walked in the throng.

---

a   Psalm 55:1 Probably a musical or liturgical term

15 Let death steal over them;
   let them go down to Sheol alive;
   for evil is in their dwelling place and in their heart.

16 But I call to God,
   and the LORD will save me.
17 Evening and morning and at noon
   I utter my complaint and moan,
   and he hears my voice.
18 He redeems my soul in safety
   from the battle that I wage,
   for many are arrayed against me.
19 God will give ear and humble them,
   he who is enthroned from of old,   *Selah*
   because they do not change
   and do not fear God.

20 My companion^b stretched out his hand against his friends;
   he violated his covenant.
21 His speech was smooth as butter,
   yet war was in his heart;
   his words were softer than oil,
   yet they were drawn swords.

22 Cast your burden on the LORD,
   and he will sustain you;
   he will never permit
   the righteous to be moved.

23 But you, O God, will cast them down
   into the pit of destruction;
   men of blood and treachery
   shall not live out half their days.
   But I will trust in you.

---

b   Psalm 55:20 Hebrew *He*

In Psalm 55, the author asks God for help because he finds himself in a dangerous city, betrayed by a close friend, and in great peril. He shares his situation in order to teach wisdom. Some have seen in this psalm a reference to Ahithophel's betrayal of David (2 Samuel 16:20–23) during the revolt led by David's son Absalom (2 Samuel 15–17). Due to a lack of specific reference in the psalm, no certain identification of the historical context is possible.

⚜ REQUEST THE SPIRIT'S HELP IN PRAYER

⚜ READ AND REPEAT THE WORD

What words or phrases stick out to you? How do those words or phrases reveal the poet's purpose for the psalm? What effect does this psalm have on you as you meditate on it?

⚜ RETURN TO THE LORD IN PRAYER

The author finds himself in a town full of wickedness and violence, betrayed by a trusted friend and colleague, with no one to help except God. He turns to the Lord in prayer, entrusting his life to God's hand with confidence. When troubles press hard, we may find it easy to give in to our feelings and give up on God. The psalmist's steadfastness challenges us to trust in God's mercy. Our Lord Jesus Christ, the Righteous One, faced a city full of violence and plots against His life. Betrayed by Judas, He endured the cross, where He turned to the Father with confidence and gave His life as the ransom price for ours.

PRAYERS OF REQUEST
For members of my household, I pray:

For my everyday work, I pray:

For my congregation, I pray:

For my neighbor in the world, I pray:

Lord, inscribe and keep Your promises in my heart. Hold me firm in faith and confidence, even if terror and distress befall me. In Christ, I am unafraid, and I look to You for help, for I know You will come and rescue me. Amen.

The 55th psalm is a psalm of prayer. Although it might have been spoken in the person of Christ against His betrayer, Judas, I rather let it remain a general prayer against those vile alley cats who lick in front and scratch in back. In appearance, they are such true friends, fathers, brothers, and sisters, so full of love and life compared to us, that their mouth is smoother than butter and oil. But behind the scene is nothing but murder, sword, warfare, and the destruction of all, as the psalm says here. That is, they can go with us to the table, to church, in house, on the street, and be the best of companions. Therefore, the devil or death and hell may carry them away, for they create a great heartache and affliction for the people. This curse, however, is a prophecy—thus it will certainly be with them, for they can say nothing better. Or rather, "they do not change and do not fear God." (Martin Luther)

PSALM 56

To the choirmaster: according to The Dove on Far-off Terebinths.
A Miktam[a] of David, when the Philistines seized him in
Gath.

1   Be gracious to me, O God, for man tramples on me;
     all day long an attacker oppresses me;
2   my enemies trample on me all day long,
     for many attack me proudly.
3   When I am afraid,
     I put my trust in you.
4   In God, whose word I praise,
     in God I trust; I shall not be afraid.
     What can flesh do to me?

5   All day long they injure my cause;[b]
     all their thoughts are against me for evil.
6   They stir up strife, they lurk;
     they watch my steps,
     as they have waited for my life.
7   For their crime will they escape?
     In wrath cast down the peoples, O God!

8   You have kept count of my tossings;[c]
     put my tears in your bottle.
     Are they not in your book?
9   Then my enemies will turn back
     in the day when I call.
     This I know, that[d] God is for me.
10   In God, whose word I praise,
     in the LORD, whose word I praise,
11   in God I trust; I shall not be afraid.
     What can man do to me?

12   I must perform my vows to you, O God;
     I will render thank offerings to you.
13   For you have delivered my soul from death,
     yes, my feet from falling,
    that I may walk before God
     in the light of life.

a   Psalm 56:1 Probably a musical or liturgical term
b   Psalm 56:5 Or *they twist my words*
c   Psalm 56:8 Or *wanderings*
d   Psalm 56:9 Or *because*

Psalm 56 recalls a time when David found himself in great peril from enemies and turned to God with confidence. In 1 Samuel 21:10–15, David fled from King Saul (who wanted to kill him) to the Philistine city of Gath. Since David had killed a great many Philistines, he feared for his life. He survived by pretending to be insane until he was able to escape back into safe territory. The title "The Dove on Far-off Terebinths" in the superscript likely indicates directions to the choirmaster for musical accompaniment.

⊛ REQUEST THE SPIRIT'S HELP IN PRAYER

⊛ READ AND REPEAT THE WORD

What words or phrases stick out to you? How do those words or phrases reveal the poet's purpose for the psalm? What effect does this psalm have on you as you meditate on it?

....
....
....
....
....
....
....
....

⊛ RETURN TO THE LORD IN PRAYER

Even in the midst of danger, David rejoices in God's love and His certain deliverance from death. When we face trials, we may be tempted to worry about our own welfare or feel like giving up in hopelessness. Instead, we can remember that our problems are nothing new and that God is able to help in every situation. Through these experiences, He strengthens our faith and draws us closer to Jesus Christ, our Savior.

PRAYERS OF REQUEST
For members of my household to delight in the Lord, I pray:
....
For faithfulness in my everyday work, I pray:
....
For my congregation, I pray:
....
For my neighbor in the world, I pray:
....

Father, by Your Spirit, help us walk before You in faith, joy,
and humble obedience. In Jesus' name, we pray. Amen.

PSALM 57

To the choirmaster: according to Do Not Destroy. A Miktam[a] of
David, when he fled from Saul, in the cave.

1   Be merciful to me, O God, be merciful to me,
     for in you my soul takes refuge;
  in the shadow of your wings I will take refuge,
     till the storms of destruction pass by.
2   I cry out to God Most High,
     to God who fulfills his purpose for me.
3   He will send from heaven and save me;
     he will put to shame him who tramples on me.   *Selah*
  God will send out his steadfast love and his faithfulness!

4   My soul is in the midst of lions;
     I lie down amid fiery beasts—
  the children of man, whose teeth are spears and arrows,
     whose tongues are sharp swords.

5   Be exalted, O God, above the heavens!
     Let your glory be over all the earth!

6   They set a net for my steps;
     my soul was bowed down.
  They dug a pit in my way,
     but they have fallen into it themselves.   *Selah*
7   My heart is steadfast, O God,
     my heart is steadfast!
  I will sing and make melody!
8   Awake, my glory![b]
  Awake, O harp and lyre!
     I will awake the dawn!
9   I will give thanks to you, O Lord, among the peoples;
     I will sing praises to you among the nations.
10   For your steadfast love is great to the heavens,
     your faithfulness to the clouds.

11   Be exalted, O God, above the heavens!
     Let your glory be over all the earth!

---

a   Psalm 57:1 Probably a musical or liturgical term
b   Psalm 57:8 Or *my whole being*

In 1 Samuel 22:1–2, David found refuge in the cave of Adullam. King Saul was after him, and he had only narrowly escaped from the Philistine city of Gath (for more, read 1 Samuel 21:10–15; Psalm 56). Since his life was in danger from a variety of enemies, David turned to God for help. The title in the superscript, "Do Not Destroy" (also mentioned in Psalm 58), may refer to a popular tune.

❀ REQUEST THE SPIRIT'S HELP IN PRAYER

❀ READ AND REPEAT THE WORD

What words or phrases stick out to you? How do those words or phrases reveal the poet's purpose for the psalm? What effect does this psalm have on you as you meditate on it?

❀ RETURN TO THE LORD IN PRAYER

David turns to God for help. Chased by Saul, his king and father-in-law, David flees for his life and hides in a cave to avoid discovery. He confidently asks God for deliverance and praises God for rescuing him even before it happens (2 Samuel 22). We often pray with uncertainty and hesitation, doubting God's love and interest in our lives. Trusting in Jesus, we have confidence that God listens to us as a loving father listens to His beloved children.

STEADFAST GOD, TODAY I PRAISE YOU:

MERCIFUL GOD, TODAY I CONFESS TO YOU:

FAITHFUL GOD, TODAY I ALSO PRAY:

*Exalted Savior, make my heart steadfast
in faith and prayer. Amen.*

PSALM 58

To the choirmaster: according to Do Not Destroy. A Miktam[a] of David.

1   Do you indeed decree what is right, you gods?[b]
      Do you judge the children of man uprightly?
2   No, in your hearts you devise wrongs;
      your hands deal out violence on earth.

3   The wicked are estranged from the womb;
      they go astray from birth, speaking lies.
4   They have venom like the venom of a serpent,
      like the deaf adder that stops its ear,
5   so that it does not hear the voice of charmers
      or of the cunning enchanter.

6   O God, break the teeth in their mouths;
      tear out the fangs of the young lions, O LORD!
7   Let them vanish like water that runs away;
      when he aims his arrows, let them be blunted.
8   Let them be like the snail that dissolves into slime,
      like the stillborn child who never sees the sun.
9   Sooner than your pots can feel the heat of thorns,
      whether green or ablaze, may he sweep them away![c]

10 The righteous will rejoice when he sees the vengeance;
      he will bathe his feet in the blood of the wicked.
11 Mankind will say, "Surely there is a reward for the righteous;
      surely there is a God who judges on earth."

---

a   Psalm 58:1 Probably a musical or liturgical term
b   Psalm 58:1 Or *you mighty lords* (by revocalization; Hebrew *in silence*)
c   Psalm 58:9 The meaning of the Hebrew verse is uncertain

Psalm 58 has many similarities to Psalm 57, except in this psalm, David does not directly refer to a historical situation or event as the inspiration. For more on this psalm, consider reading the introduction to Psalm 57.

⊛ REQUEST THE SPIRIT'S HELP IN PRAYER

⊛ READ AND REPEAT THE WORD

What words or phrases stick out to you? How do those words or phrases reveal the poet's purpose for the psalm? What effect does this psalm have on you as you meditate on it?

⊛ RETURN TO THE LORD IN PRAYER

David challenges the leaders of the people (judges and rulers) by condemning the unjust and dishonest. When you find yourself in a position of power over someone, treat that person as one precious to God, purchased by the blood of Christ. Jesus suffered unjustly before the Jewish Council (the Sanhedrin) and the Roman governor. The plans of both sets of judges came to nothing; ultimate justice was served on the cross (condemnation of sin) and at the empty tomb (public vindication of Jesus as our Savior).

LORD GOD, I THANK YOU:

MERCIFUL GOD, I CONFESS TO YOU:

PRAYERS OF REQUEST
For members of my household to delight in the Lord, I pray:

For faithfulness in my everyday work, I pray:

For my congregation, I pray:

For my neighbor in the world, I pray:

Heavenly Father, lead us to do the right thing, even when it seems no one notices. Lead us to live for You and remember that You set all things right in the end. In Jesus' name, we pray. Amen.

PSALM 59

To the choirmaster: according to Do Not Destroy. A Miktam[a] of
David, when Saul sent men to watch his house in order to
kill him.

1   Deliver me from my enemies, O my God;
      protect me from those who rise up against me;
2   deliver me from those who work evil,
      and save me from bloodthirsty men.

3   For behold, they lie in wait for my life;
      fierce men stir up strife against me.
  For no transgression or sin of mine, O LORD,
4   for no fault of mine, they run and make ready.
  Awake, come to meet me, and see!
5   You, LORD God of hosts, are God of Israel.
  Rouse yourself to punish all the nations;
      spare none of those who treacherously plot evil.   *Selah*

6   Each evening they come back,
      howling like dogs
      and prowling about the city.
7   There they are, bellowing with their mouths
      with swords in their lips—
      for "Who," they think,[b] "will hear us?"

8   But you, O LORD, laugh at them;
      you hold all the nations in derision.
9   O my Strength, I will watch for you,
      for you, O God, are my fortress.
10   My God in his steadfast love[c] will meet me;
      God will let me look in triumph on my enemies.

11   Kill them not, lest my people forget;
      make them totter[d] by your power and bring them down,
      O Lord, our shield!
12   For the sin of their mouths, the words of their lips,
      let them be trapped in their pride.
  For the cursing and lies that they utter,

a   Psalm 59:1 Probably a musical or liturgical term
b   Psalm 59:7 Hebrew lacks *they think*
c   Psalm 59:10 Or *The God who shows me steadfast love*
d   Psalm 59:11 Or *wander*

13   consume them in wrath;
       consume them till they are no more,
   that they may know that God rules over Jacob
       to the ends of the earth.   *Selah*

14 Each evening they come back,
       howling like dogs
       and prowling about the city.
15 They wander about for food
       and growl if they do not get their fill.

16 But I will sing of your strength;
       I will sing aloud of your steadfast love in the morning.
   For you have been to me a fortress
       and a refuge in the day of my distress.
17 O my Strength, I will sing praises to you,
       for you, O God, are my fortress,
       the God who shows me steadfast love.

In Psalm 59, verses 1–7 are a prayer for help in time of need, while verses 8–17 reflect the author's assurance of deliverance. Both sections of the psalm end on a note of praise for God, our strength and security. Though Scripture does not record a specific event that fits the superscription, Scripture is very clear on Saul's ongoing hatred toward David (for more, read 1 Samuel 19–31).

⦾ REQUEST THE SPIRIT'S HELP IN PRAYER

⦾ READ AND REPEAT THE WORD

What words or phrases stick out to you? How do those words or phrases reveal the poet's purpose for the psalm? What effect does this psalm have on you as you meditate on it?

⦾ RETURN TO THE LORD IN PRAYER

When surrounded by enemies (or difficult circumstances), we turn to God in confidence and trust. Whatever He wills for us is best, even if we don't understand it at the time. The world and all that is in it is passing away. Empires come and go. Only God and His promise of salvation in Jesus Christ stand firm, stand fast, and stand forever.

PRAYERS:

O God, our mighty fortress, our trusty shield and weapon, deliver us from the snaps and snarls of the wicked. Trap them with Your Law and turn their hearts by Your Gospel. Let Your people know peace amid strife. Amen.

The 59th psalm is a psalm of prayer and can very well be spoken in the person of Christ, who lamented over those who by their teachings stood arrayed against Him, to condemn and disavow Him. Thereby they have their reward: They come into the city at evening like hungry dogs, yet find nothing. The psalm, however, can also be understood from the history of David against his "Saulites," who also are finally without a kingdom and wander around like hungry dogs until they are totally destroyed. For Saul's family never again came to the kingship, though they strived for it with eagerness and effort. (Martin Luther)

PSALM 60

To the choirmaster: according to Shushan Eduth. A Miktam[a] of David; for instruction; when he strove with Aram-naharaim and with Aram-zobah, and when Joab on his return struck down twelve thousand of Edom in the Valley of Salt.

1   O God, you have rejected us, broken our defenses;
     you have been angry; oh, restore us.
2   You have made the land to quake; you have torn it open;
     repair its breaches, for it totters.
3   You have made your people see hard things;
     you have given us wine to drink that made us stagger.

4   You have set up a banner for those who fear you,
     that they may flee to it from the bow.[b]   *Selah*
5   That your beloved ones may be delivered,
     give salvation by your right hand and answer us!

6   God has spoken in his holiness:[c]
     "With exultation I will divide up Shechem
     and portion out the Vale of Succoth.
7   Gilead is mine; Manasseh is mine;
     Ephraim is my helmet;
     Judah is my scepter.
8   Moab is my washbasin;
     upon Edom I cast my shoe;
     over Philistia I shout in triumph."[d]

9   Who will bring me to the fortified city?
     Who will lead me to Edom?
10 Have you not rejected us, O God?
     You do not go forth, O God, with our armies.
11 Oh, grant us help against the foe,
     for vain is the salvation of man!
12 With God we shall do valiantly;
     it is he who will tread down our foes.

---

a   Psalm 60:1 Probably musical or liturgical terms
b   Psalm 60:4 Or *that it may be displayed because of truth*
c   Psalm 60:6 Or *sanctuary*
d   Psalm 60:8 Revocalization (compare Psalm 108:10); Masoretic Text *over me, O Philistia, shout in triumph*

Israel faced many enemies throughout her long history. During David's reign, wars were fought with Syria to the north and with Edom to the southeast (as well as other countries). Of course, biblical writers do not record every battle or even every war. Apparently, a hostile nation defeated Israel (possibly Edom), and David turned to the Lord for help. God's gracious answer and the victorious outcome are recorded in 2 Samuel 8; 1 Chronicles 18. Though God has seemingly turned a deaf ear to His people (Psalm 60:1–3), David prays for God's help in battle (vv. 4–8) and ends this psalm on a note of confidence (vv. 10–12). The title in the superscript, *Shushan Eduth*, may mean "The Lily of the Testimony," a tune or a type of musical accompaniment for the psalm. The common title, *Miktam*, probably indicates that the reader should use this psalm to be encouraged and uplifted when suffering defeat or another type of setback. Songs such as this were also often used to instruct the young and the nation.

❂ REQUEST THE SPIRIT'S HELP IN PRAYER

❂ READ AND REPEAT THE WORD

What words or phrases stick out to you? How do those words or phrases reveal the poet's purpose for the psalm? What effect does this psalm have on you as you meditate on it?

❂ RETURN TO THE LORD IN PRAYER

God disciplines those He loves, and He tests His people to build their faith and strengthen the relationship of grace. Whether you experience victory or defeat, persist in prayer and service to your Lord. In His care, you "shall do valiantly" (v. 12).

PRAYERS:

When we face defeat, O Lord, keep our eyes on Your promises. When we experience loss, keep our hearts filled with Your peace. When we don't understand Your plan for us, keep the cross of Christ always before us—the depth and breadth and height of Your love for us. Amen.

169

PSALM 61

To the choirmaster: with stringed instruments. Of David.

1   Hear my cry, O God,
        listen to my prayer;
2   from the end of the earth I call to you
        when my heart is faint.
    Lead me to the rock
        that is higher than I,
3   for you have been my refuge,
        a strong tower against the enemy.

4   Let me dwell in your tent forever!
        Let me take refuge under the shelter of your wings!   *Selah*
5   For you, O God, have heard my vows;
        you have given me the heritage of those who fear
        your name.

6   Prolong the life of the king;
        may his years endure to all generations!
7   May he be enthroned forever before God;
        appoint steadfast love and faithfulness to watch over him!

8   So will I ever sing praises to your name,
        as I perform my vows day after day.

David may have written this psalm when he fled during Absalom's attempted coup (as he says explicitly in Psalm 3; see also 2 Samuel 15–17 for more).

⊛ REQUEST THE SPIRIT'S HELP IN PRAYER

⊛ READ AND REPEAT THE WORD

What words or phrases stick out to you? How do those words or phrases reveal the poet's purpose for the psalm? What effect does this psalm have on you as you meditate on it?

....

....

....

....

....

....

⊛ RETURN TO THE LORD IN PRAYER

In this psalm, David turns once more to God for help in time of need, asking God to restore him to his throne in Jerusalem and bless him in the years and generations ahead. God often uses difficult times to strengthen our faith and redefine our priorities. If we have drifted away from the Lord, He can use a reversal of fortune in our earthly circumstances to make us aware of our precarious spiritual situation and bring us back to Him. David's prayer that the King would reign forever (v. 7) is ultimately fulfilled in Christ Jesus, who embodies God's steadfast love and faithfulness forever.

LORD GOD, I THANK YOU:

....

....

MERCIFUL GOD, I CONFESS TO YOU:

....

....

PRAYERS OF REQUEST
For members of my household to delight in the Lord, I pray:

....

For faithfulness in my everyday work, I pray:

....

For my congregation, I pray:

....

For my neighbor in the world, I pray:

....

O God, let me take refuge under the shelter of Your wings. Amen.

PSALM 62

To the choirmaster: according to Jeduthun. A Psalm of David.

1   For God alone my soul waits in silence;
      from him comes my salvation.
2   He alone is my rock and my salvation,
      my fortress; I shall not be greatly shaken.

3   How long will all of you attack a man
      to batter him,
      like a leaning wall, a tottering fence?
4   They only plan to thrust him down from his high position.
      They take pleasure in falsehood.
      They bless with their mouths,
      but inwardly they curse.   *Selah*

5   For God alone, O my soul, wait in silence,
      for my hope is from him.
6   He only is my rock and my salvation,
      my fortress; I shall not be shaken.
7   On God rests my salvation and my glory;
      my mighty rock, my refuge is God.

8   Trust in him at all times, O people;
      pour out your heart before him;
      God is a refuge for us.   *Selah*

9   Those of low estate are but a breath;
      those of high estate are a delusion;
  in the balances they go up;
      they are together lighter than a breath.
10   Put no trust in extortion;
      set no vain hopes on robbery;
      if riches increase, set not your heart on them.

11   Once God has spoken;
      twice have I heard this:
  that power belongs to God,
12   and that to you, O Lord, belongs steadfast love.
  For you will render to a man
      according to his work.

Psalm 62 is a hymn of peace and confidence in God, who alone provides security and hope. David does not identify the historical context, but the wisdom embodied in the psalm and the hint of weakness in verse 3 suggest a time late in David's life (such as David's words in 2 Samuel 23:1–7). The reference to Jeduthun in the superscript is likely either the name of a musician (or his family; see 1 Chronicles 25:1 or the introduction to Psalm 39) or a tune associated with him (see the introduction to Psalm 77).

⊛ REQUEST THE SPIRIT'S HELP IN PRAYER

⊛ READ AND REPEAT THE WORD

What words or phrases stick out to you? How do those words or phrases reveal the poet's purpose for the psalm? What effect does this psalm have on you as you meditate on it?

⊛ RETURN TO THE LORD IN PRAYER

Wealth deceives people by promising happiness. In the end, wealth, power, and fame turn out to be lies because they do not deliver what they seem to promise. Even when our lives fall apart, our center and foundation hold firm: nothing can separate us from the love of God in Christ Jesus, our Lord (Romans 8:38–39).

LORD GOD, MY ROCK AND MY SALVATION, I THANK YOU:

MERCIFUL GOD, MY REFUGE, I CONFESS TO YOU:

FAITHFUL GOD, MY HOPE, TODAY I ALSO PRAY:

"The Church's one foundation Is Jesus Christ, her Lord; She is His new creation By water and the Word. From heav'n He came and sought her To be His holy bride; With His own blood He bought her, And for her life He died" (LSB 644:1). Amen.

PSALM 63

A Psalm of David, when he was in the wilderness of Judah.

1   O God, you are my God; earnestly I seek you;
        my soul thirsts for you;
    my flesh faints for you,
        as in a dry and weary land where there is no water.
2   So I have looked upon you in the sanctuary,
        beholding your power and glory.
3   Because your steadfast love is better than life,
        my lips will praise you.
4   So I will bless you as long as I live;
        in your name I will lift up my hands.

5   My soul will be satisfied as with fat and rich food,
        and my mouth will praise you with joyful lips,
6   when I remember you upon my bed,
        and meditate on you in the watches of the night;
7   for you have been my help,
        and in the shadow of your wings I will sing for joy.
8   My soul clings to you;
        your right hand upholds me.

9   But those who seek to destroy my life
        shall go down into the depths of the earth;
10 they shall be given over to the power of the sword;
        they shall be a portion for jackals.
11 But the king shall rejoice in God;
        all who swear by him shall exult,
        for the mouths of liars will be stopped.

Psalm 63 reflects David's faith in the Lord and his willing submission to God's plans. Most likely, the psalm refers to David's flight from Absalom into the wilderness of Judea (2 Samuel 15–17), specifically a time when the king fled Jerusalem and left his fate in the Lord's hands (2 Samuel 15:24–26).

🟤 REQUEST THE SPIRIT'S HELP IN PRAYER

🟤 READ AND REPEAT THE WORD

What words or phrases stick out to you? How do those words or phrases reveal the poet's purpose for the psalm? What effect does this psalm have on you as you meditate on it?

....

....

....

....

....

🟤 RETURN TO THE LORD IN PRAYER

On the run, cut off from God's tabernacle and the capital city of Jerusalem, David turns to God in prayer and praise for His love and salvation. When we feel like we are in the wilderness and God seems distant, we may find ourselves tempted to focus on our troubles rather than turning to God in faith and confidence. David shows us the way to handle disaster and doubt: meditate on the Lord in prayer and thanksgiving (see also Philippians 4:4–7). Faith looks beyond the circumstances to the cross of Christ and sees God's love, holding fast to His promises to His children.

PRAYERS OF REQUEST

For members of my household, Lord, I pray:..

....

For those You have called me to serve in my everyday work, I pray:..............

....

For all pastors and congregations, I pray:..

....

For those You have called me to serve in society, I pray:...........................

....

"My soul clings to You; Your right hand
upholds me" (Psalm 63:8). Amen.

PSALM 64

To the choirmaster. A Psalm of David.

1   Hear my voice, O God, in my complaint;
      preserve my life from dread of the enemy.
2   Hide me from the secret plots of the wicked,
      from the throng of evildoers,
3   who whet their tongues like swords,
      who aim bitter words like arrows,
4   shooting from ambush at the blameless,
      shooting at him suddenly and without fear.
5   They hold fast to their evil purpose;
      they talk of laying snares secretly,
   thinking, "Who can see them?"
6   They search out injustice,
   saying, "We have accomplished a diligent search."
      For the inward mind and heart of a man are deep.

7   But God shoots his arrow at them;
      they are wounded suddenly.
8   They are brought to ruin, with their own tongues turned
   against them;
      all who see them will wag their heads.
9   Then all mankind fears;
      they tell what God has brought about
      and ponder what he has done.

10 Let the righteous one rejoice in the LORD
      and take refuge in him!
   Let all the upright in heart exult!

The superscript in Psalm 64, "To the choirmaster," is probably a note for the director of music that he should collect the psalm for Israel's worship services. Possibly the leader of the worship services or the leader of the choir of Levities would speak the psalm (as in Nehemiah 11:17 and elsewhere).

❀ REQUEST THE SPIRIT'S HELP IN PRAYER

❀ READ AND REPEAT THE WORD

What words or phrases stick out to you? How do those words or phrases reveal the poet's purpose for the psalm? What effect does this psalm have on you as you meditate on it?

❀ RETURN TO THE LORD IN PRAYER

The psalmist's enemies conspire against him and seek his destruction, but he turns to the Lord in prayer and receives deliverance. When false rumors fly and your reputation suffers, seek divine justice. Turn to the Lord and put the situation in His hands. Do not try to get even, but leave the outcome to God. Jesus also endured all kinds of plots against His life and slander during His ministry (see especially Mark 15:29–32). He knows how to justify you.

LORD GOD, I THANK YOU:

MERCIFUL GOD, I CONFESS TO YOU:

PRAYERS OF REQUEST
For members of my household to delight in the Lord, I pray:

For faithfulness in my everyday work, I pray:

For my congregation, I pray:

For my neighbor in the world, I pray:

Lord, I exult in You, my refuge. Amen.

PSALM 65

To the choirmaster. A Psalm of David. A Song.

1 Praise is due to you,[a] O God, in Zion,
    and to you shall vows be performed.
2 O you who hear prayer,
    to you shall all flesh come.
3 When iniquities prevail against me,
    you atone for our transgressions.
4 Blessed is the one you choose and bring near,
    to dwell in your courts!
 We shall be satisfied with the goodness of your house,
    the holiness of your temple!

5 By awesome deeds you answer us with righteousness,
    O God of our salvation,
 the hope of all the ends of the earth
    and of the farthest seas;
6 the one who by his strength established the mountains,
    being girded with might;
7 who stills the roaring of the seas,
    the roaring of their waves,
    the tumult of the peoples,
8 so that those who dwell at the ends of the earth are in awe
 at your signs.
 You make the going out of the morning and the evening to
 shout for joy.

9 You visit the earth and water it;[b]
    you greatly enrich it;
 the river of God is full of water;
    you provide their grain,
    for so you have prepared it.
10 You water its furrows abundantly,
    settling its ridges,
 softening it with showers,
    and blessing its growth.
11 You crown the year with your bounty;
    your wagon tracks overflow with abundance.
12 The pastures of the wilderness overflow,
    the hills gird themselves with joy,
13 the meadows clothe themselves with flocks,
    the valleys deck themselves with grain,
    they shout and sing together for joy.

a Psalm 65:1 Or *Praise waits for you in silence*
b Psalm 65:9 Or *and make it overflow*

Given the beauty of Psalm 65 and its close connection to Psalms 66–68, it may well have been written for a festival or as a liturgical praise song.

⊛ REQUEST THE SPIRIT'S HELP IN PRAYER

⊛ READ AND REPEAT THE WORD

What words or phrases stick out to you? How do those words or phrases reveal the poet's purpose for the psalm? What effect does this psalm have on you as you meditate on it?

⊛ RETURN TO THE LORD IN PRAYER

David praises God for the forgiveness of sins, peace in the world, and prosperity in the land—a straightforward song of praise to God for His awesome grace. We have nothing except what God gives us, and the appropriate response to such amazing generosity, both spiritual and physical, is praise. David begins the list of gifts with the most important: the forgiveness of sins and the gift of faith.

LORD GOD, I THANK YOU:

MERCIFUL GOD, I CONFESS TO YOU:

PRAYERS OF REQUEST
For members of my household to delight in the Lord, I pray:

For faithfulness in my everyday work, I pray:

For my congregation, I pray:

For my neighbor in the world, I pray:

"Blessed is the one You choose and bring
near," O Lord (Psalm 65:4)! Amen.

PSALM 66

To the choirmaster. A Song. A Psalm.

1 Shout for joy to God, all the earth;
2   sing the glory of his name;
    give to him glorious praise!
3 Say to God, "How awesome are your deeds!
    So great is your power that your enemies come cringing
    to you.
4 All the earth worships you
    and sings praises to you;
    they sing praises to your name."   *Selah*

5 Come and see what God has done:
    he is awesome in his deeds toward the children of man.
6 He turned the sea into dry land;
    they passed through the river on foot.
    There did we rejoice in him,
7   who rules by his might forever,
    whose eyes keep watch on the nations—
    let not the rebellious exalt themselves.   *Selah*

8 Bless our God, O peoples;
    let the sound of his praise be heard,
9 who has kept our soul among the living
    and has not let our feet slip.
10 For you, O God, have tested us;
    you have tried us as silver is tried.
11 You brought us into the net;
    you laid a crushing burden on our backs;
12 you let men ride over our heads;
    we went through fire and through water;
    yet you have brought us out to a place of abundance.

13 I will come into your house with burnt offerings;
    I will perform my vows to you,
14 that which my lips uttered
    and my mouth promised when I was in trouble.
15 I will offer to you burnt offerings of fattened animals,
    with the smoke of the sacrifice of rams;
    I will make an offering of bulls and goats.   *Selah*

16 Come and hear, all you who fear God,
   and I will tell what he has done for my soul.
17 I cried to him with my mouth,
   and high praise was on[a] my tongue.[b]
18 If I had cherished iniquity in my heart,
   the Lord would not have listened.
19 But truly God has listened;
   he has attended to the voice of my prayer.

20 Blessed be God,
   because he has not rejected my prayer
   or removed his steadfast love from me!

a Psalm 66:17 Hebrew *under*
b Psalm 66:17 Or *and he was exalted with my tongue*

Psalm 66 can be offered by any believer in any time of hardship. The psalm is not attributed to David, leading some scholars to think that the Lord's deliverance at the time of Hezekiah (see 2 Kings 19:8–37; Isaiah 37:8–38) may have been the original occasion that gave rise to this psalm.

❁ REQUEST THE SPIRIT'S HELP IN PRAYER

❁ READ AND REPEAT THE WORD

What words or phrases stick out to you? How do those words or phrases reveal the poet's purpose for the psalm? What effect does this psalm have on you as you meditate on it?

❁ RETURN TO THE LORD IN PRAYER

The Lord's deeds of salvation, culminating in the ministry of Christ, assure His people that He will make all things, even hardships, work out for their ultimate good (Romans 8:28). Hardships may tempt us to abandon the faith, yet knowing that the Lord uses hardship to test our faith will strengthen us to hold on to our faith.

PRAYERS:

Bless You, Lord, for Your saving deeds and promises. Amen.

PSALM 67

To the choirmaster: with stringed instruments. A Psalm. A Song.

1   May God be gracious to us and bless us
      and make his face to shine upon us,   *Selah*
2   that your way may be known on earth,
      your saving power among all nations.
3   Let the peoples praise you, O God;
      let all the peoples praise you!

4   Let the nations be glad and sing for joy,
      for you judge the peoples with equity
      and guide the nations upon earth.   *Selah*
5   Let the peoples praise you, O God;
      let all the peoples praise you!

6   The earth has yielded its increase;
      God, our God, shall bless us.
7   God shall bless us;
      let all the ends of the earth fear him!

Psalm 67 is perhaps intended for corporate worship, before or after the benediction. Verse 6 suggests the possibility of its use in connection with the harvest. The stringed instruments mentioned in the superscript may have included the harp.

⊛ REQUEST THE SPIRIT'S HELP IN PRAYER

⊛ READ AND REPEAT THE WORD

What words or phrases stick out to you? How do those words or phrases reveal the poet's purpose for the psalm? What effect does this psalm have on you as you meditate on it?

⊛ RETURN TO THE LORD IN PRAYER

There is only one way of salvation, which Israel's God provided in the work of His Son, Jesus Christ. Thus, we believe in God's salvation through Christ and proclaim it to all the world.

LORD GOD, I THANK YOU:

MERCIFUL GOD, I CONFESS TO YOU:

PRAYERS OF REQUEST
For members of my household to delight in the Lord, I pray:

For faithfulness in my everyday work, I pray:

For my congregation, I pray:

For my neighbor in the world, I pray:

"Thine over all shall be the praise And thanks of
ev'ry nation; And all the world with joy shall raise
The voice of exultation" (LSB 823:2). Amen.

PSALM 68

To the choirmaster. A Psalm of David. A Song.

1   God shall arise, his enemies shall be scattered;
      and those who hate him shall flee before him!
2   As smoke is driven away, so you shall drive them away;
      as wax melts before fire,
      so the wicked shall perish before God!
3   But the righteous shall be glad;
      they shall exult before God;
      they shall be jubilant with joy!

4   Sing to God, sing praises to his name;
      lift up a song to him who rides through the deserts;
    his name is the LORD;
      exult before him!
5   Father of the fatherless and protector of widows
      is God in his holy habitation.
6   God settles the solitary in a home;
      he leads out the prisoners to prosperity,
      but the rebellious dwell in a parched land.

7   O God, when you went out before your people,
      when you marched through the wilderness,   *Selah*
8   the earth quaked, the heavens poured down rain,
      before God, the One of Sinai,
      before God,[a] the God of Israel.
9   Rain in abundance, O God, you shed abroad;
      you restored your inheritance as it languished;
10   your flock[b] found a dwelling in it;
      in your goodness, O God, you provided for the needy.

11   The Lord gives the word;
      the women who announce the news are a great host:
12   "The kings of the armies—they flee, they flee!"
    The women at home divide the spoil—
13   though you men lie among the sheepfolds—
    the wings of a dove covered with silver,
      its pinions with shimmering gold.
14   When the Almighty scatters kings there,
      let snow fall on Zalmon.

---

a   Psalm 68:8 Or *before God, even Sinai before God*
b   Psalm 68:10 Or *your congregation*

15 O mountain of God, mountain of Bashan;
    O many-peaked[c] mountain, mountain of Bashan!
16 Why do you look with hatred, O many-peaked mountain,
    at the mount that God desired for his abode,
    yes, where the Lᴏʀᴅ will dwell forever?
17 The chariots of God are twice ten thousand,
    thousands upon thousands;
    the Lord is among them; Sinai is now in the sanctuary.
18 You ascended on high,
    leading a host of captives in your train
    and receiving gifts among men,
    even among the rebellious, that the Lᴏʀᴅ God may dwell there.

19 Blessed be the Lord,
    who daily bears us up;
    God is our salvation.   *Selah*
20 Our God is a God of salvation,
    and to Gᴏᴅ, the Lord, belong deliverances from death.
21 But God will strike the heads of his enemies,
    the hairy crown of him who walks in his guilty ways.
22 The Lord said,
    "I will bring them back from Bashan,
    I will bring them back from the depths of the sea,
23 that you may strike your feet in their blood,
    that the tongues of your dogs may have their portion from
    the foe."

24 Your procession is[d] seen, O God,
    the procession of my God, my King, into the sanctuary—
25 the singers in front, the musicians last,
    between them virgins playing tambourines:
26 "Bless God in the great congregation,
    the Lᴏʀᴅ, O you[e] who are of Israel's fountain!"
27 There is Benjamin, the least of them, in the lead,
    the princes of Judah in their throng,
    the princes of Zebulun, the princes of Naphtali.

28 Summon your power, O God,[f]
    the power, O God, by which you have worked for us.
29 Because of your temple at Jerusalem
    kings shall bear gifts to you.

c   Psalm 68:15 Or *hunch-backed*; also verse 16
d   Psalm 68:24 Or *has been*
e   Psalm 68:26 The Hebrew for *you* is plural here
f   Psalm 68:28 By revocalization (compare Septuagint); Hebrew *Your God has summoned your power*

30 Rebuke the beasts that dwell among the reeds,
  the herd of bulls with the calves of the peoples.
  Trample underfoot those who lust after tribute;
  scatter the peoples who delight in war.^g
31 Nobles shall come from Egypt;
  Cush shall hasten to stretch out her hands to God.

32 O kingdoms of the earth, sing to God;
  sing praises to the Lord,   *Selah*
33 to him who rides in the heavens, the ancient heavens;
  behold, he sends out his voice, his mighty voice.
34 Ascribe power to God,
  whose majesty is over Israel,
  and whose power is in the skies.
35 Awesome is God from his^h sanctuary;
  the God of Israel—he is the one who gives power and
  strength to his people.
  Blessed be God!

g Psalm 68:30 The meaning of the Hebrew verse is uncertain
h Psalm 68:35 Septuagint; Hebrew *your*

Psalm 68 seems to be an order of service for a procession at the Jerusalem temple (or at the tabernacle). Parts of the psalm use imagery similar to that used by the Canaanites when describing their god Baal, which is striking because the psalm describes the defeat of Canaanite kings.

⊛ REQUEST THE SPIRIT'S HELP IN PRAYER

⊛ READ AND REPEAT THE WORD

What words or phrases stick out to you? How do those words or phrases reveal the poet's purpose for the psalm? What effect does this psalm have on you as you meditate on it?

....

....

....

....

....

....

....

....

⊛ RETURN TO THE LORD IN PRAYER

In His sanctuary, God provides His salvation. Without this sanctuary, there is only judgment. Thus, we turn to the Lord and His Word in faith, and we give Him praise.

ALMIGHTY GOD, TODAY I THANK YOU:

....

....

LORD GOD, WHO HAS SHOWN MERCY ON YOUR PEOPLE THROUGH THE FORGIVENESS OF SINS POURED OUT TO US IN CHRIST, I CONFESS TO YOU:

....

....

AWESOME GOD, WHO GIVES POWER AND STRENGTH TO HIS PEOPLE, TODAY I ALSO PRAY:

....

....

*Summon Your power, O God, by which You
have worked among us. Amen.*

PSALM 69

To the choirmaster: according to Lilies. Of David.

1   Save me, O God!
      For the waters have come up to my neck.[a]
2   I sink in deep mire,
      where there is no foothold;
  I have come into deep waters,
      and the flood sweeps over me.
3   I am weary with my crying out;
      my throat is parched.
  My eyes grow dim
      with waiting for my God.

4   More in number than the hairs of my head
      are those who hate me without cause;
  mighty are those who would destroy me,
      those who attack me with lies.
  What I did not steal
      must I now restore?
5   O God, you know my folly;
      the wrongs I have done are not hidden from you.

6   Let not those who hope in you be put to shame through me,
      O Lord GOD of hosts;
  let not those who seek you be brought to dishonor
  through me,
      O God of Israel.
7   For it is for your sake that I have borne reproach,
      that dishonor has covered my face.
8   I have become a stranger to my brothers,
      an alien to my mother's sons.

9   For zeal for your house has consumed me,
      and the reproaches of those who reproach you have fallen
      on me.
10 When I wept and humbled[b] my soul with fasting,
      it became my reproach.
11 When I made sackcloth my clothing,
      I became a byword to them.

---

a   Psalm 69:1 Or *waters threaten my life*
b   Psalm 69:10 Hebrew lacks *and humbled*

12 I am the talk of those who sit in the gate,
and the drunkards make songs about me.

13 But as for me, my prayer is to you, O LORD.
At an acceptable time, O God,
in the abundance of your steadfast love answer me in your
saving faithfulness.
14 Deliver me
from sinking in the mire;
let me be delivered from my enemies
and from the deep waters.
15 Let not the flood sweep over me,
or the deep swallow me up,
or the pit close its mouth over me.

16 Answer me, O LORD, for your steadfast love is good;
according to your abundant mercy, turn to me.
17 Hide not your face from your servant,
for I am in distress; make haste to answer me.
18 Draw near to my soul, redeem me;
ransom me because of my enemies!

19 You know my reproach,
and my shame and my dishonor;
my foes are all known to you.
20 Reproaches have broken my heart,
so that I am in despair.
I looked for pity, but there was none,
and for comforters, but I found none.
21 They gave me poison for food,
and for my thirst they gave me sour wine to drink.

22 Let their own table before them become a snare;
and when they are at peace, let it become a trap.^c
23 Let their eyes be darkened, so that they cannot see,
and make their loins tremble continually.
24 Pour out your indignation upon them,
and let your burning anger overtake them.
25 May their camp be a desolation;
let no one dwell in their tents.
26 For they persecute him whom you have struck down,
and they recount the pain of those you have wounded.

---

c Psalm 69:22 Hebrew; a slight revocalization yields (compare Septuagint, Syriac, Jerome) *a snare, and retribution and a trap*

27 Add to them punishment upon punishment;
    may they have no acquittal from you.[d]
28 Let them be blotted out of the book of the living;
    let them not be enrolled among the righteous.

29 But I am afflicted and in pain;
    let your salvation, O God, set me on high!

30 I will praise the name of God with a song;
    I will magnify him with thanksgiving.
31 This will please the LORD more than an ox
    or a bull with horns and hoofs.
32 When the humble see it they will be glad;
    you who seek God, let your hearts revive.
33 For the LORD hears the needy
    and does not despise his own people who are prisoners.

34 Let heaven and earth praise him,
    the seas and everything that moves in them.
35 For God will save Zion
    and build up the cities of Judah,
and people shall dwell there and possess it;
36   the offspring of his servants shall inherit it,
    and those who love his name shall dwell in it.

d   Psalm 69:27 Hebrew *may they not come into your righteousness*

In Psalm 69, David offers this prayer for help in the midst of attacks and sufferings imposed on him by his enemies. As Jesus is the promised Son of David (2 Samuel 7:8–16), these afflictions of David foreshadow the even greater afflictions of Christ. This psalm is quoted in the New Testament in several places with reference to Christ, including John 2:17; 15:25; 19:28–29; Acts 1:20; Romans 11:9–10. The direction "according to Lilies" in the superscript likely refers to the specific melody to which the psalm was sung.

◈ Request the Spirit's Help in Prayer

◈ Read and Repeat the Word

What words or phrases stick out to you? How do those words or phrases reveal the poet's purpose for the psalm? What effect does this psalm have on you as you meditate on it?

◈ Return to the Lord in Prayer

Though afflicted, we nevertheless confess our sins before God. We also turn to Him in faith for deliverance from those who persecute us, asking for His strength and deliverance, lest we fail to remain faithful to Him.

Lord God, I thank You:

Merciful God, I confess to You:

Prayers of Request
For wisdom to trust You in my household, I pray:

For my work and livelihood, I pray:

For my congregation, I pray:

For wisdom in loving my neighbor in the world, I pray:

"Save me, O God! . . . I will praise the name of God with a song" (Psalm 69:1, 30). Amen.

PSALM 70

To the choirmaster. Of David, for the memorial offering.

1   Make haste, O God, to deliver me!
      O LORD, make haste to help me!
2   Let them be put to shame and confusion
      who seek my life!
   Let them be turned back and brought to dishonor
      who delight in my hurt!
3   Let them turn back because of their shame
      who say, "Aha, Aha!"

4   May all who seek you
      rejoice and be glad in you!
   May those who love your salvation
      say evermore, "God is great!"
5   But I am poor and needy;
      hasten to me, O God!
   You are my help and my deliverer;
      O LORD, do not delay!

The superscript of Psalm 70 mentions a special memorial offering. Parts of certain offerings were burned as a "memorial portion" for a pleasing aroma to the Lord (see Leviticus 2:2, 9, 16; 6:15). In this way, God would remember the worshiper (Psalm 8:4) and would remember his sins no more (Jeremiah 31:34). In this psalm, the worshiper asks God for such remembrance.

⊛ REQUEST THE SPIRIT'S HELP IN PRAYER

⊛ READ AND REPEAT THE WORD

What words or phrases stick out to you? How do those words or phrases reveal the poet's purpose for the psalm? What effect does this psalm have on you as you meditate on it?

⊛ RETURN TO THE LORD IN PRAYER

With the psalmist, we acknowledge our spiritual poverty before God. Part of that acknowledgment is being watchful, lest through pride or faithlessness we ourselves turn away from Him. We seek God in His Word and Sacraments; He remembers us by forgiving our sins (Matthew 26:28; 1 Corinthians 11:25). In this way, He will provide deliverance—if not in this life, then certainly in the life to come.

PRAYERS AND NOTES:

"Make haste, O God, to deliver me!" (Psalm 70:1).
You are great in Your forgiveness. Amen.

PSALM 71

1 In you, O LORD, do I take refuge;
  let me never be put to shame!
2 In your righteousness deliver me and rescue me;
  incline your ear to me, and save me!
3 Be to me a rock of refuge,
  to which I may continually come;
  you have given the command to save me,
  for you are my rock and my fortress.

4 Rescue me, O my God, from the hand of the wicked,
  from the grasp of the unjust and cruel man.
5 For you, O Lord, are my hope,
  my trust, O LORD, from my youth.
6 Upon you I have leaned from before my birth;
  you are he who took me from my mother's womb.
  My praise is continually of you.

7 I have been as a portent to many,
  but you are my strong refuge.
8 My mouth is filled with your praise,
  and with your glory all the day.
9 Do not cast me off in the time of old age;
  forsake me not when my strength is spent.
10 For my enemies speak concerning me;
  those who watch for my life consult together
11 and say, "God has forsaken him;
  pursue and seize him,
  for there is none to deliver him."

12 O God, be not far from me;
  O my God, make haste to help me!
13 May my accusers be put to shame and consumed;
  with scorn and disgrace may they be covered
  who seek my hurt.
14 But I will hope continually
  and will praise you yet more and more.
15 My mouth will tell of your righteous acts,
  of your deeds of salvation all the day,
  for their number is past my knowledge.
16 With the mighty deeds of the Lord GOD I will come;
  I will remind them of your righteousness, yours alone.

17 O God, from my youth you have taught me,
   and I still proclaim your wondrous deeds.
18 So even to old age and gray hairs,
   O God, do not forsake me,
   until I proclaim your might to another generation,
   your power to all those to come.
19 Your righteousness, O God,
   reaches the high heavens.
   You who have done great things,
   O God, who is like you?
20 You who have made me see many troubles and calamities
   will revive me again;
   from the depths of the earth
   you will bring me up again.
21 You will increase my greatness
   and comfort me again.

22 I will also praise you with the harp
   for your faithfulness, O my God;
   I will sing praises to you with the lyre,
   O Holy One of Israel.
23 My lips will shout for joy,
   when I sing praises to you;
   my soul also, which you have redeemed.
24 And my tongue will talk of your righteous help all the day long,
   for they have been put to shame and disappointed
   who sought to do me hurt.

Psalm 71 is likely for an older believer struggling with assaults on his faith, including temptations to think that his faith was in vain. Since Psalm 70 is "of David" and Psalm 72 is "of Solomon," perhaps this is a Davidic psalm composed near the end of his life. By proclaiming the saving deeds of the Lord, he meets the challenges of old age with faith, hope, faithfulness, witness, and praise. In the original Hebrew language, this psalm lacks poetic artistry, and yet it richly proclaims the faith.

◉ REQUEST THE SPIRIT'S HELP IN PRAYER

◉ READ AND REPEAT THE WORD

What words or phrases stick out to you? How do those words or phrases reveal the poet's purpose for the psalm? What effect does this psalm have on you as you meditate on it?

◉ RETURN TO THE LORD IN PRAYER

Truths of the faith learned in childhood are of no advantage if they are forsaken later in life. The Lord is faithful in His righteous, saving deeds. They are always the source of our eternal life. Let us cling to Him in faith and faithfully give witness and praise.

PRAYERS OF REQUEST
For members of my household, I pray:

For my everyday work, I pray:

For my congregation, I pray:

For my neighbor in the world, I pray:

"My mouth will tell of Your righteous acts. . . . I will remind them of Your righteousness, Yours alone" (Psalm 71:15–16). Amen.

The 71st psalm is (by my understanding) a psalm of prayer spoken from beginning to end in the person of all Christendom against all enemies and affliction. It prays especially concerning the time of old age, when one becomes feeble and gray. That is, it prays for the last Christians, for whom the times will be dangerous, and when faith—together with the Gospel—will be cast down. In the same way, Daniel also proclaimed that the truth would be cast down and unrighteousness shall conquer. Therefore, the psalmist praises God's righteousness alone, which he has learned from God since his youth, or since the beginning.

May this be a comforting prophecy for us, that God's Word shall return before the end of the world. With this Word God will call us from the depths of the earth and mightily comfort us. From this basis comes also the general statement concerning Christ: that Elijah and Enoch shall come, the lies of the antichrist shall be exposed, and all shall again be set right. (Martin Luther)

PSALM 72

Of Solomon.

1   Give the king your justice, O God,
     and your righteousness to the royal son!
2   May he judge your people with righteousness,
     and your poor with justice!
3   Let the mountains bear prosperity for the people,
     and the hills, in righteousness!
4   May he defend the cause of the poor of the people,
     give deliverance to the children of the needy,
     and crush the oppressor!

5   May they fear you[a] while the sun endures,
     and as long as the moon, throughout all generations!
6   May he be like rain that falls on the mown grass,
     like showers that water the earth!
7   In his days may the righteous flourish,
     and peace abound, till the moon be no more!

8   May he have dominion from sea to sea,
     and from the River[b] to the ends of the earth!
9   May desert tribes bow down before him,
     and his enemies lick the dust!
10   May the kings of Tarshish and of the coastlands
     render him tribute;
   may the kings of Sheba and Seba
     bring gifts!
11   May all kings fall down before him,
     all nations serve him!

12   For he delivers the needy when he calls,
     the poor and him who has no helper.
13   He has pity on the weak and the needy,
     and saves the lives of the needy.
14   From oppression and violence he redeems their life,
     and precious is their blood in his sight.

a   Psalm 72:5 Septuagint *He shall endure*
b   Psalm 72:8 That is, the Euphrates

15 Long may he live;
        may gold of Sheba be given to him!
    May prayer be made for him continually,
        and blessings invoked for him all the day!
16 May there be abundance of grain in the land;
        on the tops of the mountains may it wave;
        may its fruit be like Lebanon;
    and may people blossom in the cities
        like the grass of the field!
17 May his name endure forever,
        his fame continue as long as the sun!
    May people be blessed in him,
        all nations call him blessed!

18 Blessed be the LORD, the God of Israel,
        who alone does wondrous things.
19 Blessed be his glorious name forever;
        may the whole earth be filled with his glory!
    Amen and Amen!

20 The prayers of David, the son of Jesse, are ended.

The title "of Solomon" from the Hebrew could mean "for Solomon" or "by Solomon" (or perhaps both) for the occasion of his coronation. Psalm 72 may well have been used at the coronation of other kings from David's line. In accord with the promise of 2 Samuel 7:8–17, the line of Davidic kings prophetically pointed to the ultimate Son of David, Jesus.

⊛ REQUEST THE SPIRIT'S HELP IN PRAYER

⊛ READ AND REPEAT THE WORD

What words or phrases stick out to you? How do those words or phrases reveal the poet's purpose for the psalm? What effect does this psalm have on you as you meditate on it?

⊛ RETURN TO THE LORD IN PRAYER

The psalmist realizes that even the best of the Davidic kings fell short of the ideal. We also often fail to live as we should. Yet our hope is in David's Son and Lord, Jesus Christ, who has brought us eternal salvation.

LORD GOD, I THANK YOU:

MERCIFUL GOD, I CONFESS TO YOU:

PRAYERS OF REQUEST
For members of my household, I pray:

For my everyday work, I pray:

For my congregation, I pray:

For my neighbor in the world, I pray:

"Hail to the Lord's anointed, Great David's greater Son! Hail, in the time appointed, His reign on earth begun! He comes to break oppression, To set the captive free, To take away transgression And rule in equity" (LSB 398:1). Amen.

The 72nd psalm is an exceedingly magnificent and beautiful prophecy of Christ and His rule in the whole world. In this kingdom, neither sin nor the evil conscience shall flower and reign (as under the Law) but only righteousness, freedom, and joy of conscience. However, this is not without the cross. On account of the cross, their blood shall be shed and counted as very precious to God. And the psalm also announces the new worship, which is to call on God and to thank Him. He tells us to pray to God daily and daily to praise Him. This is our daily offering among all the Gentiles. At this time we hear nothing of circumcision, nor that the kings and Gentiles should receive the Law of Moses, but rather that they remain kings and Gentiles and receive this king as truly God by nature, call on Him, and glorify Him. For to call on God in distress and to thank Him for His help is the worship that alone pleases Him, who is alone our helper in need and our Savior. Without Him, all else is no help at all.
(Martin Luther)

PSALM 73

A Psalm of Asaph.

1 Truly God is good to Israel,
   to those who are pure in heart.
2 But as for me, my feet had almost stumbled,
   my steps had nearly slipped.
3 For I was envious of the arrogant
   when I saw the prosperity of the wicked.

4 For they have no pangs until death;
   their bodies are fat and sleek.
5 They are not in trouble as others are;
   they are not stricken like the rest of mankind.
6 Therefore pride is their necklace;
   violence covers them as a garment.
7 Their eyes swell out through fatness;
   their hearts overflow with follies.
8 They scoff and speak with malice;
   loftily they threaten oppression.
9 They set their mouths against the heavens,
   and their tongue struts through the earth.
10 Therefore his people turn back to them,
   and find no fault in them.[a]
11 And they say, "How can God know?
   Is there knowledge in the Most High?"
12 Behold, these are the wicked;
   always at ease, they increase in riches.
13 All in vain have I kept my heart clean
   and washed my hands in innocence.
14 For all the day long I have been stricken
   and rebuked every morning.
15 If I had said, "I will speak thus,"
   I would have betrayed the generation of your children.

16 But when I thought how to understand this,
   it seemed to me a wearisome task,
17 until I went into the sanctuary of God;
   then I discerned their end.

---

a Psalm 73:10 Probable reading; Hebrew *the waters of a full cup are drained by them*

18 Truly you set them in slippery places;
  you make them fall to ruin.
19 How they are destroyed in a moment,
  swept away utterly by terrors!
20 Like a dream when one awakes,
  O Lord, when you rouse yourself, you despise them as
  phantoms.
21 When my soul was embittered,
  when I was pricked in heart,
22 I was brutish and ignorant;
  I was like a beast toward you.

23 Nevertheless, I am continually with you;
  you hold my right hand.
24 You guide me with your counsel,
  and afterward you will receive me to glory.
25 Whom have I in heaven but you?
  And there is nothing on earth that I desire besides you.
26 My flesh and my heart may fail,
  but God is the strength[b] of my heart and my portion forever.

27 For behold, those who are far from you shall perish;
  you put an end to everyone who is unfaithful to you.
28 But for me it is good to be near God;
  I have made the Lord GOD my refuge,
  that I may tell of all your works.

b   Psalm 73:26 Hebrew *rock*

Psalm 73 deals with the same issues as the Book of Job (Job 21:7–15 bears many similarities to vv. 3–14). The psalmist expresses his doubts and struggles, yet he passes through them to a faith renewed by God's faithfulness and promises. Asaph was one of the tabernacle song leaders appointed by David (see 1 Chronicles 6:31, 39). His work, including that of composing songs or psalms, may have been carried on by his descendants or successors, as Asaph's name appears on many of the non-Davidic psalms.

⊛ REQUEST THE SPIRIT'S HELP IN PRAYER

⊛ READ AND REPEAT THE WORD

What words or phrases stick out to you? How do those words or phrases reveal the poet's purpose for the psalm? What effect does this psalm have on you as you meditate on it?

⊛ RETURN TO THE LORD IN PRAYER

Being troubled by doubt and envy does not mean that we have lost our faith. However, we are called to struggle against doubt and envy. We find strength to do so in the certainty of the final outcome of God's promises.

PRAYERS AND NOTES:

*Lord, forgive me for the times I have been envious and
ungrateful. Strengthen me to believe Your promises
and to seek Your eternal kingdom. Amen.*

The 73rd psalm is a psalm of instruction against the great vexation that the godless are rich and everything goes well for them. They ridicule the poor and afflicted saints as if God neither knew nor regarded them. They consider only themselves and their holy works and what they taught and said as precious, heavenly, and godly wisdom and holiness. This causes much pain, so that the psalmist says, "I was brutish and ignorant . . . toward You," that is, I was called a godless heretic and despiser of God. Then, he says: Stop! Go into the sanctuary and hear what God's Word says of them. Look at the former examples in the histories, and you will find that they all at once come to nothing, for there is no ground or foundation under them, but only slippery footing. (Martin Luther)

PSALM 74

A Maskil[a] of Asaph.

1   O God, why do you cast us off forever?
      Why does your anger smoke against the sheep of your
      pasture?
2   Remember your congregation, which you have purchased
   of old,
      which you have redeemed to be the tribe of your heritage!
      Remember Mount Zion, where you have dwelt.
3   Direct your steps to the perpetual ruins;
      the enemy has destroyed everything in the sanctuary!

4   Your foes have roared in the midst of your meeting place;
      they set up their own signs for signs.
5   They were like those who swing axes
      in a forest of trees.[b]
6   And all its carved wood
      they broke down with hatchets and hammers.
7   They set your sanctuary on fire;
      they profaned the dwelling place of your name,
      bringing it down to the ground.
8   They said to themselves, "We will utterly subdue them";
      they burned all the meeting places of God in the land.

9   We do not see our signs;
      there is no longer any prophet,
      and there is none among us who knows how long.
10   How long, O God, is the foe to scoff?
      Is the enemy to revile your name forever?
11   Why do you hold back your hand, your right hand?
      Take it from the fold of your garment[c] and destroy them!

12   Yet God my King is from of old,
      working salvation in the midst of the earth.
13   You divided the sea by your might;
      you broke the heads of the sea monsters[d] on the waters.
14   You crushed the heads of Leviathan;
      you gave him as food for the creatures of the wilderness.

a   Psalm 74:1 Probably a musical or liturgical term
b   Psalm 74:5 The meaning of the Hebrew is uncertain
c   Psalm 74:11 Hebrew *from your bosom*
d   Psalm 74:13 Or *the great sea creatures*

15 You split open springs and brooks;
    you dried up ever-flowing streams.
16 Yours is the day, yours also the night;
    you have established the heavenly lights and the sun.
17 You have fixed all the boundaries of the earth;
    you have made summer and winter.

18 Remember this, O LORD, how the enemy scoffs,
    and a foolish people reviles your name.
19 Do not deliver the soul of your dove to the wild beasts;
    do not forget the life of your poor forever.

20 Have regard for the covenant,
    for the dark places of the land are full of the habitations
    of violence.
21 Let not the downtrodden turn back in shame;
    let the poor and needy praise your name.

22 Arise, O God, defend your cause;
    remember how the foolish scoff at you all the day!
23 Do not forget the clamor of your foes,
    the uproar of those who rise against you, which goes
    up continually!

Psalm 74 seems to have been written after the destruction of Jerusalem and the temple in 587 BC. The absence of a prophet (v. 9) would reflect the time after Jeremiah was carried into Egypt (as seen in Jeremiah 43), with the ministries of Ezekiel and Daniel being confined to Babylon. The title "of Asaph" in the superscript indicates a family name. This title refers to "sons of Asaph," descendants of the man Asaph who lived during the time of David (1 Chronicles 6:31, 39), who were still active in Israelite worship at least as late as the time of Josiah (2 Chronicles 35:15).

⊛ REQUEST THE SPIRIT'S HELP IN PRAYER

⊛ READ AND REPEAT THE WORD

What words or phrases stick out to you? How do those words or phrases reveal the poet's purpose for the psalm? What effect does this psalm have on you as you meditate on it?

⊛ RETURN TO THE LORD IN PRAYER

When calamity strikes, we ought to see God calling us to repentance in it (Luke 13:1–5). In repentance, we flee to God for mercy, not because of anything in us but by what He Himself has done for our redemption.

LORD GOD, EVEN AMID THE TROUBLES OF THIS WORLD, TODAY I THANK YOU:

MERCIFUL GOD, WHO MADE A COVENANT TO NEVER ABANDON YOUR PEOPLE BUT HEAR THEIR EVERY PRAYER, I CONFESS TO YOU:

FAITHFUL GOD, WHO HEARS THE CRIES OF THE POOR AND NEEDY, TODAY I ALSO PRAY:

You, O Lord, are my Redeemer; deliver my life. Amen.

The 74th psalm is a psalm of prayer against the enemies who had laid waste Jerusalem, the temple, and all the schools of God in the land, together with the cities. Moreover, they slandered God, saying He could not help His people. However, the psalm appears as if it were a prayer against the destruction still to come, that is, of the Babylonians and thereafter by Antiochus Ephiphanes. For only in these two instances was the temple in Jerusalem and the land destroyed. Accordingly, we pray this psalm against those who devastate Christendom, tear up God's Word, Sacraments, and all of God's ordinances, and thus clearly preach abomination and slander, and who continue everywhere. (Martin Luther)

PSALM 75

To the choirmaster: according to Do Not Destroy. A Psalm of Asaph. A Song.

1 We give thanks to you, O God;
      we give thanks, for your name is near.
   We[a] recount your wondrous deeds.

2 "At the set time that I appoint
      I will judge with equity.
3 When the earth totters, and all its inhabitants,
      it is I who keep steady its pillars.   *Selah*
4 I say to the boastful, 'Do not boast,'
      and to the wicked, 'Do not lift up your horn;
5 do not lift up your horn on high,
      or speak with haughty neck.'"

6 For not from the east or from the west
      and not from the wilderness comes lifting up,
7 but it is God who executes judgment,
      putting down one and lifting up another.
8 For in the hand of the LORD there is a cup
      with foaming wine, well mixed,
   and he pours out from it,
      and all the wicked of the earth
      shall drain it down to the dregs.

9 But I will declare it forever;
      I will sing praises to the God of Jacob.
10 All the horns of the wicked I will cut off,
      but the horns of the righteous shall be lifted up.

a   Psalm 75:1 Hebrew *They*

Psalm 75 seems to have been written when Israel was assaulted by unbelieving enemies (for example, during the time of 2 Kings 18–19). The title "Do Not Destroy" in the superscript likely refers to a specific melody appropriate for the psalm.

⊛ REQUEST THE SPIRIT'S HELP IN PRAYER

⊛ READ AND REPEAT THE WORD

What words or phrases stick out to you? How do those words or phrases reveal the poet's purpose for the psalm? What effect does this psalm have on you as you meditate on it?

⊛ RETURN TO THE LORD IN PRAYER

God judges the wicked and delivers the believer according to His timetable, not ours. His seeming delay in this matter should not cause us to lose heart but to continue in repentance and faith. As He has fulfilled all His promises in the past, so He will act in both judgment and salvation.

LORD GOD, I THANK YOU:

MERCIFUL GOD, I CONFESS TO YOU:

PRAYERS OF REQUEST
For members of my household to delight in the Lord, I pray:

For faithfulness in my everyday work, I pray:

For my congregation, I pray:

For my neighbor in the world, I pray:

"We give thanks to You, O God. . . . We recount Your wondrous deeds" (Psalm 75:1). Amen.

PSALM 76

To the choirmaster: with stringed instruments. A Psalm of Asaph. A Song.

1   In Judah God is known;
     his name is great in Israel.
2   His abode has been established in Salem,
     his dwelling place in Zion.
3   There he broke the flashing arrows,
     the shield, the sword, and the weapons of war.   *Selah*

4   Glorious are you, more majestic
     than the mountains full of prey.
5   The stouthearted were stripped of their spoil;
     they sank into sleep;
all the men of war
     were unable to use their hands.
6   At your rebuke, O God of Jacob,
     both rider and horse lay stunned.

7   But you, you are to be feared!
     Who can stand before you
     when once your anger is roused?
8   From the heavens you uttered judgment;
     the earth feared and was still,
9   when God arose to establish judgment,
     to save all the humble of the earth.   *Selah*

10   Surely the wrath of man shall praise you;
     the remnant[a] of wrath you will put on like a belt.
11   Make your vows to the LORD your God and perform them;
     let all around him bring gifts
     to him who is to be feared,
12   who cuts off the spirit of princes,
     who is to be feared by the kings of the earth.

a   Psalm 76:10 Or *extremity*

Psalm 76 has a lot in common with Psalms 46; 48; 87. Many scholars have conjectured that the deliverance from the invasion of Sennacherib (Isaiah 36–37) may have been the occasion for its composition.

◉ REQUEST THE SPIRIT'S HELP IN PRAYER

◉ READ AND REPEAT THE WORD

What words or phrases stick out to you? How do those words or phrases reveal the poet's purpose for the psalm? What effect does this psalm have on you as you meditate on it?

....

....

....

....

....

....

....

....

....

◉ RETURN TO THE LORD IN PRAYER

God is majestic in both judgment and salvation. We must tremble in fear before His judgment over our sins. Yet we also trust and rejoice in His mighty deeds for our salvation, by which He has delivered us from those who would seek our eternal, spiritual harm (Colossians 2:15).

PRAYERS AND NOTES:

....

....

....

....

....

....

....

....

....

Glorious are You, O God, when You judge
and when You save. Amen.

PSALM 77

To the choirmaster: according to Jeduthun. A Psalm of Asaph.

1   I cry aloud to God,
     aloud to God, and he will hear me.
2   In the day of my trouble I seek the Lord;
     in the night my hand is stretched out without wearying;
     my soul refuses to be comforted.
3   When I remember God, I moan;
     when I meditate, my spirit faints.   *Selah*

4   You hold my eyelids open;
     I am so troubled that I cannot speak.
5   I consider the days of old,
     the years long ago.
6   I said,[a] "Let me remember my song in the night;
     let me meditate in my heart."
     Then my spirit made a diligent search:
7   "Will the Lord spurn forever,
     and never again be favorable?
8   Has his steadfast love forever ceased?
     Are his promises at an end for all time?
9   Has God forgotten to be gracious?
     Has he in anger shut up his compassion?"   *Selah*

10   Then I said, "I will appeal to this,
     to the years of the right hand of the Most High."[b]

11   I will remember the deeds of the LORD;
     yes, I will remember your wonders of old.
12   I will ponder all your work,
     and meditate on your mighty deeds.
13   Your way, O God, is holy.
     What god is great like our God?
14   You are the God who works wonders;
     you have made known your might among the peoples.
15   You with your arm redeemed your people,
     the children of Jacob and Joseph.   *Selah*

a   Psalm 77:6 Hebrew lacks *I said*
b   Psalm 77:10 Or *This is my grief: that the right hand of the Most High has changed*

16 When the waters saw you, O God,
    when the waters saw you, they were afraid;
    indeed, the deep trembled.
17 The clouds poured out water;
    the skies gave forth thunder;
    your arrows flashed on every side.
18 The crash of your thunder was in the whirlwind;
    your lightnings lighted up the world;
    the earth trembled and shook.
19 Your way was through the sea,
    your path through the great waters;
    yet your footprints were unseen.[c]
20 You led your people like a flock
    by the hand of Moses and Aaron.

c   Psalm 77:19 Hebrew *unknown*

Similarities of thought between Psalm 77:16–19 and Habakkuk 3:8–10 suggest that this psalm comes from the time of Habakkuk. The author expresses certain struggles of faith and doubt, which plague many believers.

⊛ REQUEST THE SPIRIT'S HELP IN PRAYER

⊛ READ AND REPEAT THE WORD

What words or phrases stick out to you? How do those words or phrases reveal the poet's purpose for the psalm? What effect does this psalm have on you as you meditate on it?

⊛ RETURN TO THE LORD IN PRAYER

Even strong believers and spiritual leaders among God's people may find themselves troubled by times of weakness in their faith. But God's powerful Word strengthens us. As we focus on the Gospel, the message of God's mighty deeds for our redemption, He will strengthen our faith.

LORD GOD, I THANK YOU:

MERCIFUL GOD, I CONFESS TO YOU:

PRAYERS OF REQUEST
For members of my household to delight in the Lord, I pray:

For faithfulness in my everyday work, I pray:

For my congregation, I pray:

For my neighbor in the world, I pray:

Lord, "I believe; help my unbelief!" (Mark 9:24). Amen.

The 77th psalm is a psalm of instruction. The psalmist uses himself as an example of how to find comfort when affliction comes and the conscience is troubled, as if God is angry with it. He says that he was so troubled that he could not have any sleep or even speak. But this comfort follows: The psalmist can fight off the thoughts with which he futilely suffered, and he can grasp instead the thought of the mighty works of God in the histories of old. Here we find that God's work was to help the miserable, the troubled, and the abandoned, and to throw down the self-secure, proud scoffer, for example, when He delivered the children of Israel from Egypt.

For this reason His paths are called "hidden." He is there to help when we think that we are totally abandoned. We should learn this well. God intends by this psalm to show us and teach us His manner of helping, namely that he never abandons us when things go ill. Instead, we should wait upon His help at that time with the greatest confidence and not believe our thoughts. (Martin Luther)

TELLING ISRAEL'S STORY OF RESCUE

If anything defined Old Testament Israel, it was the Passover and exodus from Egypt. These events were seared into individual and collective memory. The circumstances leading up to the exodus were important, such as God's call of Abraham, the birth of Isaac, or the interactions of Jacob's twelve sons that led first Joseph and then the whole family to Egypt. Yet it was the mass movement of a vast nation out of bondage in slavery that marked Israel as the people of God. Not surprisingly, then, the exodus is recalled frequently in the Psalter.

Sometimes the reference is brief, while in other places, the psalms set forth a virtual litany of God's mighty acts. In Psalm 81:10, the reference is quite simple: "I am the LORD your God, who brought you up out of the land of Egypt." Another brief allusion is found in the preceding psalm: "You brought a vine out of Egypt; You drove out the nations and planted it" (Psalm 80:8).

Although made in passing, such references undoubtedly served as powerful reminders of God's role in establishing His people's identity.

Brief passages such as these were so effective because of the more extensive treatment elsewhere in the psalms. The table below provides the most important references. Several of these psalms include a brief recital of many of God's dealings with His people. Psalm 136, for example, begins with creation itself. God's first great wonder was making the heavens and the earth! In Psalm 106, the psalmist carries Israel's story beyond the Exodus by recounting events such as their worship of the golden calf and their rejection of God after they were settled in the Promised Land.

Israel's Story of Rescue in the Psalms

EVENT / PSALM	66	78	105	106	135	136
plagues		vv. 12, 42–50	vv. 27–35		v. 9	
angel of death/ Passover		v. 51	v. 36		v. 8	v. 10
crossing of Red Sea	v. 6	vv. 13, 53		vv. 7–12		vv. 11–15
pillar of cloud/fire		v. 14	v. 39			
gave them water in desert		v. 15	v. 41			
gave manna and quail		vv. 23–29	v. 40			

Why these frequent recollections of God's mighty deeds? Clearly, one reason was to solidify their identity as the people of God. Again and again, God made it clear that He was the One who rescued His people, leading them out of bondage and settling them in a rich and prosperous land. All this was done to fulfill His promise:

> He remembers His covenant forever,
>   the word that He commanded,
>   for a thousand generations,
> the covenant that He made with Abraham,
>   His sworn promise to Isaac,
> which He confirmed to Jacob as a statute,
>   to Israel as an everlasting covenant,
> saying, "To you I will give the land of Canaan
>   as your portion for an inheritance." . . .
> For He remembered His holy promise,
>   and Abraham, His servant. (Psalm 105:8–11, 42)

This rehearsal of God's mighty deeds, especially those connected with the establishment of His own people, was meant to identify the proper relationship between God and His people.

The relationship is fleshed out in a subtheme found in these and other psalms. It has to do with calling Israel to account for breaking the covenant that God had made with them. Psalm 78 is especially descriptive. In the verses preceding the retelling of Israel's rescue from bondage, we are told:

1. "They did not keep God's covenant, but refused to walk according to His law. They forgot His works and the wonders that He had shown them" (vv. 10–11). This was how they repaid God after all He had done for them!

2. "Yet they sinned still more against Him, rebelling against the Most High in the desert" (v. 17). God chastised His people to wake them from their spiritual slumber.

3. "In spite of all this, they still sinned; despite His wonders, they did not believe" (v. 32). A similar pattern continues throughout this lengthy psalm. Although one might conclude that God eventually gives up on His people, His mercy comes through.

4. "Their heart was not steadfast toward Him; they were not faithful to His covenant. Yet He, being compassionate, atoned for their iniquity and did not destroy them; He restrained His anger often and did not stir up all His wrath" (vv. 37–38).

Ultimately, these verses and the pattern they show reflect all of God's dealings with His people. Today, He wants not only to show you your sin but still more to lead you to recognize His merciful heart. His love led Him, ultimately, to give His very Son to take our place by enduring God's wrath and securing the final victory for us by His cross and resurrection.

PSALM 78

A Maskil[a] of Asaph.

1 Give ear, O my people, to my teaching;
    incline your ears to the words of my mouth!
2 I will open my mouth in a parable;
    I will utter dark sayings from of old,
3 things that we have heard and known,
    that our fathers have told us.
4 We will not hide them from their children,
    but tell to the coming generation
  the glorious deeds of the LORD, and his might,
    and the wonders that he has done.

5 He established a testimony in Jacob
    and appointed a law in Israel,
  which he commanded our fathers
    to teach to their children,
6 that the next generation might know them,
    the children yet unborn,
  and arise and tell them to their children,
7   so that they should set their hope in God
  and not forget the works of God,
    but keep his commandments;
8 and that they should not be like their fathers,
    a stubborn and rebellious generation,
  a generation whose heart was not steadfast,
    whose spirit was not faithful to God.

9 The Ephraimites, armed with[b] the bow,
    turned back on the day of battle.
10 They did not keep God's covenant,
    but refused to walk according to his law.
11 They forgot his works
    and the wonders that he had shown them.
12 In the sight of their fathers he performed wonders
    in the land of Egypt, in the fields of Zoan.
13 He divided the sea and let them pass through it,
    and made the waters stand like a heap.
14 In the daytime he led them with a cloud,
    and all the night with a fiery light.

a   Psalm 78:1 Probably a musical or liturgical term
b   Psalm 78:9 Hebrew *armed and shooting*

15 He split rocks in the wilderness
   and gave them drink abundantly as from the deep.
16 He made streams come out of the rock
   and caused waters to flow down like rivers.

17 Yet they sinned still more against him,
   rebelling against the Most High in the desert.
18 They tested God in their heart
   by demanding the food they craved.
19 They spoke against God, saying,
   "Can God spread a table in the wilderness?
20 He struck the rock so that water gushed out
   and streams overflowed.
   Can he also give bread
   or provide meat for his people?"

21 Therefore, when the LORD heard, he was full of wrath;
   a fire was kindled against Jacob;
   his anger rose against Israel,
22 because they did not believe in God
   and did not trust his saving power.
23 Yet he commanded the skies above
   and opened the doors of heaven,
24 and he rained down on them manna to eat
   and gave them the grain of heaven.
25 Man ate of the bread of the angels;
   he sent them food in abundance.
26 He caused the east wind to blow in the heavens,
   and by his power he led out the south wind;
27 he rained meat on them like dust,
   winged birds like the sand of the seas;
28 he let them fall in the midst of their camp,
   all around their dwellings.
29 And they ate and were well filled,
   for he gave them what they craved.
30 But before they had satisfied their craving,
   while the food was still in their mouths,
31 the anger of God rose against them,
   and he killed the strongest of them
   and laid low the young men of Israel.

32 In spite of all this, they still sinned;
   despite his wonders, they did not believe.

33 So he made their days vanish like[c] a breath,[d]
   and their years in terror.

34 When he killed them, they sought him;
   they repented and sought God earnestly.

35 They remembered that God was their rock,
   the Most High God their redeemer.

36 But they flattered him with their mouths;
   they lied to him with their tongues.

37 Their heart was not steadfast toward him;
   they were not faithful to his covenant.

38 Yet he, being compassionate,
   atoned for their iniquity
   and did not destroy them;
   he restrained his anger often
   and did not stir up all his wrath.

39 He remembered that they were but flesh,
   a wind that passes and comes not again.

40 How often they rebelled against him in the wilderness
   and grieved him in the desert!

41 They tested God again and again
   and provoked the Holy One of Israel.

42 They did not remember his power[e]
   or the day when he redeemed them from the foe,

43 when he performed his signs in Egypt
   and his marvels in the fields of Zoan.

44 He turned their rivers to blood,
   so that they could not drink of their streams.

45 He sent among them swarms of flies, which devoured them,
   and frogs, which destroyed them.

46 He gave their crops to the destroying locust
   and the fruit of their labor to the locust.

47 He destroyed their vines with hail
   and their sycamores with frost.

48 He gave over their cattle to the hail
   and their flocks to thunderbolts.

49 He let loose on them his burning anger,
   wrath, indignation, and distress,
   a company of destroying angels.

50 He made a path for his anger;
   he did not spare them from death,
   but gave their lives over to the plague.

51 He struck down every firstborn in Egypt,
   the firstfruits of their strength in the tents of Ham.

---

c   Psalm 78:33 Hebrew *in*
d   Psalm 78:33 Or *vapor*
e   Psalm 78:42 Hebrew *hand*

52 Then he led out his people like sheep
    and guided them in the wilderness like a flock.
53 He led them in safety, so that they were not afraid,
    but the sea overwhelmed their enemies.
54 And he brought them to his holy land,
    to the mountain which his right hand had won.
55 He drove out nations before them;
    he apportioned them for a possession
    and settled the tribes of Israel in their tents.

56 Yet they tested and rebelled against the Most High God
    and did not keep his testimonies,
57 but turned away and acted treacherously like their fathers;
    they twisted like a deceitful bow.
58 For they provoked him to anger with their high places;
    they moved him to jealousy with their idols.
59 When God heard, he was full of wrath,
    and he utterly rejected Israel.
60 He forsook his dwelling at Shiloh,
    the tent where he dwelt among mankind,
61 and delivered his power to captivity,
    his glory to the hand of the foe.
62 He gave his people over to the sword
    and vented his wrath on his heritage.
63 Fire devoured their young men,
    and their young women had no marriage song.
64 Their priests fell by the sword,
    and their widows made no lamentation.
65 Then the Lord awoke as from sleep,
    like a strong man shouting because of wine.
66 And he put his adversaries to rout;
    he put them to everlasting shame.

67 He rejected the tent of Joseph;
    he did not choose the tribe of Ephraim,
68 but he chose the tribe of Judah,
    Mount Zion, which he loves.
69 He built his sanctuary like the high heavens,
    like the earth, which he has founded forever.
70 He chose David his servant
    and took him from the sheepfolds;
71 from following the nursing ewes he brought him
    to shepherd Jacob his people,
    Israel his inheritance.
72 With upright heart he shepherded them
    and guided them with his skillful hand.

Psalm 78 is the second-longest psalm in the Book of Psalms. It seems to have originated during the days of the division of the land between the Northern (Israel) and Southern (Judah) Kingdoms, after the construction of Solomon's temple (v. 69). For example, the events of verse 67 are recounted in 1 Kings 12. Thus, it may have been written by a descendant of Asaph. The psalm culminates in God's deeds to and through David, highlighting the importance of the covenant with David (2 Samuel 7:1–17) and its fulfillment in Christ.

◉ REQUEST THE SPIRIT'S HELP IN PRAYER

◉ READ AND REPEAT THE WORD

What words or phrases stick out to you? How do those words or phrases reveal the poet's purpose for the psalm? What effect does this psalm have on you as you meditate on it?

◉ RETURN TO THE LORD IN PRAYER

God's dealings with Israel of old point to His acts toward us today. Israel's history teaches us to see and to repent of our own lack of faith. Furthermore, God's saving deeds in Israel's history, especially in His acts toward and through David, point us to what Christ has done so that we may have God's ongoing forgiveness and salvation.

LORD GOD, I THANK YOU:

MERCIFUL GOD, I CONFESS TO YOU:

MIGHTY GOD, I ALSO COME BEFORE YOU WITH MY OTHER PRAYERS:

*"Blessed be the Lord God of Israel, for He has . . .
raised up a horn of salvation for us in the house of
His servant David" (Luke 1:68–69). Amen.*

The 78th psalm is a psalm of instruction. Using the example and history of the entire people of Israel from the beginning until David, it teaches us to trust and to believe in God, and it warns us against mistrust and faithlessness. The psalm declares the punishment that follows faithlessness and the grace that comes with trust. (Martin Luther)

PSALM 79

A Psalm of Asaph.

1 O God, the nations have come into your inheritance;
      they have defiled your holy temple;
      they have laid Jerusalem in ruins.
2 They have given the bodies of your servants
      to the birds of the heavens for food,
      the flesh of your faithful to the beasts of the earth.
3 They have poured out their blood like water
      all around Jerusalem,
      and there was no one to bury them.
4 We have become a taunt to our neighbors,
      mocked and derided by those around us.

5 How long, O LORD? Will you be angry forever?
      Will your jealousy burn like fire?
6 Pour out your anger on the nations
      that do not know you,
  and on the kingdoms
      that do not call upon your name!
7 For they have devoured Jacob
      and laid waste his habitation.

8 Do not remember against us our former iniquities;[a]
      let your compassion come speedily to meet us,
      for we are brought very low.
9 Help us, O God of our salvation,
      for the glory of your name;
  deliver us, and atone for our sins,
      for your name's sake!
10 Why should the nations say,
      "Where is their God?"
  Let the avenging of the outpoured blood of your servants
      be known among the nations before our eyes!

11 Let the groans of the prisoners come before you;
      according to your great power, preserve those doomed to die!
12 Return sevenfold into the lap of our neighbors
      the taunts with which they have taunted you, O Lord!
13 But we your people, the sheep of your pasture,
      will give thanks to you forever;
      from generation to generation we will recount your praise.

---

a   Psalm 79:8 Or *the iniquities of former generations*

"The 79th psalm is a psalm of prayer against the destruction to come, which was accomplished by the Babylonians and by Antiochus Ephiphanes. It is like the 78th psalm, so the same summary applies" (*RPL*, p. 190). Psalm 79 was perhaps written during the Babylonian exile, and if so, then this psalm may lament the destruction of Jerusalem in 587 BC. Recognizing the invasion as divine judgment (vv. 5, 8), the author begs for God's mercy and restoration. The Asaph mentioned in the superscript is perhaps not the one who served during David's reign (see 2 Chronicles 35:15). Perhaps the writer is instead a descendant or is of the school of Asaph.

◉ REQUEST THE SPIRIT'S HELP IN PRAYER

◉ READ AND REPEAT THE WORD

What words or phrases stick out to you? How do those words or phrases reveal the poet's purpose for the psalm? What effect does this psalm have on you as you meditate on it?

◉ RETURN TO THE LORD IN PRAYER

Originally written as a lament over Babylon's destruction of Israel, this psalm remains applicable to all Christians who suffer hardship and struggle at the hands of unbelievers. Christians throughout the world become objects of scorn by the unbelievers around them, as they are either explicitly derided or condescendingly treated because of their faith and trust in God. Such sufferers do well to pray this psalm, for it assures us that God is reliable and His deliverance is trustworthy.

PRAYERS OF REQUEST
For members of my household to delight in the Lord, I pray:

For faithfulness in my everyday work, I pray:

For my congregation, I pray:

For my neighbor in the world, I pray:

Give me steadfastness and strength, O Lord, to wait upon You in every difficulty and trial. Amen.

PSALM 80

To the choirmaster: according to Lilies. A Testimony. Of Asaph, a Psalm.

1 Give ear, O Shepherd of Israel,
    you who lead Joseph like a flock.
You who are enthroned upon the cherubim, shine forth.
2   Before Ephraim and Benjamin and Manasseh,
stir up your might
    and come to save us!

3 Restore us,[a] O God;
    let your face shine, that we may be saved!

4 O LORD God of hosts,
    how long will you be angry with your people's prayers?
5 You have fed them with the bread of tears
    and given them tears to drink in full measure.
6 You make us an object of contention for our neighbors,
    and our enemies laugh among themselves.

7 Restore us, O God of hosts;
    let your face shine, that we may be saved!

8 You brought a vine out of Egypt;
    you drove out the nations and planted it.
9 You cleared the ground for it;
    it took deep root and filled the land.
10 The mountains were covered with its shade,
    the mighty cedars with its branches.
11 It sent out its branches to the sea
    and its shoots to the River.[b]
12 Why then have you broken down its walls,
    so that all who pass along the way pluck its fruit?
13 The boar from the forest ravages it,
    and all that move in the field feed on it.

14 Turn again, O God of hosts!
    Look down from heaven, and see;
have regard for this vine,
15   the stock that your right hand planted,
    and for the son whom you made strong for yourself.

a   Psalm 80:3 Or *Turn us again*; also verses 7, 19
b   Psalm 80:11 That is, the Euphrates

16 They have burned it with fire; they have cut it down;
     may they perish at the rebuke of your face!
17 But let your hand be on the man of your right hand,
     the son of man whom you have made strong for yourself!
18 Then we shall not turn back from you;
     give us life, and we will call upon your name!

19 Restore us, O Lord God of hosts!
     Let your face shine, that we may be saved!

The reference in Psalm 80 to Ephraim, Benjamin, and Manasseh (v. 2), representing the Northern Kingdom of Israel, suggests that this psalm may have been written in response to the Assyrian campaign of 2 Kings 17:1–6. Possibly, refugees from the Northern Kingdom had come to the Jerusalem sanctuary in the Southern Kingdom to pray for restoration and peace.

❂ REQUEST THE SPIRIT'S HELP IN PRAYER

❂ READ AND REPEAT THE WORD

What words or phrases stick out to you? How do those words or phrases reveal the poet's purpose for the psalm? What effect does this psalm have on you as you meditate on it?

❂ RETURN TO THE LORD IN PRAYER

This psalm begs God to restore His people after their fall before foreign armies. The psalmist recognizes that God's acts of salvation in the past speak assurances for His salvation in the future. Israel repeatedly turned away from the Lord, thus incurring His judgment as a call to repentance. In what ways have we suffered as a result of our turning away? God's pattern of salvation throughout history provides reliable assurances: God has saved us before; He shall yet save again!

PRAYERS AND NOTES:

As You have delivered Your people of old, dear Lord, so also deliver me for the sake of Your Son, Jesus. Amen.

PSALM 81

To the choirmaster: according to The Gittith.[a] Of Asaph.

1   Sing aloud to God our strength;
     shout for joy to the God of Jacob!
2   Raise a song; sound the tambourine,
     the sweet lyre with the harp.
3   Blow the trumpet at the new moon,
     at the full moon, on our feast day.

4   For it is a statute for Israel,
     a rule[b] of the God of Jacob.
5   He made it a decree in Joseph
     when he went out over[c] the land of Egypt.
     I hear a language I had not known:
6   "I relieved your[d] shoulder of the burden;
     your hands were freed from the basket.
7   In distress you called, and I delivered you;
     I answered you in the secret place of thunder;
     I tested you at the waters of Meribah.   *Selah*
8   Hear, O my people, while I admonish you!
     O Israel, if you would but listen to me!
9   There shall be no strange god among you;
     you shall not bow down to a foreign god.
10   I am the LORD your God,
     who brought you up out of the land of Egypt.
     Open your mouth wide, and I will fill it.

11   "But my people did not listen to my voice;
     Israel would not submit to me.
12   So I gave them over to their stubborn hearts,
     to follow their own counsels.
13   Oh, that my people would listen to me,
     that Israel would walk in my ways!
14   I would soon subdue their enemies
     and turn my hand against their foes.
15   Those who hate the LORD would cringe toward him,
     and their fate would last forever.
16   But he would feed you[e] with the finest of the wheat,
     and with honey from the rock I would satisfy you."

a   Psalm 81:1 Probably a musical or liturgical term
b   Psalm 81:4 Or *just decree*
c   Psalm 81:5 Or *against*
d   Psalm 81:6 Hebrew *his*; also next line
e   Psalm 81:16 That is, Israel; Hebrew *him*

Psalm 81 was possibly written for tabernacle festival usage (v. 3), as this psalm of unknown date speaks about a time when Israel's worship practices were not impeded by war or exile. References to the exodus (vv. 5, 10) and wilderness journey (v. 7) illustrate how Israel's worship focused on God's past deeds of deliverance, anticipating the coming of the Messiah and the greater, future deliverance He would bring (v. 15).

◉ REQUEST THE SPIRIT'S HELP IN PRAYER

◉ READ AND REPEAT THE WORD

What words or phrases stick out to you? How do those words or phrases reveal the poet's purpose for the psalm? What effect does this psalm have on you as you meditate on it?

◉ RETURN TO THE LORD IN PRAYER

Even while worshiping the one true God, His people were not listening to His Word. Here, God laments that they plugged their ears (v. 11), and He longs for the day they will turn again in repentance. God loves to speak to His people! He especially loves to tell you repeatedly of His great love for you, shown to you in the death and resurrection of His Son. God feeds His people with His Word (v. 16), nourishing them with eternal life.

LORD GOD, I THANK AND PRAISE YOU:

MERCIFUL GOD, I CONFESS TO YOU:

FAITHFUL GOD, I ALSO PRAY TODAY:

Let me never grow sated, dear heavenly Father,
but allow me always to hunger for Your Word
and to listen attentively to it. Amen.

PSALM 82

A Psalm of Asaph.

1   God has taken his place in the divine council;
        in the midst of the gods he holds judgment:

2   "How long will you judge unjustly
        and show partiality to the wicked?   *Selah*

3   Give justice to the weak and the fatherless;
        maintain the right of the afflicted and the destitute.

4   Rescue the weak and the needy;
        deliver them from the hand of the wicked."

5   They have neither knowledge nor understanding,
        they walk about in darkness;
        all the foundations of the earth are shaken.

6   I said, "You are gods,
        sons of the Most High, all of you;

7   nevertheless, like men you shall die,
        and fall like any prince."[a]

8   Arise, O God, judge the earth;
        for you shall inherit all the nations!

---

a   Psalm 82:7 Or *fall as one man, O princes*

Psalm 82 alerts faithful Israelites and all believers that God concerns Himself with the care of individuals. The "gods" of verse 1 have been charged with the duty of administering justice on God's behalf. However, rather than faithfully acting as divine representatives, these "gods" have thwarted justice (vv. 2–4).

⚙ REQUEST THE SPIRIT'S HELP IN PRAYER

⚙ READ AND REPEAT THE WORD

What words or phrases stick out to you? How do those words or phrases reveal the poet's purpose for the psalm? What effect does this psalm have on you as you meditate on it?

....

....

....

....

....

....

....

....

⚙ RETURN TO THE LORD IN PRAYER

Our Father in heaven carefully looks after each believer. No believer who suffers injustice in the world will be overlooked by God. Injustice, weakness, exploitation, continued trial and suffering—such afflictions can make the believer feel isolated and forgotten by God. Your heavenly Father has already judged you impartially by laying all of your sins upon Jesus. This provides you with salvation and endurance, even in the face of worldly injustice.

PRAYERS AND NOTES:

....

....

....

....

....

....

....

Thank You, dear Jesus, that You fully bore the just sentence that was once due to me. Give me Your Holy Spirit, so that I may bear the injustices that are visited upon me. Amen.

A Song. A Psalm of Asaph.

1   O God, do not keep silence;
      do not hold your peace or be still, O God!
2   For behold, your enemies make an uproar;
      those who hate you have raised their heads.
3   They lay crafty plans against your people;
      they consult together against your treasured ones.
4   They say, "Come, let us wipe them out as a nation;
      let the name of Israel be remembered no more!"
5   For they conspire with one accord;
      against you they make a covenant—
6   the tents of Edom and the Ishmaelites,
      Moab and the Hagrites,
7   Gebal and Ammon and Amalek,
      Philistia with the inhabitants of Tyre;
8   Asshur also has joined them;
      they are the strong arm of the children of Lot.   *Selah*

9   Do to them as you did to Midian,
      as to Sisera and Jabin at the river Kishon,
10   who were destroyed at En-dor,
      who became dung for the ground.
11   Make their nobles like Oreb and Zeeb,
      all their princes like Zebah and Zalmunna,
12   who said, "Let us take possession for ourselves
      of the pastures of God."

13   O my God, make them like whirling dust,[a]
      like chaff before the wind.
14   As fire consumes the forest,
      as the flame sets the mountains ablaze,
15   so may you pursue them with your tempest
      and terrify them with your hurricane!
16   Fill their faces with shame,
      that they may seek your name, O Lord.
17   Let them be put to shame and dismayed forever;
      let them perish in disgrace,
18   that they may know that you alone,
      whose name is the Lord,
      are the Most High over all the earth.

---

a   Psalm 83:13 Or *like a tumbleweed*

Psalm 83 was likely written after King Solomon's death (1 Kings 11:41–43) but before the Assyrian invasion (2 Kings 17:1–6). The psalmist prays that God would destroy the nations that have conspired against Israel (vv. 6–8), just as He previously destroyed those who opposed Israel during the days of the judges (vv. 9–11).

⊛ REQUEST THE SPIRIT'S HELP IN PRAYER

⊛ READ AND REPEAT THE WORD

What words or phrases stick out to you? How do those words or phrases reveal the poet's purpose for the psalm? What effect does this psalm have on you as you meditate on it?

....

....

....

⊛ RETURN TO THE LORD IN PRAYER

The psalmist feels overwhelmed by his enemies, who plot against him. His only recourse is to run to God Most High, whose great deeds he remembers in prayer. God's children do not stop praying, even when He appears to keep silent. God is faithful. He answers your prayers in His time and according to His good pleasure, yet always acting for your benefit and eternal life (Romans 8:28).

LORD GOD, I THANK YOU:
....

....

MERCIFUL GOD, I CONFESS TO YOU:
....

....

PRAYERS OF REQUEST
For members of my household to delight in the Lord, I pray: ....

....

For faithfulness in my everyday work, I pray: ....

....

For my congregation, I pray: ....

....

For my neighbor in the world, I pray: ....

....

Act on my behalf, O God, as You have
acted so many times before. Amen.

PSALM 84

To the choirmaster: according to The Gittith.[a] A Psalm of the Sons of Korah.

1 How lovely is your dwelling place,
    O LORD of hosts!
2 My soul longs, yes, faints
    for the courts of the LORD;
my heart and flesh sing for joy
    to the living God.

3 Even the sparrow finds a home,
    and the swallow a nest for herself,
    where she may lay her young,
at your altars, O LORD of hosts,
    my King and my God.
4 Blessed are those who dwell in your house,
    ever singing your praise!   *Selah*

5 Blessed are those whose strength is in you,
    in whose heart are the highways to Zion.[b]
6 As they go through the Valley of Baca
    they make it a place of springs;
    the early rain also covers it with pools.
7 They go from strength to strength;
    each one appears before God in Zion.

8 O LORD God of hosts, hear my prayer;
    give ear, O God of Jacob!   *Selah*
9 Behold our shield, O God;
    look on the face of your anointed!

10 For a day in your courts is better
    than a thousand elsewhere.
I would rather be a doorkeeper in the house of my God
    than dwell in the tents of wickedness.
11 For the LORD God is a sun and shield;
    the LORD bestows favor and honor.
No good thing does he withhold
    from those who walk uprightly.
12 O LORD of hosts,
    blessed is the one who trusts in you!

---

a   Psalm 84:1 Probably a musical or liturgical term
b   Psalm 84:5 Hebrew lacks *to Zion*

References to a "dwelling place" (v. 1), "courts" (v. 2), and "altars" (v. 3) might suggest that Psalm 84 was written fairly late, and the psalmist could be referencing God's dwelling both in the Jerusalem temple and in the tabernacle that preceded it. This prayer speaks of someone separated from the sanctuary, longing to stand within its precincts in God's presence (v. 2). The unknown reason for the separation makes the psalm more universal, aptly prayed by the homebound, prisoners, travelers, Sunday workers, and all who have been temporarily separated from the congregational worship life of the Church.

⊕ REQUEST THE SPIRIT'S HELP IN PRAYER

⊕ READ AND REPEAT THE WORD

What words or phrases stick out to you? How do those words or phrases reveal the poet's purpose for the psalm? What effect does this psalm have on you as you meditate on it?

⊕ RETURN TO THE LORD IN PRAYER

Someone who has been separated from the sanctuary, where God is rightly worshiped, now longs to return. Many homebound Christians long for worship in God's house, yearning for the days they were strong enough to go. Meanwhile, many other Christians, especially those in the height of their strength, neglect the worship of the Lord to their own detriment. God gives strength to His people (vv. 5–7) through the hearing of His Word, specifically through His Gospel promises of salvation on account of Christ.

PRAYERS AND NOTES:

Teach me to love the hearing of Your Word, O Lord, and the reception of Your gifts, so that I may carry them to those in need. When I am separated from Your congregation, stir my desire to return again according to Your mercy. Amen.

PSALM 85

To the choirmaster. A Psalm of the Sons of Korah.

1   LORD, you were favorable to your land;
      you restored the fortunes of Jacob.
2   You forgave the iniquity of your people;
      you covered all their sin.   *Selah*
3   You withdrew all your wrath;
      you turned from your hot anger.

4   Restore us again, O God of our salvation,
      and put away your indignation toward us!
5   Will you be angry with us forever?
      Will you prolong your anger to all generations?
6   Will you not revive us again,
      that your people may rejoice in you?
7   Show us your steadfast love, O LORD,
      and grant us your salvation.

8   Let me hear what God the LORD will speak,
      for he will speak peace to his people, to his saints;
      but let them not turn back to folly.
9   Surely his salvation is near to those who fear him,
      that glory may dwell in our land.

10 Steadfast love and faithfulness meet;
      righteousness and peace kiss each other.
11 Faithfulness springs up from the ground,
      and righteousness looks down from the sky.
12 Yes, the LORD will give what is good,
      and our land will yield its increase.
13 Righteousness will go before him
      and make his footsteps a way.

Possibly written soon after the return of the exiles from Babylon (as referenced in vv. 1–3), Psalm 85 expresses the psalmist's feelings of distress and exposure to danger (which can also be seen in the opposition to rebuilding Jerusalem's walls after the return; for more, read Nehemiah 4:16–23).

⊛ REQUEST THE SPIRIT'S HELP IN PRAYER

⊛ READ AND REPEAT THE WORD

What words or phrases stick out to you? How do those words or phrases reveal the poet's purpose for the psalm? What effect does this psalm have on you as you meditate on it?

....

....

....

....

....

....

⊛ RETURN TO THE LORD IN PRAYER

The psalmist feels distress and fear at his exposure to his enemies. Many people, even Christians, suffer from deep fears and insecurities. Rightly heeded, these fears chase us to Jesus. When we are overcome by fears, though, they threaten us with despair and unbelief. When God forgave your iniquity and covered your sin (v. 2) through the death and resurrection of Jesus Christ, He destroyed your enemies of sin, death, and hell. Having defeated these great enemies for you, He will surely protect you from all other enemies.

RESTORING GOD, I THANK YOU: ....

....

....

FORGIVING GOD, I CONFESS TO YOU: ....

....

....

FAITHFUL GOD, I ALSO BRING MY OTHER PRAYERS AND ANXIETIES TO YOU THIS DAY: ....

....

....

Help me, Lord, amid my fears, to trust solely in You. Amen.

PSALM 86

A Prayer of David.

1 Incline your ear, O LORD, and answer me,
    for I am poor and needy.
2 Preserve my life, for I am godly;
    save your servant, who trusts in you—you are my God.
3 Be gracious to me, O Lord,
    for to you do I cry all the day.
4 Gladden the soul of your servant,
    for to you, O Lord, do I lift up my soul.
5 For you, O Lord, are good and forgiving,
    abounding in steadfast love to all who call upon you.
6 Give ear, O LORD, to my prayer;
    listen to my plea for grace.
7 In the day of my trouble I call upon you,
    for you answer me.

8 There is none like you among the gods, O Lord,
    nor are there any works like yours.
9 All the nations you have made shall come
    and worship before you, O Lord,
    and shall glorify your name.
10 For you are great and do wondrous things;
    you alone are God.
11 Teach me your way, O LORD,
    that I may walk in your truth;
    unite my heart to fear your name.
12 I give thanks to you, O Lord my God, with my whole heart,
    and I will glorify your name forever.
13 For great is your steadfast love toward me;
    you have delivered my soul from the depths of Sheol.

14 O God, insolent men have risen up against me;
    a band of ruthless men seeks my life,
    and they do not set you before them.
15 But you, O Lord, are a God merciful and gracious,
    slow to anger and abounding in steadfast love and faithfulness.
16 Turn to me and be gracious to me;
    give your strength to your servant,
    and save the son of your maidservant.
17 Show me a sign of your favor,
    that those who hate me may see and be put to shame
    because you, LORD, have helped me and comforted me.

Psalm 86 is, surprisingly, the only Davidic psalm included in Book Three (Psalms 73–89). Similar to the others in this book, this psalm asks God for protection against enemies (v. 14) and expresses confidence that the Lord shall indeed act (vv. 5, 15–17). This is a personal psalm, apparently originating as a prayer of David before God.

⊛ REQUEST THE SPIRIT'S HELP IN PRAYER

⊛ READ AND REPEAT THE WORD

What words or phrases stick out to you? How do those words or phrases reveal the poet's purpose for the psalm? What effect does this psalm have on you as you meditate on it?

⊛ RETURN TO THE LORD IN PRAYER

Ascribed to King David, this psalm points to God's steadfast love (vv. 5, 13, 15) as the reason why prayers are answered. Rather than feeling overwhelmed by the obstacles that confront you (v. 14), keep the eyes of your faith focused on the Lord, for He alone is God (v. 10). Because of the Lord's steadfast love, He cannot overlook or neglect His children. Their care and preservation are part of His very nature—He cannot and will not fail to act according to His mercy and grace.

LORD GOD, I THANK YOU:

MERCIFUL GOD, I CONFESS TO YOU:

PRAYERS OF REQUEST
For members of my household to delight in the Lord, I pray:

For faithfulness in my everyday work, I pray:

For my congregation, I pray:

For my neighbor in the world, I pray:

Lord, help me and comfort me so that I may enjoy peace of mind and spirit. Amen.

PSALM 87

A Psalm of the Sons of Korah. A Song.

1   On the holy mount stands the city he founded;
2   the LORD loves the gates of Zion
     more than all the dwelling places of Jacob.
3   Glorious things of you are spoken,
     O city of God.   *Selah*

4   Among those who know me I mention Rahab and Babylon;
     behold, Philistia and Tyre, with Cush[a]—
     "This one was born there," they say.
5   And of Zion it shall be said,
     "This one and that one were born in her";
     for the Most High himself will establish her.
6   The LORD records as he registers the peoples,
     "This one was born there."   *Selah*

7   Singers and dancers alike say,
     "All my springs are in you."

---

a   Psalm 87:4 Probably *Nubia*

Psalm 87 includes Gentiles in God's salvation (v. 4). The psalm also notes the comforting words that the Lord carefully records the name of each person born in Zion (vv. 5–6).

◉ REQUEST THE SPIRIT'S HELP IN PRAYER

◉ READ AND REPEAT THE WORD

What words or phrases stick out to you? How do those words or phrases reveal the poet's purpose for the psalm? What effect does this psalm have on you as you meditate on it?

◉ RETURN TO THE LORD IN PRAYER

God includes people of all nations among His believers, all of whom may claim to be born in Zion (v. 5). Your true identity before God is not rooted in your nationality, your language, your family ties, your wealth, or any other earthly thing. God claims you to be His own in Baptism, through which you become His own child (vv. 5–6), no matter who you are or from where you came (v. 4).

LORD GOD, I THANK YOU:

MERCIFUL GOD, I CONFESS TO YOU:

PRAYERS OF REQUEST
For members of my household to delight in the Lord, I pray:

For faithfulness in my everyday work, I pray:

For my congregation, I pray:

For my neighbor in the world, I pray:

Thank You, dear heavenly Father, that You regard me as Your child through Jesus Christ. Amen.

PSALM 88

A Song. A Psalm of the Sons of Korah. To the choirmaster: according to Mahalath Leannoth. A Maskil[a] of Heman the Ezrahite.

1 O LORD, God of my salvation,
  I cry out day and night before you.
2 Let my prayer come before you;
  incline your ear to my cry!

3 For my soul is full of troubles,
  and my life draws near to Sheol.
4 I am counted among those who go down to the pit;
  I am a man who has no strength,
5 like one set loose among the dead,
  like the slain that lie in the grave,
  like those whom you remember no more,
  for they are cut off from your hand.
6 You have put me in the depths of the pit,
  in the regions dark and deep.
7 Your wrath lies heavy upon me,
  and you overwhelm me with all your waves.   *Selah*

8 You have caused my companions to shun me;
  you have made me a horror[b] to them.
  I am shut in so that I cannot escape;
9   my eye grows dim through sorrow.
  Every day I call upon you, O LORD;
  I spread out my hands to you.
10 Do you work wonders for the dead?
  Do the departed rise up to praise you?   *Selah*
11 Is your steadfast love declared in the grave,
  or your faithfulness in Abaddon?
12 Are your wonders known in the darkness,
  or your righteousness in the land of forgetfulness?

13 But I, O LORD, cry to you;
  in the morning my prayer comes before you.
14 O LORD, why do you cast my soul away?
  Why do you hide your face from me?
15 Afflicted and close to death from my youth up,

---

a   Psalm 88:1 Probably musical or liturgical terms
b   Psalm 88:8 Or *an abomination*

I suffer your terrors; I am helpless.[c]

16 Your wrath has swept over me;
your dreadful assaults destroy me.

17 They surround me like a flood all day long;
they close in on me together.

18 You have caused my beloved and my friend to shun me;
my companions have become darkness.[d]

c   Psalm 88:15 The meaning of the Hebrew word is uncertain
d   Psalm 88:18 Or *darkness has become my only companion*

Psalm 88 is a personal psalm, prayed by someone whose suffering sounds similar to Christ's own suffering. Lamenting the troubles that God has visited upon him (vv. 7–8, 16, 18), the psalmist clings to the hope that God shall yet save him (v. 1). The term *Mahalath Leannoth* in the superscript may refer to the tune. The name *Ezrahite* in the superscript possibly refers to a descendant of Zerah (1 Chronicles 2:6), whose sons included Heman and Ethan.

❋ REQUEST THE SPIRIT'S HELP IN PRAYER

❋ READ AND REPEAT THE WORD

What words or phrases stick out to you? How do those words or phrases reveal the poet's purpose for the psalm? What effect does this psalm have on you as you meditate on it?

❋ RETURN TO THE LORD IN PRAYER

This psalm evokes feelings of sadness and abandonment. The psalmist is so overcome by troubles that he wonders if God will hear him. Surely the loneliness spoken of here has been felt by many suffering Christians! Yet even in sorrow and suffering, God inclines His ear (v. 2) toward His people, always ready to hear and answer us according to His mercy.

PRAYERS AND NOTES:

*Thank You, O Lord, that no matter how low I sink,
I never disappear from Your sight. Amen.*

PSALM 89

A Maskil[a] of Ethan the Ezrahite.

1　I will sing of the steadfast love of the LORD, forever;
　　with my mouth I will make known your faithfulness to all
　　generations.

2　For I said, "Steadfast love will be built up forever;
　　in the heavens you will establish your faithfulness."

3　You have said, "I have made a covenant with my chosen one;
　　I have sworn to David my servant:

4　'I will establish your offspring forever,
　　and build your throne for all generations.'"　　　　*Selah*

5　Let the heavens praise your wonders, O LORD,
　　your faithfulness in the assembly of the holy ones!

6　For who in the skies can be compared to the LORD?
　　Who among the heavenly beings[b] is like the LORD,

7　a God greatly to be feared in the council of the holy ones,
　　and awesome above all who are around him?

8　O LORD God of hosts,
　　who is mighty as you are, O LORD,
　　with your faithfulness all around you?

9　You rule the raging of the sea;
　　when its waves rise, you still them.

10　You crushed Rahab like a carcass;
　　you scattered your enemies with your mighty arm.

11　The heavens are yours; the earth also is yours;
　　the world and all that is in it, you have founded them.

12　The north and the south, you have created them;
　　Tabor and Hermon joyously praise your name.

13　You have a mighty arm;
　　strong is your hand, high your right hand.

14　Righteousness and justice are the foundation of your throne;
　　steadfast love and faithfulness go before you.

15　Blessed are the people who know the festal shout,
　　who walk, O LORD, in the light of your face,

16　who exult in your name all the day
　　and in your righteousness are exalted.

17　For you are the glory of their strength;
　　by your favor our horn is exalted.

18　For our shield belongs to the LORD,
　　our king to the Holy One of Israel.

---

a　Psalm 89:1 Probably a musical or liturgical term
b　Psalm 89:6 Hebrew *the sons of God,* or *the sons of might*

19 Of old you spoke in a vision to your godly one,^c and said:
   "I have granted help to one who is mighty;
   I have exalted one chosen from the people.

20 I have found David, my servant;
   with my holy oil I have anointed him,

21 so that my hand shall be established with him;
   my arm also shall strengthen him.

22 The enemy shall not outwit him;
   the wicked shall not humble him.

23 I will crush his foes before him
   and strike down those who hate him.

24 My faithfulness and my steadfast love shall be with him,
   and in my name shall his horn be exalted.

25 I will set his hand on the sea
   and his right hand on the rivers.

26 He shall cry to me, 'You are my Father,
   my God, and the Rock of my salvation.'

27 And I will make him the firstborn,
   the highest of the kings of the earth.

28 My steadfast love I will keep for him forever,
   and my covenant will stand firm[d] for him.

29 I will establish his offspring forever
   and his throne as the days of the heavens.

30 If his children forsake my law
   and do not walk according to my rules,[e]

31 if they violate my statutes
   and do not keep my commandments,

32 then I will punish their transgression with the rod
   and their iniquity with stripes,

33 but I will not remove from him my steadfast love
   or be false to my faithfulness.

34 I will not violate my covenant
   or alter the word that went forth from my lips.

35 Once for all I have sworn by my holiness;
   I will not lie to David.

36 His offspring shall endure forever,
   his throne as long as the sun before me.

37 Like the moon it shall be established forever,
   a faithful witness in the skies."   *Selah*

c   Psalm 89:19 Some Hebrew manuscripts *godly ones*
d   Psalm 89:28 Or *will remain faithful*
e   Psalm 89:30 Or *my just decrees*

38 But now you have cast off and rejected;
    you are full of wrath against your anointed.
39 You have renounced the covenant with your servant;
    you have defiled his crown in the dust.
40 You have breached all his walls;
    you have laid his strongholds in ruins.
41 All who pass by plunder him;
    he has become the scorn of his neighbors.
42 You have exalted the right hand of his foes;
    you have made all his enemies rejoice.
43 You have also turned back the edge of his sword,
    and you have not made him stand in battle.
44 You have made his splendor to cease
    and cast his throne to the ground.
45 You have cut short the days of his youth;
    you have covered him with shame.   *Selah*

46 How long, O LORD? Will you hide yourself forever?
    How long will your wrath burn like fire?
47 Remember how short my time is!
    For what vanity you have created all the children of man!
48 What man can live and never see death?
    Who can deliver his soul from the power of Sheol?   *Selah*

49 Lord, where is your steadfast love of old,
    which by your faithfulness you swore to David?
50 Remember, O Lord, how your servants are mocked,
    and how I bear in my heart the insults[f] of all the many
    nations,
51 with which your enemies mock, O LORD,
    with which they mock the footsteps of your anointed.

52 Blessed be the LORD forever!
Amen and Amen.

f   Psalm 89:50 Hebrew lacks *the insults*

Psalm 89 speaks of the rise and fall of David's kingdom, suggesting a date during the time of the kings. Because David's sons, the kings of Judah, did not remain faithful to God (v. 30), God has visited judgment upon His people (vv. 38–45). Lamenting this harsh treatment, the psalmist calls upon God to relent and to restore His people once again. For thoughts on the term *Ezrahite* in the superscript, see the introduction to Psalm 88.

◉ REQUEST THE SPIRIT'S HELP IN PRAYER

◉ READ AND REPEAT THE WORD

What words or phrases stick out to you? How do those words or phrases reveal the poet's purpose for the psalm? What effect does this psalm have on you as you meditate on it?

◉ RETURN TO THE LORD IN PRAYER

The psalm speaks primarily of David, who enjoyed God's faithfulness (vv. 2, 24) and promises. Even when David sinned and felt the weight of God's Law (vv. 38–47), he still relied completely upon God. "How long, O LORD?" (v. 46) easily comes to the lips of all who have suffered under the weight of God's Law because of their sins. God's "steadfast love of old" (v. 49) and His faithfulness (vv. 2, 24) are shown most clearly in Christ, whose death and resurrection provide the remedy for all troubles (v. 48).

LORD GOD, I THANK YOU:

MERCIFUL GOD, I CONFESS TO YOU:

STEADFAST LORD, I ALSO BRING BEFORE YOU TODAY MY CARES AND OTHER PRAYERS:

"Blessed be the LORD forever!" (Psalm 89:52).
Preserve the faithful, O Lord, and provide for their
future security and service. Amen and amen.

PSALM 90

A Prayer of Moses, the man of God.

1 Lord, you have been our dwelling place[a]
   in all generations.
2 Before the mountains were brought forth,
   or ever you had formed the earth and the world,
   from everlasting to everlasting you are God.

3 You return man to dust
   and say, "Return, O children of man!"[b]
4 For a thousand years in your sight
   are but as yesterday when it is past,
   or as a watch in the night.

5 You sweep them away as with a flood; they are like a dream,
   like grass that is renewed in the morning:
6 in the morning it flourishes and is renewed;
   in the evening it fades and withers.

7 For we are brought to an end by your anger;
   by your wrath we are dismayed.
8 You have set our iniquities before you,
   our secret sins in the light of your presence.

9 For all our days pass away under your wrath;
   we bring our years to an end like a sigh.
10 The years of our life are seventy,
   or even by reason of strength eighty;
   yet their span[c] is but toil and trouble;
   they are soon gone, and we fly away.
11 Who considers the power of your anger,
   and your wrath according to the fear of you?

12 So teach us to number our days
   that we may get a heart of wisdom.
13 Return, O Lord! How long?
   Have pity on your servants!
14 Satisfy us in the morning with your steadfast love,
   that we may rejoice and be glad all our days.
15 Make us glad for as many days as you have afflicted us,
   and for as many years as we have seen evil.

a Psalm 90:1 Some Hebrew manuscripts (compare Septuagint) *our refuge*
b Psalm 90:3 Or *of Adam*
c Psalm 90:10 Or *pride*

16 Let your work be shown to your servants,
  and your glorious power to their children.
17 Let the favor^d of the Lord our God be upon us,
  and establish the work of our hands upon us;
  yes, establish the work of our hands!

d   Psalm 90:17 Or *beauty*

Psalm 90 does not name any specific event or crisis, so this psalm is suited for any time of lament when the frailty of life stands in stark contrast to God's eternal strength.

⚬ REQUEST THE SPIRIT'S HELP IN PRAYER

⚬ READ AND REPEAT THE WORD

What words or phrases stick out to you? How do those words or phrases reveal the poet's purpose for the psalm? What effect does this psalm have on you as you meditate on it?

⚬ RETURN TO THE LORD IN PRAYER

How quickly life flies by: grass withers in the summer heat, leaves fall and blow away in autumn, trees stand bare in winter. Even more heartbreaking is standing by a casket and staring at a lifeless body or looking in a mirror and seeing age steal youth and energy. Yet in spring, the flowers bloom and the grass turns green. The grave is empty on Easter morning. Jesus has risen! God has taken pity on us and has given us everlasting life in Christ.

PRAYERS AND NOTES:

> *Lord, give us wisdom to number our days as Your*
> *servants so that we will look forward to dwelling*
> *with You from everlasting to everlasting. Amen.*

PSALM 91

1   He who dwells in the shelter of the Most High
      will abide in the shadow of the Almighty.
2   I will say[a] to the Lord, "My refuge and my fortress,
      my God, in whom I trust."

3   For he will deliver you from the snare of the fowler
      and from the deadly pestilence.
4   He will cover you with his pinions,
      and under his wings you will find refuge;
      his faithfulness is a shield and buckler.
5   You will not fear the terror of the night,
      nor the arrow that flies by day,
6   nor the pestilence that stalks in darkness,
      nor the destruction that wastes at noonday.

7   A thousand may fall at your side,
      ten thousand at your right hand,
      but it will not come near you.
8   You will only look with your eyes
      and see the recompense of the wicked.

9   Because you have made the Lord your dwelling place—
      the Most High, who is my refuge[b]—
10 no evil shall be allowed to befall you,
      no plague come near your tent.

11 For he will command his angels concerning you
      to guard you in all your ways.
12 On their hands they will bear you up,
      lest you strike your foot against a stone.
13 You will tread on the lion and the adder;
      the young lion and the serpent you will trample underfoot.

14 "Because he holds fast to me in love, I will deliver him;
      I will protect him, because he knows my name.
15 When he calls to me, I will answer him;
      I will be with him in trouble;
      I will rescue him and honor him.
16 With long life I will satisfy him
      and show him my salvation."

a   Psalm 91:2 Septuagint *He will say*
b   Psalm 91:9 Or *For you, O Lord, are my refuge! You have made the Most High your dwelling place*

Psalm 91 is a strong confession of faith and an example of a life entrusted to God's protective safety. The psalmist, who remains anonymous, urges all readers to seek the Lord's refuge when fearful times arise.

- ❀ REQUEST THE SPIRIT'S HELP IN PRAYER

- ❀ READ AND REPEAT THE WORD

What words or phrases stick out to you? How do those words or phrases reveal the poet's purpose for the psalm? What effect does this psalm have on you as you meditate on it?

....

....

....

....

....

....

- ❀ RETURN TO THE LORD IN PRAYER

How quickly life can go from smooth and routine to troubled and fearful! How encouraging it is to know of God's protection. Our security comes from His promises kept. Jesus trampled Satan once and for all when He gloriously rose from the dead. We walk in victory even during dangerous times because He is with us and will not let us be separated from His love.

LORD GOD, I THANK YOU:

....

MERCIFUL GOD, I CONFESS TO YOU:

....

....

PRAYERS OF REQUEST
For members of my household to delight in the Lord, I pray:

....

For faithfulness in my everyday work, I pray:

....

For my congregation, I pray:

....

For my neighbor in the world, I pray:

....

....

*Thank You, Lord, for Your security and
strength in this perilous world. Amen.*

PSALM 92

A Psalm. A Song for the Sabbath.

1   It is good to give thanks to the LORD,
     to sing praises to your name, O Most High;
2   to declare your steadfast love in the morning,
     and your faithfulness by night,
3   to the music of the lute and the harp,
     to the melody of the lyre.
4   For you, O LORD, have made me glad by your work;
     at the works of your hands I sing for joy.

5   How great are your works, O LORD!
     Your thoughts are very deep!
6   The stupid man cannot know;
     the fool cannot understand this:
7   that though the wicked sprout like grass
     and all evildoers flourish,
  they are doomed to destruction forever;
8   but you, O LORD, are on high forever.
9   For behold, your enemies, O LORD,
     for behold, your enemies shall perish;
     all evildoers shall be scattered.

10   But you have exalted my horn like that of the wild ox;
     you have poured over me[a] fresh oil.
11   My eyes have seen the downfall of my enemies;
     my ears have heard the doom of my evil assailants.

12   The righteous flourish like the palm tree
     and grow like a cedar in Lebanon.
13   They are planted in the house of the LORD;
     they flourish in the courts of our God.
14   They still bear fruit in old age;
     they are ever full of sap and green,
15   to declare that the LORD is upright;
     he is my rock, and there is no unrighteousness in him.

a   Psalm 92:10 Compare Syriac; the meaning of the Hebrew is uncertain

Psalm 92 is the only psalm tied specifically to the Sabbath. While the Sabbath could be described by what could not be done on that day, this psalm shows what should be done: praise and celebration of God's great works.

⊛ REQUEST THE SPIRIT'S HELP IN PRAYER

⊛ READ AND REPEAT THE WORD

What words or phrases stick out to you? How do those words or phrases reveal the poet's purpose for the psalm? What effect does this psalm have on you as you meditate on it?

⊛ RETURN TO THE LORD IN PRAYER

In worship, you receive the strength of God's steadfast love and faithfulness. No doubt, there are days that you wonder if going to worship is worth the effort. But focus on what God has done for you in Jesus, who is faithful to His promises. One day, justice will be served on the wicked, but we who believe will flourish in the strength of Christ's resurrection.

LORD GOD, I THANK AND PRAISE YOU TODAY:

RIGHTEOUS GOD, I CONFESS TO YOU THAT I HAVE SINNED AGAINST YOU AND MY NEIGHBOR, YET YOU ARE FAITHFUL TO FORGIVE. I ESPECIALLY CONFESS TO YOU TODAY THESE SINS:

PRAYERS OF REQUEST
That my household may be fruitful today, I pray:

That I may be fruitful in my work today, I pray:

That my congregation may flourish in praise, I pray:

That Your will be done in society, I pray:

Lord, bring forth praises out of our hearts, for the works of Your hands make us glad indeed. Amen.

PSALM 93

1   The LORD reigns; he is robed in majesty;
      the LORD is robed; he has put on strength as his belt.
    Yes, the world is established; it shall never be moved.
2   Your throne is established from of old;
      you are from everlasting.

3   The floods have lifted up, O LORD,
      the floods have lifted up their voice;
      the floods lift up their roaring.
4   Mightier than the thunders of many waters,
      mightier than the waves of the sea,
      the LORD on high is mighty!

5   Your decrees are very trustworthy;
      holiness befits your house,
      O LORD, forevermore.

Many religions celebrate the enthronement of their gods. In Psalm 93, the writer affirms that the Lord has always reigned and will do so forever. This confident confession celebrates God's almighty and eternal reign over even the most chaotic powers of creation. The fall Feast of Booths (or Tabernacles) may have used this psalm, along with Psalms 47; 95–99.

⊛ REQUEST THE SPIRIT'S HELP IN PRAYER

⊛ READ AND REPEAT THE WORD

What words or phrases stick out to you? How do those words or phrases reveal the poet's purpose for the psalm? What effect does this psalm have on you as you meditate on it?

⊛ RETURN TO THE LORD IN PRAYER

The Lord reigns! Yet a storm may still crash into a church. The members may come back to see destruction, not beauty. Does the Lord reign? Indeed, He does. Many years ago, Jesus spoke, and a deadly storm was silenced. Wind and waves were calmed in an instant. Such is God's power and more! By His resurrection, He rules over our lives now and forever.

MAJESTIC LORD, I THANK YOU:

HOLY LORD, I CONFESS TO YOU:

MIGHTY GOD, TODAY I ALSO PRAY:

*Lord, despite the evil we see and the destruction all around us,
lead us to confess that Your words are trustworthy. Amen.*

PSALM 94

1 O LORD, God of vengeance,
  O God of vengeance, shine forth!
2 Rise up, O judge of the earth;
  repay to the proud what they deserve!
3 O LORD, how long shall the wicked,
  how long shall the wicked exult?
4 They pour out their arrogant words;
  all the evildoers boast.
5 They crush your people, O LORD,
  and afflict your heritage.
6 They kill the widow and the sojourner,
  and murder the fatherless;
7 and they say, "The LORD does not see;
  the God of Jacob does not perceive."

8 Understand, O dullest of the people!
  Fools, when will you be wise?
9 He who planted the ear, does he not hear?
  He who formed the eye, does he not see?
10 He who disciplines the nations, does he not rebuke?
   He who teaches man knowledge—
11   the LORD—knows the thoughts of man,
   that they are but a breath.ᵃ

12 Blessed is the man whom you discipline, O LORD,
   and whom you teach out of your law,
13 to give him rest from days of trouble,
   until a pit is dug for the wicked.
14 For the LORD will not forsake his people;
   he will not abandon his heritage;
15 for justice will return to the righteous,
   and all the upright in heart will follow it.

16 Who rises up for me against the wicked?
   Who stands up for me against evildoers?
17 If the LORD had not been my help,
   my soul would soon have lived in the land of silence.
18 When I thought, "My foot slips,"
   your steadfast love, O LORD, held me up.

---

a   Psalm 94:11 Septuagint *they are futile*

19 When the cares of my heart are many,
   your consolations cheer my soul.
20 Can wicked rulers be allied with you,
   those who frame^b injustice by statute?
21 They band together against the life of the righteous
   and condemn the innocent to death.^c
22 But the Lord has become my stronghold,
   and my God the rock of my refuge.
23 He will bring back on them their iniquity
   and wipe them out for their wickedness;
   the Lord our God will wipe them out.

b   Psalm 94:20 Or *fashion*
c   Psalm 94:21 Hebrew *condemn innocent blood*

Psalms 94–99 declare that the Lord reigns! However, the social and political situation seems to say that the wicked reign. Tension between trust that the Lord is in control and agony of seeing injustice and evil prevail dominates the beginning of Psalm 94. Worse, that wickedness could very well be from Israel's religious and political leaders and not merely a foreign power attacking the people. Internal corruption in the highest places has made life oppressive. This psalm is a plea for God to repay these oppressors so that justice returns; it trusts that God will be victorious and will discipline and care for His faithful people.

⚜ REQUEST THE SPIRIT'S HELP IN PRAYER

⚜ READ AND REPEAT THE WORD

What words or phrases stick out to you? How do those words or phrases reveal the poet's purpose for the psalm? What effect does this psalm have on you as you meditate on it?

⚜ RETURN TO THE LORD IN PRAYER

The psalmist pleads for God to take vengeance on His enemies. Jesus, however, says to pray for our enemies and even love them (Matthew 5:43–44). What are we to do? Final judgment will bring vengeance on those who arrogantly reject the Lord. Meanwhile, we pray that all will see the glory of God's justice in Jesus on the cross, turn from their wicked ways, and join with us in the life of righteousness, which includes caring for and protecting widows, orphans, and others who are helpless and oppressed.

PRAYERS AND NOTES:

Lord, help us to pray—even for our enemies! Amen.

THE GOD OF BOTH THE OLD
AND NEW TESTAMENTS

But You, O Lord, are a God merciful and gracious, slow to anger
and abounding in steadfast love and faithfulness. (Psalm 86:15)

This verse from Psalm 86 gets at the heart of the Gospel, leading the reader
to understand that the God of the Old Testament is not some distant, vengeful God who is contrasted with a New Testament God of love. Rather, He
is one and the same Lord throughout Scripture, a merciful and loving God
who is faithful to His promises. God promised that Abraham would have
offspring as numerous as the stars (Genesis 15:5), and now all people who
are called to faith in Christ are counted as Abraham's offspring (Galatians
3:29). God promised to establish David's kingdom forever (2 Samuel 7:16),
and He fulfilled that promise in establishing David's Lord (Psalm 110:1)
and David's descendant Jesus Christ on His eternal throne. God promised
to crush the head of Satan in the Garden of Eden (Genesis 3:15), and He
accomplished this act in the cross and the empty tomb.

This thought, almost a formula of words, is reflected in nearly identical
language at several points in the Psalter (for example, Psalm 103:8; 145:8),
and indeed, throughout the entirety of the Old Testament. For example, when
God gave Moses the two tablets of stone with the Commandments etched on
them, He explained the basis for His mercy, using nearly identical language:

The LORD, the LORD, a God merciful and gracious, slow to anger,
and abounding in steadfast love and faithfulness. (Exodus 34:6)

The prophet Joel includes the same thought (Joel 2:13). His words
have found their way into the liturgy, as we, too, speak back to God His
own words of mercy, grace, and faithfulness when we pray the alternate
Verse appointed for Lent:

Return to the Lord, your God, for He is gracious and
merciful, slow to anger and abounding in steadfast love,
and abounding in steadfast love. (LSB, pp. 157, 173)

As we hear and read the Scriptures, we are repeatedly pointed to the
consistency of God's Word and His actions throughout all of Scripture.
God's Law in the Psalter, just like in the rest of Scripture, shows us our sin
and convicts us of our guilt before our righteous God. The Gospel, revealed
in Scripture, including the Psalter, reveals our Savior, Jesus Christ. He is the
fulfillment of all of God's promises. He shows us just how God is merciful
and gracious, slow to anger and abounding in steadfast love and faithfulness.

PSALM 95

1   Oh come, let us sing to the LORD;
     let us make a joyful noise to the rock of our salvation!
2   Let us come into his presence with thanksgiving;
     let us make a joyful noise to him with songs of praise!
3   For the LORD is a great God,
     and a great King above all gods.
4   In his hand are the depths of the earth;
     the heights of the mountains are his also.
5   The sea is his, for he made it,
     and his hands formed the dry land.

6   Oh come, let us worship and bow down;
     let us kneel before the LORD, our Maker!
7   For he is our God,
     and we are the people of his pasture,
     and the sheep of his hand.
     Today, if you hear his voice,
8   do not harden your hearts, as at Meribah,
     as on the day at Massah in the wilderness,
9   when your fathers put me to the test
     and put me to the proof, though they had seen my work.
10 For forty years I loathed that generation
     and said, "They are a people who go astray in their heart,
     and they have not known my ways."
11 Therefore I swore in my wrath,
     "They shall not enter my rest."

Amid national crisis, Psalm 95 would assure people that God is King over all, even when they suffer defeat and death (compare to Psalm 90). The psalm references temple practices such as procession and bowing; the text may have prepared people to hear the reading of God's Word, such as at the Feast of Booths (or Tabernacles).

⊛ REQUEST THE SPIRIT'S HELP IN PRAYER

⊛ READ AND REPEAT THE WORD

What words or phrases stick out to you? How do those words or phrases reveal the poet's purpose for the psalm? What effect does this psalm have on you as you meditate on it?

⊛ RETURN TO THE LORD IN PRAYER

The opening verses have been sung in the Church for centuries as the *Venite* (Latin for "O come"). Some days, we struggle to come into God's presence with such exuberance and humility. Thankfully, the psalmist directs us not to self-generated emotions but rather to remember the God we worship. He is our Creator, who has formed and protected us by His strong hands. And wonderfully more—He is our Good Shepherd, who has made us the sheep of His loving hand.

LORD, OUR MAKER, TODAY I THANK YOU:

LORD, ROCK OF OUR SALVATION, TODAY I CONFESS TO YOU:

OUR GREAT GOD, KING ABOVE ALL GODS, I ALSO PRAY TODAY:

*Shepherd and King, lead us into Your presence
with thanksgiving and joy. Amen.*

PSALM 96

1 Oh sing to the LORD a new song;
  sing to the LORD, all the earth!
2 Sing to the LORD, bless his name;
  tell of his salvation from day to day.
3 Declare his glory among the nations,
  his marvelous works among all the peoples!
4 For great is the LORD, and greatly to be praised;
  he is to be feared above all gods.
5 For all the gods of the peoples are worthless idols,
  but the LORD made the heavens.
6 Splendor and majesty are before him;
  strength and beauty are in his sanctuary.

7 Ascribe to the LORD, O families of the peoples,
  ascribe to the LORD glory and strength!
8 Ascribe to the LORD the glory due his name;
  bring an offering, and come into his courts!
9 Worship the LORD in the splendor of holiness;[a]
  tremble before him, all the earth!

10 Say among the nations, "The LORD reigns!
   Yes, the world is established; it shall never be moved;
   he will judge the peoples with equity."

11 Let the heavens be glad, and let the earth rejoice;
   let the sea roar, and all that fills it;
12   let the field exult, and everything in it!
   Then shall all the trees of the forest sing for joy
13   before the LORD, for he comes,
   for he comes to judge the earth.
   He will judge the world in righteousness,
   and the peoples in his faithfulness.

---

a Psalm 96:9 Or *in holy attire*

Psalm 96 is a psalm for two joyous occasions. In 1 Chronicles 16:23–34, David uses this song of praise as he brings the ark of the covenant into Jerusalem in victory. Also, the Septuagint, a Greek translation of the Old Testament used at the time of Christ, titles this psalm as the one used when the temple was rebuilt after the Babylonian captivity. God is the King who reigns, and His glorious victories call for all nations, indeed all creation, to join in the joyful exaltation of His holy name.

❀ REQUEST THE SPIRIT'S HELP IN PRAYER

❀ READ AND REPEAT THE WORD

What words or phrases stick out to you? How do those words or phrases reveal the poet's purpose for the psalm? What effect does this psalm have on you as you meditate on it?

❀ RETURN TO THE LORD IN PRAYER

Proclaim the marvelous deeds of God's salvation to all nations! In our world, too many people see faith in God as a relic of the past with little relevance to today. People turn away from the true God in idolatrous pursuits of money and success; they trust in technology or revel in pleasure. Do we give up? No! First, sing to the Lord. Join with others in worshiping the splendor and majesty of the Creator. Then, speak of His salvation in Jesus day after day, until the resurrected Savior returns to judge all nations in faithfulness.

PRAYERS AND NOTES:

The Lord still reigns! O Lord, proclaim
Your glory through us. Amen.

PSALM 97

1   The LORD reigns, let the earth rejoice;
      let the many coastlands be glad!
2   Clouds and thick darkness are all around him;
      righteousness and justice are the foundation of his throne.
3   Fire goes before him
      and burns up his adversaries all around.
4   His lightnings light up the world;
      the earth sees and trembles.
5   The mountains melt like wax before the LORD,
      before the Lord of all the earth.

6   The heavens proclaim his righteousness,
      and all the peoples see his glory.
7   All worshipers of images are put to shame,
      who make their boast in worthless idols;
      worship him, all you gods!

8   Zion hears and is glad,
      and the daughters of Judah rejoice,
      because of your judgments, O LORD.
9   For you, O LORD, are most high over all the earth;
      you are exalted far above all gods.

10   O you who love the LORD, hate evil!
      He preserves the lives of his saints;
      he delivers them from the hand of the wicked.
11   Light is sown[a] for the righteous,
      and joy for the upright in heart.
12   Rejoice in the LORD, O you righteous,
      and give thanks to his holy name!

---

a   Psalm 97:11 Most Hebrew manuscripts; one Hebrew manuscript, Septuagint, Syriac, Jerome *Light dawns*

Psalm 97 joins other psalms in the series (Psalms 93–99) in joyfully proclaiming the power and majesty of God's rule over all creation. However,
in this psalm, we also glimpse a fearsome side to God's rule as He comes
with destructive power against those who worship false gods.

◉ REQUEST THE SPIRIT'S HELP IN PRAYER

◉ READ AND REPEAT THE WORD

*What words or phrases stick out to you? How do those words or phrases reveal
the poet's purpose for the psalm? What effect does this psalm have on you as
you meditate on it?*

◉ RETURN TO THE LORD IN PRAYER

When people stand before God to be judged, only two responses are
possible: terrified humiliation or joyful thanksgiving. Which will it be for
us? The cross is where God's justice is served and His anger appeased on
our behalf. The empty tomb is the assurance that we are preserved for life
everlasting. We rejoice because His judgment is that we are His saints, the
upright in heart, through faith.

EXALTED LORD, I THANK YOU:

DELIVERING LORD, I CONFESS TO YOU:

PRAYERS OF REQUEST
For members of my household to delight in the Lord, I pray:

For faithfulness in my everyday work, I pray:

For my congregation, I pray:

For my neighbor in the world, I pray:

*Lord, smash the idols we are tempted to revere.
Let us worship You alone. Amen.*

PSALM 98

A Psalm.

1 Oh sing to the LORD a new song,
    for he has done marvelous things!
  His right hand and his holy arm
    have worked salvation for him.
2 The LORD has made known his salvation;
    he has revealed his righteousness in the sight of the nations.
3 He has remembered his steadfast love and faithfulness
    to the house of Israel.
  All the ends of the earth have seen
    the salvation of our God.

4 Make a joyful noise to the LORD, all the earth;
    break forth into joyous song and sing praises!
5 Sing praises to the LORD with the lyre,
    with the lyre and the sound of melody!
6 With trumpets and the sound of the horn
    make a joyful noise before the King, the LORD!

7 Let the sea roar, and all that fills it;
    the world and those who dwell in it!
8 Let the rivers clap their hands;
    let the hills sing for joy together
9 before the LORD, for he comes
    to judge the earth.
  He will judge the world with righteousness,
    and the peoples with equity.

Psalm 98 focuses exclusively on the Lord and is similar to Psalm 96. In this psalm, other gods or enemies are absent. As such, it appears that the psalm's sole purpose is to praise the victorious God and His marvelous works.

◉ REQUEST THE SPIRIT'S HELP IN PRAYER

◉ READ AND REPEAT THE WORD

What words or phrases stick out to you? How do those words or phrases reveal the poet's purpose for the psalm? What effect does this psalm have on you as you meditate on it?

◉ RETURN TO THE LORD IN PRAYER

The defeats of life are discouraging. Thanks be to God that He is victorious for us! Sin and death are conquered. Satan's head is crushed. Eternally, we are God's children. All creation is waiting for that final day of redemption. The Lord's victory is an empty tomb on Easter morning.

LORD GOD, I THANK YOU:

MERCIFUL GOD, I CONFESS TO YOU:

PRAYERS OF REQUEST
For members of my household to delight in the Lord, I pray:

For faithfulness in my everyday work, I pray:

For my congregation, I pray:

For my neighbor in the world, I pray:

Thank You, Lord, for the glorious victory of our salvation, which only You could give us! Amen.

269

1 The LORD reigns; let the peoples tremble!
   He sits enthroned upon the cherubim; let the earth quake!
2 The LORD is great in Zion;
   he is exalted over all the peoples.
3 Let them praise your great and awesome name!
   Holy is he!
4 The King in his might loves justice.[a]
   You have established equity;
   you have executed justice
   and righteousness in Jacob.
5 Exalt the LORD our God;
   worship at his footstool!
   Holy is he!

6 Moses and Aaron were among his priests,
   Samuel also was among those who called upon his name.
   They called to the LORD, and he answered them.
7 In the pillar of the cloud he spoke to them;
   they kept his testimonies
   and the statute that he gave them.

8 O LORD our God, you answered them;
   you were a forgiving God to them,
   but an avenger of their wrongdoings.
9 Exalt the LORD our God,
   and worship at his holy mountain;
   for the LORD our God is holy!

a Psalm 99:4 Or *The might of the King loves justice*

Like Psalms 93 and 97, Psalm 99 begins with "The LORD reigns" (v. 1). It proclaims Him King over all creation; it highlights God's holiness, which evokes awe, reverence, and even fear. He alone is worthy of worship, prayer, and devotion. Although Moses, Aaron, and Samuel are mentioned, the psalm cannot be dated or identified with any particular historical event. These men represent the priestly and prophetic offices of ancient Israel and demonstrate both God's justice and forgiveness for His people.

🌐 REQUEST THE SPIRIT'S HELP IN PRAYER

🌐 READ AND REPEAT THE WORD

What words or phrases stick out to you? How do those words or phrases reveal the poet's purpose for the psalm? What effect does this psalm have on you as you meditate on it?

🌐 RETURN TO THE LORD IN PRAYER

Despite the psalmist's confidence that God reigns in all His holiness, we see an ordinary world ruled by powers and people who are too often distant from God's ways and words. Yet just as He was in the Most Holy Place, our Savior is present when we, His people, gather together to praise His holy name.

EXALTED LORD, WORTHY OF PRAISE, TODAY I THANK YOU:

MIGHTY KING WHO LOVES JUSTICE, TODAY I CONFESS TO YOU:

O LORD OUR GOD, I ALSO PRAY TODAY:

O Lord, You tabernacle in ordinary bread and wine, where Your holy body and blood are given for our forgiveness. We see God's holiness in Jesus, the Holy One of God! Amen.

PSALM 100

A Psalm for giving thanks.

1 Make a joyful noise to the LORD, all the earth!
2   Serve the LORD with gladness!
  Come into his presence with singing!

3 Know that the LORD, he is God!
  It is he who made us, and we are his;[a]
  we are his people, and the sheep of his pasture.

4 Enter his gates with thanksgiving,
  and his courts with praise!
  Give thanks to him; bless his name!

5 For the LORD is good;
  his steadfast love endures forever,
  and his faithfulness to all generations.

---

a   Psalm 100:3 Or *and not we ourselves*

The previous psalm joyfully proclaims, "The LORD reigns" (Psalm 99:1). Psalm 100 is the thankful doxology, named *Jubilate* (Latin for "O be joyful") by God's people.

◉ REQUEST THE SPIRIT'S HELP IN PRAYER

◉ READ AND REPEAT THE WORD

What words or phrases stick out to you? How do those words or phrases reveal the poet's purpose for the psalm? What effect does this psalm have on you as you meditate on it?

◉ RETURN TO THE LORD IN PRAYER

The text recalls the Common Doxology (*LSB* 805), sung to the tune "Old Hundredth." Forever joined together are the Church's much-loved song of praise and the psalm that calls for such praise. How often do we fail to make a joyful noise to the Lord! Yet even then, we know that He is good. In fact, He gave His Good Shepherd, Jesus, to make one day particularly good. We call it Good Friday.

LORD GOD, I THANK AND PRAISE YOU:

STEADFAST AND FAITHFUL LORD, I CONFESS TO YOU:

PRAYERS OF REQUEST
For members of my household to praise the Lord, I pray:

That I may praise You in my everyday work, I pray:

That my congregation may praise You, I pray:

That Your Church may bear witness to Your faithfulness in the world, I pray:

We are the sheep of Your hand, O Lord. Fill us with joyful praise as we seek to serve You. Amen.

PSALM 101

A Psalm of David.

1 I will sing of steadfast love and justice;
    to you, O LORD, I will make music.
2 I will ponder the way that is blameless.
    Oh when will you come to me?
  I will walk with integrity of heart
    within my house;
3 I will not set before my eyes
    anything that is worthless.
  I hate the work of those who fall away;
    it shall not cling to me.
4 A perverse heart shall be far from me;
    I will know nothing of evil.

5 Whoever slanders his neighbor secretly
    I will destroy.
  Whoever has a haughty look and an arrogant heart
    I will not endure.

6 I will look with favor on the faithful in the land,
    that they may dwell with me;
  he who walks in the way that is blameless
    shall minister to me.

7 No one who practices deceit
    shall dwell in my house;
  no one who utters lies
    shall continue before my eyes.

8 Morning by morning I will destroy
    all the wicked in the land,
  cutting off all the evildoers
    from the city of the LORD.

Psalm 101 appears to consist of a number of promises made by the king in a coronation ceremony. Perhaps it was intended to be used at an annual celebration of the king's enthronement. David is named as author, but even this greatest of Israel's kings could not live up to these lofty standards. Only David's greatest Son, Jesus Christ, perfectly fulfills the promises.

⊛ REQUEST THE SPIRIT'S HELP IN PRAYER

⊛ READ AND REPEAT THE WORD

What words or phrases stick out to you? How do those words or phrases reveal the poet's purpose for the psalm? What effect does this psalm have on you as you meditate on it?

⊛ RETURN TO THE LORD IN PRAYER

No nation has the kind of political leaders described here. Even King David failed miserably, as his many sins involving Bathsheba demonstrate (2 Samuel 11). No nation has the kind of citizens described here. Even we in the Church know we have not always been people of integrity. But Jesus was blameless, a man of perfect integrity. He comes to us with His royal and loyal love, shown perfectly on the cross. He brings us into the one nation made blameless in Christ's blood: the Church.

PRAYERS AND NOTES:

We pray, Lord, that You would come to us and make us people of integrity in Your Church and in our nation. Amen.

PSALM 102

A Prayer of one afflicted, when he is faint and pours out his complaint before the LORD.

1   Hear my prayer, O LORD;
     let my cry come to you!
2   Do not hide your face from me
     in the day of my distress!
   Incline your ear to me;
     answer me speedily in the day when I call!

3   For my days pass away like smoke,
     and my bones burn like a furnace.
4   My heart is struck down like grass and has withered;
     I forget to eat my bread.
5   Because of my loud groaning
     my bones cling to my flesh.
6   I am like a desert owl of the wilderness,
     like an owl[a] of the waste places;
7   I lie awake;
     I am like a lonely sparrow on the housetop.
8   All the day my enemies taunt me;
     those who deride me use my name for a curse.
9   For I eat ashes like bread
     and mingle tears with my drink,
10 because of your indignation and anger;
     for you have taken me up and thrown me down.
11 My days are like an evening shadow;
     I wither away like grass.

12 But you, O LORD, are enthroned forever;
     you are remembered throughout all generations.
13 You will arise and have pity on Zion;
     it is the time to favor her;
     the appointed time has come.
14 For your servants hold her stones dear
     and have pity on her dust.
15 Nations will fear the name of the LORD,
     and all the kings of the earth will fear your glory.
16 For the LORD builds up Zion;
     he appears in his glory;

a   Psalm 102:6 The precise identity of these birds is uncertain

17 he regards the prayer of the destitute
and does not despise their prayer.

18 Let this be recorded for a generation to come,
so that a people yet to be created may praise the LORD:
19 that he looked down from his holy height;
from heaven the LORD looked at the earth,
20 to hear the groans of the prisoners,
to set free those who were doomed to die,
21 that they may declare in Zion the name of the LORD,
and in Jerusalem his praise,
22 when peoples gather together,
and kingdoms, to worship the LORD.

23 He has broken my strength in midcourse;
he has shortened my days.
24 "O my God," I say, "take me not away
in the midst of my days—
you whose years endure
throughout all generations!"

25 Of old you laid the foundation of the earth,
and the heavens are the work of your hands.
26 They will perish, but you will remain;
they will all wear out like a garment.
You will change them like a robe, and they will pass away,
27 but you are the same, and your years have no end.
28 The children of your servants shall dwell secure;
their offspring shall be established before you.

Though the writer of this penitential psalm or psalm of repentance (see also Psalms 6; 32; 38; 51; 130; 143) is not identified, his condition is. He is faint, experiencing a weariness that envelops heart, body, and soul. He is near despair. Much has gone wrong in his personal life, including the humiliation of his nation, as seen in verses 14, 17, and 20. The lament still confesses a deep faith in the Lord's care and the security that comes from God's creative, eternal strength.

◉ REQUEST THE SPIRIT'S HELP IN PRAYER

◉ READ AND REPEAT THE WORD

What words or phrases stick out to you? How do those words or phrases reveal the poet's purpose for the psalm? What effect does this psalm have on you as you meditate on it?

◉ RETURN TO THE LORD IN PRAYER

The tears, fever, lost appetite, despair, and doubt in this psalm are eerily identical to what we go through when a personal crisis erupts in our life or a disaster rips through our town or nation. Yet it is written with confident hope because attention is turned to the God who listens to the pleas of the destitute. When you lament, turn your attention to God's answer to these prayers: Jesus Christ. He stepped into our world and took on our groans and death, restoring confident hope at the appointed time on Easter morning.

MERCIFUL LORD, THOUGH I AM SURROUNDED BY MANY TROUBLES, I THANK YOU:

MERCIFUL LORD, TRUSTING IN YOUR MERCY DESPITE MY MANY SINS, I CONFESS TO YOU:

MERCIFUL LORD, WHO ALONE PROVIDES ALL GOOD THINGS, I ALSO PRAY:

Risen Lord, establish the new Jerusalem for us forever.
Answer our prayers, in Your dear name. Alleluia! Amen.

The 102nd psalm is a psalm of prayer. In it the fathers of old—weary of laws, of sins, and of death—wholeheartedly yearn and call for the kingdom of grace promised in Christ. They ask that God yet again build up Zion and set in place her stones and dust, that He would yet again enter in and let His glory be seen in all kingdoms, that He would rescue His captives from sin and death so that they may come together and thank Him—that is, that they may worship Him in the true Zion—and the Old Testament come to an end.

For without Christ there is indeed nothing but strength broken in the middle of life and days cut short, that is, a miserable, short, wretched life from which the psalmist is reluctantly removed. But in His kingdom is eternal life, and His time has no end. He is the one who was before He created heaven and earth, and will again change and renew them. Therefore, He is outside of and over all time. His year has no end and there is no dying there. This kingdom we will gladly receive.
(Martin Luther)

PSALM 103

Of David.

1   Bless the LORD, O my soul,
       and all that is within me,
       bless his holy name!
2   Bless the LORD, O my soul,
       and forget not all his benefits,
3   who forgives all your iniquity,
       who heals all your diseases,
4   who redeems your life from the pit,
       who crowns you with steadfast love and mercy,
5   who satisfies you with good
       so that your youth is renewed like the eagle's.

6   The LORD works righteousness
       and justice for all who are oppressed.
7   He made known his ways to Moses,
       his acts to the people of Israel.
8   The LORD is merciful and gracious,
       slow to anger and abounding in steadfast love.
9   He will not always chide,
       nor will he keep his anger forever.
10   He does not deal with us according to our sins,
       nor repay us according to our iniquities.
11   For as high as the heavens are above the earth,
       so great is his steadfast love toward those who fear him;
12   as far as the east is from the west,
       so far does he remove our transgressions from us.
13   As a father shows compassion to his children,
       so the LORD shows compassion to those who fear him.
14   For he knows our frame;[a]
       he remembers that we are dust.

15   As for man, his days are like grass;
       he flourishes like a flower of the field;
16   for the wind passes over it, and it is gone,
       and its place knows it no more.
17   But the steadfast love of the LORD is from everlasting to ever-
       lasting on those who fear him,
       and his righteousness to children's children,

---

a   Psalm 103:14 Or *knows how we are formed*

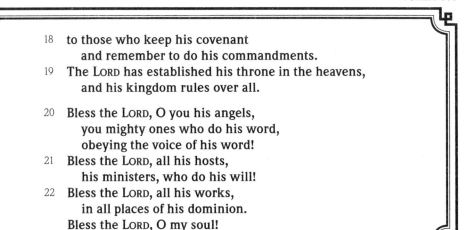

18   to those who keep his covenant
       and remember to do his commandments.
19   The LORD has established his throne in the heavens,
       and his kingdom rules over all.

20   Bless the LORD, O you his angels,
       you mighty ones who do his word,
       obeying the voice of his word!
21   Bless the LORD, all his hosts,
       his ministers, who do his will!
22   Bless the LORD, all his works,
       in all places of his dominion.
       Bless the LORD, O my soul!

Psalms 103–6 are united by their calls to praise the Lord and are a fitting conclusion to Book Four of the Psalter. While Psalm 103 is ascribed to King David, we cannot determine its particular time or situation.

⊛ REQUEST THE SPIRIT'S HELP IN PRAYER

⊛ READ AND REPEAT THE WORD

What words or phrases stick out to you? How do those words or phrases reveal the poet's purpose for the psalm? What effect does this psalm have on you as you meditate on it?

⊛ RETURN TO THE LORD IN PRAYER

How many times do we need God's forgiveness? It's impossible to count. Day after day, our transgressions should bring His anger. But over and over again, He removes our iniquities. Where are they sent? To the cross, where Jesus takes God's anger and gives us compassion instead.

PRAYERS:

> *"Bless the LORD, O my soul" (v. 1)! I thank You for redeeming*
> *me from death so that I may join the angelic hosts in praising*
> *Your holy name from everlasting to everlasting. Amen.*

1   Bless the LORD, O my soul!
     O LORD my God, you are very great!
    You are clothed with splendor and majesty,
2   covering yourself with light as with a garment,
     stretching out the heavens like a tent.
3   He lays the beams of his chambers on the waters;
    he makes the clouds his chariot;
     he rides on the wings of the wind;
4   he makes his messengers winds,
     his ministers a flaming fire.

5   He set the earth on its foundations,
     so that it should never be moved.
6   You covered it with the deep as with a garment;
     the waters stood above the mountains.
7   At your rebuke they fled;
     at the sound of your thunder they took to flight.
8   The mountains rose, the valleys sank down
     to the place that you appointed for them.
9   You set a boundary that they may not pass,
     so that they might not again cover the earth.

10   You make springs gush forth in the valleys;
     they flow between the hills;
11   they give drink to every beast of the field;
     the wild donkeys quench their thirst.
12   Beside them the birds of the heavens dwell;
     they sing among the branches.
13   From your lofty abode you water the mountains;
     the earth is satisfied with the fruit of your work.

14   You cause the grass to grow for the livestock
     and plants for man to cultivate,
    that he may bring forth food from the earth
15   and wine to gladden the heart of man,
    oil to make his face shine
     and bread to strengthen man's heart.

16   The trees of the LORD are watered abundantly,
     the cedars of Lebanon that he planted.
17   In them the birds build their nests;
     the stork has her home in the fir trees.
18   The high mountains are for the wild goats;
     the rocks are a refuge for the rock badgers.

19 He made the moon to mark the seasons;[a]
    the sun knows its time for setting.
20 You make darkness, and it is night,
    when all the beasts of the forest creep about.
21 The young lions roar for their prey,
    seeking their food from God.
22 When the sun rises, they steal away
    and lie down in their dens.
23 Man goes out to his work
    and to his labor until the evening.

24 O Lord, how manifold are your works!
    In wisdom have you made them all;
    the earth is full of your creatures.
25 Here is the sea, great and wide,
    which teems with creatures innumerable,
    living things both small and great.
26 There go the ships,
    and Leviathan, which you formed to play in it.[b]

27 These all look to you,
    to give them their food in due season.
28 When you give it to them, they gather it up;
    when you open your hand, they are filled with good things.
29 When you hide your face, they are dismayed;
    when you take away their breath, they die
    and return to their dust.
30 When you send forth your Spirit,[c] they are created,
    and you renew the face of the ground.

31 May the glory of the Lord endure forever;
    may the Lord rejoice in his works,
32 who looks on the earth and it trembles,
    who touches the mountains and they smoke!
33 I will sing to the Lord as long as I live;
    I will sing praise to my God while I have being.
34 May my meditation be pleasing to him,
    for I rejoice in the Lord.
35 Let sinners be consumed from the earth,
    and let the wicked be no more!
Bless the Lord, O my soul!
Praise the Lord!

a   Psalm 104:19 Or *the appointed times* (compare Genesis 1:14)
b   Psalm 104:26 Or *you formed to play with*
c   Psalm 104:30 Or *breath*

As in Psalm 103, the psalmist summons himself to praise the Lord. The focus, however, is on God as Creator and He who preserves creation. Genesis 1 is background, but the orderly description of creation from Genesis becomes a more spontaneous display of the wonders of God's creation. This corresponds to Luther, who wrote, "He causes all created things to serve for the uses and necessities of life" (Large Catechism II 14). The psalm became part of the temple worship and could have been used on a festival day, such as the New Year. (Similar themes are found in the Egyptian Hymn to the Aten). Lutheran scholar Martin Chemnitz commented, "There is a progression in creation, as indicated by the distinction noted in Genesis 1. No more appropriate division of the process of creation can be developed than the six day cycle of Moses" (*LTh* 1:162).

⊗ REQUEST THE SPIRIT'S HELP IN PRAYER

⊗ READ AND REPEAT THE WORD

What words or phrases stick out to you? How do those words or phrases reveal the poet's purpose for the psalm? What effect does this psalm have on you as you meditate on it?

⊗ RETURN TO THE LORD IN PRAYER

More and more, we hear about nature with no mention of the Creator. Visit a museum, read a science textbook, or watch a nature program, and you will see everything explained as some incredibly long process by which all life has evolved into what we see today. Yet God is indeed Creator of all. He continues to care for His world. Remember the word Jesus spoke over a violent storm: "Peace! Be still!" (Mark 4:39). And all was calm. Even death cannot compare to God's power—even the stone obeyed His command and rolled away from the tomb on Easter morning.

PRAYERS:

> *Lord, we make the bold confession that You in Your wisdom made the earth and all its creatures and continue to sustain it. Praise the Lord. Amen.*

The 104th psalm is a psalm of thanks for all the works that God had accomplished in heaven and on earth, beyond those done for us here on earth. He has surely ordered all things according to a wise place to produce works, fruits, and crops. The psalmist recounts these one after the other: the heavens—full of light and outstretched as a tapestry without post or rafters; the clouds—an arch without foundation or pillar; the wind flying without wings; the angels going and coming, appearing like a wind or a flame.

Thus sings the psalmist. He finds his desires and joy in God's creations, which are so wonderfully made and so beautifully ordered together. But who pays attention to this or sees that this is so? Only faith and the Spirit. (Martin Luther)

PSALM 105

1   Oh give thanks to the LORD; call upon his name;
    make known his deeds among the peoples!
2   Sing to him, sing praises to him;
    tell of all his wondrous works!
3   Glory in his holy name;
    let the hearts of those who seek the LORD rejoice!
4   Seek the LORD and his strength;
    seek his presence continually!
5   Remember the wondrous works that he has done,
    his miracles, and the judgments he uttered,
6   O offspring of Abraham, his servant,
    children of Jacob, his chosen ones!

7   He is the LORD our God;
    his judgments are in all the earth.
8   He remembers his covenant forever,
    the word that he commanded, for a thousand generations,
9   the covenant that he made with Abraham,
    his sworn promise to Isaac,
10 which he confirmed to Jacob as a statute,
    to Israel as an everlasting covenant,
11 saying, "To you I will give the land of Canaan
    as your portion for an inheritance."

12 When they were few in number,
    of little account, and sojourners in it,
13 wandering from nation to nation,
    from one kingdom to another people,
14 he allowed no one to oppress them;
    he rebuked kings on their account,
15 saying, "Touch not my anointed ones,
    do my prophets no harm!"

16 When he summoned a famine on the land
    and broke all supply[a] of bread,
17 he had sent a man ahead of them,
    Joseph, who was sold as a slave.
18 His feet were hurt with fetters;
    his neck was put in a collar of iron;

a   Psalm 105:16 Hebrew *staff*

19 until what he had said came to pass,
   the word of the LORD tested him.
20 The king sent and released him;
   the ruler of the peoples set him free;
21 he made him lord of his house
   and ruler of all his possessions,
22 to bind^b his princes at his pleasure
   and to teach his elders wisdom.

23 Then Israel came to Egypt;
   Jacob sojourned in the land of Ham.
24 And the LORD made his people very fruitful
   and made them stronger than their foes.
25 He turned their hearts to hate his people,
   to deal craftily with his servants.

26 He sent Moses, his servant,
   and Aaron, whom he had chosen.
27 They performed his signs among them
   and miracles in the land of Ham.
28 He sent darkness, and made the land dark;
   they did not rebel^c against his words.
29 He turned their waters into blood
   and caused their fish to die.
30 Their land swarmed with frogs,
   even in the chambers of their kings.
31 He spoke, and there came swarms of flies,
   and gnats throughout their country.
32 He gave them hail for rain,
   and fiery lightning bolts through their land.
33 He struck down their vines and fig trees,
   and shattered the trees of their country.
34 He spoke, and the locusts came,
   young locusts without number,
35 which devoured all the vegetation in their land
   and ate up the fruit of their ground.
36 He struck down all the firstborn in their land,
   the firstfruits of all their strength.

37 Then he brought out Israel with silver and gold,
   and there was none among his tribes who stumbled.
38 Egypt was glad when they departed,
   for dread of them had fallen upon it.

b   Psalm 105:22 Septuagint, Syriac, Jerome *instruct*
c   Psalm 105:28 Septuagint, Syriac omit *not*

39 He spread a cloud for a covering,
   and fire to give light by night.
40 They asked, and he brought quail,
   and gave them bread from heaven in abundance.
41 He opened the rock, and water gushed out;
   it flowed through the desert like a river.
42 For he remembered his holy promise,
   and Abraham, his servant.

43 So he brought his people out with joy,
   his chosen ones with singing.
44 And he gave them the lands of the nations,
   and they took possession of the fruit of the peoples' toil,
45 that they might keep his statutes
   and observe his laws.
   Praise the LORD!

Psalms 105 and 106 stand together as they recall God's promise to Abraham to bring Israel into the Promised Land and the mighty ways He kept that promise. Psalm 105 focuses on God's grace, while Psalm 106 describes the people's rebellion and their continued need for mercy. Psalm 105:1–15 appears in 1 Chronicles 16:8–22 at the joyous occasion when David brought the ark to Jerusalem, indicating it was used in worship on festival occasions celebrating the covenant God made with His people.

⊛ REQUEST THE SPIRIT'S HELP IN PRAYER

⊛ READ AND REPEAT THE WORD

What words or phrases stick out to you? How do those words or phrases reveal the poet's purpose for the psalm? What effect does this psalm have on you as you meditate on it?

⊛ RETURN TO THE LORD IN PRAYER

God frees His people from slavery. Christ has rescued us from sin and its eternal punishment. All God's promises find their fulfillment in Jesus, who hung on the cross and then ushered in a new era by rising from the grave. Abraham's true descendants are those whose faith in Christ is counted to them as righteousness (Galatians 3:6–9). Gathered together by Jesus, we now belong to the Church, which knows no geographical boundaries.

LORD GOD, I THANK YOU:

MERCIFUL GOD, I CONFESS TO YOU:

PRAYERS OF REQUEST
For wisdom to trust You in my household, I especially pray:

For my work and livelihood, I pray:

For my congregation, I pray:

For wisdom in loving my neighbor in the world, I pray:

Praise the Lord, for in Christ we received the
blessings promised to Abraham. Amen.

PSALM 106

1   Praise the LORD!
    Oh give thanks to the LORD, for he is good,
      for his steadfast love endures forever!
2   Who can utter the mighty deeds of the LORD,
      or declare all his praise?
3   Blessed are they who observe justice,
      who do righteousness at all times!

4   Remember me, O LORD, when you show favor to your people;
      help me when you save them,[a]
5   that I may look upon the prosperity of your chosen ones,
      that I may rejoice in the gladness of your nation,
      that I may glory with your inheritance.

6   Both we and our fathers have sinned;
      we have committed iniquity; we have done wickedness.
7   Our fathers, when they were in Egypt,
      did not consider your wondrous works;
      they did not remember the abundance of your steadfast love,
      but rebelled by the sea, at the Red Sea.
8   Yet he saved them for his name's sake,
      that he might make known his mighty power.
9   He rebuked the Red Sea, and it became dry,
      and he led them through the deep as through a desert.
10   So he saved them from the hand of the foe
      and redeemed them from the power of the enemy.
11   And the waters covered their adversaries;
      not one of them was left.
12   Then they believed his words;
      they sang his praise.

13   But they soon forgot his works;
      they did not wait for his counsel.
14   But they had a wanton craving in the wilderness,
      and put God to the test in the desert;
15   he gave them what they asked,
      but sent a wasting disease among them.

---

a   Psalm 106:4 Or *Remember me, O LORD, with the favor you show to your people; help me with your salvation*

16 When men in the camp were jealous of Moses
   and Aaron, the holy one of the LORD,
17 the earth opened and swallowed up Dathan,
   and covered the company of Abiram.
18 Fire also broke out in their company;
   the flame burned up the wicked.

19 They made a calf in Horeb
   and worshiped a metal image.
20 They exchanged the glory of God[b]
   for the image of an ox that eats grass.
21 They forgot God, their Savior,
   who had done great things in Egypt,
22 wondrous works in the land of Ham,
   and awesome deeds by the Red Sea.
23 Therefore he said he would destroy them—
   had not Moses, his chosen one,
   stood in the breach before him,
   to turn away his wrath from destroying them.

24 Then they despised the pleasant land,
   having no faith in his promise.
25 They murmured in their tents,
   and did not obey the voice of the LORD.
26 Therefore he raised his hand and swore to them
   that he would make them fall in the wilderness,
27 and would make their offspring fall among the nations,
   scattering them among the lands.

28 Then they yoked themselves to the Baal of Peor,
   and ate sacrifices offered to the dead;
29 they provoked the LORD to anger with their deeds,
   and a plague broke out among them.
30 Then Phinehas stood up and intervened,
   and the plague was stayed.
31 And that was counted to him as righteousness
   from generation to generation forever.

32 They angered him at the waters of Meribah,
   and it went ill with Moses on their account,
33 for they made his spirit bitter,[c]
   and he spoke rashly with his lips.

b   Psalm 106:20 Hebrew *exchanged their glory*
c   Psalm 106:33 Or *they rebelled against God's Spirit*

34 They did not destroy the peoples,
    as the Lord commanded them,
35 but they mixed with the nations
    and learned to do as they did.
36 They served their idols,
    which became a snare to them.
37 They sacrificed their sons
    and their daughters to the demons;
38 they poured out innocent blood,
    the blood of their sons and daughters,
  whom they sacrificed to the idols of Canaan,
    and the land was polluted with blood.
39 Thus they became unclean by their acts,
    and played the whore in their deeds.

40 Then the anger of the Lord was kindled against his people,
    and he abhorred his heritage;
41 he gave them into the hand of the nations,
    so that those who hated them ruled over them.
42 Their enemies oppressed them,
    and they were brought into subjection under their power.
43 Many times he delivered them,
    but they were rebellious in their purposes
    and were brought low through their iniquity.

44 Nevertheless, he looked upon their distress,
    when he heard their cry.
45 For their sake he remembered his covenant,
    and relented according to the abundance of his
    steadfast love.
46 He caused them to be pitied
    by all those who held them captive.

47 Save us, O Lord our God,
    and gather us from among the nations,
  that we may give thanks to your holy name
    and glory in your praise.

48 Blessed be the Lord, the God of Israel,
    from everlasting to everlasting!
  And let all the people say, "Amen!"
    Praise the Lord!

Psalm 106 makes up the last psalm in Book Four. Psalms 105 and 106 begin and end with praise to the Lord. Although Psalm 106 begins with praise and thanksgiving, it moves to confession. Luther wrote that "this psalm teaches the true praise of divine goodness, namely, that to confess one's own evil to God is to give thanks to the Lord, for He is good" (AE 11:345). Psalm 106 covers many of the same historical events as Psalm 105, but it praises the Lord for His wonderful salvation of a sinful people. Since verse 47 appeals to the Lord to gather His people from among the nations, many think Psalm 106 was written after the Babylonian exile. However, verses 1 and 47–48 are included in David's hymn of thanksgiving (from 1 Chronicles 16:34–36), when the ark was returned to Israel. This, along with its place at the conclusion of Book Four, indicates that it might be an earlier composition.

⊛ REQUEST THE SPIRIT'S HELP IN PRAYER

⊛ READ AND REPEAT THE WORD

What words or phrases stick out to you? How do those words or phrases reveal the poet's purpose for the psalm? What effect does this psalm have on you as you meditate on it?

⊛ RETURN TO THE LORD IN PRAYER

One of the most important words in this psalm is "nevertheless" (v. 44). Despite Israel's persistent disobedience, God consistently upheld His promises and saved them. As we struggle with temptation (Galatians 5:17), we can be sure that God will remain faithful (2 Timothy 2:13), granting us true repentance and new life in Christ.

PRAYERS:

> *O Lord, we must also confess with ancient Israel*
> *that we have sinned. Nevertheless, You have faithfully*
> *saved us through Jesus' obedience, suffering, death,*
> *and resurrection. Praise to the Lord! Amen.*

PSALM 107

1   Oh give thanks to the LORD, for he is good,
     for his steadfast love endures forever!
2   Let the redeemed of the LORD say so,
     whom he has redeemed from trouble[a]
3   and gathered in from the lands,
     from the east and from the west,
     from the north and from the south.

4   Some wandered in desert wastes,
     finding no way to a city to dwell in;
5   hungry and thirsty,
     their soul fainted within them.
6   Then they cried to the LORD in their trouble,
     and he delivered them from their distress.
7   He led them by a straight way
     till they reached a city to dwell in.
8   Let them thank the LORD for his steadfast love,
     for his wondrous works to the children of man!
9   For he satisfies the longing soul,
     and the hungry soul he fills with good things.

10   Some sat in darkness and in the shadow of death,
     prisoners in affliction and in irons,
11   for they had rebelled against the words of God,
     and spurned the counsel of the Most High.
12   So he bowed their hearts down with hard labor;
     they fell down, with none to help.
13   Then they cried to the LORD in their trouble,
     and he delivered them from their distress.
14   He brought them out of darkness and the shadow of death,
     and burst their bonds apart.
15   Let them thank the LORD for his steadfast love,
     for his wondrous works to the children of man!
16   For he shatters the doors of bronze
     and cuts in two the bars of iron.

17   Some were fools through their sinful ways,
     and because of their iniquities suffered affliction;
18   they loathed any kind of food,
     and they drew near to the gates of death.

---

a   Psalm 107:2 Or *from the hand of the foe*

19   Then they cried to the LORD in their trouble,
      and he delivered them from their distress.
20   He sent out his word and healed them,
      and delivered them from their destruction.
21   Let them thank the LORD for his steadfast love,
      for his wondrous works to the children of man!
22   And let them offer sacrifices of thanksgiving,
      and tell of his deeds in songs of joy!

23   Some went down to the sea in ships,
      doing business on the great waters;
24   they saw the deeds of the LORD,
      his wondrous works in the deep.
25   For he commanded and raised the stormy wind,
      which lifted up the waves of the sea.
26   They mounted up to heaven; they went down to the depths;
      their courage melted away in their evil plight;
27   they reeled and staggered like drunken men
      and were at their wits' end.[b]
28   Then they cried to the LORD in their trouble,
      and he delivered them from their distress.
29   He made the storm be still,
      and the waves of the sea were hushed.
30   Then they were glad that the waters[c] were quiet,
      and he brought them to their desired haven.
31   Let them thank the LORD for his steadfast love,
      for his wondrous works to the children of man!
32   Let them extol him in the congregation of the people,
      and praise him in the assembly of the elders.

33   He turns rivers into a desert,
      springs of water into thirsty ground,
34   a fruitful land into a salty waste,
      because of the evil of its inhabitants.
35   He turns a desert into pools of water,
      a parched land into springs of water.
36   And there he lets the hungry dwell,
      and they establish a city to live in;
37   they sow fields and plant vineyards
      and get a fruitful yield.
38   By his blessing they multiply greatly,
      and he does not let their livestock diminish.

b   Psalm 107:27 Hebrew *and all their wisdom was swallowed up*
c   Psalm 107:30 Hebrew *they*

39　When they are diminished and brought low
　　　through oppression, evil, and sorrow,
40　he pours contempt on princes
　　　and makes them wander in trackless wastes;
41　but he raises up the needy out of affliction
　　　and makes their families like flocks.
42　The upright see it and are glad,
　　　and all wickedness shuts its mouth.

43　Whoever is wise, let him attend to these things;
　　　let them consider the steadfast love of the LORD.

Psalms 105–7 are related by their focus on different aspects of Israel's history: Psalm 105 focuses on the early history of Israel, Psalm 106 focuses on Israel from the time of the exodus to the exile, and Psalm 107—the psalm for this meditation—focuses on the time of restoration from the exile.

⊛ REQUEST THE SPIRIT'S HELP IN PRAYER

⊛ READ AND REPEAT THE WORD

What words or phrases stick out to you? How do those words or phrases reveal the poet's purpose for the psalm? What effect does this psalm have on you as you meditate on it?

⊛ RETURN TO THE LORD IN PRAYER

History unfolds the prevailing deeds of God's steadfast love. Because of sin, this world is chaotic and inhospitable. But in Jesus, God has restored the peace we long for. Our sins are forgiven, and where there is forgiveness of sins, there is life and every blessing.

LORD GOD, I THANK YOU:

MERCIFUL GOD, I CONFESS TO YOU:

PRAYERS OF REQUEST
For wisdom to trust You in my household, I especially pray:

For my work and livelihood, I pray:

For my congregation, I pray:

For wisdom in loving my neighbor in the world, I pray:

O Lord, do not let us be overwhelmed by the confusion around us. Remind us of Your steadfast love that delivers us. Thank You, Jesus. Amen.

PSALM 108

A Song. A Psalm of David.

1   My heart is steadfast, O God!
     I will sing and make melody with all my being![a]
2   Awake, O harp and lyre!
     I will awake the dawn!
3   I will give thanks to you, O LORD, among the peoples;
     I will sing praises to you among the nations.
4   For your steadfast love is great above the heavens;
     your faithfulness reaches to the clouds.

5   Be exalted, O God, above the heavens!
     Let your glory be over all the earth!
6   That your beloved ones may be delivered,
     give salvation by your right hand and answer me!

7   God has promised in his holiness:[b]
     "With exultation I will divide up Shechem
     and portion out the Valley of Succoth.
8   Gilead is mine; Manasseh is mine;
     Ephraim is my helmet,
     Judah my scepter.
9   Moab is my washbasin;
     upon Edom I cast my shoe;
     over Philistia I shout in triumph."

10   Who will bring me to the fortified city?
     Who will lead me to Edom?
11   Have you not rejected us, O God?
     You do not go out, O God, with our armies.
12   Oh grant us help against the foe,
     for vain is the salvation of man!
13   With God we shall do valiantly;
     it is he who will tread down our foes.

a   Psalm 108:1 Hebrew *with my glory*
b   Psalm 108:7 Or *sanctuary*

Psalm 108 is surprisingly drawn from Psalm 57:7–11 and Psalm 60:5–12, with a few variations. Each of these psalms of David was a response to stress (being hunted in Psalm 57 and being defeated in Psalm 60). Psalm 108 combines the sections that emphasize God's help. Interpreters are not sure why these two psalms are pieced together here. The psalm may reflect an unresolved problem with Edom following the exile, as Edom had rejoiced at the downfall of Judah (as noted in Psalm 137:7).

⚬ REQUEST THE SPIRIT'S HELP IN PRAYER

⚬ READ AND REPEAT THE WORD

What words or phrases stick out to you? How do those words or phrases reveal the poet's purpose for the psalm? What effect does this psalm have on you as you meditate on it?

⚬ RETURN TO THE LORD IN PRAYER

From time to time, old defeats come back to haunt us. Perhaps a future challenge reminds us of a past failure. At times such as this, we remember that God, who delivered us in the past, is with us in the present and the future.

LORD GOD, I THANK AND PRAISE YOU:

STEADFAST AND FAITHFUL LORD, I CONFESS TO YOU:

PRAYERS OF REQUEST
For members of my household, I pray:

For faithfulness in my everyday work, I pray:

For my congregation, I pray:

For my neighbor in the world, I pray:

O Lord, Satan would remind me of my past failures. Forgive all my sins—past, present, and future. "Keep steady my steps according to Your promise, and let no iniquity get dominion over me" (Psalm 119:133). Amen.

The 108th psalm is a psalm of thanks, with words almost like Psalm 60, in which the psalmist gives thanks for God's kingdom. Already in the first verse, the psalm exalts the kingdom of Christ and prays that God will establish His kingdom in all the world and accordingly bring David's kingdom to its proper, final, full station. For David had only a slight, partial piece (compared to the whole world) of that which was promised to come to him. As Isaiah 9:7 also says, He will reign "on the throne of David and over his kingdom." (Martin Luther)

TYPES OF SIN

The three most common expressions in the Bible for disobedience to God's will are (1) *transgressions*, (2) *iniquity*, and (3) *sin*. Many of the psalms talk about these different ways people disobey God's will. Each of these is associated with a different action for removing sin:

1. *Transgressions* are like an ugly blotch on a page or an entry of a debt that must be blotted out or expunged from the record (Isaiah 43:25; Psalm 109:14; Numbers 5:23; Acts 3:19; Colossians 2:14).

2. *Iniquity* is like a filthy garment that must be washed thoroughly. In ancient times, this required vigorous action. Clothes were beaten on flat stones in a stream or were trampled to loosen the dirt (for more on ceremonial cleanness, see Exodus 19:10).

3. *Sin* is a stain that "lye" and "much soap" cannot remove (Jeremiah 2:22); it yields only to God's cleansing action. The blood of animals was applied to the altar in Old Testament worship to symbolize that it was hallowed "from the uncleannesses of the people of Israel" (Leviticus 16:19).

The blood of bulls and goats did not have the power to do what became a reality in the blood of Jesus, which "cleanses us from all sin" and "from all unrighteousness" (1 John 1:7, 9; see also Hebrews 10:14).

To the choirmaster. A Psalm of David.

1   Be not silent, O God of my praise!
2   For wicked and deceitful mouths are opened against me,
     speaking against me with lying tongues.
3   They encircle me with words of hate,
     and attack me without cause.
4   In return for my love they accuse me,
     but I give myself to prayer.[a]
5   So they reward me evil for good,
     and hatred for my love.

6   Appoint a wicked man against him;
     let an accuser stand at his right hand.
7   When he is tried, let him come forth guilty;
     let his prayer be counted as sin!
8   May his days be few;
     may another take his office!
9   May his children be fatherless
     and his wife a widow!
10 May his children wander about and beg,
     seeking food far from the ruins they inhabit!
11 May the creditor seize all that he has;
     may strangers plunder the fruits of his toil!
12 Let there be none to extend kindness to him,
     nor any to pity his fatherless children!
13 May his posterity be cut off;
     may his name be blotted out in the second generation!
14 May the iniquity of his fathers be remembered before
    the LORD,
     and let not the sin of his mother be blotted out!
15 Let them be before the LORD continually,
     that he may cut off the memory of them from the earth!

16 For he did not remember to show kindness,
     but pursued the poor and needy
     and the brokenhearted, to put them to death.
17 He loved to curse; let curses come[b] upon him!
     He did not delight in blessing; may it be far[c] from him!

a   Psalm 109:4 Hebrew *but I am prayer*
b   Psalm 109:17 Revocalization; Masoretic Text *curses have come*
c   Psalm 109:17 Revocalization; Masoretic Text *it is far*

18 He clothed himself with cursing as his coat;
      may it soak[d] into his body like water,
      like oil into his bones!
19 May it be like a garment that he wraps around him,
      like a belt that he puts on every day!
20 May this be the reward of my accusers from the LORD,
      of those who speak evil against my life!

21 But you, O GOD my Lord,
      deal on my behalf for your name's sake;
      because your steadfast love is good, deliver me!
22 For I am poor and needy,
      and my heart is stricken within me.
23 I am gone like a shadow at evening;
      I am shaken off like a locust.
24 My knees are weak through fasting;
      my body has become gaunt, with no fat.
25 I am an object of scorn to my accusers;
      when they see me, they wag their heads.

26 Help me, O LORD my God!
      Save me according to your steadfast love!
27 Let them know that this is your hand;
      you, O LORD, have done it!
28 Let them curse, but you will bless!
      They arise and are put to shame, but your servant will
      be glad!
29 May my accusers be clothed with dishonor;
      may they be wrapped in their own shame as in a cloak!

30 With my mouth I will give great thanks to the LORD;
      I will praise him in the midst of the throng.
31 For he stands at the right hand of the needy one,
      to save him from those who condemn his soul to death.

d   Psalm 109:18 Revocalization; Masoretic Text *it has soaked*

Falsely accused, David responds by calling for judgment and punishment. Imprecatory (cursing) psalms can be difficult to harmonize with Jesus' command to "love your enemies" (Matthew 5:44). However, we do not know the hearts of David's enemies. His calls for destruction are his prayers for salvation. If he is to be saved, and if they refuse to repent, then they must be defeated. He believes that his enemies have removed themselves beyond the reach of God's grace. Ultimately, all who persecute Christ and His followers and refuse to repent will experience God's judgment.

⊛ REQUEST THE SPIRIT'S HELP IN PRAYER

⊛ READ AND REPEAT THE WORD

What words or phrases stick out to you? How do those words or phrases reveal the poet's purpose for the psalm? What effect does this psalm have on you as you meditate on it?

⊛ RETURN TO THE LORD IN PRAYER

As we look to God for salvation, we know His justice will prevail upon our enemies who remain in sin. He declares us justified and His dear children through Jesus.

PRAYERS:

In the face of "the mystery of lawlessness" (2 Thessalonians 2:7),
we must sometimes cry out with the saints in heaven,
"O Sovereign Lord, holy and true, how long before You will
judge and avenge our blood on those who dwell on the earth?"
(Revelation 6:10). Have mercy for Jesus' sake. Amen.

The 109th psalm is a psalm of prayer, prayed in the person of Christ against Judas, His betrayer, and against the Jews, His crucifiers. (Martin Luther)

In Acts 1:20 St. Peter applied this psalm to Judas when they were selecting Matthias to replace him. He did not mean to say that the psalm speaks only about Judas. . . . The psalm begins with Judas and then extends to everyone of Judas' ilk, to all schismatics and persecutors of the Word of Christ; for they always slander the truth and persecute the genuine Christians. (From Luther's commentary on the four psalms of comfort; AE 14:257)

Christ Himself complains of these matters in Psalm 109:2. . . . For thus the enemies of the truth are accustomed to obscure, traduce, and corrupt the fruits and gains of the Gospel and of salvation among simple and godly hearers. . . . [These enemies] adorn themselves with false and counterfeit praises; but they defame us, in order to make us more obnoxious to those who are strangers to our doctrine. (From Luther's lectures on Genesis 39:13–15; AE 7:92)

PSALM 110

A Psalm of David.

1 The Lord says to my Lord:
    "Sit at my right hand,
    until I make your enemies your footstool."

2 The Lord sends forth from Zion
    your mighty scepter.
    Rule in the midst of your enemies!
3 Your people will offer themselves freely
    on the day of your power,[a]
    in holy garments;[b]
    from the womb of the morning,
    the dew of your youth will be yours.[c]
4 The Lord has sworn
    and will not change his mind,
    "You are a priest forever
    after the order of Melchizedek."

5 The Lord is at your right hand;
    he will shatter kings on the day of his wrath.
6 He will execute judgment among the nations,
    filling them with corpses;
    he will shatter chiefs[d]
    over the wide earth.
7 He will drink from the brook by the way;
    therefore he will lift up his head.

---

a Psalm 110:3 Or *on the day you lead your forces*
b Psalm 110:3 Masoretic Text; some Hebrew manuscripts and Jerome *on the holy mountains*
c Psalm 110:3 The meaning of the Hebrew is uncertain
d Psalm 110:6 Or *the head*

Psalm 110 is one the most quoted of all psalms, used seventeen times in the New Testament! Jesus quoted it (Mark 12:36) to show that He was the Messiah—David's Lord, not just David's descendant. Critics have complained that its meaning is hindered by textual problems. Yet Christ and the apostles interpret and apply the psalm boldly. Of this psalm, the Church Father Augustine declared, "We are utterly unable to doubt that Christ is announced in the Psalm, since we are now Christians, and believe the Gospel" (*NPNF*1 8:541).

⚜ REQUEST THE SPIRIT'S HELP IN PRAYER

⚜ READ AND REPEAT THE WORD

What words or phrases stick out to you? How do those words or phrases reveal the poet's purpose for the psalm? What effect does this psalm have on you as you meditate on it?

⚜ RETURN TO THE LORD IN PRAYER

The world looks for the visible manifestation of God. David sees that manifestation prophetically in one of his future descendants. In this second Lord, the divine and the human become one in order to destroy the enemies of God and of His creation.

LORD GOD, KING OF ALL CREATION, I THANK YOU:

FAITHFUL LORD, I CONFESS TO YOU:

PRAYERS OF REQUEST
For members of my household, I pray:

For faithfulness in my everyday work, I pray:

For my congregation, I pray:

For my neighbor in the world, I pray:

Dear Jesus, David's Lord and mine, I thank You that
You have come to be my Priest who sacrifices all for my
sins and to be my King to deliver me from evil. Amen.

PSALM 111

1 ᵃPraise the LORD!
   I will give thanks to the LORD with my whole heart,
      in the company of the upright, in the congregation.
2 Great are the works of the LORD,
      studied by all who delight in them.
3 Full of splendor and majesty is his work,
      and his righteousness endures forever.
4 He has caused his wondrous works to be remembered;
      the LORD is gracious and merciful.
5 He provides food for those who fear him;
      he remembers his covenant forever.
6 He has shown his people the power of his works,
      in giving them the inheritance of the nations.
7 The works of his hands are faithful and just;
      all his precepts are trustworthy;
8 they are established forever and ever,
      to be performed with faithfulness and uprightness.
9 He sent redemption to his people;
      he has commanded his covenant forever.
      Holy and awesome is his name!
10 The fear of the LORD is the beginning of wisdom;
      all those who practice it have a good understanding.
      His praise endures forever!

---

a   Psalm 111:1 This psalm is an acrostic poem, each line beginning with the successive letters of the Hebrew alphabet

In a very straightforward and powerful way, Psalm 111 praises the Lord for His words and works.

- ⊕ REQUEST THE SPIRIT'S HELP IN PRAYER

- ⊕ READ AND REPEAT THE WORD

What words or phrases stick out to you? How do those words or phrases reveal the poet's purpose for the psalm? What effect does this psalm have on you as you meditate on it?

- ⊕ RETURN TO THE LORD IN PRAYER

Praise of God for His works toward us is essential to the Christian life. We thank Him not only for His many earthly blessings but especially for the gifts of forgiveness, life, and salvation poured out on His people through Christ. Luther suggested that the words of verse 4, "The LORD is gracious and merciful," should be painted in golden letters around a portrait of the Lord's Supper (AE 13:375), for in this Supper, Christians continue to remember both the words and works of the Lord.

LORD GOD, I THANK AND PRAISE YOU:

REDEEMING GOD, I CONFESS TO YOU:

PRAYERS OF REQUEST
For members of my household to praise the Lord, I pray:

That I may praise You in my everyday work, I pray:

That my congregation may praise You, I pray:

That Your Church may bear witness to Your faithfulness in the world, I pray:

Gracious and merciful Lord, we look to You for the remission of our sins in Jesus, who speaks Your faithful words and performs the mighty work of our salvation. Alleluia! Amen.

PSALM 112

1   aPraise the LORD!
    Blessed is the man who fears the LORD,
        who greatly delights in his commandments!
2   His offspring will be mighty in the land;
        the generation of the upright will be blessed.
3   Wealth and riches are in his house,
        and his righteousness endures forever.
4   Light dawns in the darkness for the upright;
        he is gracious, merciful, and righteous.
5   It is well with the man who deals generously and lends;
        who conducts his affairs with justice.
6   For the righteous will never be moved;
        he will be remembered forever.
7   He is not afraid of bad news;
        his heart is firm, trusting in the LORD.
8   His heart is steady;b he will not be afraid,
        until he looks in triumph on his adversaries.
9   He has distributed freely; he has given to the poor;
        his righteousness endures forever;
        his horn is exalted in honor.
10 The wicked man sees it and is angry;
        he gnashes his teeth and melts away;
        the desire of the wicked will perish!

---

a   Psalm 112:1 This psalm is an acrostic poem, each line beginning with the successive letters of the Hebrew alphabet
b   Psalm 112:8 Or *established* (compare 111:8)

The emphasis in Psalm 112 is on the person who fears the Lord by keeping in mind His words and works.

❋ REQUEST THE SPIRIT'S HELP IN PRAYER

❋ READ AND REPEAT THE WORD

What words or phrases stick out to you? How do those words or phrases reveal the poet's purpose for the psalm? What effect does this psalm have on you as you meditate on it?

....

....

....

....

....

....

❋ RETURN TO THE LORD IN PRAYER

Another psalm of praise in a series of short psalms of praise, Psalm 112 adds a particular emphasis. The apostle Paul quotes verse 9 in 2 Corinthians 9:9, the great stewardship chapter of that epistle. The fear of the Lord leads us in the wisdom of generosity and contentment. As we go about our vocations as God's redeemed people, may we constantly seek to fear, love, and trust in God above all things (as emphasized in the First Commandment), so that we may live generous, content, and peaceful lives as God's people in the world.

LORD GOD, I THANK YOU FOR YOUR GIFTS TO ME:

....

....

GENEROUS LORD, WHO FORGIVES THE DEBT OF SIN THROUGH CHRIST, I CONFESS TO YOU:

....

....

MIGHTY GOD, I ALSO BRING MY OTHER PRAYERS TO YOU TODAY:

....

....

*O Lord, give us a firm heart to trust in You,
subduing our selfish nature in repentance and
reviving us in Your righteousness. Amen.*

PSALM 113

1   Praise the LORD!
Praise, O servants of the LORD,
   praise the name of the LORD!

2   Blessed be the name of the LORD
   from this time forth and forevermore!
3   From the rising of the sun to its setting,
   the name of the LORD is to be praised!

4   The LORD is high above all nations,
   and his glory above the heavens!
5   Who is like the LORD our God,
   who is seated on high,
6   who looks far down
   on the heavens and the earth?
7   He raises the poor from the dust
   and lifts the needy from the ash heap,
8   to make them sit with princes,
   with the princes of his people.
9   He gives the barren woman a home,
   making her the joyous mother of children.
Praise the LORD!

Psalms 113–18 are known as the "Egyptian Hallel," or the six alleluia ("praise the LORD") psalms sung before (113–14) and after (115–18) the Passover meal and celebration. Psalm 113 begins the Hallel. It is a general call to praise, echoing Hannah's song of praise and anticipating Mary's Magnificat (for these songs, consider reading 1 Samuel 2:1–10; Luke 1:46–55).

◉ REQUEST THE SPIRIT'S HELP IN PRAYER

◉ READ AND REPEAT THE WORD

What words or phrases stick out to you? How do those words or phrases reveal the poet's purpose for the psalm? What effect does this psalm have on you as you meditate on it?

◉ RETURN TO THE LORD IN PRAYER

Sometimes it might seem to us that the good things of this world are overwhelmed by the bad. But the Lord is not overwhelmed. He is exalted on high, and He reaches down low with His salvation.

LORD GOD, I THANK AND PRAISE YOU:

ALMIGHTY GOD, I CONFESS TO YOU:

PRAYERS OF REQUEST
For members of my household to praise the Lord, I pray:

That I may praise You in my everyday work, I pray:

That my congregation may praise You, I pray:

That Your Church may bear witness to Your faithfulness in the world, I pray:

We praise You, O Lord, because You come down to save us in Christ. Alleluia! Amen.

PSALM 114

1 When Israel went out from Egypt,
   the house of Jacob from a people of strange language,
2 Judah became his sanctuary,
   Israel his dominion.

3 The sea looked and fled;
   Jordan turned back.
4 The mountains skipped like rams,
   the hills like lambs.

5 What ails you, O sea, that you flee?
   O Jordan, that you turn back?
6 O mountains, that you skip like rams?
   O hills, like lambs?

7 Tremble, O earth, at the presence of the Lord,
   at the presence of the God of Jacob,
8 who turns the rock into a pool of water,
   the flint into a spring of water.

Psalm 114 is the second of the six alleluia psalms (113–18) sung at Passover, and it is the only one that points directly back to the exodus. Whereas Psalm 113 taught that the Lord lifts the needy, Psalm 114 shows how the Lord did this in the exodus and conquest.

◉ REQUEST THE SPIRIT'S HELP IN PRAYER

◉ READ AND REPEAT THE WORD

What words or phrases stick out to you? How do those words or phrases reveal the poet's purpose for the psalm? What effect does this psalm have on you as you meditate on it?

◉ RETURN TO THE LORD IN PRAYER

The exodus of God's people from Egypt was a time of great unrest, as seen in Pharaoh's refusal to let the people go and the uncertainty of God's people before the Red Sea. However, it was also a time of rejoicing, as the Israelites were freed from slavery after the Passover and Pharaoh's army was defeated at the Red Sea. In this psalm, which recounts those events, the word *tremble* in verse 7 could also be translated "dance." On the one hand, we tremble before the presence of the Lord because of our sins. Yet since He comes to save us through the true Passover Lamb, Jesus Christ, it is also true that we can dance with joy, as He brings us to the promised land of the new heaven and the new earth.

LORD GOD, I THANK YOU TODAY:

SAVING LORD, WHO REDEEMS ME FROM DEATH, I CONFESS TO YOU:

ALMIGHTY GOD, TODAY I ALSO PRAY:

Lord Jesus, we praise You as You come to us to lead us out of death and sin into life eternal. Amen.

PSALM 115

1 Not to us, O Lord, not to us, but to your name give glory,
  for the sake of your steadfast love and your faithfulness!

2 Why should the nations say,
  "Where is their God?"
3 Our God is in the heavens;
  he does all that he pleases.

4 Their idols are silver and gold,
  the work of human hands.
5 They have mouths, but do not speak;
  eyes, but do not see.
6 They have ears, but do not hear;
  noses, but do not smell.
7 They have hands, but do not feel;
  feet, but do not walk;
  and they do not make a sound in their throat.
8 Those who make them become like them;
  so do all who trust in them.

9 O Israel,[a] trust in the Lord!
  He is their help and their shield.
10 O house of Aaron, trust in the Lord!
  He is their help and their shield.
11 You who fear the Lord, trust in the Lord!
  He is their help and their shield.

12 The Lord has remembered us; he will bless us;
  he will bless the house of Israel;
  he will bless the house of Aaron;
13 he will bless those who fear the Lord,
  both the small and the great.

14 May the Lord give you increase,
  you and your children!
15 May you be blessed by the Lord,
  who made heaven and earth!

16 The heavens are the Lord's heavens,
  but the earth he has given to the children of man.

---

a Psalm 115:9 Masoretic Text; many Hebrew manuscripts, Septuagint, Syriac *O house of Israel*

17 The dead do not praise the LORD,
     nor do any who go down into silence.
18 But we will bless the LORD
     from this time forth and forevermore.
   Praise the LORD!

Many scholars date this psalm, the third in the series of alleluia psalms, to after the exile when Israel was at its lowest point. The psalmist encouraged Israel not to look to the outward manifestations of strength (as did the idol worshipers) but to remember God's steadfast love.

⊛ REQUEST THE SPIRIT'S HELP IN PRAYER

⊛ READ AND REPEAT THE WORD

What words or phrases stick out to you? How do those words or phrases reveal the poet's purpose for the psalm? What effect does this psalm have on you as you meditate on it?

⊛ RETURN TO THE LORD IN PRAYER

Idols, both those mentioned in the psalm and those we are tempted to bow down to in our own lives, are essentially an outward representation of human imagination. Nothing could be more fleeting or self-glorifying. Through the promises of His blessings, God calls His people beyond imagination to the truth of His existence.

PRAYERS:

Lord, we praise You for revealing Yourself to us in Your Word. Give us faith to hold fast to the truth, and grant us Your blessings. Amen.

PSALM 116

1   I love the LORD, because he has heard
      my voice and my pleas for mercy.
2   Because he inclined his ear to me,
      therefore I will call on him as long as I live.
3   The snares of death encompassed me;
      the pangs of Sheol laid hold on me;
      I suffered distress and anguish.
4   Then I called on the name of the LORD:
      "O LORD, I pray, deliver my soul!"

5   Gracious is the LORD, and righteous;
      our God is merciful.
6   The LORD preserves the simple;
      when I was brought low, he saved me.
7   Return, O my soul, to your rest;
      for the LORD has dealt bountifully with you.

8   For you have delivered my soul from death,
      my eyes from tears,
      my feet from stumbling;
9   I will walk before the LORD
      in the land of the living.

10   I believed, even when[a] I spoke:
      "I am greatly afflicted";
11   I said in my alarm,
      "All mankind are liars."

12   What shall I render to the LORD
      for all his benefits to me?
13   I will lift up the cup of salvation
      and call on the name of the LORD,
14   I will pay my vows to the LORD
      in the presence of all his people.

a   Psalm 116:10 Or *believed, indeed*; Septuagint *believed, therefore*

15 Precious in the sight of the LORD
  is the death of his saints.
16 O LORD, I am your servant;
  I am your servant, the son of your maidservant.
  You have loosed my bonds.
17 I will offer to you the sacrifice of thanksgiving
  and call on the name of the LORD.
18 I will pay my vows to the LORD
  in the presence of all his people,
19 in the courts of the house of the LORD,
  in your midst, O Jerusalem.
  Praise the LORD!

Psalm 116 is the fourth of the alleluia psalms traditionally read during the celebration of the Passover. Although originally generating from one person's experience, Psalm 116 was appropriate for Israel's celebration of the Passover, as the whole nation nearly succumbed to extinction in Egypt (Exodus 1:22). Luther viewed this psalm "as referring to Christ throughout" (AE 11:400). It is awesome to think that this was one of the last hymns our Lord sang before His "exodus" (Luke 9:31) on the cross.

⊕ REQUEST THE SPIRIT'S HELP IN PRAYER

⊕ READ AND REPEAT THE WORD

What words or phrases stick out to you? How do those words or phrases reveal the poet's purpose for the psalm? What effect does this psalm have on you as you meditate on it?

⊕ RETURN TO THE LORD IN PRAYER

All people are, at some point, "frightened to death." Death's grip is terrible because it is the result of our sin and separation from God. But this psalm reminds us that God cares deeply about our mortality and has released us from its permanent bonds through the suffering, death, and resurrection of His Son.

PRAYERS:

*Let me walk in integrity, O Lord, and
show forth Your love. Amen.*

The 116th psalm is a psalm of thanks in which the psalmist is joyful and gives thanks that God has heard his prayer and has rescued him from the distress of death and the anguish of hell. Like several other psalms above, it speaks of the deep spiritual affliction, of which few people know.

He laments in this psalm that things are so bad, yet he confesses his faith and the truth of God. He calls all human holiness, virtue, and confidence only falsehood and emptiness. This the world will not and cannot hear nor tolerate. Thus it comes that the godly suffer, tremble, and fear all kinds of misfortune.

But despite all, he is comforted by this, that God's Word is true and will only motivate us the more: "They give me to drink from the cup of their wrath. All right, then I will take the cup of grace and salvation and drink myself spiritually drunk and (through preaching) pour out from this cup on those who will drink with me and who draw their grace from the Word." This is our cup, and with this cup we will worship God and praise His name. We will fulfill our vows, namely the First Commandment, that we receive Him as the one God and praise Him as the only God worthy to preach and to be called upon. You find here also that giving thanks, preaching, and confessing God's name before all people is the true worship of God. (Martin Luther)

PSALM 117

1   Praise the LORD, all nations!
      Extol him, all peoples!
2   For great is his steadfast love toward us,
      and the faithfulness of the LORD endures forever.
      Praise the LORD!

This psalm is the fifth of six alleluia psalms associated with the celebration of Passover. Only two verses long, this shortest of all psalms has an unlimited range of vision. It celebrates God's grace, which began in Israel but is extended to all nations through Christ.

⊛ REQUEST THE SPIRIT'S HELP IN PRAYER

⊛ READ AND REPEAT THE WORD

What words or phrases stick out to you? How do those words or phrases reveal the poet's purpose for the psalm? What effect does this psalm have on you as you meditate on it?

⊛ RETURN TO THE LORD IN PRAYER

If God's love had to be merited, there would be no reason to praise Him. His love would also be severely limited. But because His love is His alone to give, it is great, and it reaches people of all nations.

LORD GOD, I THANK AND PRAISE YOU:

STEADFAST AND FAITHFUL LORD, I CONFESS TO YOU:

PRAYERS OF REQUEST
For members of my household to praise the Lord, I pray:

That I may praise You in my everyday work, I pray:

That my congregation may praise You, I pray:

That Your Church may bear witness to Your faithfulness in the world, I pray:

O Lord, I praise You for Your steadfast love
for me and for all people. Amen.

THE PSALMS IN CHRISTIAN WORSHIP

The Psalter was ancient Israel's hymnal, and it was the hymnal for Jesus and His disciples. From earliest times, Christians continued to use the psalms to give voice to their prayer and praise. The psalms have had an immense influence on Christians and their worship.

The Psalms in Worship in the Past

With the development of a daily worship life, the psalms took on even greater significance. As morning and evening services were developed for each day of the week, specific psalms were assigned to be sung at the appropriate times. By the sixth century, the development of monasticism resulted in an even more elaborate use of the psalms. One practice, specified by Benedict of Nursia, became widely accepted in the Western Church. Eight services of prayer were observed each day. The chief morning service, Matins, became the primary service at which psalms were used. The number of psalms could vary from twelve to thirty-six—in one service! Benedict's goal was recitation of the entire Psalter every week.

Martin Luther was trained in this system. Singing all 150 psalms on a weekly basis, he and others like him became steeped in the language of the psalms. Over many years, they had likely learned all the psalms by heart. Such a pressing schedule took its toll, though. Even Luther would complain during the early years of the Reformation that all his other duties left him little time to attend to the prescribed plan of prayer.

With the Reformation, monasticism met its end among the Protestants. Luther proposed simple morning and evening services (Matins and Vespers) that would be appropriate for the Christian life. These services followed the historic use of the psalms, although on a much-reduced scale. Some of Luther's earliest hymns were paraphrases of psalms. (For example, see "From Depths of Woe I Cry to Thee," *LSB* 607, a paraphrase of Psalm 130.)

The psalms also figured prominently in other churches of the Reformation. The Reformed churches in Switzerland made extensive use of the psalms, at first limiting singing in the churches to hymnlike versions of the psalms. Often these were called metrical psalms because the text was translated into a regular meter. In other words, metrical psalms were psalms set to music. Among the revisions of the daily services in Anglicanism (the Church of England), the psalms assumed a prominent place. They were usually sung to simple chant tones. Later, hymnwriters such as Isaac Watts began to write hymn paraphrases based on the psalms (for example, "From All That Dwell Below the Skies," *LSB* 816, a paraphrase of Psalm 117).

There seems to have been a general decline in sustained use of the psalms in worship until the second half of the twentieth century. With the publication of new hymnals came a renewed interest in using the psalms. Simple melodies coupled with an easy method of singing the psalms have put a premium on singing the psalms for a new generation.

The Psalms in the Liturgy Today

Portions of the psalms are built right into the liturgy. For instance, the confession of sins relies upon the blunt language of guilt for sin as found in the psalms, especially the penitential psalms, or psalms of repentance. When we confess, "I, a poor, miserable sinner" (*LSB*, p. 184), we echo the words of David, "For I know my transgressions, and my sin is ever before me" (Psalm 51:3), or again, "I acknowledged my sin to You, and I did not cover my iniquity" (Psalm 32:5a).

Many have spent years preparing to confess sins by quoting the next words: "I said, 'I will confess my transgressions to the LORD,' and You forgave the iniquity of my sin" (Psalm 32:5b). A newer setting of the Divine Service employs these words from Psalm 130: "If You, O Lord, kept a record of sins, O Lord, who could stand? But with You there is forgiveness; therefore You are feared" (*LSB*, p. 203; see Psalm 130:3–4 NIV).

The Divine Service also draws directly from the Psalter in the Offertory. For years, we sang "Create in Me" (*LSB*, pp. 192–93), from David's psalm of confession (Psalm 51), praying that God would make us new and restore the joy of His salvation to us. Recently, another psalm portion has been sung as an Offertory: "What shall I render to the Lord for all His benefits to me? I will offer the sacrifice of thanksgiving and will call on the name of the Lord. I will take the cup of salvation and will call on the name of the Lord. I will pay my vows to the Lord now in the presence of all His people, in the courts of the Lord's house, in the midst of you, O Jerusalem" (*LSB*, pp. 159–60, 176). Drawn from Psalm 116, this text teaches us that the very best we can offer God is thanksgiving in faith for the gifts He has so freely given us.

Another portion from the Psalter appears in the Sanctus, the Communion liturgy's grand hymn of praise. Our voices are joined with all the saints on earth and the whole heavenly host. At its conclusion are these words: "Blessed is He who comes in the name of the LORD" (Psalm 118:26). These words appear in the New Testament in a very intriguing place, at Jesus' entry into Jerusalem: "And the crowds that went before Him and that followed Him were shouting, 'Hosanna to the Son of David! Blessed is He who comes in the name of the Lord! Hosanna in the highest!'" (Matthew 21:9). He who came in the name of the Lord was, of course, none other than the Lord God Himself: our Savior, Jesus Christ. How fitting to sing the same words in preparation for the Lord's Supper, where this great and almighty Lord comes humbly to give communicants His body and blood under bread and wine.

PSALM 118

1   Oh give thanks to the LORD, for he is good;
      for his steadfast love endures forever!

2   Let Israel say,
      "His steadfast love endures forever."
3   Let the house of Aaron say,
      "His steadfast love endures forever."
4   Let those who fear the LORD say,
      "His steadfast love endures forever."

5   Out of my distress I called on the LORD;
      the LORD answered me and set me free.
6   The LORD is on my side; I will not fear.
      What can man do to me?
7   The LORD is on my side as my helper;
      I shall look in triumph on those who hate me.

8   It is better to take refuge in the LORD
      than to trust in man.
9   It is better to take refuge in the LORD
      than to trust in princes.

10   All nations surrounded me;
      in the name of the LORD I cut them off!
11   They surrounded me, surrounded me on every side;
      in the name of the LORD I cut them off!
12   They surrounded me like bees;
      they went out like a fire among thorns;
      in the name of the LORD I cut them off!
13   I was pushed hard,[a] so that I was falling,
      but the LORD helped me.

14   The LORD is my strength and my song;
      he has become my salvation.
15   Glad songs of salvation
      are in the tents of the righteous:
    "The right hand of the LORD does valiantly,
16   the right hand of the LORD exalts,
      the right hand of the LORD does valiantly!"

---

a   Psalm 118:13 Hebrew *You* (that is, the enemy) *pushed me hard*

17 I shall not die, but I shall live,
     and recount the deeds of the LORD.
18 The LORD has disciplined me severely,
     but he has not given me over to death.

19 Open to me the gates of righteousness,
     that I may enter through them
     and give thanks to the LORD.
20 This is the gate of the LORD;
     the righteous shall enter through it.
21 I thank you that you have answered me
     and have become my salvation.
22 The stone that the builders rejected
     has become the cornerstone.[b]
23 This is the LORD's doing;
     it is marvelous in our eyes.
24 This is the day that the LORD has made;
     let us rejoice and be glad in it.

25 Save us, we pray, O LORD!
     O LORD, we pray, give us success!

26 Blessed is he who comes in the name of the LORD!
     We bless you from the house of the LORD.
27 The LORD is God,
     and he has made his light to shine upon us.
   Bind the festal sacrifice with cords,
     up to the horns of the altar!

28 You are my God, and I will give thanks to you;
     you are my God; I will extol you.
29 Oh give thanks to the LORD, for he is good;
     for his steadfast love endures forever!

---

b   Psalm 118:22 Hebrew *the head of the corner*

Of Psalm 118, Luther wrote, "This is my own beloved psalm. Although the entire Psalter and all of Holy Scripture are dear to me as my only comfort and source of life, I fell in love with this psalm especially. Therefore I call it my own" (AE 14:45). It may have been written for celebrations at the time of David or for the celebrations of the second temple. As the last song of the Hallel, or alleluia psalms (Psalms 113–18), it was used as thanksgiving for national deliverance. However, it was destined to find greater fulfillment when sung at the triumphal entry of Jesus into Jerusalem (v. 26 was repeated by the Israelites in John 12:13) and when He Himself referred to it regarding His death and resurrection (Jesus refers to vv. 22–23 in Matthew 21:42–44).

◉ REQUEST THE SPIRIT'S HELP IN PRAYER

◉ READ AND REPEAT THE WORD

What words or phrases stick out to you? How do those words or phrases reveal the poet's purpose for the psalm? What effect does this psalm have on you as you meditate on it?

◉ RETURN TO THE LORD IN PRAYER

We may sometimes wonder, "Where is the steadfast love of God?" Where is that "good action" of God for His people? He revealed His steadfast love in humble Israel, in the Child of the Virgin Mary. He veiled His greatest gift in what is least among people so that His gift might be received by all.

PRAYERS:

O Lord, when I cry, "Hosanna! Save now!" I know
that I do not have to rise up to You, for You have
lowered Yourself to save me. Amen.

The 118th psalm is a psalm of thanks and my dearest, most beloved Confitemini *[the Latin title of the psalm]. It gives thanks and also prophesies of the Christian and of Christ, the rejected cornerstone.* (Martin Luther)

This psalm is a general statement of thanksgiving for all the kindnesses God daily and unceasingly showers on all men, both good and evil. . . . This psalm praises God especially for the greatest benefit He bestowed on the world, namely, for Christ and His kingdom of grace—first promised and now revealed. (AE 14:47)

GOD'S WORD IN PSALM 119

In Psalm 119, eight words repeatedly describe God's Word. Several of these words are used in each stanza, with all eight appearing in stanzas *Waw* (vv. 41–48), *Heth* (vv. 57–64), *Yodh* (vv. 73–80), *Kaph* (vv. 81–88), and *Pe* (vv. 129–36). Since each term describes God's Word, Hebrew poetry uses them in parallel lines, complementing one another in meaning. God's promise gives life because of God's trustworthy nature (for more, see Proverbs 30:5). Each of these eight words for God's Word in this psalm is described in some detail below.

Law   In Hebrew *torah*, meaning "instruction" or "direction," including God's Commandments as well as His proclamation of love and mercy in the Messiah, Jesus. The word *torah* eventually came to describe the Five Books of Moses (Genesis through Deuteronomy). The Torah provides God's instructions and truth, which guide our steps in all situations.

testimonies   In Hebrew *'eduth*, or the "witnesses" of the covenant. The ten "words" written on the tablets of the Law (Exodus 20:2–17) were stored by Moses in the ark of the covenant.

precepts   Hebrew *piqqudim*, or things "deserving attention," "appointed for observation" (the verb means "to visit" or "attend to"). Each teaching of God's precious Word deserves the attention of His people.

statutes   Hebrew *chuqqoth*, or thing "prescribed" or "due" (the verb means "to engrave" or "inscribe"). These were things written as decrees.

commandments   Hebrew *mitswoth*, meaning things "charged," "commanded," or "commissioned" by the Lord.

rules   In Hebrew *mishpatim*, meaning "judgments." This word denotes a legal term for the decisions of a judge. This can include rules to be followed as well as declarations of freedom and innocence. Therefore, the term frequently describes justification and God's mercy.

word   In Hebrew *dabar*, or something "spoken." This was used for all manner of messages (edicts, reports, commands, promises) or a "matter" about which one speaks.

promises   In Hebrew *'amaroth*, meaning "utterances" or "sayings," especially those of command or promise. When the saying involves fulfillment, "promise" is the preferred translation.

Some of these terms might make us think of dry, dead rules by which one has to live. Certainly, God's Word proclaims rules for us to keep. However, Psalm 119 repeatedly emphasizes that God gives life "according to" His Word. Generally, this phrase comes at the end of a verse, clinching the request with the certainty of God's previous promise. The psalmist prays according to "Your word" (vv. 9, 25, 28, 65, 107, 169, 170), "Your promise" (vv. 41, 58, 76, 133, 154), "Your rules" (v. 156), and "Your steadfast love" (vv. 124, 149, 159). He also notes that the insolent do not live according to the Law (v. 85).

"According to" God's Word, the psalmist asks for direction in life (v. 9), for life itself (vv. 25, 107), for strength (v. 28), for understanding (v. 169), for deliverance (v. 170), and he acknowledges God's blessings (v. 65). Just as God's Word created the world (Genesis 1) and God's breath gave Adam life (Genesis 2:7), God's spoken and written Word gives life, hope, and salvation. In the New Testament, Jesus, the Word, "became flesh" for our salvation (John 1:14).

PSALM 119

Aleph

1   [a]Blessed are those whose way is blameless,
     who walk in the law of the LORD!
2   Blessed are those who keep his testimonies,
     who seek him with their whole heart,
3   who also do no wrong,
     but walk in his ways!
4   You have commanded your precepts
     to be kept diligently.
5   Oh that my ways may be steadfast
     in keeping your statutes!
6   Then I shall not be put to shame,
     having my eyes fixed on all your commandments.
7   I will praise you with an upright heart,
     when I learn your righteous rules.[b]
8   I will keep your statutes;
     do not utterly forsake me!

Beth

9   How can a young man keep his way pure?
     By guarding it according to your word.
10   With my whole heart I seek you;
     let me not wander from your commandments!
11   I have stored up your word in my heart,
     that I might not sin against you.
12   Blessed are you, O LORD;
     teach me your statutes!
13   With my lips I declare
     all the rules[c] of your mouth.
14   In the way of your testimonies I delight
     as much as in all riches.
15   I will meditate on your precepts
     and fix my eyes on your ways.
16   I will delight in your statutes;
     I will not forget your word.

---

a   Psalm 119:1 This psalm is an acrostic poem of twenty-two stanzas, following the letters of the Hebrew alphabet; within a stanza, each verse begins with the same Hebrew letter
b   Psalm 119:7 Or *your just and righteous decrees*; also verses 62, 106, 160, 164
c   Psalm 119:13 Or *all the just decrees*

Gimel

17 Deal bountifully with your servant,
   that I may live and keep your word.
18 Open my eyes, that I may behold
   wondrous things out of your law.
19 I am a sojourner on the earth;
   hide not your commandments from me!
20 My soul is consumed with longing
   for your rules[d] at all times.
21 You rebuke the insolent, accursed ones,
   who wander from your commandments.
22 Take away from me scorn and contempt,
   for I have kept your testimonies.
23 Even though princes sit plotting against me,
   your servant will meditate on your statutes.
24 Your testimonies are my delight;
   they are my counselors.

Daleth

25 My soul clings to the dust;
   give me life according to your word!
26 When I told of my ways, you answered me;
   teach me your statutes!
27 Make me understand the way of your precepts,
   and I will meditate on your wondrous works.
28 My soul melts away for sorrow;
   strengthen me according to your word!
29 Put false ways far from me
   and graciously teach me your law!
30 I have chosen the way of faithfulness;
   I set your rules before me.
31 I cling to your testimonies, O LORD;
   let me not be put to shame!
32 I will run in the way of your commandments
   when you enlarge my heart![e]

---

d Psalm 119:20 Or *your just decrees*; also verses 30, 39, 43, 52, 75, 102, 108, 137, 156, 175
e Psalm 119:32 Or *for you set my heart free*

He

33 Teach me, O Lord, the way of your statutes;
  and I will keep it to the end.[f]
34 Give me understanding, that I may keep your law
  and observe it with my whole heart.
35 Lead me in the path of your commandments,
  for I delight in it.
36 Incline my heart to your testimonies,
  and not to selfish gain!
37 Turn my eyes from looking at worthless things;
  and give me life in your ways.
38 Confirm to your servant your promise,
  that you may be feared.
39 Turn away the reproach that I dread,
  for your rules are good.
40 Behold, I long for your precepts;
  in your righteousness give me life!

Waw

41 Let your steadfast love come to me, O Lord,
  your salvation according to your promise;
42 then shall I have an answer for him who taunts me,
  for I trust in your word.
43 And take not the word of truth utterly out of my mouth,
  for my hope is in your rules.
44 I will keep your law continually,
  forever and ever,
45 and I shall walk in a wide place,
  for I have sought your precepts.
46 I will also speak of your testimonies before kings
  and shall not be put to shame,
47 for I find my delight in your commandments,
  which I love.
48 I will lift up my hands toward your commandments, which
  I love,
  and I will meditate on your statutes.

f Psalm 119:33 Or *keep it as my reward*

Zayin

49 Remember your word to your servant,
in which you have made me hope.
50 This is my comfort in my affliction,
that your promise gives me life.
51 The insolent utterly deride me,
but I do not turn away from your law.
52 When I think of your rules from of old,
I take comfort, O LORD.
53 Hot indignation seizes me because of the wicked,
who forsake your law.
54 Your statutes have been my songs
in the house of my sojourning.
55 I remember your name in the night, O LORD,
and keep your law.
56 This blessing has fallen to me,
that I have kept your precepts.

Heth

57 The LORD is my portion;
I promise to keep your words.
58 I entreat your favor with all my heart;
be gracious to me according to your promise.
59 When I think on my ways,
I turn my feet to your testimonies;
60 I hasten and do not delay
to keep your commandments.
61 Though the cords of the wicked ensnare me,
I do not forget your law.
62 At midnight I rise to praise you,
because of your righteous rules.
63 I am a companion of all who fear you,
of those who keep your precepts.
64 The earth, O LORD, is full of your steadfast love;
teach me your statutes!

Teth

65 You have dealt well with your servant,
   O LORD, according to your word.
66 Teach me good judgment and knowledge,
   for I believe in your commandments.
67 Before I was afflicted I went astray,
   but now I keep your word.
68 You are good and do good;
   teach me your statutes.
69 The insolent smear me with lies,
   but with my whole heart I keep your precepts;
70 their heart is unfeeling like fat,
   but I delight in your law.
71 It is good for me that I was afflicted,
   that I might learn your statutes.
72 The law of your mouth is better to me
   than thousands of gold and silver pieces.

Yodh

73 Your hands have made and fashioned me;
   give me understanding that I may learn your
   commandments.
74 Those who fear you shall see me and rejoice,
   because I have hoped in your word.
75 I know, O LORD, that your rules are righteous,
   and that in faithfulness you have afflicted me.
76 Let your steadfast love comfort me
   according to your promise to your servant.
77 Let your mercy come to me, that I may live;
   for your law is my delight.
78 Let the insolent be put to shame,
   because they have wronged me with falsehood;
   as for me, I will meditate on your precepts.
79 Let those who fear you turn to me,
   that they may know your testimonies.
80 May my heart be blameless in your statutes,
   that I may not be put to shame!

Kaph

81 My soul longs for your salvation;
   I hope in your word.
82 My eyes long for your promise;
   I ask, "When will you comfort me?"
83 For I have become like a wineskin in the smoke,
   yet I have not forgotten your statutes.
84 How long must your servant endure?[g]
   When will you judge those who persecute me?
85 The insolent have dug pitfalls for me;
   they do not live according to your law.
86 All your commandments are sure;
   they persecute me with falsehood; help me!
87 They have almost made an end of me on earth,
   but I have not forsaken your precepts.
88 In your steadfast love give me life,
   that I may keep the testimonies of your mouth.

Lamedh

89 Forever, O LORD, your word
   is firmly fixed in the heavens.
90 Your faithfulness endures to all generations;
   you have established the earth, and it stands fast.
91 By your appointment they stand this day,
   for all things are your servants.
92 If your law had not been my delight,
   I would have perished in my affliction.
93 I will never forget your precepts,
   for by them you have given me life.
94 I am yours; save me,
   for I have sought your precepts.
95 The wicked lie in wait to destroy me,
   but I consider your testimonies.
96 I have seen a limit to all perfection,
   but your commandment is exceedingly broad.

g   Psalm 119:84 Hebrew *How many are the days of your servant?*

Mem

97 Oh how I love your law!
   It is my meditation all the day.
98 Your commandment makes me wiser than my enemies,
   for it is ever with me.
99 I have more understanding than all my teachers,
   for your testimonies are my meditation.
100 I understand more than the aged,[h]
   for I keep your precepts.
101 I hold back my feet from every evil way,
   in order to keep your word.
102 I do not turn aside from your rules,
   for you have taught me.
103 How sweet are your words to my taste,
   sweeter than honey to my mouth!
104 Through your precepts I get understanding;
   therefore I hate every false way.

Nun

105 Your word is a lamp to my feet
   and a light to my path.
106 I have sworn an oath and confirmed it,
   to keep your righteous rules.
107 I am severely afflicted;
   give me life, O Lord, according to your word!
108 Accept my freewill offerings of praise, O Lord,
   and teach me your rules.
109 I hold my life in my hand continually,
   but I do not forget your law.
110 The wicked have laid a snare for me,
   but I do not stray from your precepts.
111 Your testimonies are my heritage forever,
   for they are the joy of my heart.
112 I incline my heart to perform your statutes
   forever, to the end.[i]

h   Psalm 119:100 Or *the elders*
i   Psalm 119:112 Or *statutes; the reward is eternal*

Samekh

113 I hate the double-minded,
    but I love your law.
114 You are my hiding place and my shield;
    I hope in your word.
115 Depart from me, you evildoers,
    that I may keep the commandments of my God.
116 Uphold me according to your promise, that I may live,
    and let me not be put to shame in my hope!
117 Hold me up, that I may be safe
    and have regard for your statutes continually!
118 You spurn all who go astray from your statutes,
    for their cunning is in vain.
119 All the wicked of the earth you discard like dross,
    therefore I love your testimonies.
120 My flesh trembles for fear of you,
    and I am afraid of your judgments.

Ayin

121 I have done what is just and right;
    do not leave me to my oppressors.
122 Give your servant a pledge of good;
    let not the insolent oppress me.
123 My eyes long for your salvation
    and for the fulfillment of your righteous promise.
124 Deal with your servant according to your steadfast love,
    and teach me your statutes.
125 I am your servant; give me understanding,
    that I may know your testimonies!
126 It is time for the LORD to act,
    for your law has been broken.
127 Therefore I love your commandments
    above gold, above fine gold.
128 Therefore I consider all your precepts to be right;
    I hate every false way.

Pe

129 Your testimonies are wonderful;
    therefore my soul keeps them.
130 The unfolding of your words gives light;
    it imparts understanding to the simple.
131 I open my mouth and pant,
    because I long for your commandments.
132 Turn to me and be gracious to me,
    as is your way with those who love your name.
133 Keep steady my steps according to your promise,
    and let no iniquity get dominion over me.
134 Redeem me from man's oppression,
    that I may keep your precepts.
135 Make your face shine upon your servant,
    and teach me your statutes.
136 My eyes shed streams of tears,
    because people do not keep your law.

Tsadhe

137 Righteous are you, O LORD,
    and right are your rules.
138 You have appointed your testimonies in righteousness
    and in all faithfulness.
139 My zeal consumes me,
    because my foes forget your words.
140 Your promise is well tried,
    and your servant loves it.
141 I am small and despised,
    yet I do not forget your precepts.
142 Your righteousness is righteous forever,
    and your law is true.
143 Trouble and anguish have found me out,
    but your commandments are my delight.
144 Your testimonies are righteous forever;
    give me understanding that I may live.

Qoph

145 With my whole heart I cry; answer me, O Lord!
 I will keep your statutes.
146 I call to you; save me,
 that I may observe your testimonies.
147 I rise before dawn and cry for help;
 I hope in your words.
148 My eyes are awake before the watches of the night,
 that I may meditate on your promise.
149 Hear my voice according to your steadfast love;
 O Lord, according to your justice give me life.
150 They draw near who persecute me with evil purpose;
 they are far from your law.
151 But you are near, O Lord,
 and all your commandments are true.
152 Long have I known from your testimonies
 that you have founded them forever.

Resh

153 Look on my affliction and deliver me,
 for I do not forget your law.
154 Plead my cause and redeem me;
 give me life according to your promise!
155 Salvation is far from the wicked,
 for they do not seek your statutes.
156 Great is your mercy, O Lord;
 give me life according to your rules.
157 Many are my persecutors and my adversaries,
 but I do not swerve from your testimonies.
158 I look at the faithless with disgust,
 because they do not keep your commands.
159 Consider how I love your precepts!
 Give me life according to your steadfast love.
160 The sum of your word is truth,
 and every one of your righteous rules endures forever.

Sin and Shin

161 Princes persecute me without cause,
    but my heart stands in awe of your words.
162 I rejoice at your word
    like one who finds great spoil.
163 I hate and abhor falsehood,
    but I love your law.
164 Seven times a day I praise you
    for your righteous rules.
165 Great peace have those who love your law;
    nothing can make them stumble.
166 I hope for your salvation, O Lord,
    and I do your commandments.
167 My soul keeps your testimonies;
    I love them exceedingly.
168 I keep your precepts and testimonies,
    for all my ways are before you.

Taw

169 Let my cry come before you, O Lord;
    give me understanding according to your word!
170 Let my plea come before you;
    deliver me according to your word.
171 My lips will pour forth praise,
    for you teach me your statutes.
172 My tongue will sing of your word,
    for all your commandments are right.
173 Let your hand be ready to help me,
    for I have chosen your precepts.
174 I long for your salvation, O Lord,
    and your law is my delight.
175 Let my soul live and praise you,
    and let your rules help me.
176 I have gone astray like a lost sheep; seek your servant,
    for I do not forget your commandments.

Psalm 119 is difficult to date, as no author is given. However, the Law's central role in the author's life and the opposition he faced fit well with the sixth or fifth century BC. The psalmist likely intends that his words of devotion be as timeless as the Word of God, which he loves. The writers of the Book of Concord commented, "By this very act [of prayer] they declare that they cannot get those things that they ask of God from their own natural powers. For example, in Psalm 119 alone, David prays more than ten times that God would give him understanding, that he might rightly comprehend and learn the divine teaching" (FC SD II 15). The Hebrew word *berith*, or "covenant," does not appear in Psalm 119. The idea of a covenant as a promise from God to His people may be understood in the use of Hebrew words such as *'imrah* ("promise") or the broader *torah* ("God's Law"). Also, the concept of a covenant, if it is understood as God's distinct agreement with one people at one time, might be too narrow for the scope of Psalm 119. The psalm describes God's universal actions and nature, which are offered to all people in His Word.

❁ REQUEST THE SPIRIT'S HELP IN PRAYER

❁ READ AND REPEAT THE WORD

What words or phrases stick out to you? How do those words or phrases reveal the poet's purpose for the psalm? What effect does this psalm have on you as you meditate on it?

❁ RETURN TO THE LORD IN PRAYER

God's Word is our beloved guide to life. It reveals God's trustworthy promises and eternal mercy. The psalm's length presents God's Word like a diamond with twenty-two facets, each displaying a distinct light. By exhausting every letter of the alphabet, the psalmist demonstrates the breadth of the Word and his own boundless dedication to it. Luther spoke of the making of a theologian on the basis of Psalm 119. A theologian, he held, came from three actions: prayer (*oratio*), reading or study (*meditatio*), and affliction (*tentatio*). Psalm 119 is an excellent expression of all three. The Gospel radiates through the psalm as the psalmist describes God's promises, which save His people (for example, vv. 41, 58). God's Word is loved because of its message of steadfast love (for example, vv. 76, 88, 159). God is merciful, and this mercy brings life (for example, v. 156 and elsewhere).

Lord, teach us to love Your Word. Give us the faith to
believe that all You have said is true and that all Your
promises will be fulfilled in Christ. Let us seek You with
our whole heart and find You in Your Word. Amen.

ANCIENT USE OF PSALMS
IN WORSHIP

Different psalms were used in different ways and for different purposes for worship. The psalms called "Songs of Ascents," or pilgrimage, make up a sizable portion of the entire Book of Psalms. These shorter songs were likely sung by worshiping pilgrims as they approached the temple in Jerusalem, and their singing would have been a communal act of worship. In addition, the Jewish intertestamental book 4 Maccabees remarks that the psalms were used in the home (18:9–10, 15). Parents were responsible for teaching them to their children, thus leading their households in regular prayer and praise together. In the chart on the facing page, you can find not only descriptions of the Psalms of Ascents but also other ancient uses of the psalms in the worship life of God's people.

Ancient Use of Psalms in Worship

RITUAL ACTS	REFERENCES	NOTES
PILGRIMAGE	Psalms 120–34	Israelites were required to make annual pilgrimages to the sanctuary (Exodus 23:17). Singing psalms was part of the journey.
PROCESSION	Psalms 24:7, 9; 48; 118:19–20; 132	Psalm 132 may have been used as a reenactment of the moving of the ark of the covenant (2 Samuel 6).
DANCING	Psalms 149:3; 150:4; see also Exodus 15:20; Judges 21:16–24; 2 Samuel 6:14, 16	Dance was not an individualistic action, as in modern times, but a liturgical act of worship. For example, in Exodus 32:19, Moses was angry at the dancing before the golden calf because the Israelites were performing a ritual dance as idol worship. Israelites probably used ritual dances in processions to the sanctuary.
ENTRANCE LITURGIES	Psalms 15; 24:3–6	Priests or Levites may have asked the questions found in these psalms. The people may have voiced the responses before entering the worship area.
INVOCATION	Psalms 33:1; 111:1; 113:1; 146–50	These psalms seem to have opened a service of praise, prayer, or sacrifice. They invite the congregation to participate with the priests and Levites.
VERSICLE AND RESPONSE	Psalms 124; 129; 136	Psalms 124:1 and 129:1 command, "Let Israel now say." This may be a cue from a priest or Levite for the congregation to recite a response.
CHOIRS	Psalms 4; 5; 6; many others	Many psalms were written for the choirmaster.
CEREMONIAL WASHINGS	Psalms 26:6; 51:7	Washing was a regular part of service at the temple because of the animal sacrifices, but it was also an expression of forgiveness and purity.
OFFERING	Psalm 66:13–15	The Law of Moses does not prescribe words to accompany the sacrificial acts of the priests. The psalms seem to serve as "words of institution" for the sacrifices.
LAMENT/ FASTING	Psalms 44; 60; 74; 79; many others	In times of national crisis, and perhaps also during festivals, Israelites used lament psalms and fasted.

PSALM 120

A Song of Ascents.

1   In my distress I called to the LORD,
        and he answered me.
2   Deliver me, O LORD,
        from lying lips,
        from a deceitful tongue.

3   What shall be given to you,
        and what more shall be done to you,
        you deceitful tongue?
4   A warrior's sharp arrows,
        with glowing coals of the broom tree!

5   Woe to me, that I sojourn in Meshech,
        that I dwell among the tents of Kedar!
6   Too long have I had my dwelling
        among those who hate peace.
7   I am for peace,
        but when I speak, they are for war!

Psalms 120–34 are collectively known as the "Psalms of Ascents," based on their titles. The exact meaning of the title is unknown, but two possibilities are likely. *Ascents* could refer to the fifteen steps in the temple between the Court of the Women and the Court of the Israelites. The psalms were perhaps read or sung on the steps during the great festivals. The title could also refer to the religious pilgrimages each year going up to Jerusalem. These psalms would be sung as the worshipers approached Jerusalem's hills (as referenced in Psalms 121:1; 122:1–2). The Psalms of Ascents have no single theme, though they are all short and frequently mention Zion and Jerusalem. The historic background for this particular psalm, Psalm 120, is uncertain, as no specific author or setting is given. Perhaps it was written after the exile (587 BC) when enemies oppressed God's people.

⚙ REQUEST THE SPIRIT'S HELP IN PRAYER

⚙ READ AND REPEAT THE WORD

What words or phrases stick out to you? How do those words or phrases reveal the poet's purpose for the psalm? What effect does this psalm have on you as you meditate on it?

⚙ RETURN TO THE LORD IN PRAYER

The tongue is a powerful tool of peace or war. We can use it to call on God for help, but we might be surrounded by others who use the tongue for deceit. God warns us of His approaching judgment on lying lips that are eager for war. However, He also invites us to call on Him for peace and salvation.

PRAYERS AND NOTES:

*O Lord, answer us with Your sure Word
and rescue us by its power. Amen.*

PSALM 121

A Song of Ascents.

1   I lift up my eyes to the hills.
     From where does my help come?
2   My help comes from the LORD,
     who made heaven and earth.

3   He will not let your foot be moved;
     he who keeps you will not slumber.
4   Behold, he who keeps Israel
     will neither slumber nor sleep.

5   The LORD is your keeper;
     the LORD is your shade on your right hand.
6   The sun shall not strike you by day,
     nor the moon by night.

7   The LORD will keep you from all evil;
     he will keep your life.
8   The LORD will keep
     your going out and your coming in
     from this time forth and forevermore.

Psalm 121 is either written for a pilgrim viewing Jerusalem's hills or by a psalmist when he is feeling overwhelmed. He finds that God, who created all things, is his helper.

⊛ Request the Spirit's Help in Prayer

⊛ Read and Repeat the Word

What words or phrases stick out to you? How do those words or phrases reveal the poet's purpose for the psalm? What effect does this psalm have on you as you meditate on it?

⊛ Return to the Lord in Prayer

We are pilgrims on a journey to our heavenly home (Philippians 3:20–21). This psalm reminds us to focus on the Lord, who oversees our journey. Do not allow the mountains, moon, sun, or anything else in creation to frighten you. Our God is eternally alert and goes above and before us.

Lord God, I thank You:

Merciful God, I confess to You:

Prayers of Request
For those in my household and in my family both near and far, I pray:

That I may remain focused and faithful in my everyday work, I pray:

For the sick and hurting in my congregation, I pray:

For my neighbor and those who suffer in society, I pray:

Notes:

O Lord, we trust in Your vigilant love. You will preserve us in order to bring us home. Amen.

PSALM 122

A Song of Ascents. Of David.

1   I was glad when they said to me,
     "Let us go to the house of the LORD!"
2   Our feet have been standing
     within your gates, O Jerusalem!

3   Jerusalem—built as a city
     that is bound firmly together,
4   to which the tribes go up,
     the tribes of the LORD,
   as was decreed for[a] Israel,
     to give thanks to the name of the LORD.
5   There thrones for judgment were set,
     the thrones of the house of David.

6   Pray for the peace of Jerusalem!
     "May they be secure who love you!
7   Peace be within your walls
     and security within your towers!"
8   For my brothers and companions' sake
     I will say, "Peace be within you!"
9   For the sake of the house of the LORD our God,
     I will seek your good.

---

a   Psalm 122:4 Or *as a testimony for*

Psalm 122 focuses on the entry to Jerusalem as the place of God's judgment and the peaceful gathering of His people. From the time of David onward, Jerusalem served as the center of worship and justice. Peace with God and peace between the people of Israel are both found in Jerusalem.

⊛ REQUEST THE SPIRIT'S HELP IN PRAYER

⊛ READ AND REPEAT THE WORD

What words or phrases stick out to you? How do those words or phrases reveal the poet's purpose for the psalm? What effect does this psalm have on you as you meditate on it?

⊛ RETURN TO THE LORD IN PRAYER

Like David, we are welcomed to the Lord's house and can rejoice at the invitation. We are drawn to a heavenly Jerusalem (Hebrews 12:22). At the throne of Christ, the eternal Son of David, we find a place of peace (Romans 5:1; 8:1).

LORD OUR GOD, I THANK YOU TODAY:

LORD OUR GOD, I CONFESS TO YOU:

LORD OUR GOD, TODAY I ALSO PRAY:

May God give us a place among all His people who walk by faith in Christ (Galatians 6:16). Amen.

PSALM 123

A Song of Ascents.

1   To you I lift up my eyes,
       O you who are enthroned in the heavens!
2   Behold, as the eyes of servants
       look to the hand of their master,
    as the eyes of a maidservant
       to the hand of her mistress,
    so our eyes look to the LORD our God,
       till he has mercy upon us.

3   Have mercy upon us, O LORD, have mercy upon us,
       for we have had more than enough of contempt.
4   Our soul has had more than enough
       of the scorn of those who are at ease,
       of the contempt of the proud.

Psalm 123, the fourth in the series of Psalms of Ascents, lacks the travel imagery of Psalms 121–22. The psalm could describe pilgrims who act as servants, following God's direction to appear annually before Him. During the time of Ezra and Nehemiah, refugees returning to Jerusalem were especially mocked for their hope in the Lord and His plans (Nehemiah 2:10, 19; 4:1–4), which means this psalm may have been from this time period.

❀ REQUEST THE SPIRIT'S HELP IN PRAYER

❀ READ AND REPEAT THE WORD

What words or phrases stick out to you? How do those words or phrases reveal the poet's purpose for the psalm? What effect does this psalm have on you as you meditate on it?

❀ RETURN TO THE LORD IN PRAYER

Our eyes are to be upon God, both to receive His blessings and to do His bidding. We are servants of a merciful Lord. However, when our time of service is filled with contempt from others, we grow tired of waiting for God's justice. The Lord does indeed have mercy for us in Christ Jesus.

LORD GOD, I THANK YOU:

MERCIFUL GOD, I CONFESS TO YOU:

PRAYERS OF REQUEST
For those in my household, I pray:

For faithfulness in my everyday work, I pray:

For the sick and hurting in my congregation, I pray:

For my neighbor in the world, I pray:

I do not despair, O Lord, but pray to You, who sees my service and my enemies. May Your reward and Your justice come. Amen.

PSALM 124

A Song of Ascents. Of David.

1   If it had not been the LORD who was on our side—
     let Israel now say—
2   if it had not been the LORD who was on our side
     when people rose up against us,
3   then they would have swallowed us up alive,
     when their anger was kindled against us;
4   then the flood would have swept us away,
     the torrent would have gone over us;
5   then over us would have gone
     the raging waters.

6   Blessed be the LORD,
     who has not given us
     as prey to their teeth!
7   We have escaped like a bird
     from the snare of the fowlers;
   the snare is broken,
     and we have escaped!

8   Our help is in the name of the LORD,
     who made heaven and earth.

Ascription to David suggests a time of his own conflicts with Saul and the Philistines. The psalm might also recall the struggles of the exodus and the entry into the Promised Land. If used by the pilgrims going up to Jerusalem, along with the other Psalms of Ascents (120–134), then it recalls all that God did in leading Israel to their land.

◉ REQUEST THE SPIRIT'S HELP IN PRAYER

◉ READ AND REPEAT THE WORD

What words or phrases stick out to you? How do those words or phrases reveal the poet's purpose for the psalm? What effect does this psalm have on you as you meditate on it?

....

....

....

....

....

....

....

....

....

....

◉ RETURN TO THE LORD IN PRAYER

We need this psalm's reminder that our strength and safety come only by God's hand. We are in danger from flood and snare, the overwhelming and the enticing. But God is faithful for His name's sake. He rescues us so that we will continue to bless and call on His name.

PRAYERS:

*Lead us safely, Lord, so we may always
give glory to Your name. Amen.*

PSALM 125

A Song of Ascents.

1   Those who trust in the LORD are like Mount Zion,
        which cannot be moved, but abides forever.
2   As the mountains surround Jerusalem,
        so the LORD surrounds his people,
        from this time forth and forevermore.
3   For the scepter of wickedness shall not rest
        on the land allotted to the righteous,
    lest the righteous stretch out
        their hands to do wrong.
4   Do good, O LORD, to those who are good,
        and to those who are upright in their hearts!
5   But those who turn aside to their crooked ways
        the LORD will lead away with evildoers!
        Peace be upon Israel!

Psalm 125 was possibly written at the time of Nehemiah, following the exile. The mountains surrounding Jerusalem (v. 2) are reminders of the lasting apportionment of the land and the promise that God will be gracious to the righteous.

◉ REQUEST THE SPIRIT'S HELP IN PRAYER

◉ READ AND REPEAT THE WORD

What words or phrases stick out to you? How do those words or phrases reveal the poet's purpose for the psalm? What effect does this psalm have on you as you meditate on it?

◉ RETURN TO THE LORD IN PRAYER

God's blessing transforms us into mountains surrounding His dwelling place. We are built on His Word as an unchanging rock, and we become pillars by His grace.

LORD GOD, I THANK YOU:

MERCIFUL GOD, I CONFESS TO YOU:

PRAYERS OF REQUEST
For those in my household, I pray:

For faithfulness in my everyday work, I pray:

For the sick and hurting in my congregation, I pray:

For my neighbor in the world, I pray:

NOTES:

Make us upright in heart, Lord, that we might be preserved before You. Amen.

PSALM 126

A Song of Ascents.

1   When the LORD restored the fortunes of Zion,
      we were like those who dream.
2   Then our mouth was filled with laughter,
      and our tongue with shouts of joy;
   then they said among the nations,
      "The LORD has done great things for them."
3   The LORD has done great things for us;
      we are glad.

4   Restore our fortunes, O LORD,
      like streams in the Negeb!
5   Those who sow in tears
      shall reap with shouts of joy!
6   He who goes out weeping,
      bearing the seed for sowing,
   shall come home with shouts of joy,
      bringing his sheaves with him.

This psalm, the seventh in the series of Psalms of Ascents, was likely written after the captives returned from the Babylonian exile. Like dreaming sleepwalkers who wake to find the dream is true, the captives return to Jerusalem.

⊛ REQUEST THE SPIRIT'S HELP IN PRAYER

⊛ READ AND REPEAT THE WORD

What words or phrases stick out to you? How do those words or phrases reveal the poet's purpose for the psalm? What effect does this psalm have on you as you meditate on it?

....

....

....

....

....

....

....

....

⊛ RETURN TO THE LORD IN PRAYER

God's people are overjoyed at returning to Jerusalem. May God give us the expectation that times of sudden refreshing will come from Him. Perhaps now you are in a time of sowing with bitter tears; do not despair of His grace. Trust in His power to do the unimaginable through overflowing kindness. God restores—and through the cross of Christ, you have been rightly restored to God our Father.

RESTORING GOD, I THANK YOU TODAY: ....

....

....

RESTORING GOD, I CONFESS TO YOU: ....

....

....

RESTORING GOD, TODAY I ALSO PRAY: ....

....

....

*By faith, we rejoice, O Lord, in the sowing of Jesus'
body on Good Friday and the harvest of blessings
He prepared on Easter morn. Amen.*

PSALM 127

A Song of Ascents. Of Solomon.

1   Unless the LORD builds the house,
     those who build it labor in vain.
   Unless the LORD watches over the city,
     the watchman stays awake in vain.
2   It is in vain that you rise up early
     and go late to rest,
   eating the bread of anxious toil;
     for he gives to his beloved sleep.

3   Behold, children are a heritage from the LORD,
     the fruit of the womb a reward.
4   Like arrows in the hand of a warrior
     are the children[a] of one's youth.
5   Blessed is the man
     who fills his quiver with them!
   He shall not be put to shame
     when he speaks with his enemies in the gate.[b]

---

a   Psalm 127:4 Or *sons*
b   Psalm 127:5 Or *They shall not be put to shame when they speak with their enemies in the gate*

Unique among the Psalms of Ascents, Psalm 127 is credited to Solomon. It may well be read with his advice in the Book of Proverbs concerning the building of the home and the value of children. The psalm may also refer to his building of the temple. Solomon was considered the master builder in Israel.

❀ REQUEST THE SPIRIT'S HELP IN PRAYER

❀ READ AND REPEAT THE WORD

What words or phrases stick out to you? How do those words or phrases reveal the poet's purpose for the psalm? What effect does this psalm have on you as you meditate on it?

....

....

....

....

....

....

....

....

....

....

❀ RETURN TO THE LORD IN PRAYER

Our houses and the families within them are God's gifts. However, our walls are fragile and our rooms are empty without His blessing. The Lord leads us to value His gifts and to commit them to His watchful care. He will preserve us to life everlasting.

LORD GOD, YOU WATCH OVER ME AND OVER ALL. I BRING MY PRAYERS TO YOU, ESPECIALLY FOR MY HOUSEHOLD, THAT ALL OUR DOINGS AND LIFE MAY PLEASE YOU. TODAY I ESPECIALLY PRAY:

....

....

....

....

....

....

....

Fill our homes with devout children, our heritage from You. Give us this faith and help us build our homes and families on the security of Your Word. Amen.

PSALM 128

A Song of Ascents.

1   Blessed is everyone who fears the LORD,
        who walks in his ways!
2   You shall eat the fruit of the labor of your hands;
        you shall be blessed, and it shall be well with you.

3   Your wife will be like a fruitful vine
        within your house;
    your children will be like olive shoots
        around your table.
4   Behold, thus shall the man be blessed
        who fears the LORD.

5   The LORD bless you from Zion!
        May you see the prosperity of Jerusalem
        all the days of your life!
6   May you see your children's children!
        Peace be upon Israel!

Psalm 128, the ninth listed Psalm of Ascents, is likely a pilgrim song, recited by the travelers in the company of their families as the mountains of Jerusalem came into view.

- REQUEST THE SPIRIT'S HELP IN PRAYER

- READ AND REPEAT THE WORD

What words or phrases stick out to you? How do those words or phrases reveal the poet's purpose for the psalm? What effect does this psalm have on you as you meditate on it?

- RETURN TO THE LORD IN PRAYER

May God grant us the blessings of a life lived under the fear and respect of God. May we see our families as the kindness of God. In our relationships with our children and our grandchildren, God shows His power and mercy.

LORD GOD, I THANK YOU:

MERCIFUL GOD, I CONFESS TO YOU:

PRAYERS OF REQUEST
For my household, that we may live in the peace of God, I pray:

That I may be fruitful in my work, I pray:

For blessings on my pastor and my congregation, I pray:

That my neighbor and those in authority over me in society may fear the Lord, I pray:

NOTES:

*O Lord, open our eyes to appreciate Your gifts
and praise You for their richness. Amen.*

PSALM 129

A Song of Ascents.

1 "Greatly[a] have they afflicted me from my youth"—
   let Israel now say—
2 "Greatly have they afflicted me from my youth,
   yet they have not prevailed against me.
3 The plowers plowed upon my back;
   they made long their furrows."
4 The LORD is righteous;
   he has cut the cords of the wicked.
5 May all who hate Zion
   be put to shame and turned backward!
6 Let them be like the grass on the housetops,
   which withers before it grows up,
7 with which the reaper does not fill his hand
   nor the binder of sheaves his arms,
8 nor do those who pass by say,
   "The blessing of the LORD be upon you!
   We bless you in the name of the LORD!"

---

a   Psalm 129:1 Or *Often*; also verse 2

This psalm was likely written after the Babylonian exile, though any time of oppression against Israel is possible. Some measure of God's protection and justice has already been seen (vv. 2–4), but a more complete judgment is still looked for (vv. 5–8).

- ⊛ REQUEST THE SPIRIT'S HELP IN PRAYER

- ⊛ READ AND REPEAT THE WORD

What words or phrases stick out to you? How do those words or phrases reveal the poet's purpose for the psalm? What effect does this psalm have on you as you meditate on it?

....

....

....

....

....

....

- ⊛ RETURN TO THE LORD IN PRAYER

We may feel some part of the afflictions of this psalm. Often, we feel deep afflictions for the faith, as if we were run over by a plow (something much more punishing even than a whip!). Yet the afflictions shall not prevail! The blessings of the Lord are with us through Christ. One day, He will return and restore His creation for His chosen people. As we await that day, with the psalmist and all who spoke this psalm together on their way to Jerusalem, we call upon the name of the Lord in prayer and praise.

LORD GOD, I THANK YOU TODAY:

....

....

LORD GOD, I CONFESS TO YOU:

....

....

LORD GOD, TODAY I ALSO PRAY:

....

....

Lord, show Your power and justice over our enemies.
Lead us to call on Your name and receive the
blessings that come from You. Amen.

PSALM 130

A Song of Ascents.

1   Out of the depths I cry to you, O LORD!
2   O Lord, hear my voice!
Let your ears be attentive
   to the voice of my pleas for mercy!

3   If you, O LORD, should mark iniquities,
    O Lord, who could stand?
4   But with you there is forgiveness,
    that you may be feared.

5   I wait for the LORD, my soul waits,
    and in his word I hope;
6   my soul waits for the Lord
    more than watchmen for the morning,
    more than watchmen for the morning.

7   O Israel, hope in the LORD!
    For with the LORD there is steadfast love,
    and with him is plentiful redemption.
8   And he will redeem Israel
    from all his iniquities.

Though titled "A Song of Ascents," Psalm 130 is also considered the sixth of the seven penitential psalms, or psalms of repentance, along with Psalms 6; 32; 38; 51; 102; 143. Because of its eloquent expression of desperate sorrow, the Church has often used it in the funeral liturgy. When Luther was asked what were the best psalms of all, he cited Psalm 130—along with 32, 51, and 143—calling them the "Pauline Psalms." For Luther, these are like Paul's epistles in setting forth the realities of human sin, God's grace, and Christ's redemption.

⊛ REQUEST THE SPIRIT'S HELP IN PRAYER

⊛ READ AND REPEAT THE WORD

What words or phrases stick out to you? How do those words or phrases reveal the poet's purpose for the psalm? What effect does this psalm have on you as you meditate on it?

....
....
....
....
....
....

⊛ RETURN TO THE LORD IN PRAYER

The psalmist is in a state of emotional desolation, overwhelmed with misery and guilt. Yet as he realizes God hears his pleas and grants him full forgiveness, his darkness slowly gives way to light and the hope of "plentiful redemption" (v. 7). If we are honest with ourselves, we must admit the depths of our sinfulness. When we are overwhelmed, God hears our pleas for mercy. He does not remember our sins but rather grants us free forgiveness through the work of Christ, who gives us hope. Christ plunges into our depths to raise us in salvation.

PRAYERS: ....
....
....
....
....
....

O Lord, in our happy times, we often forget You, but in our suffering, we turn to You, and in our weakness, we find Your strength. Speak to us the word of Your promise. Amen.

PSALM 131

A Song of Ascents. Of David.

1   O Lord, my heart is not lifted up;
    my eyes are not raised too high;
  I do not occupy myself with things
    too great and too marvelous for me.
2   But I have calmed and quieted my soul,
    like a weaned child with its mother;
    like a weaned child is my soul within me.

3   O Israel, hope in the Lord
    from this time forth and forevermore.

Because the next psalm, Psalm 132, refers to David's triumphant entry with the ark of the covenant, some scholars relate this psalm of David, Psalm 131, to his expression of humility in 2 Samuel 6:20–22.

⊛ REQUEST THE SPIRIT'S HELP IN PRAYER

⊛ READ AND REPEAT THE WORD

What words or phrases stick out to you? How do those words or phrases reveal the poet's purpose for the psalm? What effect does this psalm have on you as you meditate on it?

⊛ RETURN TO THE LORD IN PRAYER

We are like little children before God and the mysteries of existence. And like little children, we can find solace in God's love for us in Jesus Christ, who likewise became a little child on our behalf. While some believe that a child cannot have faith, Christ points to children as models for faith.

LORD GOD, I THANK YOU:

MERCIFUL GOD, I CONFESS TO YOU:

PRAYERS OF REQUEST
For those in my household, I pray:

For faithfulness in my everyday work, I pray:

For the sick and hurting in my congregation, I pray:

For my neighbor in the world, I pray:

NOTES:

Give us the faith of children, Lord. Calm us and quiet us by Your presence in Word and Sacrament. In the name of the Christ Child, we pray. Amen.

PSALM 132

A Song of Ascents.

1 Remember, O LORD, in David's favor,
      all the hardships he endured,
2 how he swore to the LORD
      and vowed to the Mighty One of Jacob,
3 "I will not enter my house
      or get into my bed,
4 I will not give sleep to my eyes
      or slumber to my eyelids,
5 until I find a place for the LORD,
      a dwelling place for the Mighty One of Jacob."

6 Behold, we heard of it in Ephrathah;
      we found it in the fields of Jaar.
7 "Let us go to his dwelling place;
      let us worship at his footstool!"

8 Arise, O LORD, and go to your resting place,
      you and the ark of your might.
9 Let your priests be clothed with righteousness,
      and let your saints shout for joy.
10 For the sake of your servant David,
      do not turn away the face of your anointed one.

11 The LORD swore to David a sure oath
      from which he will not turn back:
   "One of the sons of your body[a]
      I will set on your throne.
12 If your sons keep my covenant
      and my testimonies that I shall teach them,
   their sons also forever
      shall sit on your throne."

a   Psalm 132:11 Hebrew *of your fruit of the womb*

13 For the Lord has chosen Zion;
　　he has desired it for his dwelling place:
14 "This is my resting place forever;
　　here I will dwell, for I have desired it.
15 I will abundantly bless her provisions;
　　I will satisfy her poor with bread.
16 Her priests I will clothe with salvation,
　　and her saints will shout for joy.
17 There I will make a horn to sprout for David;
　　I have prepared a lamp for my anointed.
18 His enemies I will clothe with shame,
　　but on him his crown will shine."

This psalm remembers how David brought the ark of the covenant into Jerusalem (2 Samuel 6–7). It was likely written by Solomon to underscore the significance of him bringing the ark out of the tabernacle and into the new temple he had built (see 2 Chronicles 5; see also 2 Chronicles 6:41–42, when Solomon uses Psalm 132:8–11). The psalm is also a meditation on God's promises to David and his descendants.

◉ REQUEST THE SPIRIT'S HELP IN PRAYER

◉ READ AND REPEAT THE WORD

What words or phrases stick out to you? How do those words or phrases reveal the poet's purpose for the psalm? What effect does this psalm have on you as you meditate on it?

....

....

....

....

....

◉ RETURN TO THE LORD IN PRAYER

One of David's sons, the Anointed One, will be enthroned forever. He will clothe His people with righteousness and salvation. This psalm curses the enemies of God's Anointed, and He "will clothe [them] with shame" (v. 18). Our sins would make us God's enemies. And yet, God dwells with us and clothes us with His righteousness and salvation. In David's Son, Jesus Christ, the incarnate God tabernacles with His people. He is still actually present in His Church through His Word and Sacraments. God swore an oath to work this salvation, and, like David, we can trust His promises.

PRAYERS: ....

....

....

....

O, Lord, we praise You for dwelling with us. Clothe us
with the righteousness and salvation of Your Anointed One,
Jesus Christ, our King. In His name, we pray. Amen.

The 132nd psalm is a psalm of prayer in which Solomon, or the people of Israel, pray for the preservation of the priesthood and the kingdom. That is, they pray for the spiritual and worldly authorities: for God's Word and temporal peace. For where these both stand well, things go well. The psalmist goes on to tell how such a prayer is not only heard, but that God has promised with an oath to preserve the kingdom and priesthood in Jerusalem and to dwell there Himself. He will give all blessing and grace Himself and bring their enemies down to disgrace, so long as they also keep His Commandments and be obedient to Him. Why, however, he called the place of God's dwelling "Ephrathah" and the "fields of Jaar" is too long to comment on here and belongs in a commentary. (Martin Luther)

PSALM 133

A Song of Ascents. Of David.

1 Behold, how good and pleasant it is
   when brothers dwell in unity![a]
2 It is like the precious oil on the head,
   running down on the beard,
  on the beard of Aaron,
   running down on the collar of his robes!
3 It is like the dew of Hermon,
   which falls on the mountains of Zion!
  For there the LORD has commanded the blessing,
   life forevermore.

---

a   Psalm 133:1 Or *dwell together*

All of the Israelites would come from far and near to Mount Zion to offer their sacrifices (Deuteronomy 12). Though perhaps unusual to modern readers, the image of putting oil on someone's head, or anointing someone with oil, would be familiar to those in the Old Testament. Pressed oil from olives could be used as a medicine to soothe the skin, and anointing a visitor to one's home with oil was likely associated with mutual care and hospitality. Additionally, in this psalm, oil represents the anointing of Aaron as priest (Exodus 30:22–33). As Aaron and the priests felt the oil pouring over them in the presence of the congregation, they must have felt a great sense of unity with the people they were ordained to represent. The psalm celebrates the unity the people felt with one another as they gathered to worship the one God and to receive His blessings.

⊛ REQUEST THE SPIRIT'S HELP IN PRAYER

⊛ READ AND REPEAT THE WORD

What words or phrases stick out to you? How do those words or phrases reveal the poet's purpose for the psalm? What effect does this psalm have on you as you meditate on it?

⊛ RETURN TO THE LORD IN PRAYER

Living in unity is as soothing as being anointed with oil, as refreshing as dew from the mountains on a parched desert. Descriptions of the goodness and pleasure of unity and brotherhood remind us that we often experience discord, strife, and disunity instead. This is true of our families, our communities, and our churches. Yet Christ's prayer is "that they may be one, even as We are one" (John 17:11). He bestows that unity through the Holy Spirit in the refreshing waters of Baptism.

PRAYERS:

We praise You, Lord, for the unity we have through You with all our fellow Christians. Amen.

PSALM 134

A Song of Ascents.

1 Come, bless the LORD, all you servants of the LORD,
   who stand by night in the house of the LORD!
2 Lift up your hands to the holy place
   and bless the LORD!

3 May the LORD bless you from Zion,
   he who made heaven and earth!

Psalm 134 is the last, and the shortest, of the Psalms of Ascents.

⚘ REQUEST THE SPIRIT'S HELP IN PRAYER

⚘ READ AND REPEAT THE WORD

What words or phrases stick out to you? How do those words or phrases reveal the poet's purpose for the psalm? What effect does this psalm have on you as you meditate on it?

⚘ RETURN TO THE LORD IN PRAYER

The priests on duty at the temple during the night are urged to bless the Lord, and yet the Lord blesses us. The night is an emblem of darkness and sorrow. Yet Christ is present in the darkness. He gives His blessing from the sacrificial mountain in Jerusalem by the continual ministry of the Church through Word and Sacrament.

LORD GOD, I THANK YOU:

MERCIFUL GOD, I CONFESS TO YOU:

PRAYERS OF REQUEST
That those in my household may receive Your blessing, I pray:

That my daily work may be blessed, I pray:

For blessing upon those who work in my congregation, I pray:

That the blessing You have given me may be extended to the world, I pray:

NOTES:

We bless You, Lord, even in the darkness. And You bless us through Your Son, who went into the darkness of death to bring us into His light. Amen.

PSALM 135

1 Praise the LORD!
Praise the name of the LORD,
give praise, O servants of the LORD,
2 who stand in the house of the LORD,
in the courts of the house of our God!
3 Praise the LORD, for the LORD is good;
sing to his name, for it is pleasant!^a
4 For the LORD has chosen Jacob for himself,
Israel as his own possession.

5 For I know that the LORD is great,
and that our Lord is above all gods.
6 Whatever the LORD pleases, he does,
in heaven and on earth,
in the seas and all deeps.
7 He it is who makes the clouds rise at the end of the earth,
who makes lightnings for the rain
and brings forth the wind from his storehouses.

8 He it was who struck down the firstborn of Egypt,
both of man and of beast;
9 who in your midst, O Egypt,
sent signs and wonders
against Pharaoh and all his servants;
10 who struck down many nations
and killed mighty kings,
11 Sihon, king of the Amorites,
and Og, king of Bashan,
and all the kingdoms of Canaan,
12 and gave their land as a heritage,
a heritage to his people Israel.

13 Your name, O LORD, endures forever,
your renown,^b O LORD, throughout all ages.
14 For the LORD will vindicate his people
and have compassion on his servants.

a Psalm 135:3 Or *for he is beautiful*
b Psalm 135:13 Or *remembrance*

15 The idols of the nations are silver and gold,
   the work of human hands.
16 They have mouths, but do not speak;
   they have eyes, but do not see;
17 they have ears, but do not hear,
   nor is there any breath in their mouths.
18 Those who make them become like them,
   so do all who trust in them.

19 O house of Israel, bless the LORD!
   O house of Aaron, bless the LORD!
20 O house of Levi, bless the LORD!
   You who fear the LORD, bless the LORD!
21 Blessed be the LORD from Zion,
   he who dwells in Jerusalem!
   Praise the LORD!

Psalm 135 was evidently sung as a celebration in the temple by the whole worshiping community.

◉ REQUEST THE SPIRIT'S HELP IN PRAYER

◉ READ AND REPEAT THE WORD

What words or phrases stick out to you? How do those words or phrases reveal the poet's purpose for the psalm? What effect does this psalm have on you as you meditate on it?

◉ RETURN TO THE LORD IN PRAYER

God's almighty power is evident in His creation and in His acts of redemption. The true God is contrasted with the man-made deities of false religions. When we know God only through His creation—the lightning and the storm—He can be terrifying. And in His dealings with human beings, He punishes sin, as He did with Pharaoh, the Canaanite kings, and worshipers of false gods. Yet God has compassion on His people, those whom He has chosen and claims as His own. The true God was incarnate in Jesus Christ as true man, one with us. In Baptism, He makes us His possession.

PRAYERS AND NOTES

O Lord, we praise You for redeeming us and all Your people throughout history. May pastors, teachers, musicians, choirs, and the whole congregation bless You for Your presence in Your Church. Amen.

The 135th psalm is a psalm of thanks. It calls the priests to give thanks, preach, and praise God for the wonders that He showed to the people in Egypt and Canaan, so that they never forget God and seek idols or other gods. This happens when one does not occupy oneself with—and diligently hold to—preaching and the praise of God, as it says in the next psalm. But where His Word is silenced and He does not judge or teach, there truly shall be great anger and no grace. Therefore think, you servants in the house of the Lord, and preach diligently of God and His works. (Martin Luther)

1 Give thanks to the LORD, for he is good,
   for his steadfast love endures forever.
2 Give thanks to the God of gods,
   for his steadfast love endures forever.
3 Give thanks to the Lord of lords,
   for his steadfast love endures forever;

4 to him who alone does great wonders,
   for his steadfast love endures forever;
5 to him who by understanding made the heavens,
   for his steadfast love endures forever;
6 to him who spread out the earth above the waters,
   for his steadfast love endures forever;
7 to him who made the great lights,
   for his steadfast love endures forever;
8 the sun to rule over the day,
   for his steadfast love endures forever;
9 the moon and stars to rule over the night,
   for his steadfast love endures forever;

10 to him who struck down the firstborn of Egypt,
   for his steadfast love endures forever;
11 and brought Israel out from among them,
   for his steadfast love endures forever;
12 with a strong hand and an outstretched arm,
   for his steadfast love endures forever;
13 to him who divided the Red Sea in two,
   for his steadfast love endures forever;
14 and made Israel pass through the midst of it,
   for his steadfast love endures forever;
15 but overthrew[a] Pharaoh and his host in the Red Sea,
   for his steadfast love endures forever;
16 to him who led his people through the wilderness,
   for his steadfast love endures forever;

a   Psalm 136:15 Hebrew *shook off*

17 to him who struck down great kings,
   for his steadfast love endures forever;
18 and killed mighty kings,
   for his steadfast love endures forever;
19 Sihon, king of the Amorites,
   for his steadfast love endures forever;
20 and Og, king of Bashan,
   for his steadfast love endures forever;
21 and gave their land as a heritage,
   for his steadfast love endures forever;
22 a heritage to Israel his servant,
   for his steadfast love endures forever.

23 It is he who remembered us in our low estate,
   for his steadfast love endures forever;
24 and rescued us from our foes,
   for his steadfast love endures forever;
25 he who gives food to all flesh,
   for his steadfast love endures forever.

26 Give thanks to the God of heaven,
   for his steadfast love endures forever.

The psalm's refrain, "For His steadfast love endures forever," suggests that it was used liturgically in the temple, with a solo voice recounting God's works in the first half of the verse and the whole community responding with the recognition of His mercy in the second half. Verses 1–3 highlight how He is the God of gods; verses 4–9 extol the wonders of creation; verses 10–16 recall the wonders of the exodus; verses 17–22 recount the wonders of the conquest; verses 23–25 tell of God's loving care; and finally, verse 26 gives a closing refrain. Simple oral responses were probably common in biblical worship since many participants could not read written responses.

◉ REQUEST THE SPIRIT'S HELP IN PRAYER

◉ READ AND REPEAT THE WORD

What words or phrases stick out to you? How do those words or phrases reveal the poet's purpose for the psalm? What effect does this psalm have on you as you meditate on it?

....

....

....

....

....

....

....

....

....

◉ RETURN TO THE LORD IN PRAYER

This great psalm of thanksgiving praises God for His acts of creation and redemption, both in history and in the lives of His people. Every detail, at every stage, is a sign of God's steadfast love, which, throughout human history, endures forever. The psalm is all about God's action, not ours.

PRAYERS: ....

....

....

....

....

....

*O Lord, we thank You that as we live our lives, with
all the highs and lows, joys and trials, Your steadfast
love is there for us at every moment—it endures forever.
Through Christ, our redemption, we pray. Amen.*

The 136th psalm is a psalm of thanks and is perhaps the text to show priests how they should sing and preach. Namely, they should sing and preach of God and His wonderful deeds, that He is gracious and merciful and a true Savior. Therefore, in each verse the psalmist repeats the line, "His steadfast love endures forever," with which the psalm is nearly overwhelmed. Truly nothing but grace, not human works or doctrines, should ever be preached. For human works and words have done no wonders such as these. They are not deserving of this worship, but rather only the grace and pure goodness of Him who gives all. Gift! Gift, he says! Gift—free of charge! And Christ also stands hidden in the phrase. Such doctrine keeps in the people a pure faith and a right understanding of grace and the forgiveness of sins, against the rebellious and stiff-necked work-saints. (Martin Luther)

PSALM 137

1 By the waters of Babylon,
    there we sat down and wept,
    when we remembered Zion.
2 On the willows[a] there
    we hung up our lyres.
3 For there our captors
    required of us songs,
  and our tormentors, mirth, saying,
    "Sing us one of the songs of Zion!"

4 How shall we sing the LORD's song
    in a foreign land?
5 If I forget you, O Jerusalem,
    let my right hand forget its skill!
6 Let my tongue stick to the roof of my mouth,
    if I do not remember you,
  if I do not set Jerusalem
    above my highest joy!

7 Remember, O LORD, against the Edomites
    the day of Jerusalem,
  how they said, "Lay it bare, lay it bare,
    down to its foundations!"
8 O daughter of Babylon, doomed to be destroyed,
    blessed shall he be who repays you
    with what you have done to us!
9 Blessed shall he be who takes your little ones
    and dashes them against the rock!

---

a   Psalm 137:2 Or *poplars*

Psalm 137 is one of the imprecatory psalms, and likely one of the most troubling to read. Generation after generation, God's unfaithful people practiced idolatry. They refused to heed the warnings of God's prophets, choosing instead to conform to the dominant cultures of the pagan world, including infant sacrifice. At last, God's people experienced His judgment. In the Babylonian captivity, God's people mourned for their sin and its consequences. As the captives are mocked by their captors, they recall the violence that the Babylonians once inflicted upon them, and they experience a desire for violent revenge against God's enemies (much like in Revelation 6:10). While they experienced these feelings of God's judgment upon them and their desire for God's judgment on their enemies, the exiles learned to cling to God's promises of deliverance in His Word as delivered by the prophets.

◉ REQUEST THE SPIRIT'S HELP IN PRAYER

◉ READ AND REPEAT THE WORD

What words or phrases stick out to you? How do those words or phrases reveal the poet's purpose for the psalm? What effect does this psalm have on you as you meditate on it?

◉ RETURN TO THE LORD IN PRAYER

By abandoning God for false religions and the evil ways of the surrounding cultures, the people lost everything. Now, in their exile, they appreciate what they threw away. We, too, are exiles in the new Babylon—the world, with its abominations and its beast (Revelation 18)—and we must endure its temptations and tribulations. We, too, know that sin brings regret, grief, self-loathing, and bitterness. (Such emotions are signs of repentance.) Yet we can also look for our deliverance, clinging to God's promises of redemption delivered by one who is wholly innocent, Jesus, God's own Child.

PRAYERS:

> *O Lord, as we, too, are exiles in this ungodly world, teach us to mourn for our sins. Give us the gift of repentance, so that we may escape the judgment we deserve. Deliver us from our captivity to sin, through Your Son, Jesus Christ. Amen.*

PSALM 138

Of David.

1 I give you thanks, O LORD, with my whole heart;
    before the gods I sing your praise;
2 I bow down toward your holy temple
    and give thanks to your name for your steadfast love and
    your faithfulness,
    for you have exalted above all things
    your name and your word.[a]
3 On the day I called, you answered me;
    my strength of soul you increased.[b]

4 All the kings of the earth shall give you thanks, O LORD,
    for they have heard the words of your mouth,
5 and they shall sing of the ways of the LORD,
    for great is the glory of the LORD.
6 For though the LORD is high, he regards the lowly,
    but the haughty he knows from afar.

7 Though I walk in the midst of trouble,
    you preserve my life;
    you stretch out your hand against the wrath of my enemies,
    and your right hand delivers me.
8 The LORD will fulfill his purpose for me;
    your steadfast love, O LORD, endures forever.
    Do not forsake the work of your hands.

a   Psalm 138:2 Or *you have exalted your word above all your name*
b   Psalm 138:3 Hebrew *you made me bold in my soul with strength*

Psalm 138 is a psalm of David, who exults in how God delivered him from one of the many crises he endured.

⚇ REQUEST THE SPIRIT'S HELP IN PRAYER

⚇ READ AND REPEAT THE WORD

What words or phrases stick out to you? How do those words or phrases reveal the poet's purpose for the psalm? What effect does this psalm have on you as you meditate on it?

⚇ RETURN TO THE LORD IN PRAYER

God's name and Word are above everything, including all of the claims of the false gods. He cares for His children, the work of His hands, and His hands will protect them and bring His plans for them to completion. God's hand is against His enemies. David's victories prefigure the victories of David's Son, Jesus Christ, and the victories of those who have been baptized into Him. Salvation is not only for David or for the Israelites but also for all nations who will come to faith through God's Word.

LORD GOD, I THANK YOU:

PRESERVING GOD, I CONFESS TO YOU:

PRAYERS OF REQUEST
For those in my household, I pray:

For faithfulness in my everyday work, I pray:

For the sick and hurting in my congregation, I pray:

For my neighbor in the world, I pray:

O Lord, we thank You that in Your Word You extend to us such great promises. Grant us full assurance of Your grace, protection, and spiritual care. Fulfill Your purpose in our lives through Jesus Christ. Amen.

LIFE'S GOD-GIVEN VALUE

In 1920, two German physicians published a book called *The Permission to Destroy Life Unworthy of Life*. In it, they argued that "death assistance" should be extended to "empty shells of human beings" such as those with brain damage, some psychiatric conditions, and mental disabilities. They argued that money spent to care for "meaningless life" could be used by those socially and physically fit. It was just a matter of determining which lives were worthy of life. History demonstrates that such thinking led to brutal Nazi experiments and death camps, forced sterilization programs in some European countries, and radical "eugenics" movements in Britain and the United States.

God Gives Value to Life

The value of human life does not depend upon what someone is able to do or not to do. God creates life. God made the first two human beings in His image (Genesis 1:26–27). Even though this image was lost when sin came into the world, this original, lofty position still gives value to human life (Genesis 9:6).

First, when God told Adam and Eve to be fruitful and multiply (Genesis 1:28), He set in motion a biological process for procreation. But God is still involved in this process. "For You formed my inward parts; You knitted me together in my mother's womb. I praise You, for I am fearfully and wonderfully made. Wonderful are Your works" (Psalm 139:13–14; see also Job 10:8–12; 31:15). You are handmade by God! Everyone is. Whether you are an embryo growing in a womb, a young man in his prime, or a grandma in a nursing-home bed—every human life has this God-given value.

Second, God redeemed human life. God loved what He made with His hands so much that He sent His Son to pay the price to buy all human life back from sin and death. "You were bought with a price," Paul says (1 Corinthians 6:20). You know what that price was. It was not with "silver or gold, but with the precious blood of Christ" (1 Peter 1:18–19). The hands that knit you in your mother's womb stretched out on a cross, were pierced with nails, and bled the cleansing blood of forgiveness. Every human being is a human being for whom Jesus Christ died. The embryo in the Petri dish, the child with Down syndrome yet to be born, the young woman who has brain injuries, and the elderly man with Alzheimer's disease have all been bought with a price. That price gives them value regardless of their stage of development or their condition.

Finally, God gives special value to those He calls as His own. God's grace given in Baptism flows to the infirm as well as to the healthy. The little girl with cognitive disabilities is as much a child of God as the pastor who baptizes her. Value comes from what God is able to do in and through His children, not from the capabilities of His children. Paul says that God "is able to do far more abundantly than all that we ask or think" and that this abundant power of God is "at work within us" (Ephesians 3:20; see also Ephesians 4:24; Colossians 3:10 for more). We minimize God's power when we say He cannot be at work in and give value to the baby born with birth defects who lives only a few hours. We minimize God's power when we say He cannot be at work in and give value to the grandma who has lived ninety-five years but no longer remembers her family.

Life Worthy of Life!
An elderly pastor living in a nursing home struggled each day to care for his wife, who had lost virtually all physical strength and the ability to communicate. Despite these troubles, her husband visited with her each day, recalling the life of love and commitment they still shared. They little realized that their simple gestures were carefully and thoughtfully observed by a young man working at the nursing home. The couple's loving interaction moved the young man to consider dedicating himself to the pastoral ministry.

"Why is God keeping me around?" "The quality of Grandma's life just isn't what it used to be." You may have said similar things. Take note: such statements reflect a view of the value of life based on people's abilities rather than on God's ability. Assigning value to human life based on mental or physical capacity can lead to the foreboding conclusion that maybe there is life not worthy of life.

Not so! All life is worthy of life because God makes it so. He created life with His hands. You and every life have handmade value! God redeemed life with His outstretched hands. You and every life have been bought with a price! God's power is at work in those He calls His own. You and every child of God are instruments of His power (Jeremiah 1:5). Thank God for the gift of life! Thank God for the value He gives to every life!

—Adapted from James I. Lamb, executive director, Lutherans For Life

PSALM 139

To the choirmaster. A Psalm of David.

1   O LORD, you have searched me and known me!
2   You know when I sit down and when I rise up;
      you discern my thoughts from afar.
3   You search out my path and my lying down
      and are acquainted with all my ways.
4   Even before a word is on my tongue,
      behold, O LORD, you know it altogether.
5   You hem me in, behind and before,
      and lay your hand upon me.
6   Such knowledge is too wonderful for me;
      it is high; I cannot attain it.

7   Where shall I go from your Spirit?
      Or where shall I flee from your presence?
8   If I ascend to heaven, you are there!
      If I make my bed in Sheol, you are there!
9   If I take the wings of the morning
      and dwell in the uttermost parts of the sea,
10   even there your hand shall lead me,
      and your right hand shall hold me.
11   If I say, "Surely the darkness shall cover me,
      and the light about me be night,"
12   even the darkness is not dark to you;
      the night is bright as the day,
      for darkness is as light with you.

13   For you formed my inward parts;
      you knitted me together in my mother's womb.
14   I praise you, for I am fearfully and wonderfully made.[a]
    Wonderful are your works;
      my soul knows it very well.
15   My frame was not hidden from you,
    when I was being made in secret,
      intricately woven in the depths of the earth.
16   Your eyes saw my unformed substance;
    in your book were written, every one of them,
      the days that were formed for me,
      when as yet there was none of them.

a   Psalm 139:14 Or *for I am fearfully set apart*

17 How precious to me are your thoughts, O God!
   How vast is the sum of them!
18 If I would count them, they are more than the sand.
   I awake, and I am still with you.

19 Oh that you would slay the wicked, O God!
   O men of blood, depart from me!
20 They speak against you with malicious intent;
   your enemies take your name in vain.^b
21 Do I not hate those who hate you, O LORD?
   And do I not loathe those who rise up against you?
22 I hate them with complete hatred;
   I count them my enemies.

23 Search me, O God, and know my heart!
   Try me and know my thoughts!^c
24 And see if there be any grievous way in me,
   and lead me in the way everlasting!^d

---

b   Psalm 139:20 Hebrew lacks *your name*
c   Psalm 139:23 Or *cares*
d   Psalm 139:24 Or *in the ancient way* (compare Jeremiah 6:16)

Though the notation "to the choirmaster" suggests a use in public worship, this psalm of David is deeply personal and contemplative.

⊛ REQUEST THE SPIRIT'S HELP IN PRAYER

⊛ READ AND REPEAT THE WORD

What words or phrases stick out to you? How do those words or phrases reveal the poet's purpose for the psalm? What effect does this psalm have on you as you meditate on it?

....

....

....

....

....

⊛ RETURN TO THE LORD IN PRAYER

Psalm 139 is a classic meditation on God's attributes: His omniscience, His omnipresence, His omnipotence, and His holiness. The psalmist's wonder segues into anger at those who hate God and destroy His gift of life. That God knows our every thought, word, and deed can be terrifying to a sinner. This psalm also gives a clear answer to today's controversy about the value of human life and when life begins, clearly condemning abortion and other assaults on developing children. And yet, this psalm above all proclaims God's love, which He expresses in His personal care and involvement in all of His creation. God's knowledge, power, and presence were manifest most fully when He Himself assumed our substance, with a human body knit together in the womb of the Virgin Mary, and grew up to bear in that body God's hatred of sin at the cross.

PRAYERS: ....

....

....

....

....

....

O Lord, thank You for knowing us so completely! Confound the abortionists, the "men of blood" (v. 19), and others who would abuse and harm the bodies You have made. Lead us to agree with Your judgment against sin, especially with the sin in our own lives. Cleanse us with the blood of Christ, born of the Virgin Mary and present for our salvation in His Word and Sacraments. Amen.

The 139th psalm is a psalm of thanks that praises God that He has provided for them so wonderfully and still reigns in all of His works, words, and thoughts. Whether the psalmist stands, walks, sleeps, or wakes—yes, even in his mother's womb, before he was made—God has been with him as he was being formed and will be with him as long as he lives.

It is as if the psalmist should say: Every human ability or power—how we live, what we do, speak, think, wherever and whenever, from where we come and to where we should go—it is all clearly God's work and art. What then do the abominable ungodly do, those who do not believe this but want to make themselves pious through their vexatious work? They want to have done what they do and then want to receive worship, honor, and glory from God on account of it. But they do not create so much as one word by themselves, indeed cannot create one thought by their own power. Moreover, they do not understand what they do, how they are created, how they live, speak, and think. Because all that we are and do are God's work and powers, how can they consider it to be their own noble work to make themselves godly, praise their free will, and deliver themselves from sin and death? Such people cannot rightly speak about God and His work. Protect us from this, O God, and bless my heart, so that I may remain in the true way that stands forever.
(Martin Luther)

PSALM 140

To the choirmaster. A Psalm of David.

1   Deliver me, O LORD, from evil men;
     preserve me from violent men,
2   who plan evil things in their heart
     and stir up wars continually.
3   They make their tongue sharp as a serpent's,
     and under their lips is the venom of asps.   *Selah*

4   Guard me, O LORD, from the hands of the wicked;
     preserve me from violent men,
     who have planned to trip up my feet.
5   The arrogant have hidden a trap for me,
     and with cords they have spread a net;[a]
     beside the way they have set snares for me.   *Selah*

6   I say to the LORD, You are my God;
     give ear to the voice of my pleas for mercy, O LORD!
7   O LORD, my Lord, the strength of my salvation,
     you have covered my head in the day of battle.
8   Grant not, O LORD, the desires of the wicked;
     do not further their[b] evil plot, or they will be exalted!
                               Selah

9   As for the head of those who surround me,
     let the mischief of their lips overwhelm them!
10 Let burning coals fall upon them!
     Let them be cast into fire,
     into miry pits, no more to rise!
11 Let not the slanderer be established in the land;
     let evil hunt down the violent man speedily!

12 I know that the LORD will maintain the cause of the afflicted,
     and will execute justice for the needy.
13 Surely the righteous shall give thanks to your name;
     the upright shall dwell in your presence.

---

a   Psalm 140:5 Or *they have spread cords as a net*
b   Psalm 140:8 Hebrew *his*

Psalm 140 is one of the imprecatory psalms, in which David calls on God to bring judgment on his enemies. David was the target of the plots and slanders of "evil men" (v. 1) throughout his life. For example, King Saul tried to kill him (1 Samuel 19); David's own son Absalom usurped his throne (2 Samuel 15); Shimei cursed him (2 Samuel 16:5–13); Sheba persuaded his subjects to reject his kingship (2 Samuel 20). Surrounded by so much opposition, it is understandable that David would desire God's justice against those who opposed God.

⊛ REQUEST THE SPIRIT'S HELP IN PRAYER

⊛ READ AND REPEAT THE WORD

What words or phrases stick out to you? How do those words or phrases reveal the poet's purpose for the psalm? What effect does this psalm have on you as you meditate on it?

....

....

....

....

....

⊛ RETURN TO THE LORD IN PRAYER

God's judgment is harsh against those who use their words to harm others—through lies, gossip, slander, or other poisonous speech—as well as those who harm others through violence or subtle traps. God is on the side of the poor, the weak, and the oppressed. Those who are persecuted for righteousness' sake are blessed with the kingdom of heaven (Matthew 5:10–11). They are bearing the cross, in that Jesus too—the Son of David prefigured in this psalm—endured the vicious words and violent actions of "evil men" (v. 1; Matthew 26:57–68; 27:32–44). In Christ, we receive our vindication, our forgiveness, and assurance.

PRAYERS: ....

....

....

....

....

> *O Lord, protect us from "evil men." Protect us, too, from being evil ourselves—forgive us for hurting other people through our words or deeds. We turn to Christ, who was despised and afflicted, for our refuge and healing. Amen.*

A Psalm of David.

1 O LORD, I call upon you; hasten to me!
    Give ear to my voice when I call to you!
2 Let my prayer be counted as incense before you,
    and the lifting up of my hands as the evening sacrifice!

3 Set a guard, O LORD, over my mouth;
    keep watch over the door of my lips!
4 Do not let my heart incline to any evil,
    to busy myself with wicked deeds
  in company with men who work iniquity,
    and let me not eat of their delicacies!

5 Let a righteous man strike me—it is a kindness;
    let him rebuke me—it is oil for my head;
    let my head not refuse it.
  Yet my prayer is continually against their evil deeds.
6 When their judges are thrown over the cliff,[a]
    then they shall hear my words, for they are pleasant.
7 As when one plows and breaks up the earth,
    so shall our bones be scattered at the mouth of Sheol.[b]

8 But my eyes are toward you, O GOD, my Lord;
    in you I seek refuge; leave me not defenseless![c]
9 Keep me from the trap that they have laid for me
    and from the snares of evildoers!
10 Let the wicked fall into their own nets,
    while I pass by safely.

---

a Psalm 141:6 Or *When their judges fall into the hands of the Rock*
b Psalm 141:7 The meaning of the Hebrew in verses 6, 7 is uncertain
c Psalm 141:8 Hebrew *refuge; do not pour out my life!*

Psalm 141 may reflect the time when David, driven out of Jerusalem by his son Absalom, could not worship on Mount Zion, where sacrifices were held. Yet he associates his prayers with the evening service, with its incense and sacrifices (v. 2).

⊛ REQUEST THE SPIRIT'S HELP IN PRAYER

⊛ READ AND REPEAT THE WORD

What words or phrases stick out to you? How do those words or phrases reveal the poet's purpose for the psalm? What effect does this psalm have on you as you meditate on it?

⊛ RETURN TO THE LORD IN PRAYER

Sinners will fall into the traps they have made for themselves and will ultimately be cast down. God, through pastors and other authorities, rebukes us for our sins. These are all to bring us to repentance. "The evening sacrifice" (v. 2) of Christ's final atonement for sin makes our prayers acceptable before God. In Him, we will "pass by" (v. 10) the snares and punishments of the wicked, and He will be our refuge.

LORD GOD, I THANK YOU:

PRESERVING GOD, I CONFESS TO YOU:

PRAYERS OF REQUEST
For those in my household, I pray:

For faithfulness in my everyday work, I pray:

For the sick and hurting in my congregation, I pray:

For my neighbor in the world, I pray:

> *O Lord, keep me from sinning! Guard my mouth, lest I say something I should not. Keep me away from people who would lead me into sin. Make me open to correction and utterly dependent on Your grace in Christ. Amen.*

PSALM 142

A Maskil[a] of David, when he was in the cave. A Prayer.

1 With my voice I cry out to the LORD;
      with my voice I plead for mercy to the LORD.
2 I pour out my complaint before him;
      I tell my trouble before him.

3 When my spirit faints within me,
      you know my way!
   In the path where I walk
      they have hidden a trap for me.
4 Look to the right and see:
      there is none who takes notice of me;
   no refuge remains to me;
      no one cares for my soul.

5 I cry to you, O LORD;
      I say, "You are my refuge,
      my portion in the land of the living."
6 Attend to my cry,
      for I am brought very low!
   Deliver me from my persecutors,
      for they are too strong for me!
7 Bring me out of prison,
      that I may give thanks to your name!
   The righteous will surround me,
      for you will deal bountifully with me.

a   Psalm 142:1 Probably a musical or liturgical term

When David was pursued by King Saul, he hid in a cave, both in Adullam (1 Samuel 22:1–2) and at Engedi (1 Samuel 24). A sense of imprisonment, of being buried, of being in the depths—both literally and emotionally—provoked fervent and honest prayer. Since his persecutors were too strong for him, David could only depend on God, who indeed did deliver and exalt him.

◉ REQUEST THE SPIRIT'S HELP IN PRAYER

◉ READ AND REPEAT THE WORD

What words or phrases stick out to you? How do those words or phrases reveal the poet's purpose for the psalm? What effect does this psalm have on you as you meditate on it?

◉ RETURN TO THE LORD IN PRAYER

David prays to the Lord, pouring out his complaints and troubles. God restores him to the fellowship of faith. We often find ourselves in a prison of our own making. Our sins isolate us from others. We are shut out of the community of the righteous. These words of David are even more true of David's Son, Jesus Christ. He, more than anyone, was persecuted, deserted, imprisoned, and tormented. At His burial, He was imprisoned in a cave. But His Father raised Him from the dead to live in the company of those made righteous through His blood.

DELIVERING GOD, I THANK YOU TODAY:

MERCIFUL GOD, I CONFESS TO YOU:

RIGHTEOUS GOD, TODAY I ALSO PRAY:

Heavenly Father, when I have no one to turn to, help me realize that I can turn to You. Be my defender, my refuge, and my portion in Christ. Bring me out of my prison and into the company of Your Church, now on earth and in eternity. Amen.

PSALM 143

A Psalm of David.

1   Hear my prayer, O LORD;
     give ear to my pleas for mercy!
  In your faithfulness answer me, in your righteousness!

2   Enter not into judgment with your servant,
     for no one living is righteous before you.

3   For the enemy has pursued my soul;
     he has crushed my life to the ground;
     he has made me sit in darkness like those long dead.

4   Therefore my spirit faints within me;
     my heart within me is appalled.

5   I remember the days of old;
     I meditate on all that you have done;
     I ponder the work of your hands.

6   I stretch out my hands to you;
     my soul thirsts for you like a parched land.   *Selah*

7   Answer me quickly, O LORD!
     My spirit fails!
  Hide not your face from me,
     lest I be like those who go down to the pit.

8   Let me hear in the morning of your steadfast love,
     for in you I trust.
  Make me know the way I should go,
     for to you I lift up my soul.

9   Deliver me from my enemies, O LORD!
     I have fled to you for refuge.[a]

10   Teach me to do your will,
     for you are my God!
  Let your good Spirit lead me
     on level ground!

11   For your name's sake, O LORD, preserve my life!
     In your righteousness bring my soul out of trouble!

12   And in your steadfast love you will cut off my enemies,
     and you will destroy all the adversaries of my soul,
     for I am your servant.

---

a   Psalm 143:9 One Hebrew manuscript, Septuagint; most Hebrew manuscripts *To you I have covered*

The original context of this penitential psalm, or psalm of repentance, is thought to be David's desolation after being driven from his throne by his son Absalom. The last of the seven penitential psalms, it has historically been used in the Church during Lent. Concerning the power of Scripture, Luther wrote, "Every psalm, all Scripture, calls to grace, extols grace, searches for Christ, and praises only God's work, while rejecting all the works of man. . . . The life of a saint is more a taking from God than a giving; more a desiring than a having; more a becoming pious than a being pious. . . . Not on account of the work I do, but on account of the faith Thou givest me" (AE 14:196).

⊛ REQUEST THE SPIRIT'S HELP IN PRAYER

⊛ READ AND REPEAT THE WORD

What words or phrases stick out to you? How do those words or phrases reveal the poet's purpose for the psalm? What effect does this psalm have on you as you meditate on it?

⊛ RETURN TO THE LORD IN PRAYER

The psalmist pleads for God's mercy, admitting that neither he nor anyone else can stand before God's judgment. He trusts in God's righteousness and in His name, not his own. This penitential psalm is a profound description of a repentant heart, which receives God's grace. The psalmist, giving up on himself, trusts in God's "steadfast love" (v. 8).

PRAYERS:

> *O Lord, I confess that I am sinful and unclean. By Your steadfast love, take away from me every shred of pride and self-righteousness. Trusting in Your grace, I come before You not in my own righteousness but clothed in Jesus' righteousness. Amen.*

PSALM 144

Of David.

1 Blessed be the LORD, my rock,
    who trains my hands for war,
    and my fingers for battle;
2 he is my steadfast love and my fortress,
    my stronghold and my deliverer,
  my shield and he in whom I take refuge,
    who subdues peoples[a] under me.

3 O LORD, what is man that you regard him,
    or the son of man that you think of him?
4 Man is like a breath;
    his days are like a passing shadow.

5 Bow your heavens, O LORD, and come down!
    Touch the mountains so that they smoke!
6 Flash forth the lightning and scatter them;
    send out your arrows and rout them!
7 Stretch out your hand from on high;
    rescue me and deliver me from the many waters,
    from the hand of foreigners,
8 whose mouths speak lies
    and whose right hand is a right hand of falsehood.

9 I will sing a new song to you, O God;
    upon a ten-stringed harp I will play to you,
10 who gives victory to kings,
    who rescues David his servant from the cruel sword.
11 Rescue me and deliver me
    from the hand of foreigners,
  whose mouths speak lies
    and whose right hand is a right hand of falsehood.

---

a Psalm 144:2 Many Hebrew manuscripts, Dead Sea Scroll, Jerome, Syriac, Aquila; most Hebrew manuscripts *subdues my people*

12 May our sons in their youth
    be like plants full grown,
  our daughters like corner pillars
    cut for the structure of a palace;
13 may our granaries be full,
    providing all kinds of produce;
  may our sheep bring forth thousands
    and ten thousands in our fields;
14 may our cattle be heavy with young,
    suffering no mishap or failure in bearing;[b]
  may there be no cry of distress in our streets!
15 Blessed are the people to whom such blessings fall!
    Blessed are the people whose God is the Lord!

b   Psalm 144:14 Hebrew *with no breaking in or going out*

Psalm 144 is a joyful song of victory by King David—who mentions his own name in verse 10—after defeating enemies in battle.

⚫ REQUEST THE SPIRIT'S HELP IN PRAYER

⚫ READ AND REPEAT THE WORD

What words or phrases stick out to you? How do those words or phrases reveal the poet's purpose for the psalm? What effect does this psalm have on you as you meditate on it?

⚫ RETURN TO THE LORD IN PRAYER

We are indeed like a breath, a shadow, before God. In our sins—such as our propensity for lying and swearing falsely, as mentioned here—we are God's enemies. And yet God shows us His favor, despite our insignificance, particularly through the Son of Man, the Son of David, Jesus Christ. The Church has historically seen this psalm as foreshadowing Christ, our true King.

PRAYERS:

Blessed are You, Lord Christ, our King! You have come down to us, not in Your glory, but as one of us. You have won the victory over sin, the devil, and death itself. May we share Your victory and its blessings as we cling to You in faith. Amen.

The 144th psalm is a psalm of thanks for kings and those in authority. David, a king who has to wage war and rule, gives thanks to God with this psalm. He confesses that victory, good fortune, and success—whether in conflict or in government—are gifts of God and do not come from human power and ability. Little does human wisdom know how to keep subjects under authority and to rule land and people well. For how should he be capable of these great things when he is nothing and passes away like a shadow?

Instead, the Lord does this. He sends for the lightning—sending discouraged and frightened hearts to the army and humble hearts among the people. Where He thus touches the mountains and the multitudes, so that they are in fear before Him, there it is good to fight and rule, for there victory and good fortune follow—as well as this fear. Yet how can one, being only flesh and blood, bring about this fear?

Then he prays against his own people and rebukes their foolishness. For the people of Israel, having the renown of being the people of God, were nevertheless proud, stiffnecked, disobedient, rebellious, covetous, jealous, and faithless, as indeed they showed by their opposition to Moses, David, and other kings. And though they saw that David fought and ruled with miraculous wonders, as did Moses, yet they were no better and did not inquire about God or faith in God.

"What God? What faith? As long as we have beautiful children, houses, cattle, many possessions, and enjoyable days, we are a blessed people. And, in addition, we have prophets enough, who teach us that God's people are those for whom things go well. Those for whom things go badly are not of God." However, things do go badly for all the saints—for the reason that they trust in God.

You have now rescued me, David says, from the murderous sword of Goliath. You have given me victory over other kings. Therefore, preserve me also from this ungodly, evil, false people, who listen to neither God nor man. They are peasants and brutes, yes, truly swine, who are concerned for nothing but their own belly. It is harder and more dangerous to rule over them than to continually be at war.

He calls them foreign children, for they want to be the foremost children of God, yet they are foreigners, strangers, and worse than heathen. They praise God with their mouths, while their heart is far from Him. (Martin Luther)

PSALM 145

ªA Song of Praise. Of David.

1 I will extol you, my God and King,
  and bless your name forever and ever.
2 Every day I will bless you
  and praise your name forever and ever.
3 Great is the LORD, and greatly to be praised,
  and his greatness is unsearchable.

4 One generation shall commend your works to another,
  and shall declare your mighty acts.
5 On the glorious splendor of your majesty,
  and on your wondrous works, I will meditate.
6 They shall speak of the might of your awesome deeds,
  and I will declare your greatness.
7 They shall pour forth the fame of your abundant goodness
  and shall sing aloud of your righteousness.

8 The LORD is gracious and merciful,
  slow to anger and abounding in steadfast love.
9 The LORD is good to all,
  and his mercy is over all that he has made.

10 All your works shall give thanks to you, O LORD,
  and all your saints shall bless you!
11 They shall speak of the glory of your kingdom
  and tell of your power,
12 to make known to the children of man your[b] mighty deeds,
  and the glorious splendor of your kingdom.
13 Your kingdom is an everlasting kingdom,
  and your dominion endures throughout all generations.

---

a Psalm 145:1 This psalm is an acrostic poem, each verse beginning with the successive letters of the Hebrew alphabet
b Psalm 145:12 Hebrew *his*; also next line

[The Lord is faithful in all his words
and kind in all his works.]^c

14 The Lord upholds all who are falling
and raises up all who are bowed down.
15 The eyes of all look to you,
and you give them their food in due season.
16 You open your hand;
you satisfy the desire of every living thing.
17 The Lord is righteous in all his ways
and kind in all his works.
18 The Lord is near to all who call on him,
to all who call on him in truth.
19 He fulfills the desire of those who fear him;
he also hears their cry and saves them.
20 The Lord preserves all who love him,
but all the wicked he will destroy.

21 My mouth will speak the praise of the Lord,
and let all flesh bless his holy name forever and ever.

c   Psalm 145:13 These two lines are supplied by one Hebrew manuscript, Septuagint, Syriac (compare Dead Sea Scroll)

Psalm 145 is named in the superscript "A Song of Praise," a word literally translated as "psalm." This is the only poem so labeled, though the entire collection goes by that name. It is a poetic acrostic, each line beginning with one of the letters in the Hebrew alphabet (though one letter, *nun*, is mysteriously left out). Other acrostic psalms are 9; 10; 25; 34; 37; 111; 112; 119; 146. As a psalm of David, we have a king paying homage to his King, whose dominion goes beyond Israel, to "all flesh" (v. 21) and to the universe itself. Of special note to the psalm are the lines, in brackets in the text, at the end of verse 13, which were only provided by one ancient manuscript and may or may not have been original to the text. Regardless, this "Mission Psalm" describes the calling of God's people to proclaim His Word.

⊛ REQUEST THE SPIRIT'S HELP IN PRAYER

⊛ READ AND REPEAT THE WORD

What words or phrases stick out to you? How do those words or phrases reveal the poet's purpose for the psalm? What effect does this psalm have on you as you meditate on it?

⊛ RETURN TO THE LORD IN PRAYER

God is our King, and all generations and all the earth must hear about Him. He abounds in mercy, which extends to all His works. The Lord will draw near to those who fear Him (who have been broken by the Law). He drew near to us in Christ, our King. His Word resounds from generation to generation, bringing the kingdom of God to all the world and to us.

PRAYERS:

> *O Christ, our King, Your righteousness is unsearchable. Though I should be counted among the wicked, You have redeemed me. Proclaim this Good News to all the world through me. Amen.*

The 145th psalm is a psalm of thanks for the kingdom of Christ, which was to come. It strongly urges the high, exalted work of praising God and glorifying His power and kingdom. For Christ's kingdom and power are hidden under the cross. If the cross were not extolled through preaching, teaching, and confession, who could have ever thought of it, to say nothing of knowing it? But such is His kingdom and power, that He aided the fallen, called the needy to Himself, made sinners godly, and brought the dead to life. Yes, He is the one who gives food to all, who hears the call of His saints, does what they desire, and protects them. (Martin Luther)

GIVE US A KING?

Imagine Samuel's shock. After he had served God's people for so many years, how did they express their gratitude? They demanded a king. They wanted a king to rule over them, to be just like their neighbors. Had the Israelites forgotten that they were not like the surrounding nations? They were the Lord's. He was their King. But how could God be their King if they had a human king?

Rejecting God's Way

With a mighty hand, the Lord had rescued His people from slavery in Egypt. He brought them safely through the Red Sea, and then He gathered them at Mount Sinai to establish His covenant with them, saying, "Now therefore, if you will indeed obey My voice and keep My covenant, you shall be My treasured possession among all peoples, for all the earth is Mine; and you shall be to Me a kingdom of priests and a holy nation" (Exodus 19:5–6). This was the kingdom God intended for His people. They would be His treasured possession, and He would be their King.

That was not the way of the other nations. Israel's neighbors had kings who wielded great power. God's people had come to desire, yes, even covet this path. The Lord told Samuel to give them their king, but not to take it personally. "They have not rejected you, but they have rejected Me from being king over them," said the Lord (1 Samuel 8:7).

Imagine rejecting God as king! Every year as the Israelites celebrated the Passover, they would recount the story of God's miraculous dealings with their enemies. How could they reject this mighty King, asking instead for a mere mortal to lead them?

"Be Careful What You Ask For"

As an old saying puts it, "Be careful what you ask for." God granted Israel's request for a king, to be sure. But He also instructed Samuel to make clear to the Israelites just what they would be getting. Samuel told the people what they could expect from a king. Their new king would take their sons to build his army, use others to plow the ground and reap the harvest, take their daughters to cook and bake, and take the best of their fields, vineyards, and olive orchards. In addition, for those who kept their land, the king would require a tenth of all their produce and flocks. In effect, they would become slaves. "And in that day you will cry out because of your king, whom you have chosen for yourselves, but the LORD will not answer you in that day" (1 Samuel 8:18; see also vv. 11–18).

Despite these stern warnings, the people were sure of themselves and continued to demand a king. God chose for them Saul, of the tribe of Benjamin (1 Samuel 9). At first, Saul was all the people could have imagined. Tall and handsome, he soon showed himself brave in battle. Little by little, though, Saul took matters into his hands, offering sacrifices he was not authorized to offer and failing to deal with enemies as God had prescribed.

Live by God's Promise!

God eventually rejected Saul and commanded Samuel to anoint another king. God's choice was not one of Jesse's older sons, but his youngest, David (1 Samuel 16:1–13). David, of course, would soon be the talk of the nation when he defeated the giant Goliath and otherwise proved himself in battle. As time went on, David also would demonstrate his capacity to disobey God, going so far as to take another man's wife and use his authority as king to arrange for that man's death (2 Samuel 11–12).

Yet God promised David that one of his descendants would reign on his throne forever and that this king would be to God as a Son (2 Samuel 7:1–17). This is none other than the promised Messiah. Jesus is the eternal Son of God who is also the Son of David (Matthew 1:1; Romans 1:3). Jesus, David's son, is indeed David's Lord. In other words: with King Jesus, the old problem is solved. The one who is God and man reigns to all eternity!

Which King for You?

Kings in the line between David and Jesus turned out, overall, to be a great disappointment. Although a few were God-fearing and attempted to lead the people back to the Lord, most succumbed to the temptations of the foreign gods. The storied history of the kings of Israel reinforces the truth of Psalm 146:3: "Put not your trust in princes." Trust the true and living God, in whom alone is salvation. Despite the failings of David and his descendants, God remained faithful. At the right time, He sent His Son to do what a good King does. He saved His people. He redeemed you from sin and death.

Many of the psalms talk about kings or rulers anointed by God (such as Psalm 2). On one hand, we should see that God had expectations for those whom He chose to rule. As we see in the Scriptures, however, each one of these kings or leaders was a sinner. On the other hand, these psalms point us to the one true King promised to David (in 2 Samuel 7 and elsewhere), the Messiah, Jesus Christ. As you read the psalms about royalty, look for both. See not only what God's Word tells us about how God treated His chosen kings during the Old Testament, but look also for how Jesus fulfilled the role perfectly to be our ultimate King of kings.

PSALM 146

1   Praise the LORD!
    Praise the LORD, O my soul!
2   I will praise the LORD as long as I live;
        I will sing praises to my God while I have my being.

3   Put not your trust in princes,
        in a son of man, in whom there is no salvation.
4   When his breath departs, he returns to the earth;
        on that very day his plans perish.

5   Blessed is he whose help is the God of Jacob,
        whose hope is in the LORD his God,
6   who made heaven and earth,
        the sea, and all that is in them,
    who keeps faith forever;
7   who executes justice for the oppressed,
        who gives food to the hungry.

    The LORD sets the prisoners free;
8   the LORD opens the eyes of the blind.
    The LORD lifts up those who are bowed down;
        the LORD loves the righteous.
9   The LORD watches over the sojourners;
        he upholds the widow and the fatherless,
        but the way of the wicked he brings to ruin.

10 The LORD will reign forever,
        your God, O Zion, to all generations.
    Praise the LORD!

Psalm 146 is the first of five alleluia psalms (*alleluia* means "Praise the LORD!") that conclude the Book of Psalms. These are also known as the final Hallel. An acrostic poem, each line of Psalm 146 begins with the next letter in the Hebrew alphabet. Notations in the Septuagint, or the Greek translation of the Old Testament used at the time of Jesus, associate this psalm with the postexilic prophets Haggai and Zechariah.

◉ REQUEST THE SPIRIT'S HELP IN PRAYER

◉ READ AND REPEAT THE WORD

What words or phrases stick out to you? How do those words or phrases reveal the poet's purpose for the psalm? What effect does this psalm have on you as you meditate on it?

◉ RETURN TO THE LORD IN PRAYER

Do not put your faith in human beings—in politicians, social elites, or individuals, none of whom can save and all of whom will die. Rather, put your trust in God. Your Lord is Christ, the Son of Man in whom there is salvation, who on earth fed the hungry, healed the blind, and ministered to everyone in need. You were buried with Him in Baptism so you can share His new life and claim all of these promises.

LORD GOD, I THANK YOU:

PRESERVING GOD, I CONFESS TO YOU:

PRAYERS OF REQUEST
For those in my household, I pray:

For faithfulness in my everyday work, I pray:

For the sick and hurting in my congregation, I pray:

For my neighbor in the world, I pray:

> *O Lord, help us not to put our trust in people, but in You alone. Forgive us for mistreating others and for looking down on people different from ourselves. Thank You for keeping all of Your promises through Christ. Amen.*

PSALM 147

1   Praise the LORD!
     For it is good to sing praises to our God;
       for it is pleasant,[a] and a song of praise is fitting.
2   The LORD builds up Jerusalem;
       he gathers the outcasts of Israel.
3   He heals the brokenhearted
       and binds up their wounds.
4   He determines the number of the stars;
       he gives to all of them their names.
5   Great is our Lord, and abundant in power;
       his understanding is beyond measure.
6   The LORD lifts up the humble;[b]
       he casts the wicked to the ground.

7   Sing to the LORD with thanksgiving;
       make melody to our God on the lyre!
8   He covers the heavens with clouds;
       he prepares rain for the earth;
       he makes grass grow on the hills.
9   He gives to the beasts their food,
       and to the young ravens that cry.
10   His delight is not in the strength of the horse,
       nor his pleasure in the legs of a man,
11   but the LORD takes pleasure in those who fear him,
       in those who hope in his steadfast love.

12   Praise the LORD, O Jerusalem!
       Praise your God, O Zion!
13   For he strengthens the bars of your gates;
       he blesses your children within you.
14   He makes peace in your borders;
       he fills you with the finest of the wheat.
15   He sends out his command to the earth;
       his word runs swiftly.

---

a   Psalm 147:1 Or *for he is beautiful*
b   Psalm 147:6 Or *afflicted*

16 He gives snow like wool;
        he scatters frost like ashes.
17 He hurls down his crystals of ice like crumbs;
        who can stand before his cold?
18 He sends out his word, and melts them;
        he makes his wind blow and the waters flow.
19 He declares his word to Jacob,
        his statutes and rules[c] to Israel.
20 He has not dealt thus with any other nation;
        they do not know his rules.[d]
    Praise the LORD!

c   Psalm 147:19 Or *and just decrees*
d   Psalm 147:20 Or *his just decrees*

Psalm 146 is the second of five alleluia psalms. Jerusalem had been destroyed and God's people had been sent into exile in Babylon. But, as recorded in Ezra and Nehemiah, God brought His people back to the land He had promised them. Jerusalem and its walls were rebuilt and the temple reestablished. This psalm was perhaps composed to celebrate this restoration. As with Psalm 146, notations in the Septuagint, the Greek translation of the Old Testament used at the time of Jesus, associate this psalm with the postexilic prophets Haggai and Zechariah.

❋ REQUEST THE SPIRIT'S HELP IN PRAYER

❋ READ AND REPEAT THE WORD

What words or phrases stick out to you? How do those words or phrases reveal the poet's purpose for the psalm? What effect does this psalm have on you as you meditate on it?

❋ RETURN TO THE LORD IN PRAYER

God has built Jerusalem and brought the exiles home. His Word that governs nature has been given to the children of Israel in Scripture. The Lord has forgiven those whom He had punished, gathered them from exile, and restored the Holy City. We need not depend on our strength, but we can "hope in His steadfast love" (v. 11). The same Word that called the universe into existence and still governs its every detail is manifest in the Holy Scriptures and proclaimed in the Church for our salvation.

PRAYERS:

O Lord, You have made the crystals of ice, and You have made the stars. And yet, You show Your love for us. You have forgiven our sins and gathered us to Yourself. Above all of Your other blessings, You have given us Your Word. And that Word became flesh and dwelt among us. In His name, we come before You. Amen.

The 147th psalm is a psalm of thanks for various kindnesses and mighty works of God—first, toward Israel and Jerusalem, then to all who thirst. He gives rain and water to all creatures and does not let the least little bird go hungry, even the most useless raven. How much more then shall He care for us, especially those who trust in His goodness and not in human strength or horses? But above all, to Jerusalem, where His Word and His dwelling are, He gives peace, grain, and all they need. For Jerusalem and Israel have the advantage that they have God's Word and worship before all the nations; therefore, He has done more miracles from them. He will also be much more recognized there in the daily wonders such as rain, snow, ice, than by the faithless who do not have God's Word or do not heed it. These people cannot see any work or wonder of God, though they enjoy them daily with their five senses, root in them, and devour them like swine. They did not know God because they do not hear or pay attention to His Word. (Martin Luther)

PSALM 148

1 Praise the LORD!
  Praise the LORD from the heavens;
    praise him in the heights!
2 Praise him, all his angels;
    praise him, all his hosts!

3 Praise him, sun and moon,
    praise him, all you shining stars!
4 Praise him, you highest heavens,
    and you waters above the heavens!

5 Let them praise the name of the LORD!
    For he commanded and they were created.
6 And he established them forever and ever;
    he gave a decree, and it shall not pass away.[a]

7 Praise the LORD from the earth,
    you great sea creatures and all deeps,
8 fire and hail, snow and mist,
    stormy wind fulfilling his word!

9 Mountains and all hills,
    fruit trees and all cedars!
10 Beasts and all livestock,
    creeping things and flying birds!

11 Kings of the earth and all peoples,
    princes and all rulers of the earth!
12 Young men and maidens together,
    old men and children!

13 Let them praise the name of the LORD,
    for his name alone is exalted;
    his majesty is above earth and heaven.
14 He has raised up a horn for his people,
    praise for all his saints,
    for the people of Israel who are near to him.
  Praise the LORD!

---

a Psalm 148:6 Or *it shall not be transgressed*

The third of five final alleluia psalms, the Greek Septuagint notations associate this psalm with the postexilic prophets Haggai and Zechariah. Moving from the heavens to the earth, it catalogs the whole range of the created order, from angels to children, from stars to snowflakes. The praise of creation culminates with praise for God's own redeemed people.

⊛ REQUEST THE SPIRIT'S HELP IN PRAYER

⊛ READ AND REPEAT THE WORD

What words or phrases stick out to you? How do those words or phrases reveal the poet's purpose for the psalm? What effect does this psalm have on you as you meditate on it?

⊛ RETURN TO THE LORD IN PRAYER

Our insensibility to God's goodness and glory is a sign of how far we have fallen. In all of His manifold creation, God "has raised up a horn for His people" (v. 14). This is a prophecy of Christ, as evident in the words of Zechariah, John the Baptist's father (Luke 1:68–69). Through Christ, God has gathered together His own people into the Church, declaring them to be His saints and dwelling near them with His very presence in Word and Sacrament.

ALMIGHTY GOD, I THANK YOU TODAY:

ALMIGHTY GOD, I CONFESS TO YOU:

ALMIGHTY GOD, TODAY I ALSO PRAY:

O Lord, may the nebulas of outer space and each atom that You have crafted praise You! May everything living praise You, from archangels to microorganisms! May men and women, old and young, from every nation and culture praise You! O Christ, come quickly and bring all things to their fulfillment. Amen.

PSALM 149

1   Praise the LORD!
Sing to the LORD a new song,
   his praise in the assembly of the godly!
2   Let Israel be glad in his Maker;
   let the children of Zion rejoice in their King!
3   Let them praise his name with dancing,
   making melody to him with tambourine and lyre!
4   For the LORD takes pleasure in his people;
   he adorns the humble with salvation.
5   Let the godly exult in glory;
   let them sing for joy on their beds.
6   Let the high praises of God be in their throats
   and two-edged swords in their hands,
7   to execute vengeance on the nations
   and punishments on the peoples,
8   to bind their kings with chains
   and their nobles with fetters of iron,
9   to execute on them the judgment written!
   This is honor for all his godly ones.
Praise the LORD!

Psalm 149 is the fourth of the five alleluia psalms. The psalm describes a festival procession to the Temple Mount, apparently in celebration of a victory. The date of the writing of this psalm is uncertain.

⊛ REQUEST THE SPIRIT'S HELP IN PRAYER

⊛ READ AND REPEAT THE WORD

What words or phrases stick out to you? How do those words or phrases reveal the poet's purpose for the psalm? What effect does this psalm have on you as you meditate on it?

⊛ RETURN TO THE LORD IN PRAYER

In this psalm, joyous praise of God is interrupted with invocations for God's "vengeance" and "punishments" (v. 7). And yet, despite God's judgment, "He adorns the humble with salvation" (v. 4). Salvation is a gift, a kind of clothing, and the pleasure the Lord takes in His people is not on account of their works. They rejoice in their King, who was bound and suffered the punishment due to the nations. We have fellowship with Him in the Church.

LORD GOD OUR MAKER, I THANK YOU:

LORD GOD OUR KING, I CONFESS TO YOU:

PRAYERS OF REQUEST
That my household may praise You, I pray:

That my daily work may be pleasing to You, I pray:

That my congregation may praise You, I pray:

That I may proclaim You to the world, I pray:

> *O Christ, our King, we praise You in the Church! When we worship and when we are alone, we adore You. Give us courage to engage in spiritual warfare—against the world, our flesh, and the devil—with the two-edged sword of Your Word, and grant us the victory. Amen.*

PSALM 150

1 Praise the LORD!
Praise God in his sanctuary;
    praise him in his mighty heavens!^a
2 Praise him for his mighty deeds;
    praise him according to his excellent greatness!

3 Praise him with trumpet sound;
    praise him with lute and harp!
4 Praise him with tambourine and dance;
    praise him with strings and pipe!
5 Praise him with sounding cymbals;
    praise him with loud clashing cymbals!
6 Let everything that has breath praise the LORD!
Praise the LORD!

a   Psalm 150:1 Hebrew *expanse* (compare Genesis 1:6–8)

Psalm 150 is the final alleluia psalm and the final psalm in the Book of Psalms. In it, we learn how sacred music played an important role in ancient worship. This particular psalm seems to describe a festival procession.

⊛ REQUEST THE SPIRIT'S HELP IN PRAYER

⊛ READ AND REPEAT THE WORD

What words or phrases stick out to you? How do those words or phrases reveal the poet's purpose for the psalm? What effect does this psalm have on you as you meditate on it?

....

....

....

....

....

....

....

⊛ RETURN TO THE LORD IN PRAYER

Psalm 150 is a tenfold "alleluia!" in the heavens and in the place of worship, with every musical instrument. Everything that breathes should praise the Lord because of His mighty deeds and His "excellent greatness" (v. 2)! Of the many reasons to praise God, for us the most joyous are "His mighty deeds" (v. 2), by which He has redeemed us in Christ and brought us to faith.

ALMIGHTY GOD, I THANK YOU:

....

ALMIGHTY GOD, I CONFESS TO YOU:

....

PRAYERS OF REQUEST
That my household may praise You, I pray:

That my daily work may be pleasing to You, I pray:

That my congregation may praise You, I pray:

That I may proclaim You to the world, I pray:

> *O Lord, may the praises in the Psalms, the praises in the Church, and the praises in heaven equip me to join in praising You! Amen.*

BIBLE STUDY RESOURCES

Using the Bible Studies

Engaging the Psalms: A Guide for Reflection and Prayer will not only serve you as a great resource for individual lifelong learning, but it can also serve as a group study of God's Word. Using the Psalms in a group setting, such as a small-group Bible study or a Sunday morning large-group study, allows for the community of God's people to learn together. Not only does this group study allow for sharing experiences and insights but it also helps model what meditation on the Psalms for life can look like. As a group practices the art of requesting the Spirit's help in prayer, reading and repeating the Word, and returning to the Lord in prayer together, each member of the group will be better equipped and encouraged in their daily discipleship.

The Bible studies in this book are self-contained, and no separate student and leader guides are needed. Pages 428–42 present the individual student pages that each member of the group will use during the study. Pages 443–49 serve as a leader guide, one guide per Bible study, providing some prompts and aids in reflecting on the different questions.

The format of the Bible study is straightforward and follows the same format as the reflection prompts for each psalm. The study can take as long or as short as you would like, as many of the questions require self-reflection and sharing and time will vary from group to group. A potential format for these studies, written primarily for a group leader, is presented below.

1. Encourage your learners to share any insights from the previous lesson's suggested readings from the page "For Next Time" (except for Psalm 1). Allow people who did prepare to share one or two valuable insights, but be mindful not to let this take too much time.

2. "Request the Spirit's Help in Prayer": Each study has printed out one of the prayers from the suggested prayer reading list on page 450. This is a great opportunity to learn to use these prayers.

3. "Opening Reflections": This question is meant to hook the attention of your learners. As a leader, don't necessarily look for particular answers. These questions are meant to stimulate thought and conversation. Consider having each learner turn and share their reflections in pairs or small

groups before opening up your group to whole-group
sharing.

4. "Read and Repeat the Word": Read through the introduction in the Bible study together. Then, direct your learners
(either individually or out loud together) to read the text
of the psalm. Some Bible studies highlight points from
different verses, so pay attention to these. As they read,
encourage your learners to underline or circle words or
phrases that jump out to them or to write down their
thoughts on the reflection page. Give them some time to
reflect on their own, and try not to rush. After a set time,
encourage your learners to share any major insights from
reading with your group, perhaps limiting each learner to
one or two points.

5. "Discuss": Lead your learners in further reflection through
the discussion questions. The leader guide provides suggested information that may be helpful in this discussion.
Know your group. Some are more talkative than others.
Encourage everyone to participate, and look for ways to
keep the more talkative members of your group (if you
have them) from dominating the conversation.

6. "Return to the Lord in Prayer": Read the devotional message in the psalm meditation out loud, then discuss the
different application questions as a group.

7. "Closing Reflection": Each Bible study contains a final
reflection, meant to encourage your group to use their
learning outside the study. Consider asking each learner
to write down their reflection privately first before going
around the group to share. This practice will help encourage greater engagement from each learner. Then, consider
using the prayer prompts in the psalm meditation as a
springboard for closing in prayer, using the different ideas
and understandings from the psalm to help guide your
requests to God.

8. "For Next Time": After the session, there are five different
psalms that each participant is encouraged to meditate on
individually between group sessions, along with an article
from *Engaging the Psalms* that will help elaborate some of
the themes from the writing. This is not required for the
next study, but it will enhance the experience.

BIBLE STUDY 1:
GOD'S WISDOM—PSALM 1

Request the Spirit's Help in Prayer

Pray: Blessed Lord, You have caused all Holy Scriptures to be written for our learning. Grant that we may so hear them, read, mark, learn, and inwardly digest them that, by patience and comfort of Your holy Word, we may embrace and ever hold fast the blessed hope of everlasting life; through Jesus Christ, our Lord. Amen. (*LSB*, p. 308)

Opening Reflections

In your experience, how do people define the word *wisdom*? According to the world, what are the marks of someone who lives wisely?

Read and Repeat the Word

Psalm 1 serves as an introduction to Book One of the Psalms, Psalms 1–41. (The Psalms are made up of five books, or collections, of psalms.) It also introduces the entire Book of Psalms, showing God's blessings on those who follow His Word. Read through Psalm 1 in the front of this book, noting and sharing any words or phrases that stick out to you as you go. In particular, pay attention to the following points.

Verse 1: Notice how a person's association with sin progresses: *walk*; *stand*; *sit*. It is difficult to be near a sinful situation and not to be influenced by it.

Verse 2, "The law of the LORD": This refers to both Law and Gospel.

Verse 3, "Leaf does not wither": Such a tree withstands the forces of nature. So do the righteous withstand the winds of trials and troubles.

Verse 6: Hebrew poetry does not rhyme as English poetry often does. Rather, it uses various language devices. For instance, in this verse the psalmist uses parallelism. The first and second parts of verse 6 are parallel; in this case, they express parallel but opposite thoughts.

Discuss

1. What are three characteristics of the wise and godly, according to verses 1–3?

2. In what ways is a Christian like a fruit tree?

3. What does being blown away by the wind symbolize in this psalm?

4. How will the lives of the righteous and the wicked end?

Return to the Lord in Prayer

Read the devotional section after "Return to the Lord in Prayer" in Psalm 1 of this book. Then, discuss the following questions.

5. What are ways in which Christians might gradually be corrupted by the world's standards?

6. How can we and our children guard ourselves against these dangers?

7. What are the only two roads people can travel?

Closing Reflection

How has this psalm helped you better understand what the Christian life looks like?

Write down some prayer requests, and share some that you would like others to pray for with you during the week.

....

....

....

....

....

....

For Next Time

Meditate on Psalms 2; 62; 72; 121; 131, and read the article "Sheep and Shepherds" on pages 59–61 in preparation for the next session.

BIBLE STUDY 2:
OUR SHEPHERD—PSALM 23

Request the Spirit's Help in Prayer

Pray: O almighty Father, lead us to Your Word, that we may find healing of heart, soul, and mind in the Gospel of Jesus. Be near us as we read for ourselves that Jesus has indeed died and has risen again for us. Keep us steadfast in Your grace and mercy, that we may spread Your love to those who haven't heard the Good News and to those who have heard but have forgotten it. Let us do all we can to win souls for You, that they may go out and do the same. In Jesus' most holy name, we pray. Amen. (*TLSB*, inside front cover)

Opening Reflections

Who are some of the most charismatic and powerful leaders that people follow in the world? Think of politicians, celebrities, or thought leaders. Make a short list, and consider what qualities these leaders have that cause others to follow them and do what they say.

Read and Repeat the Word

Psalm 23 is perhaps the most familiar and best-loved of the psalms. It describes God's loving care for us in shepherd terms. Recall that David once served as a shepherd, so it is very personal. Note other Old Testament references to God as the Shepherd of Israel (Isaiah 40:11; Ezekiel 34:11–16) and the New Testament reference to Christ as the Good Shepherd (John 10:1–18). Read through Psalm 23 in this book, noting and sharing any words or phrases that stick out to you as you go.

Discuss

1. Verses 1–3 picture how a shepherd cares for his sheep. How do these pictures describe our Father's care for us?

    "The LORD is my shepherd."

    ....

    ....

    "He makes me lie down in green pastures."

    ....

    ....

"He leads me beside still waters."

"He restores my soul."

2. "Righteousness" refers to God's covenant. The heart of God's righteousness is His faithfulness to His promises. With that in mind, interpret what David means by "paths of righteousness." Why does God lead us along those paths?

3. How does a shepherd protect his sheep? From what does the Shepherd protect us?

4. At one point in the psalm, the picture shifts from the shepherd to the Shepherd King. What does our Shepherd King do for us, according to verse 5?

Return to the Lord in Prayer

Read the devotional section after "Return to the Lord in Prayer" for Psalm 23 in this book. Then, discuss the following questions.

5. As God's redeemed child in Christ, in what ways is God your Shepherd?

6. When you attend the funeral of a Christian loved one, you often hear Psalm 23. What comfort does it bring you? Note especially verse 6.

Closing Reflection

Take another look at Psalm 23, looking for specific verses and phrases that catch your eye. Using these, consider different ways you can intentionally seek to follow God as your Shepherd in different aspects of your life this week. Think about your different roles, or vocations, in life, and how you can more diligently trust in God's care and listen to His voice rather than the voices of the world in those times.

Write down some prayer requests, and share some that you would like others to pray for with you during the week.

For Next Time

Meditate on Psalms 8; 76; 78; 84; 100, and read the article "Telling Israel's Story of Rescue" on pages 218–19 in preparation for the next session.

BIBLE STUDY 3:
OUR FORTRESS—PSALM 46

Request the Spirit's Help in Prayer

Pray: Gracious and Blessed God, You have taught and commanded us above all things first to seek the kingdom of God and His righteousness. Grant us grace, that Your holy Word may be preached in all the world in all its truth and purity. May we submit our reason to the obedience of faith and live holy lives, as is proper for the children of God, to Your pleasing. Then Your kingdom may come to us and increase, and many people who do not yet believe in the Word may be won through Christian conduct. Help us, dear God, who are delivered from the power of darkness and are translated into the kingdom of Your dear Son, Jesus Christ. In Him, we have redemption through His blood, even the forgiveness of sin. May we remain in His kingdom, faithfully continue in the wholesome doctrine, and live worthily as children of light in all piety and godliness. Amen. (*TLWA*, p. 315)

Opening Reflections

What are different people, places, and things that people in society turn to when life gets difficult? Think of the top three in your experience. Are these good or bad things to turn to, and why?

Read and Repeat the Word

The event in the history of Israel that best fits the powerful deliverance described in Psalm 46 occurred during the reign of Hezekiah when the Lord destroyed the Assyrian army of Sennacherib (2 Kings 19:35–37). Luther based his famous hymn, "A Mighty Fortress Is Our God" (*LSB* 656), on this psalm. Luther said that the words of this psalm gave him the strength he needed for the Reformation. Read through Psalm 46 in this book, noting and sharing any words or phrases that stick out to you as you go. In particular, pay attention to the following points.

Verse 7, "The LORD of hosts": The Hebrew word translated "host" means "an army." It may be interpreted to mean that our God is the Lord of the "army of the heavenly angels," or that He is the Lord of "all armies," both earthly and heavenly.

Verse 7, "The God of Jacob is our fortress": The word for *fortress* literally means "a lofty place," "a rock affording shelter," or "a stronghold." It can also be translated as "refuge."

Discuss

1. From what kinds of calamities does the Lord protect His own (vv. 2–3)? Does this mean that believers will never be hurt by any of these calamities? In what sense does God protect us?

2. What is "the city of God" (v. 4)? Why can God's people find perfect safety there (vv. 4–7)?

3. Verses 8–9 call us to remember that the Lord of hosts also has power over another kind of calamity. What is that calamity? Cite some examples of this in modern history.

Return to the Lord in Prayer

Read the devotional section after "Return to the Lord in Prayer" for Psalm 46 in this book. Then, discuss the following questions.

4. The admonition of the Lord in verse 10 is very often ignored by Christians. Explain.

5. Recall a time in your life when you should have waited patiently for God's help but didn't. Recall a time when you did wait on Him. How did He help you?

Closing Reflection

What is your one biggest takeaway from studying this psalm? How has it helped you better understand what it is to trust in God above all things? Write down some prayer requests, and share some that you would like others to pray for with you during the week.

....

....

....

....

For Next Time

Meditate on Psalms 6; 22; 32; 102; 130, and read the article "Law and Gospel in the Psalms" on pages 144–45 in preparation for the next session.

BIBLE STUDY 4:
GOD'S MERCY–PSALM 51

Request the Spirit's Help in Prayer

Pray: Blessed Lord, You have caused all Holy Scriptures to be written for our learning. Grant that we may so hear them, read, mark, learn, and inwardly digest them that, by patience and comfort of Your holy Word, we may embrace and ever hold fast the blessed hope of everlasting life; through Jesus Christ, our Lord. Amen. (*LSB*, p. 308)

Opening Reflections

Think of a time you felt really broken by something you had done. What was your response, and how did you try to make things right (if at all)?

Read and Repeat the Word

The heading tells us that Psalm 51 was written after the prophet Nathan visited David. See 2 Samuel 11–12 for the background. This is the most highly regarded of the penitential psalms (6; 32; 38; 51; 102; 130; 143) because it so clearly states both the sinner's grief over his sin and God's great mercy. Read through Psalm 51 in this book, noting and sharing any words or phrases that stick out to you as you go. In particular, pay attention to the following points.

Verses 1–2: The word pictures used to describe God's rejection and David's disobedience tell the story in this psalm. Such disobedience is like an ugly blotch that must be removed and like a filthy garment that must be thoroughly washed.

Verse 7, "Hyssop": This is a branch from a bush with fragrant leaves, used for sprinkling blood or water in rituals prescribed by God.

Discuss

1. With what truth does David begin this psalm? How do many people approach sin and guilt?

....

....

2. David provides us with a very clear picture of his sin. Against whom, above all, had he sinned? How well is this concept understood today? See also Genesis 39:9.

3. Verse 5 gets to the very root of humankind's problem with sin. What is the problem?

4. What does David ask God to do with him (v. 6)?

5. What words in verse 7 show that David is confident the Lord will answer his prayer?

6. How had God crushed David's bones (v. 8)? How did David find relief?

7. Verses 10–12 are used in the Divine Service (*LSB*, pp. 192–193) immediately after the sermon. How do these verses help us respond to a sermon in which both Law and Gospel have been preached?

8. What do all sinners do when they know they have been forgiven (vv. 13–15)?

Return to the Lord in Prayer

Read the devotional section after "Return to the Lord in Prayer" for Psalm 51 in this book. Then, discuss the following situation.

Your friend attends a church where the Law is not preached and the issue of sin is not treated. He comes home each Sunday feeling good about himself.

He finds fault with your church because your pastor speaks about the Law and the consequences of sin. How could you answer him with verses from this psalm? What kind of joy do you have when you return from church services on Sunday?

Closing Reflection
Write down some prayer requests, and share some that you would like others to pray for with you during the week.

....

....

....

....

For Next Time
Meditate on Psalms 2; 8; 104; 118; and 144, and read the article "Life's God-Given Value" on pages 390–91 in preparation for the next session.

BIBLE STUDY 5:
LORD OF LIFE–PSALM 139

Request the Spirit's Help in Prayer

Pray: Eternal God and Father of our Lord Jesus Christ, grant us Your Holy Spirit who writes the preached word into our hearts so that we may receive and believe it, and be gladdened and comforted by it in eternity. Glorify Your Word in our hearts. Make it so bright and warm that we may find pleasure in it, and through Your inspiration think what is right. By Your power fulfill the Word, for the sake of Jesus Christ, Your Son, our Lord. Amen. (*TLWA*, p. 38)

Opening Reflections

In what ways does society value human life, and in what ways does society downplay or neglect human life? What are the biggest factors, in your own experience, that contribute to these discrepancies?

Read and Repeat the Word

In Psalm 139, David looks at his relationship with God in light of God's qualities. David evaluates himself (and all Christians) in view of four qualities. In the spaces below, describe which attributes of God David is speaking about, and then describe what effect these have on him. Read through Psalm 139 in this book, noting and sharing any words or phrases that stick out to you as you go.

....
....
....
....

Discuss

1. Verses 1–6: David knows that God .... about him.
    What effect does this have on David? (Note vv. 5–6.)

....
....

2. Verses 7–12: David is aware that God is present ....
    What effect does this have on David?

....
....

3. Verses 13–18: When David considers how he was formed, he reflects on God's ...., and when he consider how God guides his life, he reflects on God's

   ....

   What effect does this have on David? (Note the transition in v. 13.)

   ....

   ....

4. Verses 19–24: When David prays that God would defeat the wicked and then considers his own behavior, he reflects on God's ....

   What effect does this have on David?

   ....

   ....

Return to the Lord in Prayer

Read the devotional section after "Return to the Lord in Prayer" for Psalm 139 in this book. Then, discuss the following questions.

5. What does this psalm say about God's view of life? How do Christians align with God's view, and how do we often fail to align with God's view?

   ....

   ....

6. Does this psalm give you comfort? Why or why not?

   ....

   ....

7. When in your life does God feel most present and most absent?

   ....

   ....

8. Knowing that God truly is with you regardless of how you feel (see Psalm 139; Matthew 28:20), what is one thing you can do in your daily life to remind yourself constantly of God's presence and care?

   ....

   ....

Closing Reflection

How has this psalm helped you better understand what God thinks about you and all human life?

....

....

....

Write down some prayer requests, and share some that you would like others to pray for with you during the week. Then consider how you and those in your group will continue to find ways to meditate on the psalms now that the study is complete.

....

....

BIBLE STUDY 1: LEADER NOTES

Opening Reflections

In the world, *wisdom* could be defined as having the ability to make good decisions. Marks of worldly wisdom include success, friends, and power. These are not the marks of godly wisdom, as Psalm 1 will show.

Discuss

1. They refuse to be among sinners (v. 1). They love the Word and meditate on it (v. 2). They produce fruits of faith (v. 3).

2. A Christian is joined to the Lord by faith, is nurtured by the Word, and bears fruits of faith.

3. The chaff is worthless and is blown away. It symbolizes not being able to stand before God on Judgment Day. It symbolizes that a person is not part of God's people.

4. The Lord watches over the way of the righteous. The way of the wicked leads to eternal death.

Return to the Lord in Prayer

5. Christians might begin to tolerate the ways of the world. Then they may start hanging around people who practice the world's sins. Eventually, they will find themselves joining in with the sinful actions of these people. Specifics will vary.

6. We can delight in God's Word and meditate on it. Regular Bible study, daily family devotions, and personal Bible study are all things we can do.

7. The two roads are the road of obedience and the road of rebellion. Note these two options in verse 6.

Closing Reflection

This psalm shows us that Christians are to meditate on God's Word and let it strengthen our faith and life. As we live in God's Word, we are to follow God's ways and wisdom above the ways and wisdom of the world.

BIBLE STUDY 2:
LEADER NOTES

Opening Reflections

Lists of leaders will vary, but reasons for their appeal may include political power, wealth, attractiveness, success, or platform for speaking.

Discuss

1. Verses 1–3: "The LORD is my shepherd." I am part of the flock that the Lord guides and nourishes. "He makes me lie down in green pastures." He gives me nourishment and refreshment in the Word. "He leads me beside still waters. He restores my soul." He gives me rest from the guilt and power of sin.

2. Verse 3: "Paths of righteousness" are the paths that lead us on the way of enjoying the blessings of God's covenant promises. Think of the well-known passage in Romans, "We know that for those who love God all things work together for good" (8:28). God does all this for us not because of our own goodness but for the sake of His name, which means love and blessing through Jesus.

3. Verse 4: A shepherd protects his sheep with his shepherd's rod and staff. Our Shepherd protects us from the wicked people of this world, especially from false teachers and from all the attacks of Satan. This protection forces what seems bad in our lives to serve for our good.

4. Verse 5: He spreads out rich banquet tables at which we are anointed with oil as a symbol of honor and joy at being in the royal court. He sets these banquets in the sight of our enemies, who see clearly that we have put our trust in the right person. In this position, we can be sure we are safe from all our enemies.

Return to the Lord in Prayer

5. God is our Shepherd in that through His Word, He not only gives us life but also leads and guides us. By the Sacrament of the Altar, He likewise feeds and sustains us.

6. All God's people can say that the Lord has bestowed His goodness and love on them throughout their lives. They can be assured they are dwelling in the house of the Lord and will live there forever.

Closing Reflection

Vocations include being a parent, worker, citizen, or member of a congregation. Habits include prayer, reading and meditating on God's Word, and remembering your Baptism. The greatest habit of faith is regularly attending the Divine Service and receiving the Means of Grace.

BIBLE STUDY 3: LEADER NOTES

Opening Reflections

People turn to many different things. Encourage your group to divide up into pairs or small groups to write a list before sharing with the rest of the group. Some things are good, such as turning to God for help or relying on loving family who is there for you. Other things, such as turning to substance abuse or idle distractions, can be dangerous.

Discuss

1. Verses 2–3: The calamities are described as natural disasters. They are symbolic of everything that threatens to harm the Church, whether natural disasters or spiritual attacks. Even though God's people will experience hardships and difficulties in life, God has promised to be with His people always. He may or may not protect us from all earthly harm, but in Christ, He gives us the promise of eternal security through the forgiveness of sins.

2. Verses 4–7: The "city of God" is the refuge of God's Church. The Church has life-giving water. God is within her. God will help her at the break of day; He is always awake and ready to defend her whenever the enemy attacks. When God lifts His voice, the earth melts.

3. Verses 8–9: Here we have a reference to warfare of all kinds. There is no army or nation that our Lord cannot defeat. He may forcefully stop wars by His power. He may

lead people to put down their hatred and weapons by the power of His Gospel. Recent examples include World Wars and other conflicts around the world that either directly or indirectly impact our daily lives.

Return to the Lord in Prayer

4. Too often, we lose ourselves in nervous, incessant chatter when faced with a calamity. We need to stop, be quiet, and listen carefully to God's Word, waiting for His help.

5. Answers will vary, but encourage your learners to share their experiences with one another.

Closing Reflection

Answers will vary but may include points such as God does not change, God is more powerful than any of the enemies of Gods' people, and God is with us regardless of the circumstances.

BIBLE STUDY 4: LEADER NOTES

Opening Reflections

This is a very personal question, so pay special attention to your particular group and their needs. The most important part of this reflection is giving your learners space to think through how they react to times when their personal sins are before them. If your group is not open to sharing, consider having them each consider this question privately on their own.

Discuss

1. Verse 1: David begins with the truth of God's mercy. Some people get no farther than the Law of God, which convicts them of sin, fills them with guilt, and leaves them only with self-pity or self-righteousness. Others seek to rationalize their conduct, ignore the Law, and go forward calling good bad and bad good.

2. Verse 4: While it is true that he sinned against Uriah, Bathsheba, and God's people in general (2 Samuel 11–12), David's sin was against God. Today, many leave God out

of the equation. If they can convince themselves that no one is getting hurt by their sins, they justify them.

3. Verse 5: David here speaks of original sin, that is, the sin we were born with that Jesus referred to in Matthew 15:19. David did not say that he couldn't help doing what he did; rather, he placed the blame squarely where it belonged, on himself.

4. Verse 6: David asks God to teach him wisdom—the wisdom to get rid of sin by confessing it.

5. Verse 7: The words "I shall be" make clear David's complete confidence that he would be washed, cleansed, and made whiter than snow.

6. Verse 8: David lived in guilt, which no doubt took its mental and physical toll. David found relief when he realized that God had forgiven him.

7. Having heard the Law, we are eager to have God's promised forgiveness. Having heard the Gospel, we are confident that God will renew our spirits and restore us with the joy of salvation.

8. Forgiven sinners cannot help but want others to know the joy they have found.

Return to the Lord in Prayer
True joy can only come from knowing that sin is forgiven. People need to be taught that feeling good about oneself is not the most important thing. Feeling good about Christ is.

Closing Reflection
Close with prayer, taking special note of prayers of thanks for forgiveness.

BIBLE STUDY 5:
LEADER NOTES

Opening Reflections

People often celebrate birthdays and gender reveals while also supporting abortion and physician-assisted suicide. As in anything, sinful humans tend to craft their morals on life issues around what they desire at the moment.

Discuss

1. Verses 1–6: David knows that God **knows everything** about him. David realizes that since God knows everything, God has His hand on him. God shapes and controls his entire life—for David's good. David says he cannot fathom God's knowledge about him. He does not know how the Lord will deal with him next.

2. Verses 7–12: David is aware that God is present **everywhere**. David knows that there is no place where he can flee to escape the Lord. On the negative side, David could not escape God after his sin with Bathsheba and subsequent unrepentance. The positive side, however, he would experience during most of his life. David knows that no matter where he goes, the Lord is always there.

3. Verses 13–18: When David considers how he was formed, he reflects on God's **power**, and when he considers how God guides his life, he reflects on God's **power and goodness**. David focuses on one particular place the Lord was with him: namely, in the womb. God displayed His power and goodness there by shaping and fashioning David in a wonderful way. David also confesses that God ordained all his days, pointing out how God's power controls his life and how God's goodness makes a wonderful plan for David's life.

4. Verses 19–24: When David prays that God would defeat the wicked and then considers his own behavior, he reflects on God's **holiness**. David wants to be far from the wicked. He asks God to destroy those who hate the Lord and want to destroy His people. David also asks the Lord to chasten him and correct him so that he continues to walk in the Lord's ways forever.

Return to the Lord in Prayer

5. The psalm shows how God cares about and values life. He forms us in our mothers' wombs and cares for us throughout our lives, wherever we may be. Christians often fail to love as God loves, as we are sinful human creatures. In Christ, however, God can still use us to love our neighbor as ourselves; through the Spirit and the Word, God continues to form our lives of faith to be more loving.

6. Answers will vary. For some, this psalm gives comfort as it tells of God's relentless care. For others who are convicted in their sins, this psalm may trouble them, as it shows how God knows and sees all. Be assured that God's presence is for our benefit. Through the Word, God continually calls us to lives of repentance and forgiveness, and He is with us always, even to the end of the age.

7. This is a personal reflection. God may feel present or absent at different times in life, but that does not change the reality that He has promised to be with us always, regardless of how we feel. We can rejoice greatly that God has promised to be with us through the Means of Grace, in Word and Sacrament, as we gather together for worship. As we gather around the Word in our daily lives, either on our own or with others, the Spirit is still working through the Word to form us in Christ. In times when God feels absent, we should always turn back to God's Word and gather with others in worship.

8. Reminders may include creating a prayer list, doing daily devotions, listening to sermons, leaving Scripture reminders around your house or wherever you live, and gathering with others to pray, praise, and give thanks to God.

Closing Reflection

God values human life, from conception until death. There are no boundaries to His love for His human creatures. We can always be assured that God will never abandon us. Likewise, this love should prompt us to love all human life, from conception to death. As Christians, we live in a world with confused priorities about human life. We should show genuine care and compassion to all human life, regardless of circumstance.

SUGGESTED PRAYERS FOR REQUESTING THE SPIRIT'S HELP

The Great Psalm of the Word
Let my cry come before You, O LORD; give me understanding according to Your word! Let my plea come before You; deliver me according to Your word. My lips will pour forth praise, for You teach me Your statutes. My tongue will sing of Your word, for all Your commandments are right. Let Your hand be ready to help me, for I have chosen Your precepts. I long for Your salvation, O LORD, and Your law is my delight. Let my soul live and praise You, and let Your rules help me. I have gone astray like a lost sheep; seek Your servant, for I do not forget Your commandments. [Amen.] (Psalm 119:169–76)

Grace to Receive the Word
Blessed Lord, You have caused all Holy Scriptures to be written for our learning. Grant that we may so hear them, read, mark, learn, and inwardly digest them that, by patience and comfort of Your holy Word, we may embrace and ever hold fast the blessed hope of everlasting life; through Jesus Christ, our Lord. [Amen.] (*LSB*, p. 308)

Luther's Prayer for Growth
[God our Father,] help us to grow in the knowledge of Your dear Son, our Lord Jesus Christ, and to remain firm in the confession of His blessed Word. Give us the love to be of one mind and to serve one another in Christ. Then we will not be afraid of that which is disagreeable, nor of the rage of the arsonist (Satan) whose torch is almost extinguished. Dear Father, guard us so that his craftiness may not take the place of our pure faith. Grant that our cross and sufferings may lead to a blessed and sure hope of the coming of our Savior, Jesus Christ, for whom we wait daily. Amen. (*TLWA*, p. 35)

Luther's Prayer to Receive the Word
Eternal God and Father of our Lord Jesus Christ, grant us Your Holy Spirit who writes the preached word into our hearts so that we may receive and believe it, and be gladdened and comforted by it in eternity. Glorify Your Word in our hearts. Make it so bright and warm that we may find pleasure in it, and through Your inspiration think what is right. By Your power fulfill the Word, for the sake of Jesus Christ, Your Son, our Lord. Amen. (*TLWA*, p. 38)

Bless Our Hearts and Minds

Heavenly Father, almighty and everlasting God, we come before You in humble awe. You are the one true God, and there is none other like You. Come, we pray, and bless our hearts and minds as we study Your Word. Send Your Holy Spirit into our lives so that we may grow in love and grace, and that we may go forth into all the world, proclaiming Your Gospel so that others may learn of Your saving grace. Amen. (*TLSB*, inside front cover)

Lead Us to Your Word

O almighty Father, lead us to Your Word, that we may find healing of heart, soul, and mind in the Gospel of Jesus. Be near us as we read for ourselves that Jesus has indeed died and has risen again for us. Keep us steadfast in Your grace and mercy, that we may spread Your love to those who haven't heard the Good News and to those who have heard but have forgotten it. Let us do all we can to win souls for You, that they may go out and do the same. In Jesus' most holy name, we pray. Amen. (*TLSB*, inside front cover)

Lord Jesus Christ, with Us Abide

Lord Jesus Christ, with us abide,
For round us falls the eventide.
O let Your Word, that saving light,
Shine forth undimmed into the night.

In these last days of great distress
Grant us, dear Lord, true steadfastness
That we keep pure till life is spent
Your holy Word and Sacrament. [Amen.]
(*LSB* 585:1–2, © 1982 CPH)

Prayer for God's Kingdom

Gracious and Blessed God, You have taught and commanded us above all things first to seek the kingdom of God and His righteousness. Grant us grace, that Your holy Word may be preached in all the world in all its truth and purity. May we submit our reason to the obedience of faith and live holy lives, as is proper for the children of God, to Your pleasing. Then Your kingdom may come to us, and increase, and many people, who do not yet believe in the Word, may be won through Christian conduct. Help us, dear God, who are delivered from the power of darkness and are translated into the kingdom of Your dear Son, Jesus Christ. In Him we have redemption through His blood, even the forgiveness of sin. May we remain in His kingdom, faithfully continue in the wholesome doctrine, and live worthily as children of light in all piety and godliness. Amen. (*TLWA*, p. 315)

Prayer for Faith in the Word
O Lord, our God, how blessed are we! Not only have You given us Your Word, which offers and imparts to us all the fruits of the redemption of Your dear Son, Jesus Christ, but You have also opened our eyes, so that we may know Your grace and in firm confidence receive it. Though the world, the Law, our heart, and our conscience condemn us, what do we care? Your Word declares us free of all guilt. O keep us in such faith unto our end and grant that all the members of our congregation may appreciate the great treasure which they possess. Help them and us to triumph over all attacks of the devil, the world, and our flesh and finally to depart this life in peace and to be received into Your eternal kingdom. Hear us for the sake of our risen and victorious Champion, Jesus Christ. Amen. (*TLWA*, p. 317)

Prayer for Blessing on the Word
Lord Jesus Christ, giver and perfecter of our faith, we thank and praise You for continuing among us the preaching of Your Gospel for our instruction and edification. Send Your blessing upon the Word, which has been spoken to us, and by Your Holy Spirit increase our saving knowledge of You, that day by day we may be strengthened in the divine truth and remain steadfast in Your grace. Give us strength to fight the good fight and by faith to overcome all the temptations of Satan, the flesh, and the world so that we may finally receive the salvation of our souls; for You live and reign with the Father and the Holy Spirit, one God, now and forever. [Amen.] (*LSB*, p. 308)

Prayer for Obedience to the Word
O holy and most merciful God, You have taught us the way of Your commandments. We implore You to pour out Your grace into our hearts. Cause it to bear fruit in us that, being ever mindful of Your mercies and Your laws, we may always be directed to Your will and daily increase in love toward You and one another. Enable us to resist all evil and to live a godly life. Help us to follow the example of our Lord and Savior, Jesus Christ, and to walk in His steps until we shall possess the kingdom that has been prepared for us in heaven; through Jesus Christ, our Lord. [Amen.] (*LSB*, p. 308)

God's Word Is Our Great Heritage
God's Word is our great heritage
And shall be ours forever;
To spread its light from age to age
Shall be our chief endeavor.
Through life it guides our way,
In death it is our stay.
Lord, grant, while worlds endure,
We keep its teachings pure
Throughout all generations. [Amen.]

(*LSB* 582)

Speak, O Lord, Your Servant Listens

Speak, O Lord, Your servant listens,
Let Your Word to me come near;
Newborn life and spirit give me,
Let each promise still my fear.
Death's dread pow'r, its inward strife,
Wars against Your Word of life;
Fill me, Lord, with love's strong fervor
That I cling to You forever! [Amen.]
(*LSB* 589:1)

Lord, Keep Us Steadfast in Your Word

Lord, keep us steadfast in Your Word;
Curb those who by deceit or sword
Would wrest the kingdom from Your Son
And bring to naught all He has done. [Amen.]
(*LSB* 655:1)

Open to Me Your Word

Jesus, Key of David, I have tried to open the gates of heaven by clever reason. I have pounded them by my own strength. My efforts always end with a frustrated mind and a battered conscience. Open to me Your Word. Take away my burdens of body and soul and bear me feather-light over the threshold of heaven. Amen. (*TLWA*, p. 37)

Prayer to Abide by God's Revealed Will

Merciful Father, Your Word was written for our instruction so that by steadfastness and by encouragement of the Scriptures we might have hope. Grant us sound interpretation of all the Scriptures that we may receive all their comfort and hope according to Your Holy Spirit's will and intent. Grant that we abide in this simple, direct, and useful exposition that is permanently and well-grounded in Your revealed will. Teach us to flee all abstruse and specious questions and disputations so that we reject and condemn all things contrary to Your true, simple, and useful teachings; through Christ Jesus, our Savior. Amen. (*TLSB*, inside back cover)

KEY TERMS

arm In Israelite thought, an image of strength. See *hand* and *right hand*.

bless In Hebrew *barak*, "To bestow ability for success" (from the greater person to the lesser) or "to praise a person's ability for success" (from the lesser person to the greater). Refers to bending the knees, perhaps to kneel and receive a pronouncement of inheritance with all its wealth (see Genesis 27). "Bless the Lord" has the sense of "greet" and is common in the Psalms, expressing thanks and praise (see 34:1; 145:1, 10). In faith, praise is the greatest gift we can offer to our Lord. The blessing that came from the temple at Jerusalem now resonates through the Church, brought by pastors, missionaries, teachers, and other Christians who proclaim the Gospel of Christ's sacrifice.

blessed In Hebrew *'ashar*, "happy, blissful," having God's gifts.

call In Hebrew *qara'*, "to call upon," "name," or "summon." "Call on God's name" describes speaking God's name in prayer, repentance, or consulting the Lord by Urim and Thummim, administered by the high priest. See *seek*.

courts of the Lord The various courtyards that surrounded the tabernacle and temple were restricted by the various standards of holiness. To enter these holy places was to enter God's presence. See also *presence*.

deliver Translates various Hebrew terms. Primarily *natsal*, which has the sense "to pull or draw out," therefore, "to rescue, save" as the Lord delivered Israel in the exodus from Egypt (see Colossians 1:13).

faithfulness   From Hebrew *'aman*, "to be steady, faithful, true," from which our term "Amen" comes. An attribute of God celebrated in the Psalms. See *steadfast love.*

fear   In Hebrew *yare'*, as in "fear the Lord" and "fear God"—common expressions in the Psalms. They mean to "trust in the Lord."

for Your name's sake   That is, "for the sake of the Lord's good reputation." The preciousness of God's name is illustrated by the way He guards it and by the delight He takes when people use His name well. Everything God does for His people reveals Himself and demonstrates His character. It brings glory to His name. See *name.*

gracious   From Hebrew *chanan*, "to be gracious, generous, compassionate." An attribute of God celebrated in the Psalms.

great congregation   From Hebrew *qahal*, "assembly." The gathering of God's people at the tabernacle or temple.

hand   In Hebrew *yad*, "hand, including the forearm." An image for God's saving power. See *right hand* and *arm.*

horn   An image of power. Animals with horns are bold; in Israelite thought, a horned animal with its head held high symbolized strength and triumph.

just   See *righteous.*

justice   See *righteousness.*

meditate   Translates Hebrew *hagah* and *siach*, terms about speaking. A person holds his attention by uttering words of Scripture or prayers to focus his thoughts. The Israelites meditated on God's Word by reciting it. The believer explores God's Word, since "there is always something left over to understand and to do. Therefore you must never be proud, as if you were already full" (AE 11:434). Lutheran scholar Chemnitz wrote, "Each person, in whatever station or calling he has, may meditate on the law of the Lord and speak of His testimonies" (*LTh* 2:380). Luther suggests that this verb recalls the singing of the birds, "so the church continuously fills its mouth with preaching in joy and gladness like that of the little birds" (AE 11:437, n 23).

mercy Translates various Hebrew terms (see *steadfast love* and *gracious*). Hebrew *rachamim*, "tender mercy," "compassion" from the term for "womb," it pictures the tender love a mother has for her children.

name In Hebrew *shem*. Its meanings can include "reputation," "fame," and "memory." Yahweh's name bears His being and power to save (Psalm 54:1). See *call*, *seek*, and *for Your name's sake*.

new song In Hebrew *shir chadash*, a song written to celebrate God's new work of salvation. The "old song" was the Song of Moses, which celebrated the redemption from Egypt (Exodus 15:1–18). The "new song" in the Psalms often celebrated redemption from exile (see Nehemiah 12:27). Revelation 5:8–9 says the "new song" is about the final redemption through Jesus.

path(s) See *way(s)*.

Praise the Lord In Hebrew *hallelu yah*, "praise Yah[weh]." An exclamation of thankful praise to the one true God.

presence In Hebrew *panim*, "face," so "to be in front of someone or something." To "enter God's presence" typically refers to visiting the temple or tabernacle for worship. See *courts of the Lord*. An advancing warrior naturally "faced" his enemies, so the Lord's "presence" or "face" is fearsome to His enemies.

redeem   Translates two terms. Hebrew *ga'al*, "to ransom, deliver, buy back," and *padah*, "to ransom," used especially by Moses for the ransoming of the firstborn from sacrifice (see Exodus 13:13). The Lord redeemed Israel by rescuing them from slavery. In the New Testament, "redeem" and "ransom" describe Jesus' work (see Ephesians 1:7; 1 Peter 1:18–19).

remember   In Hebrew *zakar*, "to recall" or "keep in mind." God could not forget His covenant with His people. When He "remembers" them, He actively works to keep His promise to protect and save them.

right hand   In Israelite thought, the right hand was the favored one. As such, it symbolized the place of privilege or strength. The chief court official was seated at the king's right hand as a symbol of his power and authority. The term can describe God's chosen servant (for example, King David). See *hand*.

righteous   In Hebrew *tsadaq*, "proved right" or "in good order." Used to describe a person in a right relationship with God, trusting God's promised salvation and living by the covenant promise. The Psalms describe how the wicked plot against the righteous, but the Lord watches over the righteous and delivers them. God is righteous because He faithfully and justly keeps His Word.

righteousness   Hebrew *tsedaqah*, "blamelessness, honesty, justice." An attribute of God praised in the Psalms. The expression "in Your righteousness deliver me" (Psalm 71:2; see also Psalms 5:8; 31:1; 89:16; 119:40; 143:11) describes the psalmist asking God to keep His promise of salvation (see "righteous acts" and "deeds of salvation" in 71:15). He is the source of righteousness (4:1), which is the basis for the biblical teaching of righteousness or justification through faith (see also Genesis 15:6; Romans 3:21–5:11).

rock   Translates two terms: Hebrew *sela'*, "rock" or "cliff face," and *tsur*, "massive rock" or "boulder."

Psalms use the terms interchangeably for a place of refuge or hiding. The Lord is "the Rock of my salvation" (89:26). See *Zion.*

saints
Translates two terms: Hebrew *qedoshim*, those "set apart, holy," God's chosen people who serve Him, and *chasidim*, those "loyal, devout, faithful" (see *steadfast love*). Nearly always with a possessive pronoun (for example, "His saints"). God's people are declared holy because of God's work, not their own.

salvation
In Hebrew *yeshu'ah*, "deliverance." Sometimes translated as "victory" because of military imagery. God defeated Pharaoh and his army during the exodus, and subsequently conquered all enemies that would separate His people from Him. His righteousness is victorious over wickedness, and thus salvation comes to His people solely because of Him. See *redeem* and *deliver.* Martin Chemnitz wrote, "In the Psalms for the first time the word *yāsha*, from which is derived the name 'Jesus' begins to be used in reference to the matter of salvation" (*LTh* 2:458).

seek
Translates two terms: Hebrew *baqash*, "look for," and *darash*, "care about, examine, inquire." The Lord is sought in three ways: (1) through calling on His name in prayer, (2) by consulting Him through Urim and Thummim administered by the high priest, and (3) through the study of His Word. A visit to the tabernacle or temple is frequently implied. Unbelievers do not seek God. Believers seek Him in an attitude of repentance, not selfishness. See *call.*

Selah
A Hebrew musical notation, but untranslatable. It is used mostly in the first two books of the Psalms. It probably refers to the accompaniment of the harps during the psalm.

steadfast love
In Hebrew *chesed*, "loyalty" to one's community; most common term for God's grace in the Psalms (125 times). Luther described *chesed* as "goodness in action" (AE 14:50). God's unwavering

devotion to the salvation of His people finds its
fulfillment in the cross of Christ.

*steadfast love
and
faithfulness* A common word pair in the Psalms, epitomizing
the Lord's care for His people. See *steadfast love,
faithfulness.*

*Urim and
Thummim* Two sacred lots that were used by the high priest
to receive answers from the Lord. It seems that
the technique used in determining God's will
involved questions that could be answered by yes
or no. Answers were given by means of the Urim
and Thummim, which may have been sticks,
some kind of dice, or black and white stones.

upholds In Hebrew *samak*, "sustain, support." The arms of
the wicked will not support them before God on
the Last Day, while the Lord's arms are under the
righteous to hold them up. See *arm*, *hand*, and
right hand.

way(s) In Hebrew *derek*, "trodden path," used for a "pattern
of behavior or custom." "The way of the Lord"
is twofold: He punishes sinfulness, but He also
shows mercy to the repentant.

Zion A Hebrew name that could be derived from a
Semitic term for "defend" (as in a fortress) or
"to be bald" (as in a defendable rocky space; see
rock). Zion is the defensive hill before the temple
mount, between the Kidron and Tyropean valleys. It was captured by David from the Jebusites
(see 2 Samuel 5:6–7). In the Psalms, *Zion* often
describes the Temple Mount, where God dwelt
among His people and where they sought Him;
by extension, it can include Jerusalem, Israel, and
God's people here and in eternity (that is, the
Church). See *presence*.